Politico's Guide to

The General Election

Simon Henig

and

Lewis Baston

First published in Great Britain 2000
by Politico's Publishing
8 Artillery Row
Westminster
London
SW1P 1RZ

Tel 020 7931 0090
Fax 020 7828 8111
Email publishing@politicos.co.uk
www.politicos.co.uk/publishing

First published in paperback 2000

A catalogue record of this book is available from the British Library.

ISBN 1 902301 50 1

Printed and bound in Great Britain by St Edmundsbury Press.
Cover Design by Advantage

Contents

Preface / by David Butler

Over the last 60 years elections have been transformed. The coming of television did much to nationalise campaigning. The new arts of public relations and the new technologies of communications have transformed the role of central headquarters, and opinion polling has made politicians and voters far more self-aware.

The reporting of elections has also been transformed. Quantification is in. The results of past elections and the relation between seats and votes are percentaged and analysed in a way that was quite unknown two generations ago.

As one who has contributed to the process of explanation in every election since 1945, I am delighted to endorse this effort by Simon Henig and Lewis Baston, both (like contributor Roger Mortimore) former pupils of mine, psephologically expert, to expound in advance what we should be looking for in the General Election of 2001. They have assembled the basic facts about the electorate and the constituencies, as well as about the opinion polls and the basic practical and tactical considerations involved in contemporary electioneering. One is a political scientist, and one is a historian, and the *Politico's Guide to the General Election* is a synthesis of these approaches. For the next few months and above all during the campaign this is certainly a work for the political cognoscenti, as well as for the ordinarily curious, to keep by their side.

Nuffield College Oxford
July 2000

Notes on Authors and Contributors

Simon Henig is a Lecturer in Politics at the Centre for Contemporary Political Issues, University of Sunderland. He is the co-author of Women and Political Power (2000) and has previously written on the 1997 General Election campaign. He correctly predicted the Conservative election victory in 1992 and Labour landslide in 1997, and is a regular election commentator in the North East.

Lewis Baston is Senior Research Fellow of the Centre for the Understanding of Society and Politics at Kingston University, and biographer of Reginald Maudling. His most recent publication was *Sleaze* (2000) which accompanied a series on Channel Four. He was associate author of *Major: A Political Life* and contributed two chapters to the centenary history of the Labour party. He wrote on the 1997 election in the *Financial Times*.

Russell Deacon is Senior Lecturer in Government and Politics at the University of Wales Institute Cardiff, Business School. He has worked in both the Welsh Office and the National Assembly for Wales. He has also written widely on the subject of Welsh elections and acted as a consultant and broadcaster to both Welsh and UK media on this area.

Roger Mortimore has worked for MORI since 1993 as Political Analyst and Senior Political Assistant to the chairman, Robert Worcester. He was extensively involved with MORI's election polling in 1997, in particular the weekly surveys for *The Times* and the ITN exit poll. He is also responsible for editing the British Public Opinion newsletter, and was co-author with Robert Worcester of *Explaining Labour's Landslide* (1999) and with Dick Leonard of *Elections in Britain – A Voter's Guide*. He was also a semi-finalist in the BBC's 'Brain of Britain' in 1999.

Mark Shephard is a Lecturer in the Department of Government at the University of Strathclyde. His interests include British and Scottish politics and government, comparative legislatures and executives (especially Holyrood, Westminster and the European Parliament), American government and politics, constitutional issues, elite behaviour and election campaigns.

Glenn Simpson (key events 1997–2000) is a politics research student at the Centre for Contemporary Political Issues, University of Sunderland. He has previously written on the campaign for regional government in the North East of England.

Introduction

No event in our political calendar is more important than a general election. Our votes will determine the future of individual MPs, political parties, and the government in almost brutal fashion, as pictures of removal vans in Downing Street on 2nd May 1997 amply demonstrated. Some elections, such as those in 1945 and 1979, are seen as marking sea changes in our political history, while all elections will end individual political careers and mark the beginning of others. The campaign itself, officially a few weeks but unofficially several months long, will be exhaustively covered by the media, rounded off on election night itself, which in the case of the last election produced one of the most dramatic nights in recent memory.

The aim of this guide is to survey the political landscape in Britain as we again move onto an election footing. We examine all the main indicators of likely success and failure in some detail, including opinion polls, by-elections and historical precedents, and include profiles of the 200 marginal constituencies which will determine the overall result. Our first section provides a reminder of key political events in Britain since Labour's landslide election victory on 1st May 1997, whether cabinet reshuffles, ministerial resignations, or the development of the peace process in Northern Ireland. After a summary of general election results since 1945, we then move on to look at what has happened to previous Labour governments, particularly those which followed previous landslide victories in 1945 and 1966. This does not make happy reading for Labour supporters, as the party has never succeeded in winning a second full parliamentary term, even after the 1945 Attlee government, universally regarded as the most successful period for the Labour party. Conservative recoveries have been aided by a regular tale of economic crisis and loss of confidence in the government, and Labour have found themselves back in opposition only a few years after what seemed a permanent (or at least long-term) leftward shift in political attitudes. Changing this pattern and winning a second full term has become the key aim of Tony Blair's government.

Our next sections look at political indicators since 1997. We analyse the results of parliamentary by-elections since May 1997, including likely implications for the result of the next full election, though this exercise is hampered to some extent by the fact that, up to July 2000, there had not been a single by-election in a Labour-held marginal constituency. Nevertheless the by-elections do reveal tumbling levels of turnout, particularly in safe Labour seats, where traditional Labour voters have stayed at home. Labour voters have been more likely to turn out where it matters (for example at the Eddisbury by-election) or even vote tactically to defeat the Conservatives (Winchester, Romsey). If these patterns are repeated at the General Election, the overall Labour vote will drop without the loss of a significant number of seats. As a result the present bias in the electoral system towards Labour (assuming a uniform swing at the election, the Conservatives require a national lead of over 8% for a majority, Labour could retain a majority even if 1% behind) seems likely to widen still further. In addition, turnouts below 50% in several inner-city constituencies seem highly likely.

Roger Mortimore from MORI analyses opinion poll data since 1997, which reveals continuing Labour leads, though these have fallen somewhat since the heady days immediately following the last election. Despite the fall in Labour's popularity from late 1999 into 2000, the ratings of the government have remained unprecedented, partly as a result of opposition weakness. The polls section includes ratings for each of the main party leaders, the issues which are seen as important by voters and finally the 'economic optimism' index which assesses whether voters believe the economy will improve or get worse over the next year. For all these poll findings, we have given figures back to 1992, which provide stark comparisons between the Major and Blair governments.

The prospects of each of the main parties, Labour, the Conservatives and Liberal Democrats are then examined, including a look back at key events for each since the last General Election. Of course, events are unpredictable, and the fact this guide went to press in July 2000 obviously means changes may occur before the election is called. Labour will hope to keep the political and election agenda tied to that around Gordon Brown's comprehensive spending review, in terms of promised improvements to health, education and transport, while the Conservatives will hope to regain ground lost to Labour in 1997 on taxation and law and order. Above all, the Conservatives will hope to elevate the question of Britain's relationship with Europe to that of a key election issue, perhaps fusing this with fears of asylum, and will play to older voters, who it is clear are far more likely to vote than younger age groups. Ultimately, the result of the election could well depend on which party is the more successful at keeping 'its issues' at the forefront during the campaign.

Before reaching our regional and constituency profiles, two shorter sections deal with changes to electoral law and retiring MPs. Although the Representation of the People Act which governs British elections has not been greatly altered since 1997, there have been changes to the framework surrounding political parties. From 1999, party symbols have appeared on ballot papers, with parties now required to centrally register their candidates, in an attempt to prevent the candidatures of bogus Labour, Conservative and 'Literal Democrat' candidates, who have previously siphoned off a significant number of votes from the main candidates. More recently, a change in the law anticipated for autumn 2000 will limit national campaign spending for the first time and force parties to reveal the identity of their donors. Meanwhile, the list of retiring MPs (correct up to July 2000) includes some notable names from all three main parties who will be bowing out at the next election. It is clear from this section that the replacements selected thus far are overwhelmingly male, suggesting that the overall number of women in parliament is unlikely to rise.

A large part of this guide consists of our surveys of the 200 or so marginal constituencies which will determine the final outcome of the election. We have attempted to include in the surveys some idea of where a constituency is located (most would be unaware of the location of Amber Valley or Castle Point for example) and we have also examined election results on a local and European level since 1997. Of course electors are increasingly voting differently in different elections, but nevertheless these results do provide some sort of indication as to what has happened in each marginal seat since the last election. Finally, each profile also includes the name of the MP and main opposition candidate, where this was known at the time of going to press.

The constituency profiles are divided into 11 regions (plus a separate summary of the rather different electoral contest in Northern Ireland), and in the main consists of the 170 or so seats which the Conservatives need to gain if they are to win the election outright. Given that some of the Labour leads in these seats (relating to the 1997 results) exceed 20%, the task facing William Hague will not be an easy one. For ease of reference, each of these constituencies has been given a Conservative target number, which is repeated in the individual profiles, regional tables and national battleground summary table towards the end of the guide. The target numbers are an indicator of marginality: as a rough rule of thumb William Hague must win the top 50 if he is to remain party leader after the next election, approximately 90–100 if he is to deprive Labour of a workable majority (a loss of 90 Labour seats ends their majority) and up to 165 and beyond to return the Tories to power with an overall majority.

We have also included constituency profiles for a small number of Labour and Liberal Democrat targets, as although it would be surprising if either party increased their overall number of MPs from the high totals achieved in 1997 (a record number for Labour, the highest since 1929 for the Liberals), it is not impossible for parties to gain seats 'against the tide'. Indeed, there were notable examples in 1964 (Labour won nationally but lost four seats including Smethwick and Norfolk South West) and 1987 (the Conservatives lost 27 seats nationally but gained 6 including Battersea and Walthamstow). Finally, we include the handful of marginal constituencies which Labour are defending against the Liberal Democrats and Nationalist parties. The regional summaries at the start of each section include tables of all the profiled constituencies within that region, and also give an indication in the text of possible 'shock' results outside of the profiled seats.

The final section of the guide contains election predictions from political experts, journalists and others, who have bravely made their best guesses several months before the election itself. Of course the exact date of the election will be uncertain until officially declared by the Prime Minister: though May 3rd 2001 (four years after the last General Election) is widely assumed to be the overwhelming favourite, an earlier date should not be discounted. It does seem unlikely to be in June, because Labour are likely to suffer losses in the May (county) council elections, which would provide a bad start to the 'official' campaign period. Any later date risks the government becoming boxed in by events, and five-year parliaments generally end with a change in government (for example 1964 and 1979) or a much reduced majority (1950). The exception was 1992, though on that occasion a change of Prime Minister (Major replacing Thatcher) convinced electors there already had been a change of government. The best election results for governments tend to come four years after the last election (majorities were increased in 1955, 1959 and 1983, and a majority of over 100 retained in 1987); Labour will aim to repeat this hitherto Conservative pattern and go to the country in spring 2001.

Acknowledgements

We would like to acknowledge the assistance of all individuals who have helped us locate information, notably John Lodge, Michael Steed and Simon Carter, party staff from all the main political parties and also the staff in several council election departments, who enabled us to include data from the 2000 local council elections. We would also like to particularly thank David Butler, who fired our enthusiasm for electoral studies, Bob Worcester and all our other contributors for their input. Work colleagues at both the University of Sunderland and Kingston University have been helpful, particularly Brian Brivati at Kingston. Finally this book would not have appeared without the support of Iain Dale from Politico's, a true political enthusiast. We dedicate this book to all those other enthusiasts (on all sides and none) whose unrecorded and unrewarded hard work keeps our electoral process going.

Key Events / 1997–2000

1997

May

1st — Labour wins the General Election, gaining 419 seats to give the party a massive 179-seat majority with 43.2% of the vote. This is the largest majority for a single party since 1924. The Conservatives manage to win only 165 seats, the Liberal Democrats see their total increase to 46. Tony Blair (43) becomes the youngest Prime Minister in 185 years.

2nd — John Major resigns as leader of the Conservative Party.

3rd — Former Conservative Deputy PM Michael Heseltine admitted to hospital after suffering an attack of angina.

4th — Foreign Secretary Robin Cook announces that the government will sign the European social chapter.

6th — Chancellor Gordon Brown gives the Bank of England 'independence'. The Bank's monetary policy committee becomes responsible for setting interest rates.

8th — The new Labour government holds its first Cabinet meeting. A record five women are included in Tony Blair's first Cabinet.

8th — Sir Michael Shersby (64), Conservative MP for Uxbridge since 1972, dies.

9th — Changes are announced to the format of Prime Minister's Question Time. One session lasting for 30 minutes on Wednesdays replaces the twice-weekly sessions of 15 minutes each on Tuesdays and Thursdays.

14th — The state opening of Parliament. In the Queen's Speech the government announces that 26 Bills will be put before Parliament.

16th   Prime Minister Blair visits Northern Ireland in an attempt to re-start the stalled peace process.

16th   Labour lifts the ban on trade unions at the top secret GCHQ base in Cheltenham. The ban was originally imposed by the Thatcher government in 1984.

29th   US President Bill Clinton meets Blair for the first time at 10 Downing Street.

June

2nd   Tony Blair apologises for Britain's role in the Irish famine between 1845-50.

11th   Parliament votes to make the ownership of all handguns illegal in Great Britain.

16th–17th   Prime Minister Blair meets his EU counterparts for the first time at the Amsterdam Summit.

18th   Bob Wareing MP is suspended by the Labour Party after allegations that he failed to declare a financial interest in the Commons register of members interests.

19th   William Hague defeats Ken Clarke by 92 votes to 70 in the final round of the Conservative Party leadership contest. He becomes the youngest leader of the Tories since William Pitt in 1783.

20th   The libel trial of former Conservative Cabinet Minister Jonathan Aitken against the *Guardian* newspaper and Granada TV collapses.

30th   The UK returns Hong Kong to China, ending 156 years of British rule.

July

2nd   Gordon Brown's first budget. An extra £3 billion is promised for health and education. The Chancellor pledges to raise £5 billion through the 'windfall tax' levied on privatised utilities. However, the Chancellor states the government will stay within the public spending limits of the previous Conservative administration.

2nd   The Downey Report is published. Sir Gordon Downey (Parliamentary Commissioner for Standards) finds five former MPs – Michael Brown, Tim Smith, Sir Andrew Bowden, Sir Michael Grylls and Neil Hamilton – had broken Parliamentary rules by accepting money from Harrods owner Mohammed Fayed.

6th   Violent incidents erupt following the decision by Northern Ireland Secretary Mo Mowlam to allow the Drumcree Orange Parade to march down the Nationalist Garvaghy Road in Portadown.

10th   An estimated 100,000 pro-hunt campaigners converge on Hyde Park in London to protest against a proposed bill that would ban fox-hunting with dogs.

19th   The IRA announces the restoration of its cease-fire broken on 9 February 1996.

22th   The government publishes a White Paper outlining its proposals for a Welsh Assembly.

22nd   Blair announces the establishment of a new Cabinet Committee on the constitution to include not only members of the government but also the Leader of the Liberal Democrats, Paddy Ashdown and four of his colleagues.

22nd   Respected political broadcaster Vincent Hanna dies (57).

24th   The government publishes a White Paper outlining its proposals for a Scottish Parliament.

28th   Gordon McMaster, MP for Paisley South, found dead. He leaves a suicide note accusing fellow Labour MP Tommy Graham and other colleagues of instigating a whispering campaign against him concerning his health and sexual orientation.

29th   The government announces plans to create a Greater London Authority comprising a directly elected mayor and assembly.

31st	Conservative John Randall wins the Uxbridge by-election with a 3,766 majority (see by-elections).

August

2nd	Foreign Secretary Robin Cook announces that he is leaving his wife to live with his secretary Gaynor Regan. This follows a statement by a tabloid newspaper which said it would publish revelations about Cook's personal life.
5th	Trade Minister, Lord Simon, sells his £2 million of shares in British Petroleum (BP), after attacks from the Conservative Party accusing him of a conflict of interest.
19th	After an internal party enquiry following the death of Gordon McMaster, Tommy Graham MP is suspended from the Parliamentary Labour Party for bringing the party into disrepute.
23rd	International Development Secretary Clare Short causes controversy by criticising the government of Montserrat in the Caribbean for raising unrealistic expectations among islanders for compensation following the eruption of a volcano. She was quoted as saying: 'they will want golden elephants next'.
25th–26th	David Shayler, a former agent for the British Intelligence Service alleges MI5 has kept secret files on leading Labour politicians such as Home Secretary Jack Straw and Peter Mandelson, the Minister without Portfolio.
29th	Northern Ireland Secretary Mo Mowlam invites Sinn Fein, the political wing of the IRA to all party peace talks on 15th September.
31st	Diana Princess of Wales (36) is killed in a car crash in Paris.

September

6th	The funeral of Diana Princess of Wales takes place at Westminster Abbey

9th   Sinn Fein agrees to subscribe to the six 'Mitchell principles'.

11th   In the devolution referendum in Scotland, 74.3% vote in favour of establishing a Scottish Parliament on a 60% turnout. A further 63.5% vote in favour of the Parliament having tax varying powers.

18th   In the Welsh devolution referendum 50.3% of voters approve the creation of a National Assembly on a 50% turnout. The result is only confirmed by the final declaration.

19th   Southall (London) rail crash leaves seven dead and 160 injured.

22nd   Former Speaker of the Commons, Viscount Tonypandy (George Thomas) dies (88).

24th   An agenda is agreed for future negotiations on peace in Northern Ireland. A new independent commission will deal with decommissioning terrorist weapons.

29th   Peter Mandelson, Minister without Portfolio and close confidant of the Prime Minister, fails to be elected to the Labour Party's National Executive Committee.

30th   Tony Blair makes his first speech as Prime Minister to the Labour Party Conference (held in Brighton).

October

7th   The High Court rules that the General Election result in the constituency of Winchester (Hampshire) is void due to procedural errors during the count. The Court orders that the election must be re-run. Conservative candidate Gerry Malone had lost by two votes to Liberal Democrat Mark Oaten.

10th   William Hague's first speech as leader to the Conservative Party Conference (held in Blackpool).

13th   British PM Tony Blair meets the leader of Sinn Fein, Gerry Adams at Stormont. This is the first meeting of its kind since 1921.

14th   The Conservative MP Piers Merchant resigns after newspaper reports of an alleged affair with former night-club hostess Anna Cox.

14th   Keith Hellawell leaves his post as Chief Constable of West Yorkshire police to become the UK's first 'drugs tsar'.

23rd   The Conservatives announce that they will rule out joining the Single European Currency in the next Parliament.

25th   Four Labour MEPs, Alec Falconer, Ken Coates, Hugh Kerr and Michael Hindley, are suspended from the European Parliamentary Labour Party for opposing the introduction of a new code of conduct preventing MEPs from publicly criticising party policy.

27th   Chancellor Gordon Brown tells the Commons that the UK will not join the launch of the European Single Currency in 1999. The Chancellor goes on to state government support for joining the Single Currency in principle, but only when the economic conditions are right and subject to a referendum.

29th   Ian Taylor MP, Conservative spokesperson on Northern Ireland, resigns from the front bench after disagreeing with party policy on the European Single Currency.

November

6th   The Commons Committee on Standards and Privileges criticises former Minister and MP Neil Hamilton for accepting 'cash for questions'.

6th   In the Paisley South by-election, called after the suicide of Gordon McMaster, Labour retain the seat but with a significantly reduced majority (see by-elections)

10th   The Labour Party promises to return a £1 million donation made by Bernie Ecclestone President of the Formula One Association. This revelation followed an announcement by the government on 5th November that it would seek to exempt Formula One racing from a proposed ban on tobacco advertising.

20th	Liberal Democrat Mark Oaten wins the Winchester by-election by a majority of 21,536 over Conservative Gerry Malone. The by-election was called after the Conservatives successfully challenged the original result in High Court. In a second by-election, the Conservatives hold Beckenham with a reduced majority. (see by-elections)
21st	Pro-European MP, Peter Temple-Morris is expelled from the Conservative Parliamentary Party for opposing the party's policy of ruling out British membership of the Single European Currency in the next Parliament.
25th	Chancellor Gordon Brown announces his pre-budget report, including plans for a radical overhaul of the welfare system.
28th	The Commons votes 411-151 in support of a private members bill banning hunting with dogs. However the Bill does not become law after failing to receive sufficient time from the government in order to progress through Parliament.
30th	Protesters in Wales dump imported beef from Ireland in the water at Holyhead harbour.

December

1st	The government sets up an independent commission to examine alternatives to the current first-past-the-post electoral system. Chairman of the commission is Liberal Democrat peer Lord Jenkins.
2nd	Social Security Secretary Harriet Harman announces that the government will freeze the level of benefit paid to single parents. This leads to the first significant opposition to government policy from Labour back-benchers.
3rd	The Agriculture Secretary, Jack Cunningham, announces that the government will ban the sale of beef on the bone after scientific advice suggests it could transmit the BSE agent.
10th	47 Labour MPs vote against government plans to reduce the level of lone parents benefits to new claimants.

11th   Tony Blair meets Sinn Fein leader Gerry Adams at 10 Downing Street.

16th   The Labour MP for Glasgow Govan, Mohammed Sarwar appears in court on charges relating to electoral irregularities. He was late acquitted.

19th   Conservative leader William Hague marries Ffion Jenkins in a ceremony at the Palace of Westminster.

22nd   Agriculture Secretary Jack Cunningham announces £85 million of aid for hill and beef farmers.

24th   The Mirror newspaper 'entraps' the son of Home Secretary, Jack Straw, when a journalist reports she bought marijuana from the 17 year old.

27th   Billy Wright, the leader of the terrorist group the Loyalist Volunteer Force, is gunned down at the Maze Prison by two members of the republican terrorist group the Irish National Liberation Army. A series of revenge murders follows, which seriously threatens the peace process.

1998

January

8th   Scottish Secretary Donald Dewar announces that he intends to stand as a candidate for the new Scottish Parliament. Dewar is tipped to become Scotland's 'First Minister'.

8th   The Labour Party expels MEPs Hugh Kerr and Ken Coates for continuing to criticise party policy in public and the candidate selection process for the forthcoming June elections.

11th   Robin Cook, announces that he will marry his secretary Gaynor Regan after he divorces his wife. The announcement comes after persistent rumours in the press concerning Cook's private life.

12th   Tony Blair visits Japan, where he receives an apology from

Japanese Premier Ryutaro Hashimoto for Japan's treatment of British POW's during the Second World War.

14th   Agriculture Secretary Jack Cunningham announces that the government will establish an independent Food Standards Agency, to monitor the safety of food.

20th   Paymaster General Geoffrey Robinson, is criticised by the Parliamentary Commissioner for Standards after failing to record a £12.5 million off-shore trust in the register of members interests.

26th   The ban on the possession of handguns comes into effect in Great Britain.

29th   PM Blair announces that the government will launch a fresh inquiry into the 'Bloody Sunday' killings in 1972, when 14 unarmed Catholic protesters were killed by British paratroopers in Londonderry / Derry.

February

4th–7th   Tony Blair makes his first official visit to the United States as Prime Minister.

8th   The former Conservative and Ulster Unionist MP, Enoch Powell dies (85).

9th   A gunman kills Catholic Brendan Campbell in Belfast. Although officially on cease-fire, the IRA is suspected.

10th   A gunman kills Protestant Robert Dougan, who allegedly has links with loyalist paramilitaries. The IRA is again suspected of involvement in the murder.

15th   Revelations appear in the media concerning the cost of refurbishing the official residence of the Lord Chancellor (Lord) Derry Irvine, which run to a reported £650,000.

20th   The UK and Irish governments suspend Sinn Fein, the political wing of the IRA, from the peace talks after the IRA was blamed for murders on the 9–10 February.

March

1st   Over 200,000 people join the 'countryside march' on London. The aim is to draw attention to the problems faced by rural areas such as the crisis in farming.

3rd   The Loyalist Volunteer Force gun down two men in a pub at Poyntzpass in County Armagh.

8th   Reports in the media allege that Deputy Prime Minister John Prescott failed to register a donation of over £27,000 towards campaigning expenses in 1996.

12th   After meeting Tony Blair, President of Sinn Fein Gerry Adams, announces that the party will soon rejoin the all-party peace talks on the future of Northern Ireland.

13th   Mike Foster's (Labour MP for Worcester) Private Member's Bill to ban hunting with hounds fails to become law after running out of Parliamentary time.

17th   Labour's second budget since coming to power. Changes to the tax and benefits system are announced including the working families tax credit.

23rd   Sinn Fein returns to the all-party peace talks in Northern Ireland.

27th   Former Labour MPs Joan Maynard (76) and Joan Lestor (66) die.

27th   Gunmen kill retired policeman Cyril Stewart in Armagh, Northern Ireland.

April

1st   Deputy PM John Prescott is cleared of any impropriety for failing to declare a donation of over £27,000 by the Parliamentary Commissioner for Standards, Sir Gordon Downey.

10th   The UK and Irish governments and the political parties in Northern Ireland sign a historic peace accord, known as the 'Good Friday Agreement'. The agreement creates an elected assembly, north-south institutions and a British-Irish Council, bringing together the two governments and members of devolved bodies around the British Isles.

18th   The Ulster Unionist Party leader receives the formal backing of his party for the peace agreement. 72% of the party's ruling Council endorse the agreement, with 28% voting against.

25th   The loyalist paramilitary group the Ulster Defence Association release a statement supporting the Good Friday Agreement.

30th   The Irish Republican Army endorse the Good Friday Agreement but refuse to surrender any weaponry.

May

2nd   Dutchman Wim Duisenberg is confirmed head of the European Central Bank that will manage the Single European Currency, the Euro, from 1999.

6nd   Robin Cook announces an inquiry into the so-called 'arms to Africa' affair. A Sunday newspaper had alleged that the government had known that British company Sandline International had sent arms to support forces loyal to deposed President Kabbah, in defiance of an arms embargo imposed by the United Nations.

7th   In local government elections in England, the Conservatives improve on their 1994 performance, with both Labour and Liberal Democrats suffering some losses. Nevertheless Labour still remains the largest party in local government. In the referendum on establishing a Greater London Authority, 72% (on a 34% turnout) of Londoners vote in favour of setting up the new body.

10th   Delegates to a special Sinn Fein conference vote to endorse the Northern Ireland peace agreement.

21th   Jonathan Aitken, the former Conservative Cabinet Minister, is charged with perjury and perverting the course of justice.

22nd   Voters in Northern Ireland and the Irish Republic vote in favour of the Good Friday Agreement.

25th
The Japanese Emperor Akihito faces protests from British World War Two veterans who are demanding compensation for their time spent in prisoner of war camps.

June

1st
Conservative leader William Hague reshuffles his shadow cabinet. Ann Widdecombe takes the Health portfolio, David Willetts takes over at Education and Employment, while Peter Lilley is appointed deputy leader of the party.

7th
Veteran rockers the Rolling Stones announce they will cancel concerts in the UK because of changes in the tax laws introduced by the Labour government.

8th
Harriet Harman, the Secretary of State for Social Security, announces legislation that will allow women the right to a share of their husband's pension if they become divorced.

18th
Trade and Industry Secretary, Margaret Beckett announces the government's plans for a national minimum wage. The minimum wage will be introduced in April 1999, at £3.60 an hour for workers aged 22 and over.

20th
The government announces the appointment of 27 new life peers.

21st
Former Conservative MP Peter Temple-Morris announces that he has joined the Labour Party. The new Labour MP previously had been suspended from the Conservative Parliamentary Party for opposing their policy on Europe.

22nd
The Commons votes 336-129 to lower the homosexual age of consent from 18 to 16, thus equalising the law with heterosexuals.

25th
Elections take place to the Northern Ireland assembly, with parties supporting the Good Friday agreement winning the majority of seats.

July

1st   The newly elected Northern Ireland assembly meets for the first time. Ulster Unionist leader David Trimble is elected First Minister, while Seamus Mallon of the nationalist SDLP becomes Deputy First Minister.

5th   A Sunday newspaper alleges that lobbyists are using contacts within the government and Labour Party to gain special access to Ministers for their clients.

9th   Margaret McDonagh becomes the first woman to hold the influential post of General Secretary of the Labour Party.

15th   The parliamentary Standards and Privileges Committee clears Paymaster General Geoffrey Robinson of allegations that he had not registered a payment of £200,000 made by a company owned by the disgraced tycoon, the late Robert Maxwell.

22nd   The House of Lords causes an outcry among gay rights and civil liberties campaigners when it votes against the government amendment to reduce the age of consentfor homosexuals from 18 to 16. As a result the government announces that the amendment would be withdrawn and any changes to the law postponed until the next session of parliament.

27th   A new code of conduct regulating contacts between Ministers and lobbyists is issued by the Cabinet Office following allegations made in the media.

27th   A report into the 'arms to Africa' affairs clears Ministers of any wrong-doing, although the High Commissioner in Sierra Leone, Peter Penfold is criticised.

27th–29th   PM Blair carries out his first Cabinet reshuffle. Four Cabinet Ministers are sacked: Gavin Strang (Transport), Harriet Harman (Social Security), David Clark (Chancellor of the Duchy of Lancaster) and Lord Richard (Leader of the House of Lords). Blair also promotes Minister without Portfolio, Peter Mandelson to Trade and Industry Secretary, while Margaret Beckett moves sideways from Trade and Industry to

Leader of the House of Commons; Chief Whip Nick Brown becomes Agriculture Secretary; Jack Cunningham moves from Agriculture to the new post of Cabinet 'enforcer'; Chief Secretary to the Treasury, Alistair Darling takes over as Social Security Secretary; Stephen Byers becomes Chief Secretary to the Treasury and Baroness Jay is appointed Leader of the House of Lords.

August

1st
Former MI5 intelligence operative, David Shayler, is detained in France after the UK government request his extradition to face charges of revealing state secrets.

3rd
The head of Scottish Television and friend of the Prime Minister, Gus MacDonald is made a life peer and appointed to the Scottish Office as Minister for business and industry.

15th
The single greatest loss of life in the history of Northern Ireland 'troubles' occurs when republican dissenters, the so-called 'Real IRA' explode a bomb in Omagh, County Tyrone, killing 28 civilians and injuring 220 others.

25th
In the wake of the Omagh bombing, the government unveils plans for new anti-terrorism measures.

September

2nd
Parliament is recalled early from its summer recess. This allows the Criminal Justice (Terrorism and Conspiracy) Bill to be passed by both Houses of Parliament in just 27 hours.

4th
Japanese company Fujitsu announces that it is closing its modern semi-conductor plant in Tony Blair's Sedgefield constituency in North East England. Job losses of 570 at Fujitsu come after 1100 jobs were lost a few weeks earlier at the Siemens semi-conductor plant, also in the North East. The government faces criticism that it is not doing enough to help industry in struggling regions.

9th
Labour MP Tommy Graham (Renfrewshire West) is expelled

from the party for misconduct and bringing the party into disrepute.

19th   Donald Dewar, the Secretary of State for Scotland is chosen as Labour's candidate for the position of First Minister in the Scottish executive.

October

1st   The government order UK citizens to leave Yugoslavia because of the threat of NATO air strikes over the conflict in the province of Kosovo between the Yugoslav military and the local Albanian population.

8th   Conservative MEP James Moorhouse joins the Liberal Democrats in protest at Tory policy on the Single European Currency.

13th   The Committee on Standards in Public Life publishes a report that recommends reform in the way political parties are funded. One of the main recommendations is that the parties should be able to spend a maximum of £20 million on General Election campaigning (see changes in electoral law section).

14th   The government announces that a Royal Commission, chaired by Conservative peer Lord Wakeham, will be established to examine various options for reforming the House of Lords.

16th   David Trimble, the leader of the Ulster Unionists and John Hume, the leader of nationalist SDLP are jointly awarded the Nobel Peace Prize for their work in bringing peace to Northern Ireland.

17th   Senator Augusto Pinochet, the former Chilean dictator, is arrested at a hospital in London following a request by the Spanish government for his extradition to face charges of murdering Spanish citizens in Chile.

26th   Former Conservative MP Nicholas Budgen dies (60).

27th   Secretary of State for Wales, Ron Davies resigns after a 'moment of madness' on Clapham Common in London, when he was robbed and had his car stolen. Lurid allegations are made in the press following the incident. Alun Michael is appointed to the vacant post.

27th   Matthew Parris, former Conservative MP and newspaper columnist causes controversy by alleging on BBC television's Newsnight programme, that Trade and Industry Secretary Peter Mandelson is one of several Cabinet Ministers who are gay.

28th   The High Court rejects the Spanish government request to extradite Senator Pinochet on the grounds that he enjoys diplomatic immunity from extradition.

29th   The Independent Commission on Electoral Reform chaired by Liberal Democrat peer Lord Jenkins publishes its report. It recommends the present voting system for electing the Commons, 'first-past-the-post' should be replaced by a combined alternative vote system and 'top-up' proportional list system, known as 'alternative vote plus'.

29th   Ron Davies resigns as Labour's prospective candidate for First Secretary of the Welsh Assembly.

November

3rd   Chancellor Gordon Brown presents his second pre-budget report to the Commons.

5th   Secretary of State for Wales Alun Michael announces that he will stand to become Labour's candidate for First Secretary of the Welsh Assembly.

7th   Agriculture Secretary Nick Brown admits he is gay after revelations made by a Sunday tabloid newspaper.

11th   Tony Blair and Liberal Democrat leader Paddy Ashdown announce that the remit of the special joint Labour-Liberal Democrat Cabinet Committee will be expanded to policy areas such as education and welfare. Prior to this the Committee had limited its discussions to constitutional issues.

16th   Nick Brown, the Agriculture Secretary announces a £120 million package of government assistance for farmers who are suffering from a collapse in prices.

18th   The Paymaster General, Geoffrey Robinson makes a formal apology to the Commons for failing to declare some of his business interests.

18th   A Court in France refuses Britain's request to extradite former MI5 intelligence officer, David Shayler, to answer charges of divulging state secrets.

18th   The House of Lords defeats the government's European Parliamentary Elections Bill for a fifth time. The Bill seeks to establish a 'closed list' system of proportional representation for European elections. The government announces that it will force legislation through in the next session of Parliament, so that a Bill is introduced in time for the European elections in June 1999.

23rd   European Union Agriculture Ministers agree to lift the ban on British beef (introduced in March 1996) providing certain conditions are met.

24th   The state opening of Parliament and Queen's speech set out the government's legislative programme. The main Bills to be introduced in the new session of Parliament include welfare reform, youth justice, lowering the age of consent for homosexuals and reforming the National Health Service.

25th   The Law Lords rule by three to two that Senator Pinochet is not entitled to diplomatic immunity from extradition.

26th   Tony Blair becomes the first British Prime Minister to address both Houses of the Irish Parliament.

26th   The Scottish National Party retains the Scotland North East European Parliamentary seat in a by-election.

December

2nd   Conservative Party leader William Hague sacks Viscount Cranborne, the Conservative leader in the Lords. Cranborne had unilaterally reached an agreement with the government, without informing Hague, to allow 91 hereditary peers to remain in the Lords on an interim basis until the Upper House is fully reformed. Lord Strathclyde becomes the new Conservative leader in the Lords.

15th   The European Parliamentary Elections Bill is rejected by the Lords for a sixth time. Nevertheless, this does not prevent the Bill receiving Royal Assent as the government invokes the Parliament Act, overriding the decision of the Upper House. This is only the third time the Parliament Act has been used since World War Two.

16th   US and UK military forces launch cruise missile and air attacks on targets in Iraq.

17th   An emergency debate takes place in the Commons on the UK's role in air attacks on Iraq.

17th   The Law Lords make the unprecedented decision of over-ruling their previous decision on Senator Pinochet, taken on 25 November, on the grounds that one of the Law Lords, Lord Hoffman, had links with Amnesty International, who supported Pinochet's extradition to Spain.

23th   Trade and Industry Secretary Peter Mandelson and Paymaster General Geoffrey Robinson both resign from their posts after a newspaper reveals that Mandelson had received a loan of £373,000 from Robinson in order to purchase a property in London. Chief Secretary to the Treasury Stephen Byers replaces Mandelson, while Alan Milburn takes over Byers former post. Dawn Primarolo becomes the new Paymaster General.

31st   Former Conservative Prime Minister John Major is made a Companion of Honour in the New Year's Honours List.

1999

January

1st   The Euro replaces national currencies in 11 countries, though notes and coins will not come into circulation until 2002.

17th   It is revealed that Conservative MEP Tom Spencer was caught carrying drugs and homosexual pornography by customs officers at Heathrow Airport. Spencer later announces that he will not seek re-election.

19th   Former Conservative Cabinet Minister Jonathan Aitken admits he is guilty of charges of perjury and perverting the cause of justice in his libel action against the *Guardian* newspaper and Granada Television. Aitken is notified that he will be sentenced in June.

20th   Liberal Democrat leader Paddy Ashdown announces that he will stand down as party leader after the European parliamentary elections in June.

25th   The Northern Ireland Secretary Mo Mowlam calls for an end to punishment beatings by paramilitaries.

27th   Former IRA informer and occasional media commentator on Irish Republicanism Eamon Collins is found murdered in South Armagh.

February

6th   Peace talks to resolve the conflict in Kosovo begin in Paris, under the threat of NATO air strikes.

9th   The Foreign Affairs Select Committee publishes a highly critical report of the role played by Foreign Office officials during the so-called 'arms to Africa' affair.

20th   Secretary of State for Wales, Alun Michael, narrowly beats challenger Rhodri Morgan in the contest to become the leader of the Labour Party in Wales.

20th   Home Secretary Jack Straw obtains a Court injunction preventing the Sunday Telegraph newspaper publishing details of the Macpherson report into the murder of black teenager Stephen Lawrence in 1993. The leaked report accidentally contains the names and addresses of individuals who had given evidence to the police.

23rd PM Blair launches the 'national change-over plan' which aims to prepare the UK for entry into the Single European Currency.

24th The Macpherson report on the murder of Stephen Lawrence is published in full. It accuses the Metropolitan Police Authority in London of 'institutional racism' and incompetence.

March

8th The government announces that it intends to introduce a statutory 'right to roam' that will open up millions of acres of private land to public access across England and Wales.

9th The Chancellor Gordon Brown presents his third budget to the Commons. The Chancellor announces a new starting rate of income tax at 10p, and promises to reduce the basic rate to 22p.

16th The European Commission resigns en masse after an auditor's report concludes that there has been fraud and corruption in the Commission.

19th Fiona Jones, the Labour MP for Newark and her agent are convicted in court of falsifying election expenses from the 1997 General Election campaign. She is temporarily disqualified from Parliament; however the two are later cleared on appeal.

23rd Peace talks over the future of Kosovo finally collapse, after the Yugoslav government opposes the free and uninhibited movement of NATO troops across its territory. President Milosevic accuses NATO of seeking to undermine Yugoslav sovereignty.

24th NATO air strikes are launched against targets in Yugoslavia, the first aggressive action taken by the organisation in its history.

24th The Law Lords rule that Senator Pinochet does not have immunity from extradition.

24th Italian Romano Prodi is nominated as the candidate to succeed out-going European Commission President Jacques Santer.

25th   Labour MP for Glasgow Govan Mohammed Sarwar is cleared by a court in Edinburgh of seeking to bribe a rival candidate in the 1997 General Election.

April

6th   NATO rejects an offer for a cease-fire made by the Yugoslav President Slobodan Milosevic.

13th   The Prime Minister informs the Commons that a further 2000 UK troops are to be sent to the Former Yugoslav Republic of Macedonia as part of an international force to be deployed in Kosovo.

13th   The Lords vote against giving a second reading to the Sexual Offences (Amendment) Bill that seeks to reduce the gay age of consent from 18 to 16.

17th   Dozens of people are injured after a nail bomb explodes in a street in multi-ethnic Brixton in London.

24th   A second nail bomb explodes in the Brick Lane area of London, injuring six people.

25th   The first group of Kosovar refugees arrives in the UK.

27th   The Conservative Party's Director of Membership, Michael Simmonds leaves his post after details of a speech by deputy leader Peter Lilley are leaked to the press.

30th   Another nail bomb explodes in a gay bar in London, killing three people and injuring 73 others.

30th   The former Conservative leader of Westminster City Council Dame Shirley Porter who was found guilty of wilful miscon-duct and gerrymandering by the District Auditor in 1996, is cleared of the charges by the Court of Appeal.

May

1st   The Amsterdam Treaty becomes law across the EU.

1st

More than 40 Kosovar civilians are killed when a NATO aircraft mistakenly attacks a bus.

2nd

A man is charged with causing explosions and murder following the nail bomb attacks in London in April.

3rd

PM Blair visits refugee camps on the Kosovo – Macedonia border.

6th

Elections to the Scottish Parliament and Welsh Assembly are held. In Scotland, Labour is the largest party with 56 seats but fails to achieve an overall majority in the 129 member Parliament. A similar situation occurs in Wales where Labour wins 28 of the 60 seats in the assembly, losing the strongholds of the Rhondda and Islwyn to Plaid Cymru. In local elections, the Conservatives make a modest recovery to secure the position of leader William Hague. Labour lose control of 30 councils but remain 4% ahead of the Conservatives in share of the vote.

7th

NATO accidentally bombs the Chinese embassy in Belgrade, killing three people.

12th

Alun Michael is elected First Secretary of the Welsh Assembly. Labour decide against a coalition, instead forming a minority Administration.

13th

Labour and the Liberal Democrats agree to form a coalition government in the Scottish Parliament. Labour's Donald Dewar becomes First Minister, while the leader of the Scottish Liberal Democrats, Jim Wallace, becomes Deputy First Minister.

16th

The British and Irish governments announce a 30 June deadline for the talks aimed at breaking the deadlock on the issue of decommissioning terrorist weapons in Northern Ireland

17th

John Reid is appointed Secretary of State for Scotland replacing Donald Dewar. Helen Liddell replaces John Reid as the Transport Minister.

24th

The Yugoslav military forces thousands of Kosovar Albanians from their homes, further escalating the Kosovo conflict. This increases criticism that NATO's bombing policy is not working.

26th   The Queen formally opens the Welsh Assembly.

June

2nd   European Union and Russian peace negotiators meet Yugoslav President Milosevic.

3rd   President Milosevic accepts a peace plan for Kosovo. The peace deal means all Yugoslav forces must withdraw from Kosovo and international peace keepers allowed to enter the province.

8th   Former Conservative Cabinet Minister Jonathan Aitken is sentenced to 18 months imprisonment for perjury and perverting the cause of justice.

10th   Yugoslav generals sign the peace deal with NATO. The Secretary General of NATO, Javier Solana, formally suspends air operations against Yugoslavia, bringing to an end the conflict in Kosovo.

10th   European Parliamentary elections are held. The Conservatives win 36 seats, Labour 29, Liberal Democrats 10, the UK Independence Party 3, with the Scottish National Party, Plaid Cymru (the Party of Wales) and the Green Party all winning 2 each, but on a turnout of just 24%. On the same day, Hilary Benn, son of veteran Labour MP Tony Benn, wins the Leeds Central by-election for the Labour Party. However turnout was under 20%, the lowest in any post-war parliamentary election (see by-elections section).

12th   British troops enter Kosovo as part of the international KFOR peace force.

15th   Conservative leader William Hague reshuffles his shadow Cabinet team. Deputy leader Peter Lilley is sacked, in what is seen as a clear-out of the Thatcher and Major generation of Conservatives. Those promoted include Ann Widdecombe to shadow Home Secretary and John Maples to shadow Foreign Secretary.

17th   Tessa Jowell, the Public Health Minister announces that tobacco advertising will be banned in the UK from December 1999.

27th	Left-wing MP Tony Benn, announces that he will stand down at the next election (see retiring MPs section).
30th	The deadline passes on talks in Northern Ireland aimed at breaking the deadlock on decommissioning.

July

1st	The Queen formally opens the Scottish Parliament.
4th	PM Blair announces that if the IRA does not meet its obligation to decommission, Sinn Fein will be removed from the Northern Ireland executive once it is established.
12th	Emergency legislation is passed through Parliament to establish a Northern Ireland assembly.
15th	The Ulster Unionists boycott the inaugural session of the Northern Ireland assembly in protest at the IRA's refusal to begin the decommissioning process. Seamus Mallon of the nationalist SDLP and Deputy First Minister resigns as a result of Unionist refusal to join the assembly.
22nd	The Conservatives hold Eddisbury in a by-election (see by-elections section) though there is virtually no swing away from Labour after a tightly-fought contest.
28th	Paul Murphy becomes the new Secretary of State for Wales, replacing Alun Michael.
31st	Prime Minister Tony Blair visits Kosovo.

August

1st	The EU lifts the export ban on British beef.
4th	Defence Secretary George Robertson is appointed NATO's new Secretary General.
9th	Charles Kennedy is elected leader of the Liberal Democrats.
26th	Northern Ireland Secretary, Mo Mowlam, announces that in her opinion the IRA cease-fire remains intact, despite the murder of a taxi-driver in July, continuing punishment

beatings and gun running in the United States.

September

7th   The death is announced of Conservative MP Alan Clark (71) from a brain tumour.

9th   Former Defence Secretary Michael Portillo puts his name forward as a candidate for the Kensington and Chelsea seat left vacant following the death of Alan Clark.

9th   Chris Patten, Chairman of the Independent Commission on Policing in Northern Ireland, publishes proposals to transform the Royal Ulster Constabulary.

9th   The new EU Commission is formally endorsed by MEPs.

20th   UN peacekeeping forces, including a contingent from the UK, arrive in East Timor following violence in the wake of a 'yes' vote in the independence referendum.

21st   The government announces £150 million of new aid to help livestock farmers.

27th   The ban on gay men and women joining the armed forces is effectively lifted following a ruling by the European Court of Human Rights. The Court ruled the ban illegal after a 3 year battle by three gays expelled from the armed forces.

28th   PM Blair promises to free Britain of 'all forms of conservatism' in his speech to the Labour Party Conference at Bournemouth.

October

4th   William Hague launches the Conservative Party's platform for the next general election, the so-called 'Common Sense Revolution'. A list of guarantees includes reducing taxes as a share of the UK's income over the term of the next Parliament.

5th   The Paddington rail crash claims 30 lives, after two trains collide.

11th   PM Blair announces a Cabinet reshuffle. Former Trade and Industry Secretary, Peter Mandelson returns as the new

Northern Ireland Secretary. Mo Mowlam moves from the Northern Ireland office to replace Jack Cunningham (who leaves the government) as the Cabinet 'enforcer'. Alan Milburn fills the Health Secretary post vacated by London Mayoral candidate Frank Dobson and Geoff Hoon becomes Defence Secretary replacing George Robertson, the new NATO Secretary General.

14th   Tony Blair joins a platform with Michael Heseltine, the former Conservative Deputy Prime Minister, Charles Kennedy, the Liberal Democrat leader and former Conservative Chancellor Ken Clarke to launch the 'Britain in Europe' campaign. The campaign focuses on the merits of EU membership for the UK.

17th   PM Blair warns French Premier Lionel Jospin, that the UK will take France to the European Court if the French ban on British beef is not lifted. The row overshadows the EU Council summit in Finland.

18th   Pakistan is suspended from the Commonwealth after a military coup six days earlier (12 October).

19th   Public protests greet the visit to the UK of Chinese President Jiang Zemin. Protesters accuse China of human rights abuses in Tibet and other areas of China.

21st   Two Labour MPs are suspended from the Commons. Don Touhig (Islwyn) is suspended for three days for leaking a Social Security Select Committee report, while Kali Mountford (Colne Valley) is suspended for five days for also leaking the report. Mountford resigns from the Select Committee.

26th   The right of hereditary peers to sit in the House of Lords ends. Under a deal brokered between the government and Conservative peers, 91 hereditaries will remain in the transitional House until the long term future of the Lords is decided.

November

3rd   Fifty-two Labour MPs vote against the government's Welfare Reform and Pensions Bill in protest at plans to reduce claimants entitlement to incapacity benefit. Ten other Labour MPs abstain in spite of a 3-line whip.

8th   The House of Lords inflict a defeat on the government's Welfare Reform and Pensions Bill by 216 votes to 127.

9th   In the Chancellor of the Exchequer's pre-budget report, Gordon Brown announces 4 key aims for the next century: higher productivity, more students taking degrees; more people in employment; and halving of child poverty.

17th   The government introduces a 28 Bill Queen's speech. Bills covering transport, gay rights, local government, welfare reform, freedom of information and the countryside will be introduced over the next 18 months.

17th   The IRA appoints an interlocutor to General John de Chastelain's International Commission on Decommissioning. It is hoped that this will break the deadlock concerning the decommissioning of IRA arms and seats for Sinn Fein in the Northern Ireland Cabinet.

18th   Tony Blair announces that his wife Cherie (45) is pregnant with their fourth child.

18th   Left-wing Labour MP Ken Livingstone is included on Labour's shortlist for the Mayor of London.

20th   Conservative Party candidate for the London mayoral contest, Jeffrey Archer, stands down after press revelations that he asked a friend to provide a false alibi in his successful libel action against the Daily Star newspaper. The paper alleged Archer had slept with a prostitute.

25th   Allegations are made in the press that Conservative Party Treasurer, Michael Ashcroft, gave the party £2 million while he was not registered to vote in the UK.

27th   Ulster Unionist leader David Trimble wins the support of his ruling Council for the party to join the Cabinet of the Northern Ireland assembly, even though the IRA has not decommissioned its weapons. However support for joining the Cabinet is conditional on the IRA handing in arms after ten weeks.

27th The stolen diary of former Liberal Democrat leader Paddy Ashdown is published by a Sunday newspaper. It revealed that Tony Blair had considered including two Liberal Democrats in his Cabinet in 1997.

29th Northern Ireland's first ever inclusive government is established. Ulster Unionist leader David Trimble becomes First Minister, while Seamus Mallon of the SDLP is appointed Deputy First Minister. The Cabinet includes two Sinn Fein Ministers, Martin McGuinness as Education Minister and Bairbre de Brun as Health, Social Services and Public Safety Minister.

30th Westminster Hall, the new £1 million semi-circular debating chamber, holds its first session. The new chamber aims to provide extra opportunities for debates and to scrutinise the government.

31st Michael Portillo, the former Conservative Defence Secretary, who lost his seat at the 1997 General Election, returns to the Commons as the MP for Kensington and Chelsea (see by-elections section).

31st Agriculture Secretary Nick Brown, announces that the 'beef on the bone' ban will be lifted. It ends a two year ban after fears it could transmit the BSE agent to humans.

December

1st Deputy PM John Prescott, the Secretary of State for the Environment, receives heavy criticism from Labour back-benchers and unions over the government's plans to privatise the Air Traffic Control system.

2nd Irish Taoiseach Bertie Ahern signs the Good Friday Agreement, which sweeps away Articles Two and Three of the Irish constitution, laying a territorial claim to Northern Ireland.

2nd   Conservative leader William Hague sacks his front-bench spokesman for London, Shaun Woodward. Woodward refused to support party policy of opposing the repeal of section 28 of the Local Government Act on the 'promotion' of homosexuality in schools.

10th   The UK blocks plans by the EU to introduce a European-wide tax on savings after securing a six month delay at the Helsinki summit.

12th   Allegations are made in a BBC TV programme that Labour's London mayoral candidate, Frank Dobson, received the Labour Party's membership list for London in breach of party rules.

15th   Alan Donnelly, leader of the UK's Labour MEP's resigns suddenly because he is tired of 'excessive travelling' and work caused by having to move between two Parliamentary sites in Brussels and Strasbourg.

17th   The inaugural meeting of the British – Irish Council takes place in London.

18th   Former Conservative spokesman for London and MP for Witney, Shaun Woodward, defects from the party to join Labour. He claims the Conservatives have abandoned their commitment to one-nation politics.

18th   Newspapers report that the UK government will write-off all debts owed by the world's poorest states.

21st   The Scottish Parliament announces it will abolish tuition fees for students and reintroduce student grants. This runs counter to UK government policy, where students pay tuition fees.

21st   Former Conservative Minister Neil Hamilton, loses a libel action against the owner of Harrods, Mohammed Fayed, over the so-called 'cash for questions' affair.

26th   A Department for Trade and Industry inquiry is launched into an engineering company founded by the former Labour Paymaster General, Geoffrey Robinson, after allegations of 'accounting irregularities'.

31st   The New Years Honours list is published. Scottish National

Party supporter, the actor Sean Connery receives a Knighthood, as does businessman Richard Branson.

2000

January

4th

A leaked government report passed to the BBC highlights a number of problems with equipment used by the British Army in Kosovo.

7th

Former Conservative Cabinet Minister Jonathan Aitken is released from prison but will spend the final two months of his sentence electronically tagged.

7th

Rumours emerge in the press that the Cabinet Office Minister Mo Mowlam is 'on trial' and will not been given another chance if she fails in her present post.

7th

Jeff Rooker (59), the Social Security Minister announces that he is standing down as an MP for Birmingham Perry Barr at the next General Election (see Retiring MPs section).

10th

The government faces criticism over its handling of the Health Service after an outbreak of flu leaves hospitals claiming they do not have enough capacity to deal with the epidemic.

10th

The PM's wife Cherie Booth QC is fined £10 for boarding a train without a ticket.

12th

Lord Neill, the Parliamentary Commissioner for Standards publishes his report. Among other things the report recommends that MPs who take bribes should face criminal charges, Ministers must record all their meetings with lobbyists and that limits should be set on the numbers of special advisers.

12th

Simon Murphy (37) is elected the leader of Labour's MEPs, replacing Alan Donnelly.

13th

Labour peer Lord Winston, accuses the government of

deceiving the public over their handling of the Health Service.

16th   Mo Mowlam admits to smoking cannabis when she was a student.

16th   PM Tony Blair pledges to bring spending on the Health Service up to the European average by 2006.

17th   Former Transport Minister Stephen Norris is selected as Conservative candidate for the London Mayor.

20th   Lord Wakeham's Royal Commission on Reform of the House of Lords publishes its report. Among other things it recommends that the second chamber should have approximately 550 members, the majority chosen by an independent commission and that either 65, 87 or 195 members be elected from the 12 UK nations and regions.

20th   The Lords defeat the government's Criminal Justice (Mode of Trial) Bill that seeks to limit the right of defendants to trial by jury.

26th   Labour's 1,000th day in office.

26th   Prime Minister's Question Time is called off for the first time in 14 years after an all night session of Parliament over a Bill to allow members of the Northern Irish Parliament to sit in the Commons and the Northern Ireland Assembly at the same time.

27th   PM Blair announces an annual Holocaust Memorial Day to be held on the 27th January, beginning in 2001.

28th   Andy Pennington, an aide of the Liberal Democrat MP Nigel Jones (Cheltenham), is stabbed to death in the MP's constituency office by a man armed with a sword.

30th   Peter Kilfoyle resigns from his post as Junior Minister of Defence. The Liverpool Walton MP said he wished to be a 'critical friend' of the government from the back-benches. He is replaced by Lewis Moonie, MP for Kirkcaldy.

February

1st   GP Dr. Harold Shipman is found guilty of murdering 15 female patients. He is suspected of being involved in the deaths of scores of other patients. Health Secretary Alan Milburn announces a public enquiry into the affair.

1st   William Hague announces a surprise reshuffle of the Conservative Shadow Cabinet. John Redwood is sacked as Shadow Minister for Environment, Transport and the Regions; Michael Portillo replaces Francis Maude as Shadow Chancellor, who in turn becomes Shadow Foreign Secretary; John Maples is sacked as Shadow Foreign Secretary, with Archie Norman becoming Shadow Minister for Environment, Transport and the Regions;

4th   The formation of a new coalition government in Austria, composed of the People's Party and the controversial far-right Freedom Party, leads to international protests from the other 14 EU member states. The EU effectively places Austria in diplomatic isolation by refusing to deal directly with the new government.

9th   First Secretary of the Welsh Assembly, Alun Michael resigns, moments before a motion of no-confidence is tabled on his leadership by the opposition parties in the Assembly.

15th   The IRA withdraws its interlocutor from General John De Chastelain's decommissioning body following Northern Ireland Secretary Peter Mandelson's decision to re-impose direct rule from London five days previously.

15th   Labour's Rhodri Morgan is formally elected First Secretary of the Welsh Assembly.

15th   The government raises the basic adult hourly rate of the minimum wage by 10p from £3.60 to £3.70. The rate for workers aged 21 and under is increased from £3 to £3.20.

17th   Veteran Labour MP Robert Sheldon (76) collapses after a suspected heart attack while walking to the Commons. The MP for Ashton-under-Lyne was given first aid by the 1980 Olympic swimming gold medalist Duncan Goodhew, who happened to be in the area at the time.

17th   Teresa Gorman MP (Billericay) is suspended from the Commons for one month for repeatedly failing to declare business interests.

20th   Frank Dobson is selected as Labour's candidate for London Mayor. Dobson wins by 51.5% against 48.5% for Ken Livingstone, in a three-way electoral college.

24th   Conservative MP Michael Colvin (67) dies with his wife in a fire at their country manor in Hampshire.

24th   The official inquiry into the Southall rail crash in September 1997 blames the 'unexplained inattention' of the driver as the main reason for the crash. The report is also critical of the rail company Great Western Trains for failures of communication.

March

2nd   General Pinochet finally leaves the UK to return home to Chile after he is deemed unfit to stand trial.

2nd   Divisions emerge between two government departments over UK disaster relief effort in the wake of massive floods in Mozambique. International Development Secretary Clare Short accuses the Ministry of Defence of charging too much for hiring helicopters used for search and rescue missions.

5th   The PM and his wife take out an injunction against the Mail on Sunday over an article containing revelations about the family life of the Blairs. The article was based on an interview given by their former nanny.

6th   The runner-up in Labour's mayoral selection contest, Ken Livingstone, announces that he will stand as an independent candidate. As a result Livingstone is expelled from the Labour Party.

10th   Former Conservative Prime Minister John Major announces that he will stand down as an MP at the next election (see retiring MPs section).

11th	PM Blair visits Russia and meets acting President Vladimir Putin. The meeting is controversial after media reports alleging Russia had committed atrocities in the war-torn Republic of Chechnya.
15th	The Parliamentary Standards and Privileges Committee finds the independent candidate for London, Ken Livingstone, guilty of failing to declare £158,000 of income made from speeches and newspaper articles.
16th	German firm BMW announces that it is to sell-off or close its UK subsidiary Rover. British ministers express dismay at BMW's decision after not being informed by the company.
24th	Former Conservative Minister, Tony Baldry (Banbury), apologises to the Commons after admitting he had proposed a CBE award for a lawyer who provided him with a loan of £5,000.
25th	Ulster Unionist leader, David Trimble, wins the leadership contest at the party's Executive Council, Trimble beating challenger Rev. Martin Smith (South Belfast), by 56.8% to 43.2% of the vote.
28th	The government rejects a number of findings produced in a report by the Police Foundation. The report recommended that ecstasy and LSD be downgraded from a Class A to Class B drug, and Cannabis moved from Class B to Class C status.
31st	The government announces 33 new 'working peers', 20 of them Labour, 9 Liberal Democrats and 4 Conservatives. The most controversial new peer is millionaire Conservative Michael Ashcroft. The Public Honours Scrutiny Committee rules that Ashcroft must return from tax exile to live permanently in the UK as a condition of his peerage.

April

2nd	Foreign Secretary Robin Cook urges EU Foreign Ministers to send monitors to observe elections due to take place in Zimbabwe. This follows violence in Zimbabwe between President Mugabe's ruling Zanu-PF party and opposition groups and white farmers.

3rd   Former Conservative Minister Charles Wardle, the MP for Bexhill and Battle accepts a £120,000 a year directorship from Mohammed Fayed, whose allegations of sleaze undermined John Major's government.

4th   Former Defence Secretary, Tom King (66), announces he will not contest his Bridgwater seat at the next General Election (see retiring MPs section).

5th   Trade and Industry Secretary, Stephen Byers, defends his handling of the BMW-Rover crisis at a meeting of the Commons Trade and Industry Select Committee.

6th   The Speaker of the House of Commons, Betty Boothroyd, rules that breast-feeding is banned in the debating chamber and all committee rooms.

8th   Labour MP Bernie Grant (56) the MP for Tottenham, dies after suffering a heart attack. Grant was a powerful campaigner on behalf of the UK's Afro-Caribbean community.

9th   Former Conservative Home Office Minister, Charles Wardle MP, announces he is to stand down at the next General Election, following strong criticism over his links with Mohammed Fayed from his constituency association. Ironically Wardle was the Minister who turned down Fayed's application for UK citizenship in 1993.

10th   Shadow Chancellor Michael Portillo apologises to the Commons after he broke parliamentary rules for not declaring an interest in a multi-national oil company during a debate on petrol duty.

14th   The leader of the TGWU union, Bill Morris, attacks the government for 'creating a climate of fear' in its handling of asylum seekers and immigration policy.

25th   The National Union of Teachers, the biggest teaching union in England, votes to ballot members on strike action in protest at the introduction of performance related pay.

27th   Former Conservative Deputy Prime Minister, Michael Heseltine, announces that he will not stand as the MP for

Henley at the next General Election (see retiring MPs section).

27th   Ulster Unionist MP, Clifford Forsythe (70) dies. He was the MP for South Antrim.

May

4th   Ken Livingstone is elected as the first Mayor of London beating nearest rival Steven Norris by 776,427 votes to 564,137. Labour's Frank Dobson comes third in the contest. In the elections for the Greater London Assembly, Labour win 9 seats, the Conservatives 9, the Liberal Democrats 4 and the Greens 3.

4th   In local elections elsewhere in England, Labour suffers badly losing 573 council seats in total. The Conservatives increase their total by 593, with Liberal Democrats losing 18 and the Greens gaining 4 seats. In a by-election for the parliamentary seat of Romsey, held on the same day, the Conservatives are defeated by Liberal Democrat Sandra Gidley, who wins with a majority of over 3,000 (see by-elections section).

6th   The IRA issues a statement pledging to put its weapons 'beyond use'. The statement is seen as an attempt to encourage the Ulster Unionists to agree to re-enter the suspended Northern Ireland Assembly.

8th   First Minister of the Scottish Parliament, Donald Dewar undergoes surgery to correct a heart problem.

8th   UK military forces evacuate British, EU and Commonwealth nationals from war-torn Sierra Leone, after rebel forces launch a series of attacks.

9th   The Phoenix consortium purchase the Rover car company for a symbolic £10. The deal saves thousands of jobs in the West Midlands.

9th   45 Labour MPs vote against the government on their policy to partly privatise the UK's air traffic control system. Despite this opposition the government manages to win the vote in the Commons.

10th   Nicky Gavron, a Labour member of the London Assembly, becomes the Deputy Mayor of London at the request of the Independent Mayor Ken Livingstone.

15th   Defence Secretary, Geoff Hoon, makes a statement to the Commons ruling out UK forces becoming involved in the civil war in Sierra Leone.

18th   Ulster Unionist leader, David Trimble, cancels a planned meeting of the Ulster Unionist Council scheduled for the 20th May, in order to gain more time to persuade party members to re-enter the Northern Ireland Assembly alongside Sinn Fein.

19th   Tess Kingham, the Labour MP for Gloucester, says she will not stand at the next General Election. She blames the male culture and practice of the Westminster Parliament for her decision to step down (see retiring MPs section).

20th   The PM's wife Cherie Blair gives birth to a baby boy, named Leo after Tony Blair's father.

26th   Gordon Brown attacks admissions practices at Oxford University as elitist after the rejection of state school pupil Laura Spence by Magdalen College.

27th   Ulster Unionist leader, David Trimble, wins a crucial vote at his Ulster Unionist Council by 53% to 47%, saving the Northern Ireland peace process. The vote permits the Ulster Unionist Party to re-enter the power-sharing Northern Ireland Executive along with Sinn Fein.

31st   Plaid Cymru leader Dafydd Wigley (57) announces that he will stand down as President of the party. Mr. Wigley said he was stepping down for medical reasons following advice from his doctors.

June

1st   Cardinal Thomas Winning, the leader of Scotland's Catholic community launches an outspoken attack on the Scottish Parliament, describing it as an 'utter failure'. The Cardinal was annoyed at the decision of the Parliament to rescind 'section

28' preventing the promotion of homosexuality in schools.

5th   Liberal Democrat MP Ronnie Fearn announces that he will stand down from his Southport seat at the next general election.

6th   Liberal Democrat deputy leader, Alan Beith, returns from a parliamentary visit to Germany following the sudden death of his son Christopher aged 23.

7th   Prime Minister Tony Blair is jeered and heckled while making a speech at the Women's Institute national conference in London. The incident is seen as a major public relations disaster for Blair and the government.

12th   The government announces that it will introduce a bill to ban hunting with hounds.

17th   In the Queen's birthday honours list, former Liberal Democrat leader Paddy Ashdown receives a Knighthood, as does Bank of England Governor Eddie George and Conservative party treasurer, Michael Ashcroft.

18th   English football fans are involved in clashes with German fans and local North African youths during the Euro 2000 tournament in Belgium. The UK government is criticised by the UEFA football governing body and the Conservatives for not introducing legislation to prevent suspected hooligans from travelling abroad.

19th   Customs officers at Dover find 58 people dead in the back of a lorry. Two men in the lorry managed to survive the ordeal. Police suspect they are illegal immigrants, who were being smuggled into the UK.

23th   27 year old David Lammy wins the Tottenham by-election for Labour, and in so doing becomes the youngest MP in the Commons.

26th   The IRA opens up some of its weapons dumps for inspection by two international inspectors, former ANC Secretary Cyril Ramaphosa and former Finnish President Martti Ahtisaari.

30th   David Copeland, who conducted a nail bombing campaign against black and gay people in London, is jailed for six life terms. His bombing campaign killed 3 people and injured 139 others.

July

2nd   Author and long-standing Labour Party supporter, Ken Follett attacks Tony Blair and his government for making 'malicious gossip' a tool of government. He also attacks spin-doctors, describing them as 'rent boys' and launches a personal attack on Blair for his tolerance of such behaviour.

6th   The PM's son Euan (16) is arrested in the early hours of the morning for being 'drunk and incapable'. Euan was found lying semi-conscious in the centre of London after a night drinking to celebrate his GCSE exam results. The incident comes soon after the announcement (and abandonment) of a plan by Tony Blair to impose cash penalties on 'drunken yobs'.

11th   William Hague backtracks on his 'tax guarantee' by admitting a future Conservative government would not cut taxes as a proportion of national income if the economy ran into trouble. The policy change is widely interpreted as a victory for Shadow Chancellor, Michael Portillo.

12th   Betty Boothroyd (70) announces that she will stand down as Speaker and MP for her West Bromwich West seat before the next general election.

17th   Scottish National Party leader Alex Salmond (45) announces that he will stand down as party leader in September.

17th   The *Sun* and *The Times* newspapers publish a leaked confidential memo written by Tony Blair. The leak causes Blair and his government serious political embarrassment. In the memo the PM admits that his government is perceived to be 'out of touch with gut British instincts'. The leaked memo is followed by a series of other leaked documents written by Blair and pollster Philip Gould.

18th   Chancellor Gordon Brown announces in the Comprehensive Spending Review that public services will receive an extra

£43 billion over the next three years. Health, education and transport receive the largest increases in the spending review.

UK General Election Results, 1945–97

1945 (Turnout: 72.7%)

Party	Votes	% vote	Seats
Labour	11,995,152	47.8	393
Conservative	9,988,306	39.8	213
Liberal	2,248,226	9.0	12
Communist	102,780	0.4	2
Common Wealth	110,634	0.4	1
Others	640,880	2.6	19

1950 (Turnout: 84.0%)

Party	Votes	% vote	Seats
Labour	13,266,592	46.1	315
Conservative	12,502,567	43.5	298
Liberal	2,621,548	9.1	9
Communist	91,746	0.3	–
Others	290,218	1.0	3

1951 (Turnout: 82.5%)

Party	Votes	% vote	Seats
Labour	13,948,605	48.8	295
Conservative	13,717,538	48.0	321
Liberal	730,556	2.5	6
Others	198,969	0.7	3

1955 (Turnout: 76.7%)

Party	Votes	% vote	Seats
Labour	12,404,970	46.4	277
Conservative	13,286,569	49.7	344
Liberal	722,405	2.7	6
Others	346,554	1.2	3

1959 (Turnout: 78.8%)

Party	Votes	% vote	Seats
Labour	12,215,538	43.8	258
Conservative	13,749,830	49.4	365
Liberal	1,638,571	5.9	6
Others	142,670	0.9	1

1964 (Turnout 77.1%)

Party	Votes	% vote	Seats
Labour	12,205,814	44.1	317
Conservative	12,001,396	43.4	304
Liberal	3,092,878	11.2	9
Others	347,905	1.3	—

1966 (Turnout: 75.8%)

Party	Votes%	vote	Seats
Labour	13,064,951	47.9	363
Conservative	11,418,433	41.9	253
Liberal	2,327,533	8.5	12
Others	452,959	1.6	2

1970 (Turnout: 72.0%)

Party	Votes	%vote	Seats
Labour	12,179,341	43.0	287
Conservative	13,145,123	46.4	330
Liberal	2,117,035	7.5	6
SNP	306,802	(11.4*)	1
Plaid Cymru	175,016	(11.5**)	–
Others	383,511	1.4	6

* % vote in Scotland, ** % vote in Wales

February 1974 (Turnout: 78.7%)

Party	Votes	% vote	Seats
Labour	11,639,243	37.1	301
Conservative	11,868,906	37.9	297
Liberal	6,063,470	19.3	14
SNP	632,032	(21.9*)	7
Plaid Cymru	171,364	(10.7**)	2
Others	958,651	3.0	14

* % vote in Scotland, ** % vote in Wales

October 1974 (Turnout: 72.8%)

Party	Votes	% vote	Seats
Labour	11,457,079	39.2	319
Conservative	10,464,817	35.8	277
Liberal	5,346,754	18.3	13
SNP	839,617	(30.4*)	11
Plaid Cymru	166,321	(10.8**)	3
Others	914,590	3.2	12

* % vote in Scotland, ** % vote in Wales

1979 (Turnout: 76.0%)

Party	Votes	% vote	Seats
Labour	11,532,148	36.9	269
Conservative	13,697,690	43.9	339
Liberal	4,313,811	13.8	11
SNP	504,259	(17.3★)	2
Plaid Cymru	132,544	(8.1★★)	2
Others	1,039,563	3.3	12

★ % vote in Scotland, ★★ % vote in Wales

1983 (Turnout: 72.7%)

Party	Votes	% vote	Seats
Labour	8,456,934	27.6	209
Conservative	13,012,315	42.4	397
Liberal / SDP	7,780,949	25.4	23
SNP	331,975	(11.8★)	2
Plaid Cymru	125,309	(7.8★★)	2
Others	996,979	3.8	17

★ % vote in Scotland, ★★ % vote in Wales

1987 (Turnout: 75.3%)

Party	Votes	% vote	Seats
Labour	10,029,778	30.8	229
Conservative	13,763,066	42.3	376
Liberal / SDP	7,341,633	22.5	22
SNP	416,473	(14.0★)	3
Plaid Cymru	123,599	(7.3★★)	3
Others	881,671	2.7	17

★ % vote in Scotland, ★★ % vote in Wales

1992 (Turnout: 77.7%)

Party	Votes	% vote	Seats
Labour	11,559,735	34.4	271
Conservative	14,092,891	41.9	336
Liberal Dem	5,999,384	17.8	20
SNP	629,552	(21.5*)	3
Plaid Cymru	154,439	(8.8**)	4
Others	1,176,692	3.2	17

* % vote in Scotland, ** % vote in Wales

1997 (Turnout: 71.5%)

Party	Votes	% vote	Seats
Labour	13,517,911	43.2	419
Conservative	9,600,940	30.7	165
Liberal Dem	5,243,440	16.8	46
SNP	622,260	(22.1*)	6
Plaid Cymru	161,030	(9.9**)	4
Referendum	811,827	2.6	–
Others	1,340,652	4.2	19

* % vote in Scotland, ** % vote in Wales

That Difficult Second Term

Tony Blair is well aware that the Labour Party has never enjoyed two successive full terms of office; proud though he was of the victory of 1997 he would probably be even more proud of winning in 2001. Clement Attlee and Harold Wilson won landslide Labour election victories, in 1945 and 1966 respectively, but failed to establish firm control of the political environment and were out of power surprisingly rapidly. The 147-seat majority of July 1945 was replaced by an unworkably small majority of six in February 1950. Attlee carried on government for a year and a half, but called another election in October 1951 in which the Conservatives won a narrow victory. Labour's 97-strong majority of 1966 vanished in one go, as Edward Heath won a surprising and impressive victory in 1970.

Labour has also been in power on several occasions without the benefit of a large majority, and in each case the party has had a short lease on power. Labour took office for the first time in January 1924 despite being only the second largest party in a hung parliament. Labour lost a confidence vote a few months later, and the Conservatives won a big majority in October 1924. The world had not come to an end, and Labour also improved its vote in 1924 at the expense of the Liberals and went on to become the biggest party in another hung parliament after the May 1929 election. It was another single term government, as the Labour Party split in 1931 and the October 1931 election was the biggest landslide – to the Conservatives and allies – in British history.

More recently, Labour slunk into power after the February 1974 election despite the party's vote falling, and won a narrow overall majority in October 1974, but were booted out again in May 1979. Second terms have certainly been a problem for the Labour Party. Can 'New' Labour break this jinx, win another election, and enjoy the party's longest ever stretch of power?

Labour's Record in Power

The Blair government is the fifth period of Labour government in Britain. The first was for nine months in 1924, when Labour was a minority government with only 191 seats. Ramsay MacDonald became Prime Minister with Liberal acquiescence. The 1924 government's achievements were limited, although it reformed council housing finance and reopened diplomatic relations with Russia. It fell on a vote of confidence and lost the October 1924 election thanks to a collapse in Liberal support in favour of the Conservatives.

Labour formed another minority government in June 1929. It was an unfortunate moment to take power. The Wall Street Crash of October 1929 started a slump in the world economy, and Britain was hit hard. Unemployment rose from 1.2m to 2.9m. The crisis deepened in summer 1931 when the government was urged by a committee of inquiry to make deep cuts in public spending, including unemployment benefit. The Cabinet split, and MacDonald formed a 'National' government with the Conservatives and Liberals and smashed his old party in the election.

Labour's first majority government took power in July 1945 under Clement Attlee. Despite the precarious position of Britain after the Second World War, the Attlee government presided over massive changes in British society. Nye Bevan founded the NHS in 1948; Labour also introduced a comprehensive system of National Insurance covering unemployment, disability and a basic pension. Coal, rail, road transport and steel were taken into public ownership. Labour also made Britain a founder member of NATO and sent troops to Korea in 1950. The Labour government withdrew from India in 1947, a decisive retreat from an imperial role. The Attlee government's record defined much of the post-war world. Despite remaining very popular with its core voters, Labour only won narrowly in 1950 and lost power in 1951 thanks to the consolidation of the middle class vote around the much-reformed Conservatives.

Harold Wilson's narrow victory in the October 1964 election was confirmed with a landslide in March 1966, and for a while Labour appeared on the way to becoming the 'natural party of government'. However, the 1970 election produced a sharp swing to the Conservatives and Labour was out again. The Wilson government was greeted with very high expectations, but the reality proved disappointing, particularly in the central area of economic management. Nevertheless, the Labour government expanded access to education, abolished capital punishment, liberalised society through reforms on homosexual law, abortion and divorce, and somewhat by stealth reformed the tax system to make it much more progressive. The Wilson government left a permanent legacy, although it changed Britain much less than Attlee's.

Labour's accidental victory in February 1974, again under Harold Wilson, put the party back into power with a weak parliamentary position and deep internal divisions, facing a severe economic crisis. Another election in October 1974 only improved the parliamentary position slightly and the overall majority vanished days after Callaghan took over from Wilson in April 1976. Much of the time and energy of this government was spent dealing with severe economic problems and the government's medicine proved unpalatable for many on the left and in the unions. The legacy of the 1974-79 government is surprisingly substantial – employment rights legislation, health and safety law, liberalising measures on race relations and sex discrimination, reduced violence in Northern Ireland and a referendum that settled Britain's membership of the EC. However, much parliamentary time was wasted on enacting legislation to devolve power to Scotland and Wales that was cancelled by failed referendums in March 1979. It was no surprise when Labour lost the 1979 election.

Blair's government elected in May 1997 has also changed Britain in lasting ways. Devolution in Scotland and Wales has become reality and Sinn Fein has been brought into the government of Northern Ireland. Other constitutional reforms have removed most hereditary peers from the legislature and changed the electoral system for the European Parliament. Labour have introduced a minimum wage and new employment rights, and passed the far-reaching Human Rights Act.

Labour's Popularity in Power

The mid-term blues of the Blair government have been of the palest hue. Previous Labour governments have suffered long and deep periods of unpopularity, except for 1924 when the party had no time to do so. Labour popularity slumped at the end of 1929 and kept on falling until the October 1931 wipe-out.

The Labour government of 1945-51 did not lose a single seat in a by-election although it suffered from high swings against the party in local government elections in 1947-49, and lagged in the opinion polls for much of that time. Labour held seats in such tricky conditions as the by-elections in Gravesend and Sowerby, each of whose MPs had resigned under a cloud, and the highly marginal Hammersmith South.

The Labour government of 1964–70 had a bumpier ride. Its first by-election loss was in January 1965 at Leyton but it recovered strongly in 1965 and 1966. However, it was highly unpopular for the latter half of its tenure; until the Major government of 1992–97 the Wilson government of 1966–70 had the worst record ever in opinion polls. The party was behind continuously from April 1967 until May 1970, often by more than 20 points. The Conservatives won a succession of previously safe Labour seats such as Walthamstow West and Dudley in by-elections on massive swings. Very few Labour councils survived the disastrous local elections of 1967–69 – even Lambeth and Stoke-on-Trent went Tory. A Labour lead of 7% in the opinion polls in May 1970 caused massive Labour euphoria, rather than the 'what went wrong?' feeling that greeted similar figures in summer 2000.

The 1974–79 Labour government's popularity slipped badly in 1975, and was particularly low at the end of 1976 and through most of 1977. 'Safe' seats like Ashfield and Workington were lost in by-elections. Local elections, though less bad than 1967–69, saw heavy Labour defeats in 1975–77. The government was popular again in autumn 1978 but this was destroyed in the 'Winter of Discontent'.

By contrast, three years into Blair's government no by-elections have been lost and Labour has stayed well ahead in the polls (see by-election and polls sections). Although Labour performed patchily or poorly in local and devolution elections in May 1999, the only electoral beating the party has received was in the June 1999 European elections. The May 2000 local elections were bad for the party in many areas but there was no national wipe-out of the sort that happened in 1947, 1968 or 1977.

Labour and the Economy

The reason for New Labour's popularity as a government, compared to past Labour governments, is mainly because of the favourable economic conditions linked to a superior political-economic strategy that has learned from past errors. Every previous Labour government has faced a serious economic crisis about two years into power. In summer 1931 the Labour government collapsed during a crisis of confidence in sterling and the budget deficit. Unemployment discredited the government with its own supporters. The party was not believed to be a responsible guardian of the economy and was wiped out in the 1931 election.

The Attlee government faced several severe economic crises during its time in office, which perhaps unfairly gave Labour a renewed reputation for unsteady economic management. Crisis struck in 1947, with the run on the pound caused by restoring convertibility with the dollar; in 1949, with a large devaluation; and again in 1951 as the economic consequences of the Korean War unfolded. The ambitious spending plans of the first two years were mostly kept up, but there was diminishing room for further expansion. Rationing was applied to more goods in 1947 than had been controlled during the war, and although rationing was gradually lifted from 1948 onwards the budgets of 1949 and 1951 were particularly severe.

The first four years of the 1964–70 government were dominated by economic crisis, centred around the value of sterling. The honeymoon of 1966 came to an abrupt end in July 1966 when the government responded to a sterling crisis with harsh cuts that destroyed the National Plan and a restriction on travellers taking more than £50 out of the country. Even after devaluation in November 1967 crisis conditions continued, with a harsh budget in 1968 and a further crisis during which a second devaluation loomed. The more placid last two years were not enough to soothe the wounds of the previous period and in 1970 the electorate were willing to listen to Conservative warnings that yet another economic crisis lay just around the corner. Labour had promised increased investment in public services and help for modernising industry in 1964, but many promises had to be torn up, particularly in the period between the July 1966 crisis and autumn 1968. Particularly wounding retreats took place by delaying the raising of the school leaving age to 16 and reintroducing prescription charges.

Labour took power in March 1974 in conditions of considerable disorder. As in 1964–68, repeated crises of confidence shook the government and initial plans for expanding public expenditure had to be progressively torn up as 1975 and 1976 wore on. The government lost a Commons vote on the 1976 public expenditure plans thanks to a left wing revolt. The IMF crisis at the end of 1976 led to the rapid imposition of cuts across the range of public spending, particularly capital investment. Healey's retreat from Heathrow in September 1976, and the conditions attached to the IMF loan in December, gave a humiliating impression of Britain at the mercy of events. Although Healey was able to cut taxes, restore some of the spending cuts and pay off the IMF in 1978, Labour once again was associated with crisis and decline.

The association of Labour with economic crisis has blighted the party's reputation for decades – although the Conservatives have had their crises too, such as the 'pots and pans' budget in October 1955 and sterling crisis over Suez in 1956, the pay pause of 1961, repeated crises in 1970–74, the 1979–81 slump and 1992's Black Wednesday. Labour has been particularly vulnerable for a number of reasons. In 1929 and 1974 the party came to power just as world economic conditions were entering dangerous and uncharted territory. In 1964 and 1974 Labour inherited a mess from Conservative governments that had over-stimulated the economy. Labour have also showed incompetence and lack of imagination at dealing with what the left calls 'capital', tending to be over-impressed by warnings of doom from bankers. This hobbled the Labour government of 1929–31, which rejected the expansionist ideas of Lloyd George and (the then Labour) Oswald Mosley; instead, it convened a committee of bankers to advise on cuts. Labour also wasted opportunities through attempting to pacify foreign exchange markets in 1964–67. Financial markets have tended to lack confidence in Labour, a problem in itself and a handicap in achieving other aims.

The effect of these crises has been pretty uniform. Each one has compounded the perception that Labour governments are incompetent and lack grip, denting the party's general image. The Conservatives were able to taunt Labour for many years after the IMF crisis of 1976 for being 'bailed out' by an international organisation. As well as the general image problem, restrictive measures lead to slower growth, and the build up of dissatisfaction among the electorate, as after July 1966. Spending cuts also tend to break the party's promises, further irritating the electorate and causing division in the party – as after devaluation in 1967. Internal divisions, of the sort that broke out particularly in 1976, harm the party's prospects even further. 1931 broke the Labour Party; the crises of 1947, 1967 and 1976 also did severe damage and broke the morale and self-confidence of the government in each case.

The situation after 1997 has been very different from any that Labour has faced in the past. Labour's inheritance in 1997 was better than at the time of most previous election victories. The outgoing Conservative government had not generated an irresponsible boom or left the public finances grossly out of balance. World economic conditions have been surprisingly positive, particularly considering the Asian crisis at the end of 1997.

Blair and Brown's most explicit lesson from the past was to keep the previous government's spending plans for 1997–99 and allow funds to build up to allow a mid term shift towards expansion rather than panic cuts. Perhaps in retrospect 24 months was too long, but it has seemed to work. Labour's relations with capital have, if anything, been too good. Far from falling as in 1949, 1967 and 1976, sterling has risen to levels that endanger British industry. Giving independence to the Bank of England's Monetary Policy Committee in May 1997 was a very early signal of financial prudence; it, and the success of public spending restraint and balancing the budget in 1997–99, meant that Gordon Brown has enjoyed much more credibility in the financial markets than any previous Labour Chancellor.

The purpose behind the prudence became clearer in July 2000, with Brown's statement on the Comprehensive Spending Review and a massive planned increase in spending on public services and public sector invest-ment. This is a contrast to previous experience, when initial planned expansion was abandoned and harmful and divisive cuts introduced, as in 1966–68 and 1976. New Labour, so far, has managed to avoid the economic pitfalls of the past.

A Band of Brothers?

Newspapers enjoy discussing the resentments and jealousies at the heart of government, and the Blair government has seen its share of infighting. The basic divide is widely assumed to be between Tony Blair and Gordon Brown, which in turn spills over into factional allegiances among other ministers and MPs. The 1994 leadership election, in which Brown reluc-tantly did not stand, has left wounded feelings and personality conflicts. Accounts of other personality conflicts, involving Robin Cook, Peter Mandelson, John Prescott and various others, are also sometimes made public. Downing Street is much criticised for 'spin' and allegedly briefing against fellow ministers. It is difficult, at such close range, to assess how true and how important such tensions really are, but this government has suffered rather less so far from personality clashes than previous Labour administrations.

Perhaps the worst government of all for personal feuding was the successful Labour government of 1945–51. Having led Labour to a landslide victory in July 1945, Clement Attlee had to proceed directly to Buckingham Palace to accept the King's commission before Herbert Morrison had a chance to organise a coup among the new Parliamentary Labour Party against his leadership. There was a very serious attempt to get rid of Attlee in 1947, led by Stafford Cripps and the ever-plotting Hugh Dalton, and organised by the then junior George Brown. There were also strong resent-ments at the heart of the Cabinet particularly between Ernie Bevin and Herbert Morrison. It is often recalled that when someone made the remark that Morrison was his own worst enemy, Bevin growled, 'Not while I'm alive, he ain't.' Towards the end of the government the duel between Nye Bevan and Hugh Gaitskell was sharpening up, leading to the resignation of Bevan in April 1951 and a deep ideological split in the party for the next six years. None of these were junior figures: Dalton, Cripps and Gaitskell were Chancellors, Bevin and Morrison Foreign Secretaries, and Bevan was responsible for the creation of the NHS. Attlee, for his part, remained aloof from the plotting and infighting.

The Wilson governments' feuds are well chronicled by talented diarists and memoir writers. George Brown's envy and resentment of Harold Wilson, who defeated him in the 1963 leadership election, was barely held in check even when he was sober; Brown's resignation from the government was finally accepted in 1968 although he continued as Deputy Leader of the Labour Party. Brown was a good hater; when his enemy Len Williams was appointed Governor of Bermuda Brown asked whether he would have to wear a plumed hat. Williams confirmed that he would. 'I hope your fucking feathers fall out,' was Brown's charming response.

Wilson's Number 10 was criticised in ways that should seem familiar. He brought a personal retinue to Downing Street, who were often seen as forming a protective shell that kept him remote from the outside world. Wilson's government was very leaky and he frequently ticked off his Cabinet for leaking; one day Crosland spoke up and told Wilson that such lectures were pointless as most of the leaking came from Downing Street and everyone knew it. Wilson was always suspicious of the 'Gaitskellites' in his government, and to some extent he was justified. Roy Jenkins, a tough but successful Chancellor in 1967–70, was a focus of loyalty for Gaitskellites unreconciled to, or disillusioned with, the Wilson leadership. Although he was not a direct participant in plots against Wilson, the aim of some plotters was to install him as Prime Minister and Wilson made several pointed remarks about his alleged ambition. Plotting against Wilson was frequent in 1968 and 1969, leading the Prime Minister to announce in May 1968 'I know what's going on – I'm going on.'

There was brutal infighting over trade union law in 1969: Jim Callaghan, then Home Secretary, led a revolt against Barbara Castle's Industrial Relations Bill and voted against the government line in Labour's National Executive. Wilson was in too weak a position to sack him. Callaghan and Castle had never liked each other and the enmity continued: one of the first things Callaghan did when he became Prime Minister in 1976 was to sack her. When Wilson was forced to withdraw the Bill he raged against his Cabinet, shouting at them that they were spineless and implying that he might resign soon and denounce the decision. Wilson survived mainly because his critics were divided between Callaghan supporters and Jenkins supporters.

In the 1970s, the Labour Cabinet was publicly divided over Europe in 1975, and feuding continued behind the scenes. Tony Benn became progressively more disenchanted, even disgusted, with the government. Some colleagues thought he was playing to the gallery of the increasingly left wing Labour Party membership. The National Executive and the Conference produced and approved left-wing policies that had next to nothing in common with the government's attitudes. The widening divisions that led to the SDP breakaway in 1981 were opening up. The tension was relieved by occasional self-mocking wit and gallows humour. Tony Benn recorded Harold Wilson's farewell dinner in his Diaries; Benn reminded Wilson that 'When I was young and naïve many years ago I asked you, Harold, at Chequers what we should do if you were run over by a bus, and you said, 'Find out who was driving the bus.''

Labour Landslides and the Election After*

	1906	1945	1966	1997
Labour MPs (Lib & Lab in 1906)	427	399	363	419
Conservative and other MPs	133	217	265	222
Labour lead (Lib & Lab in 1906)	294	182	98	197

	Jan 1910	1950	1970
Labour MPs (Lib & Lab in 1910)	314	315	286
Conservative and other MPs	255	298	332
Labour lead (Lib & Lab in 1910)	59	17	(– 46)

*Table includes only British seats, not Irish (or Northern Irish) or university seats. Left wing independents are listed with Labour in 1945.

Labour's Election Record Reassessed

Past failures to maintain control after a landslide need some examination. As a rough rule of thumb, Labour (and the Liberals after their great victory of 1906) has seen something like a net loss of 75 seats after a landslide, reducing the majority by 150. The losses in 1950 were inflated by adverse boundary changes (for instance, seven depopulated East End seats in 1945 were collapsed into three in 1950). There are no boundary changes due until approximately 2005, when admittedly Labour will probably lose out a little from the reduction of Scottish representation. In this current election, a repeat of the average loss of 75 seats would still leave Labour with a lead of 47 over other parties in Britain (29 including Northern Ireland), which should be enough to last a full parliament.

The position at the margins is more favourable to Labour than in 1970, or 1950. Irish MPs boosted the progressive majority in 1910 but in 1950 and 1970 most Northern Ireland MPs were aligned with the Conservatives. In 1950–51 the rump of the Liberals were closer to the Conservatives than Labour. Since 1970, however, Liberal Democrats and Nationalists of various shades have won greater representation and drawn closer to Labour. Labour's October 1974 majority of three (and lead over the Tories of 42) was enough to sustain a government for over four years. A Labour majority of 29 would imply a lead over the Tories of at least 80, easily enough to sustain that elusive second term to its conclusion.

There is a lesser-known historical jinx that works against the Conservatives this time. There has only been one election in the last century in which a government with a clear majority was defeated in an election and replaced by a clear majority for another party. In 1905-06, 1918, 1922 and 1931 new governments were formed before the election and confirmed in office; in 1923–24, 1929 and 1974 there was no majority in the new parliament; in 1924, 1979 and 1997 the outgoing government had no majority in parliament; in 1964 the new government's majority was insufficient for a full term, as was that of the outgoing government in 1951. 1945 is the only arguable case; a Conservative led caretaker government held office during the election campaign itself, although until the election was called there was an all-party coalition. Edward Heath's achievement in winning the 1970 election outright therefore stands alone in recent history – 1880 was the previous 'clean' transfer of power.

Many Conservatives have attempted to draw solace from the failure of Labour, or the 1906 Liberals, to maintain landslide majorities. David Willetts has written an interesting paper, focusing on the experience of 1906 and 1945 in particular and the lessons the Tories might learn. The precedents seem to show that a clean transfer of power to the Conservatives is unlikely at the next election, but that a substantial recovery is possible – maybe substantial enough to deprive Labour of a working majority.

Looking at votes rather than seats, Labour in government, despite its poor record at winning re-election, leaves its electoral base more or less intact. The Conservatives prosper at the expense of the centre party, and overhaul Labour by rallying anti-Labour voters rather than slicing into Labour's support:

Periods of Labour Government

Change in Support. (%)

	1945–51	1964–70	Feb 1974–79
Labour vote	+0.5	–1.1	–0.1
Conservative vote	+8.2	+3.0	+6.1
Liberal vote	–6.6	–3.7	–5.5

In general, periods of Conservative government have done more to erode Labour's electoral base, with the dramatic exception of the 1992–97 parliament. When Conservative governments lose elections, it is generally because there has been a third party revival eating into the share of both major parties but taking more from the Tories. If Labour had squeaked ahead in 1992, this would have been repeated, but victory in 1997 was more like that of 1945 when Labour also gained votes.

Periods of Conservative Government

Change in Support (%)

	1951–64	1970–Feb 74	1979–92
Labour vote	–4.7	–5.9	–2.6
Conservative vote	–4.6	–8.6	–2.0
Liberal vote	+8.7	+11.8	+4.0

The generally stable pattern of Labour support under Labour government, however, disguises different reactions to long and short parliaments under Labour rule:

Full Term Labour Parliaments

Change in Support (%)

	1945–50	1966–70	Oct 1974–79
Labour vote	–2.2	–4.9	–2.2
Conservative vote	+3.7	+4.5	+8.1
Liberal vote	0	–1.0	–4.5

Short Parliaments with Labour Governments

Change in Support(%)

	1950–51	1964–66	Feb–Oct 1974
Labour vote	+2.7	+3.8	+2.1
Conservative vote	+4.5	–1.5	–2.0
Liberal vote	–6.6	–2.7	–1.0

Labour's vote was also up 2.6% in 1924 but down 6.2% in 1931.

If Labour disappointed as badly as the 1966–70 Labour government, their share of the vote would fall to a little over 38%. If the Conservatives manage to rally anti-Labour votes as well as they did between October 1974 and 1979, this would put them a little under 39%. Because of the way the electoral system operated in 1997, a uniform swing of this size would return Labour to power with a single-figure majority in 2001.

It seems quite improbable, given the extreme travails endured by the Wilson government after 1966 in by-elections, opinion polls, policy reverses, splits and general humiliation that Blair could suffer as badly. The current thrust of Conservative policy, coupled with the lack of middle class fear of Labour and union power, is unlikely to rally as much centre support as in the past to the Conservatives. It is therefore pretty unlikely on past performance that the Conservatives will come so close, and it is more likely that Labour will retain a popular vote lead and an adequate overall majority. According to Philip Gould's leaked memorandum, this rough guess aligns with the views of New Labour pessimists such as pollster Stan Greenberg. But if, as the economic record seems to suggest, Labour are now in a qualitatively stronger position than ever in the past, Blair should do better than that.

No doubt the memory of 1970 haunts the Labour party and its leadership, and gives hope to the Conservatives. It was a very unusual election, not only for being a clean transfer of power but also because the result was a complete shock to a Labour government blithely confident of re-election until the first results were declared. The pre-1997 mantra of 'no complacency' is surely due for a revival. But no Labour government has been in a better position to ask the electorate for a second term.

By-Elections of the 1997 Parliament

The 1997 parliament has so far been short of classic by-elections. From about 1962 to 1997, by-elections were occasions of huge media and public interest, and a travelling circus of party activists and journalists toured between them. They were capable of sending shocks through the political system, as Liberal or SDP gains in Orpington (1962), Isle of Ely (1973), Crosby (1981), Greenwich (1987) and Newbury (1993) did; of massive government losses to the main opposition like Dudley (1968), Ashfield (1977) and Dudley West (1994); and of bleeding away government majorities as in 1965, 1975-79 and 1993-97. By-elections have fuelled the growth of nationalism in Scotland and Wales since the 1960s. Nothing since 1997 has been quite as dramatic, although Romsey (2000) was certainly a jolt to the Conservatives. In fact, the most unusual fact about by-elections so far was that none took place in 1998; it is the first year in British democratic history in which no election took place at all for any seat in Parliament.

Blair's is the first government to have reached this stage of a parliament without losing a seat in a by-election since the high tide of two party stability in 1945-55, although this is partly luck in not defending any vulnerable seats. During the first 40 months of the Blair government Labour did not have to defend any of the marginal seats it gained in the 1997 election – the last time any of the contested Labour seats failed to elect a Labour MP was in 1935. The front line and the supporting fortifications remain untested in by-elections. So far by-elections have not only spared Labour marginals but also some other interesting types of seat. There have been none in the South West, where Euroscepticism is strongest and the Tories did well in the Euro election, and none in the Midlands. There have been none in Labour cities that have seen strong Liberal Democrat showings in local elections such as Liverpool or Sheffield. As a result we have a rather odd assortment of seats from which to try to glean some information about electoral trends.

By-election Results May 1997–June 2000

TO:	Turnout
C:	Conservative
L:	Labour
LD:	Liberal Democrat
N:	Nationalist

			TO(%)	C (%)	L(%)	LD(%)	N(%)
31.7.97	Uxbridge	Con hold	55.5	51.1	39.3	5.6	
6.11.97	Paisley South	Lab hold	42.9	7.0	44.1	11.0	32.5
20.11.97	Beckenham	Con hold	43.6	41.2	37.4	18.4	
20.11.97	Winchester	LD hold	68.7	28.4	1.7	68.0	
10.6.99	Leeds Central	Lab hold	19.6	12.3	48.4	30.8	
22.7.99	Eddisbury	Con hold	51.4	44.8	40.2	13.8	
23.9.99	Hamilton South	Lab hold	41.3	7.2	36.9	3.3	34.0
23.9.99	Wigan	Lab hold	25.0	18.0	59.6	13.3	
25.11.99	Kensington & Chelsea	Con hold	29.8	56.4	22.0	9.4	
3.2.00	Ceredigion	PC hold	45.7	16.5	14.4	23.0	42.8
4.5.00	Romsey	LD gain	55.4	42.0	3.7	50.6	
22.6.00	Tottenham	Lab hold	25.4	16.0	53.5	19.1	

It should be noted that Labour defended Ayr (first gained in 1997 and won by 25 votes in the 1999 Scottish parliament election) in a by-election for the Scottish parliament in March 2000, and achieved a very bad result. Labour won 22.1% of the vote, compared to 39.4% for the victorious Conservative and 28.9% for the SNP. The turnout was relatively high, at 57%. It is not yet clear how the electorate regard by-elections for the devolved assemblies, but at the very least the Ayr result was a warning for the administration in Edinburgh (Labour's partners, the Lib Dems, were fifth with 2.5%) and possibly for Westminster too not to take Scotland for granted.

The By-elections: a Summary

Five of the 12 Westminster by-elections have taken place in safe Labour seats:

Paisley South was caused by the suicide of Labour MP Gordon McMaster, and was a safe Labour hold despite the unsavoury nature of Paisley politics it revealed. Douglas Alexander, a high-flying New Labour

MP, was elected in McMaster's stead without much difficulty against an SNP challenge.

Leeds Central was caused by the sudden death of Foreign Office minister Derek Fatchett, and was held on the same day as the Euro election. It was notable mainly for its dismal turnout, but also put in a strong Lib Dem showing. The new MP, Hilary Benn, son of Tony, is the fourth generation of Benn in the Commons.

Wigan was caused by the early death of Callaghan's one-time PPS, Roger Stott, and aroused massive indifference in Wigan as elsewhere. Labour's Neil Turner held the seat comfortably.

Hamilton South was a more dramatic election. It was caused by the grant of a peerage to George Robertson prior to his taking office as NATO Secretary General. SNP candidate Annabelle Ewing was the daughter of Winnie, the woman who had shaken Scottish Labour in 1967 by taking the Hamilton seat in a by-election. The younger Ewing missed narrowly in 1999 despite a collapse in the Labour vote, and Bill Tynan was welcomed to Labour's parliamentary ranks.

Tottenham was caused by the death of Bernie Grant, a tabloid ogre when he first won in 1987 but a much respected and missed figure. Choice of his successor caused some ructions in the local Labour Party, but David Lammy, a formidably bright and energetic black barrister from Tottenham, held the seat. Lammy is now the youngest MP in the House of Commons.

Three by-elections have taken place in seats in which the Conservative majority, once large, was severely eroded in 1997:

Uxbridge was the first by-election of the new parliament. Conservative MP Michael Shersby died within a week of narrowly holding the seat, and Labour were optimistic of a gain at a time when the government's popularity was stratospheric. It was not to be; local Tory John Randall held the seat with a swing in his favour. The last Tory to hold a seat in a by-election, at Richmond (North Yorkshire) in 1989, had just become party leader.

Beckenham was called for an embarrassing reason – the Conservative MP Piers Merchant, who had been given the benefit of the doubt in

May, had been spotted behaving foolishly again with a Soho nightclub hostess in October 1997 and resigned. The Conservatives were at a disadvantage and held on despite a swing to the government; their new MP, Jacqui Lait, had managed to lose Hastings & Rye in May 1997.

Eddisbury in rural Cheshire, was produced by the machinations of public appointments. Former Conservative Chief Whip Alastair Goodlad had been tipped for a European Commissionership, but the job went to Chris Patten instead. Goodlad was appointed British High Commissioner in Australia. Eddisbury was a pitched battle between Conservatives and Labour; the Tory Stephen O'Brien held the seat with a similar majority to 1997.

Two of the by-elections have been in ostensibly safe Conservative seats:

Kensington and Chelsea hosted Alan Clark's brief return to the Commons in 1997–99; it is perhaps the safest Conservative seat in the country and one of few which could have withstood a by-election in the 1992–97 parliament (Chelsea was considered as an alternative berth for Chris Patten when he lost Bath in 1992). The Conservatives, with another charismatic candidate in Michael Portillo, held it easily in 1999, although turnout was very low.

Romsey in Hampshire had been represented by Tory MP Michael Colvin until his death in a house fire, and was not expected to present significant difficulties for the Conservatives. It was a considerable surprise when the Liberal Democrat Sandra Gidley managed to gain the seat in May 2000, when the Conservatives seemed to be riding high nationally.

Finally, two by-elections have been in seats defended by smaller parties:

Winchester was a strange by-election, caused by a petition against the two-vote victory of Lib Dem Mark Oaten in May 1997. Defeated Tory Gerry Malone argued in court that had some votes not been inadvertently disallowed, he would have won, and he was given another chance in November 1997. There was no doubt about the result this time; Malone was trounced by over 20,000 votes on the highest turnout of any by-election this parliament and Oaten returned in triumph.

Ceredigion was called because its Plaid Cymru MP Cynog Dafis, having been elected to the Welsh Assembly, decided to concentrate on his work in Cardiff and give up the Westminster seat. His successor Simon Thomas held the seat in a low-temperature by-election, the first of the year 2000.

The table below summarises the changes in major party share of the vote and turnout in the 12 by-elections.

Change Since 1997 General Election

TO: Turnout
C: Conservative
L: Labour
LD: Liberal Democrat
N: Nationalist

			TO(%)	C(%)	L (%)	LD (%)	N (%)
31.7.97	Uxbridge	Con hold	-16.9	+7.5	-2.5	-5.3	
6.11.97	Paisley South	Lab hold	-26.2	-1.7	-13.4	+1.6	+11.1
20.11.97	Beckenham	Con hold	-30.7	-1.3	+4.0	+0.3	
20.11.97	Winchester	LD hold	-9.6	-13.7	-8.8	+25.9	
10.6.99	Leeds Central	Lab hold	-34.6	-1.4	-21.4	+19.5	
22.7.99	Eddisbury	Con hold	-24.2	+2.3	+0.1	+0.6	
23.9.99	Hamilton South	Lab hold	-29.8	-1.4	-28.7	-1.8	+16.4
23.9.99	Wigan	Lab hold	-42.7	+1.1	-9.0	+3.3	
25.11.99	Kensington & Chelsea	Con hold	-19.8	+2.8	-6.0	-5.9	
3.2.00	Ceredigion	PC hold	-28.2	+1.6	-9.9	+6.5	+1.2
4.5.00	Romsey	LD gain	-21.6	-4.0	-14.9	+21.2	
22.6.00	Tottenham	Lab hold	-29.6	+0.3	-15.8	+8.3	

The Categories of By-election

1. Labour defences Labour does indeed have a problem in its 'heartlands' in by-elections. ('Vote retention' is the by-election vote expressed as a percentage of the party's vote in the general election.)

	Fall in TO (%)	Fall in Lab share(%)	Lab vote retention (%)
Paisley South	16.2	-13.4	48.2
Leeds Central	-34.6	-21.4	24.7
Hamilton South	-29.8	-28.7	33.0
Wigan	-42.7	-9.2	32.1
Tottenham	-29.6	-15.8	33.6

Labour is vulnerable on two fronts; from apathy among its supporters and attack from non-Conservative opposition forces. Turnout sank to dismal levels in Leeds Central, Wigan and Tottenham; 19.1% in Leeds Central was the worst turnout in any peacetime parliamentary contest, as was the turnout drop in Wigan. There have been low turnout by-elections in safe Labour seats in previous parliaments, but very few below 30% and the occasional very high turnout (Bassetlaw in 1968 saw 68% of electors voting, and in Batley and Morley in 1949 an astonishing 81.3% voted in a routine by-election in a Labour seat).

Labour has been unable to bring its support to the polls – in this measure it is hardly doing any better than John Major's 1992–97 government – but has been fortunate in that opposition parties have in general failed to bring their supporters out either, although the SNP in particular has been able to make some headway in by-elections against Labour.

These two factors have combined to produce some remarkably poor showings in safe Labour seats. Hamilton South is the worst so far, with the Labour share of the vote falling by 28.7 percentage points. There have only been three worse Labour showings in post-war by-elections: Bermondsey in 1983, Birmingham Ladywood in 1969 and Hamilton in 1967. Even Dudley (1968) and Ashfield (1977) were less severe.

However, Labour's cushion of votes gained in 1997 is so comfortable, and the gains from the Labour slump have been so scattered among other parties and minor candidates, that Labour has held on even in such circumstances. If the SNP had been able to monopolise the gains in Hamilton South, as they did in the 1967 by-election in the same town, they would have won comfortably. In the event, socialist and minor party candidates absorbed over half the Labour losses. A similar pattern was apparent in Tottenham, where the Lib Dems were the main beneficiary but the London Socialist Alliance also saved its deposit. Left wing opponents have increased their share of the vote in all the Labour seats, winning 10.7% in Hamilton South and over 5% in Tottenham and Leeds Central. There is clearly a small groundswell of opinion on the left that the Blair government has not been left wing enough.

The Conservatives have failed to make any headway in the Labour heartland seats. Their share of the vote was down in three, and very feebly up in Wigan and Tottenham. There was no sign at Tottenham that the political climate has turned sharply against Labour, and certainly none that the Tories have recovered.

2. Conservative marginals. The three by-election seats in which Labour ran the Tories relatively close in 1997 were all retained by the new Conservative candidates; only three such seats have been lost by the opposition to the government since the 1920s, so it is not too surprising than none of them changed hands. However, these contests have a disturbing message for the Conservatives.

	Uxbridge	Beckenham	Eddisbury
Change in turnout (%)	-16.9	-28.7	-24.2
Change in Con vote (%)	+7.5	-1.3	+2.3
Con vote retention rate (%)	90.0	57.0	74.4
Change in Lab vote (%)	-2.5	+4.0	+0.1
Lab vote retention rate (%)	72.1	65.8	69.8

The best Tory showing was in Uxbridge, held at the height of the Blair honeymoon in July 1997, when the party enjoyed a 5% swing in its favour. Labour probably had more to learn from Uxbridge than the Tories; it was an early straw in the wind that demonstrated that when the electorate detected a fix going on, they disliked it. The Millbank-approved Hammersmith council leader abruptly replaced Labour's candidate from the general election a few weeks earlier, and was vulnerable to a strong local Conservative candidate and the defensive independence of a semi-metropolitan town like Uxbridge. Wales, Falkirk and London followed where Uxbridge led.

The worst Tory showing was in Beckenham, a south east London suburb, in November 1997, where there was a 2.6% swing to Labour in an extremely embarrassing, inconvenient and rather unnecessary contest of the sort voters often seem to resent. The most recent to date was at Eddisbury in July 1999. Both parties campaigned hard for the seat and the result was a near repeat of the 1997 election with a puny swing to the Conservatives of 1.1%. The Labour share of the vote was a tiny fraction up on 1997, a very unusual mid-term result. The July result was very different from the Euro election in June 1999, when the Conservatives led 48–22%. Labour's record at retaining its 1997 voters is much better in the Tory marginals than its own heartlands, and the Conservatives have not inspired their 1997 deserters to return.

In both Beckenham and Eddisbury the Conservatives should have been able to profit from the withdrawal of Eurosceptic candidates who had won 4% in 1997, but they seem to have failed to do so. Serious election analysts did stress that the 1997 Referendum and UKIP vote could not be regarded simply as a split-off from the Conservative vote, and it has not simply 'returned' to the Tories despite the increasingly anti-European tone of the Conservative leadership. In a couple of seats (Wigan and Kensington) the share of the anti-European minor parties has increased, as of course it did in the 1999 Euro election.

3. The Rest. The Liberal Democrats or Liberals have won at least one startling victory in every parliament since 1955-59, and the current one is no exception, with the surprise gain from the Conservatives in Romsey in May 2000. They also held Winchester, where their two-vote gain in May 1997 was disputed, with a massive swing against the Conservatives in November 1997. In both seats the number of Liberal Democrat voters rose on 1997; only in Hamilton South has another main party (SNP) managed this. In both these elections the Labour vote collapsed, with some connivance from the leadership of the party, in favour of the Lib Dems – from 10.5% to 1.7% in Winchester and 18.6% to 3.7% in Romsey. Turnout dropped 9.6% in Winchester and 21.6% in Romsey.

The devastatingly bad result for the Conservatives in Romsey in May 2000, against the backdrop of a reasonably strong showing in local elections, was the most notable of the parliament. It is quite unusual for the main opposition party to lose a by-election, and there is no real precedent for it to lose a reasonably safe seat in such circumstances. The Tories have only lost one other by-election from opposition since the war – Roxburgh, Selkirk and Peebles in 1965 – and that was in a seat with a Liberal tradition and an MP as recently as 1950–51. Romsey was, like Christchurch in the previous parliament, an 'assemble from kit form' Lib Dem campaign in a previously patchily organised area. That the Conservatives are still vulnerable to such efforts is significant.

The two remaining seats are an odd couple in every respect. Kensington and Chelsea is one of only two Conservative remnants of a once solid category of seats – affluent, but urban rather than suburban, parts of big cities. It is a concentration of some of the most intractable Tory areas in London, and even in local elections it has always been a strong Conservative seat. Michael Portillo returned to parliament without much trouble with a small swing in his favour although on a turnout (under 30%) that was comparable to the Labour held by-elections.

The remaining by-election, at Ceredigion in rural west Wales, is a long way from Sloane Square. The Lib Dems, who held the seat from 1974 to 1992, gained a respectable second place to Plaid Cymru and Labour slipped from second to fourth, although the party's vote fell rather less than it has in their heartlands and was only 1.8% down on the Welsh election of 1999. Labour's relative success in Eddisbury and the worse result in Ceredigion sent mixed signals about whether there is much of a 'countryside effect'.

The Lessons of the By-elections

In parliaments that precede a change of government, there are by-elections which show ferocious swings to the main opposition party – such as Labour's 29.1% swing at Dudley West in 1994 and the Conservatives' 22.5% at Walsall North in 1976. The next general elections, in 1997 and 1979, produced the largest swings that have ejected governments since 1945; the Tories before 1970 also achieved massive swings in by-elections, for instance at Dudley (21.2%).

More moderate, but still double-figure, swings to the main opposition took place before the elections of 1951, 1964 and February 1974, all of which saw a change of government, and 1959 which did not. Double-figure swings also took place before the elections of 1950, 1987 and 1992 in which the opposition improved its position; failures to achieve this benchmark preceded opposition losses at general elections in 1955, 1966 and October 1974. In all previous parliaments (even the short parliament of 1974) the best opposition performance in a by-election would, if replicated nationally, be enough to put it into office with a majority – usually a substantial one although only just adequate in the short 1974 parliament and the 1983–87 parliament. Swings to the Tories in the by-elections so far since 1997 are not enough to deprive Labour of an overall majority. When past Labour governments have been genuinely unpopular, the Conservatives have managed to obtain high swings in Labour's heartland seats and easily see off challenges in their own marginals, not to mention not losing their own seats.

Other than Uxbridge, when the Conservatives have been seriously challenged their results have been mediocre against Labour (Beckenham, Eddisbury) and disastrous against the Lib Dems (Winchester, Romsey). The Lib Dems can clearly still benefit from tactical voting by Labour sympathisers to keep the Conservatives out, even three years into a Labour government. Perhaps Labour supporters are even more willing to vote Lib Dem in tactical situations as a way of making a mild protest at the government's departures from traditional Labour policies and kicking the Tories, all in one go. As of May 2000, there is no evidence from the by-elections that the electorate are willing to trust the Tories again.

Turnout in Labour's heartlands is continuing to fall faster than in the rest of the country. The five Labour heartland seats accounted for 36.0% of the votes cast in the twelve seats in 1997 (and 37.2% in 1992) but only 27.3% in the by-elections. The change in turnout in the Labour heartlands compared to the rest accounts for 3.6% of Labour's 13.2% fall in support taking the by-elections as a whole – over a quarter. If anything like this were to happen in the next general election Labour's lead in the national share of the vote can narrow without loss of marginal seats and the electoral system will become even more biased in the party's favour.

By-elections are far from infallible indicators of the way the next general election will go, but the general pattern by which changes of government are preceded by high swings to the main opposition holds good. The only counter-examples are the way in which Labour's strong showings in 1956–58 and 1989–91 were followed up by losing in 1959 and 1992, and – after an initial burst of good results in 1971 – Labour's bad results in 1972–73 preceded a return to government – albeit minority government on a very low share of the vote. So far, the by-elections of the 1997 parliament seem to point to the election in 2001 or 2002 being a lot like 1997, although with significantly lower turnout.

Opinion Polls 1997-2000

by Roger Mortimore, Political Analyst, MORI

The most difficult aspect of interpreting the polls since 1997 is that their findings have been quite unprecedented. Other Prime Ministers have occasionally, in a single poll, touched the same heights of approval as Tony Blair, other governments have now and then briefly attained comparable voting intention leads, but no Prime Minister or government in the sixty-odd years that opinion polls have existed in Britain has ever been able to bask in the sustained popularity found by the polls in the first two-and-a half years of the 1997 parliament.

The peaks came in the autumn of 1997, when the 'honeymoon effect' that a new government could have expected in any case was clearly enhanced by approval of the Prime Minister's handling of events following the death of Diana, Princess of Wales, at the start of September. But even apart from this exceptional event, it was more than two years before the government slipped 'into the red' in satisfaction ratings, and over three years before more said they were dissatisfied than satisfied with Tony Blair for the first time. Taking all the trends together, it is clear that the government's honeymoon period, when the majority of the public were prepared to give it the benefit of the doubt, lasted for an unprecedented period, but disillusionment began to be increasingly reflected in the findings from the end of 1999.

This sharp drop in the government's and Tony Blair's own approval ratings restores the political scene in Britain to what we generally assume to be its normal state, after more than three years when it seemed as if the laws of political gravity had been suspended. In the past, it has been taken for granted that governments are unpopular for most of the time; for the first time, Mr Blair's ratings are beginning to be comparable to those of his predecessors. Not that he should necessarily consider this cause for real alarm: for example, Margaret Thatcher consistently scored worse than Tony Blair has ever done throughout 1986, yet won the 1987 election comfortably. Nevertheless, it is a considerable comedown for a Prime Minister who as recently as April 1999 had more than 60% of the country satisfied with how he is doing his job. Normal service has been restored, so to speak.

There have been signs, notably a flurry of leaked memos between senior members of the government, that Mr Blair was concerned by the messages coming from his private polls over the first four months of 2000, and that the government attempted a series of 'eye-catching initiatives' to win back the lost ground. If so, the result was counter-productive. At the end of April, satisfaction with the government had dropped eight points in four months and with Mr Blair personally by 5 points; nevertheless, the figures on almost every front were still at a level most previous Prime Ministers could only have dreamed of. Following a disastrous series of initiatives and statements between April and the end of June, satisfaction with the government dropped by a further 12 points in two months, to just 28%, with Mr Blair by 13 points (giving him for the first time negative net ratings), and the voting intentions though still showing a Labour lead have also taken a perceptible knock. The apparent panicky reaction to disappointing poll ratings more sharply undermined the government's position than anything that had gone before.

Although, for most of the period, the government's satisfaction ratings looked healthy, this was not necessarily an indication that the public thought the country was being governed well. For example, in December 1999 only 26% thought that since the election the government had improved law and order, 28% that it had kept taxes down, 23% that it had helped to improve their own living standards and, overall, 35% thought it had kept its promises while 49% did not. So how could the voters be 'satisfied' with such a government? The answer, essentially, is that their expectations were low to start with and, probably that by comparison with the previous government even a low level of perceived achievement was considered an improvement. Even before the election, only two in five, 42%, expected a Blair government to keep its promises and almost as many, 40%, did not; and 63% said they expected a Labour government to increase income tax, even though Tony Blair had given a pledge that he would not do so. Intriguingly, these figures were little different from those applying to Neil Kinnock in 1992, when 66% expected him to raise income tax if elected, even though many politicians and commentators remain convinced that it was fear of tax rises under a Kinnock government that led to Labour's defeat in 1992.

Falling satisfaction ratings in 2000 have reflected falling performance ratings on individual issues, and perhaps indicate that public patience is wearing thin over what they see as lack of delivery on the government's objectives. At the start of June, only 25% of the public thought the government had kept its promises, while 60% thought it had not; 24% believed that since 1997 the government had improved law and order, 25% that it had improved the NHS and 36% that it had improved the standard of education.

Nevertheless, falling satisfaction with the government has not been matched by any precipitous movement in the voting intention polls. Labour's share has not dipped far below 50% (table A), and that only occasionally, while the Conservatives were steady on 30% or below until May 2000. While there has been a definite (and sustained) improvement for the Tories since the end of 1999, they are still not even close to shaking Mr Blair's grip on power if the election were held tomorrow. At the time of writing, the closest that any poll has put the parties is the 41% to 38% Labour lead in a MORI poll for the Mail on Sunday (not part of the regular monthly series shown in the table). But this poll, conducted in the immediate aftermath of Tony Blair's disastrous speech to the Women's Institute, clearly measured only a transient 'blip' in public opinion; and even were it to be translated into reality at the polls, on uniform swing such a lead in votes would give Labour an overall majority of more than 60 seats; and all the other polls before and since have put Labour's share higher and the Conservative share lower.

There is little mystery as to why this is. Although the public is no longer prepared to give the government the benefit of the doubt, and seems dissatisfied with its record on many fronts, it doesn't think much of the Conservative alternative. Even the Mail on Sunday MORI poll in which the gap between the parties narrowed to three points and the government was judged a failure in every one of eight key policy areas also found that Mr Blair beat Mr Hague by 37% to 18% as most capable Prime Minister.

From the start it has been apparent that one major factor in the government's high ratings has been the public's distaste for the Conservatives. William Hague's personal approval ratings as Conservative leader have never risen above the dismal (see table B), and for a long period even the party's supporters were dissatisfied with his performance, although from the time of the victory in the 1999 European Elections onwards he has at least managed to win approval from more of this dwindled band than are dissatisfied. Mr Hague's failure has been a negative rather than a positive one – he has not made a significant impact with the public in his own right, and has therefore come to be seen as being generally representative of all the aspects of the Conservative party's image which contributed to the sweeping defeat in 1997. In May 2000, just 18% of the public agreed that 'William Hague is

ready to be Prime Minister' (64% disagreed), and 23% agreed that 'The
Conservatives are ready to form the next government'. Nevertheless, in one
respect Mr Hague has made an impact, drawing upon his party's traditional
strengths. MORI's leader image poll for The Times in April 2000 found, as
had the previous one in October 1999, that more people chose 'patriotic' as
a description of William Hague than Tony Blair – but this is the only one of
14 measures on which Hague beats or has ever beaten Blair.

Maintaining public distaste for the Tories is, mostly, out of Mr Blair's
hands and in Mr Hague's. However, the signs are that, for the moment, Mr
Hague is doing a good job – for Mr Blair. Not that there is an obvious alternative: when tested, Michael Portillo's ratings have been worse, and moving
downwards.

Meanwhile in the same leader image surveys (table B), Charles Kennedy
has yet to make much of an impact, though this is only to be expected for
a third party leader who has yet to lead his party in a general election. In
April 2000, 51% of the public said they had no opinion of him and could
not apply any of the 14 descriptions to him. (By way of comparison, only
7% had no opinion of Mr Blair and 21% of Mr Hague.) His profile is lower
among women than men (43% of men but 58% of women had no opinion).
The same is true of his party in the voting intention polls. Their monthly
share has almost invariably been lower than they achieved at the last
election, but this has been a familiar pattern in previous parliaments and the
Liberal Democrats can probably in the next election, as in those of the past,
expect to pick up support in the last months and weeks as polling day
looms.

The main issues concerning the public (table C) have remained substantially the same ever since Mr Blair's election. The National Health Service is
the almost invariable number one; education, crime and unemployment
regularly fill the next ranks, with only sporadic appearances by other issues
when they become a topical matter of concern. The most noticeable change
from the previous parliament is the low priority given to unemployment,
once the unchallenged 'top dog' in the issues facing Britain question,
testimony to the effect of economic success in reducing joblessness.

More relevant for a forthcoming election is the generally low showing
of two of the issues on which the Conservatives might be tempted to fight
their campaign, Europe and tax. The Tories have already got their message
about tax rises under this government home to the electorate – in June
2000, only 26 per cent of Britons thought that since May 1997 this
Government has 'kept taxes down'. But taxation is nowhere to be found

among the top few issues: as the table shows, the percentage has not been in double figures in any MORI poll under Blair's premiership. The public may believe that Mr Blair has raised taxes, but for the moment it is not preying on their minds. Similarly, although the instinct of the public seems to back Mr Hague's generally Euro-sceptic policy, only occasionally is the issue at the front of the public's minds, and even then it has no impact on Conservative support.

A similar pattern is seen when respondents are asked which issues they think will be important to them in deciding the way they will vote. Although the Conservatives had a comfortable lead in July 2000 as being the party with the best policy on both of these issues among those who think it will be important, only 36% rate taxation and 26% Europe as an issue that will be important in deciding their vote – and most of these are Tory already. The vote-wining potential is therefore decidedly limited. By contrast, 67% think healthcare will be important to their vote, and of these 43% think Labour has the best policy while only 17% back the Tories.

The Economic Optimism Index (EOI, sometimes called the Consumer Confidence Index or simply the Feelgood Factor, see table D) has fluctuated since 1997 but has been negative throughout 2000. In the 1980s this would have been a portent of doom for the government – the correlation between the EOI and voting intentions was always high, and a negative EOI would be likely to presage electoral defeat. But this relationship broke down in the 1990s, perhaps especially as a result of 'Black Wednesday' in autumn 1992 when sterling dropped out of the ERM. The public apparently no longer demands confidence in the government's economic competence as a pre-requisite for its support at the ballot box. The EOI remains a useful economic indicator, but unless trends change Tony Blair need not lose too much sleep even if it remains negative into the election campaign.

Yet public opinion is volatile, and the polls indicate that very trivial factors can swing opinions and perhaps even affect the results of elections. The birth of a fourth child to the Prime Minister offers a prime example. In MORI's monthly poll for The Times in May, as it happened, almost half the interviews were completed before Leo Blair's birth was announced, and the remainder in the next couple of days. The effect was dramatic; in voting intention, there was a 3% swing to Labour from the Conservatives, and Mr Blair's personal satisfaction score rose six points, from 45% to 51%. To understand the scale of the impact a little better, we ought to convert the percentages into numbers. Tony Blair's satisfaction score rose by 6%: in other words, two-and-a-half million people went to bed on Saturday night apparently dissatisfied with his performance as Prime Minister, only to change their minds the following morning.

Who was it who swung? Almost exclusively those who live in households with no children – apparently the sight of Tony and Cherie cuddling Leo is less impressive to those who have kids of their own – and C2DEs rather than ABC1s – probably because they are less likely to take a deep interest in politics, and are therefore more susceptible to changing impressions and image. Broadsheet readers showed no 'Leo effect' at all; indeed, Labour's share of their vote fractionally fell over the weekend. But tabloid readers swung, and those reading no daily regularly at all swung even more.

People often criticise opinion polls because they seem to fluctuate wildly over time. But if a single event, so apparently irrelevant, can have this much effect on public opinion then it would hardly be surprising if events of real political moment can produce swings over days and weeks. Indeed, we already know how volatile public opinion has become: during the last general election MORI interviewed a panel of voters twice for the Evening Standard, once towards the start of the campaign and again the day before polling, and found that a quarter of them had changed their answers. Wise political leaders bear this in mind, which is why 'spin doctors' have become so important in modern elections: the superficially trivial can swing millions of minds and millions of votes.

There is a final factor to be borne in mind – turnout, which may possibly have more effect in the next general election than at any for generations. The Conservatives have achieved dramatic victories in European and local elections in 1999 and 2000 on derisory turnouts, because they have proved better at persuading their supporters to vote. Polling questions on likelihood of voting at the next general election confirm that more Conservatives say they are 'certain' or 'very likely' to vote than Labour supporters: in March 2000, for example, Labour led by 48% to 29% among all adults, but only by 45% to 33% among those certain to vote. So the 'real' lead – what would happen if there really were 'a general election tomorrow', as the time-honoured poll question puts it – is probably smaller than the raw poll figures suggest. But whether that will still be the case when the election comes, or whether the government can motivate its more disillusioned supporters to vote against the risk of a Conservative government, remains to be seen.

Table A: Voting Intentions*

Question: How would you vote if there were a General Election tomorrow?

Question: (If Undecided or Refused) Which party are you most inclined to support?

*All figures shown are percentages

	Con	Lab	LibDem	Other	Con lead
1992					
Election	43	35	18	4	+8
2nd Quarter	43	38	16	3	+5
3rd Quarter	39	43	14	4	-4
4th Quarter	34	47	15	4	-13
1993					
1st Quarter	34	47	16	3	-13
2nd Quarter	29	45	22	4	-16
3rd Quarter	28	43	25	4	-15
4th Quarter	28	47	22	3	-19
1994					
1st Quarter	28	48	21	3	-20
2nd Quarter	25	49	22	4	-24
3rd Quarter	24	54	17	5	-30
4th Quarter	23	58	15	4	-35
1995					
1st Quarter	25	58	13	4	-33
2nd Quarter	25	57	15	3	-32
3rd Quarter	26	56	14	4	-30
4th Quarter	27	56	13	4	-29
1996					
1st Quarter	27	56	14	3	-29
2nd Quarter	27	56	13	4	-29
3rd Quarter	29	54	13	4	-25
4th Quarter	29	53	13	5	-24
1997					
1st Quarter	29	54	12	5	-25
Election	31	44	17	8	-13

	Con	Lab	LibDem	Other	Con lead
June 20-23	24	58	15	3	-34
July 25-28	23	57	15	5	-34
Aug 21-25	28	54	15	3	-26
Sept 26-29	25	59	13	3	-34
Oct 24-27	24	60	12	4	-36
Nov 21-24	24	56	16	4	-32
Dec 12-15	26	55	15	4	-29

1998

Jan 23-26	28	54	14	4	-26
Feb 20-23	28	52	15	5	-24
March 20-23	28	53	14	5	-25
April 24-27	27	55	14	4	-28
May 21-24	26	55	14	5	-29
June 25-30	27	56	13	4	-29
July 17-21	28	53	14	5	-25
Aug 21-24	28	52	14	6	-24
Sept 18-21	24	56	15	5	-32
Oct 23-26	26	53	16	5	-27
Nov 20-23	29	53	13	5	-24
Dec 11-14	27	54	12	7	-27

1999

Jan 22-25	24	56	14	6	-32
Feb 19-22	30	51	14	5	-21
March 19-22	27	54	13	6	-27
April 23-26	25	56	13	6	-31
May 21-24	28	52	14	6	-24
June 18-21	28	51	13	8	-23
July 23-26	28	51	14	7	-23
Aug 20-23	27	49	17	7	-22
Sept 24-27	25	52	17	6	-27
Oct 22-25	28	56	11	5	-28
Nov 19-22	25	55	14	6	-30
Dec 10-14	28	54	13	5	-26

2000

Jan 21-24	30	50	15	5	-20
Feb 17-22	29	50	15	6	-21

	Con	Lab	LibDem	Other	Con lead
March 23-28	29	50	14	7	-21
April 13-18	27	51	15	7	-24
May 18-23	32	48	15	5	-16
June 22-27	33	47	13	7	-14
July 20-24	33	49	12	6	-16

Source: MORI/The Times

Base: c. 2,000 interviews with British adults aged 18+ each month from 1997, c. 5,000-18,000 each quarter 1992-97.

Table B: Satisfaction Ratings*

Question: Are you satisfied or dissatisfied with the way the Government is running the country?

Question: Are you satisfied or dissatisfied with the way Mr Major / Mr Blair is doing his job as Prime Minister?

Question: Are you satisfied or dissatisfied with the way Mr Kinnock / Mr Smith / Mr Blair / Mr Hague is doing his job as leader of the Labour / Conservative Party?

Question: Are you satisfied or dissatisfied with the way Mr Ashdown / Mr Kennedy is doing his job as Leader of the Liberal Democrats?

*All figures shown are percentages

	Government			Mr Major			Mr Kinnock			Mr Ashdown		
	Sat	Dis	Net	Sat	Dis	Net	Sat	Dis	Net	Sat	Dis	Net
1992												
2nd Quarter	38	52	-14	54	36	+18	30	57	-27	50	29	+21
							Mr Smith					
3rd Quarter	23	69	-46	43	49	-6	31	19	+12	49	26	+24
4th Quarter	12	82	-70	25	68	-44	38	28	+11	44	31	+12
1993												
1st Quarter	15	79	-64	28	64	-36	35	35	0	42	31	+11
2nd Quarter	13	80	-67	22	69	-47	35	40	-5	48	29	+20

	Government			Mr Major			Mr Smith			Mr Ashdown		
	Sat	Dis	Net	Sat	Dis	Net	Sat	Dis	Net	Sat	Dis	Net
3rd Quarter	12	81	-69	20	71	-51	35	39	-4	49	26	+23
4th Quarter	12	81	-69	23	69	-47	40	35	+5	45	30	+16
1994												
1st Quarter	12	81	-69	21	70	-49	37	37	0	42	31	+12
2nd Quarter	11	83	-72	20	73	-53	36	40	-4	46	28	+18
							Mr Blair					
3rd Quarter	11	83	-72	20	73	-52	34	26	+8	37	32	+6
4th Quarter	11	82	-71	23	70	-47	44	18	+26	39	32	+8
1995												
1st Quarter	10	84	-74	21	71	-51	48	22	+26	38	32	+7
2nd Quarter	11	81	-70	24	68	-44	50	24	+27	40	29	+11
3rd Quarter	13	79	-66	26	64	-38	47	27	+20	41	29	+12
4th Quarter	15	78	-63	27	65	-38	52	26	+26	42	28	+13
1996												
1st Quarter	14	78	-64	26	65	-39	50	27	+23	42	27	+15
2nd Quarter	16	75	-60	28	63	-35	49	29	+20	43	26	+17
3rd Quarter	16	75	-59	28	62	-34	43	34	+9	39	28	+11
4th Quarter	19	72	-53	32	59	-27	49	29	+20	43	25	+19
1997												
1st Quarter	22	70	-48	32	59	-27	50	31	+19	45	23	+22

	Government			Mr Blair			Mr Hague			Mr Ashdown		
1997												
May 9-12	46	9	+37	65	5	+60				66	8	+58
June 20-23	53	15	+38	72	7	+65	12	13	-1	61	10	+51
July 25-28	53	20	+33	70	11	+59	21	24	-3	62	11	+51
Aug 21-25	48	27	+21	65	19	+46	22	28	-6	58	15	+43
Sept 26-29	57	20	+37	75	13	+62	18	46	-28	60	15	+45
Oct 24-27	55	22	+33	72	15	+57	23	41	-18	59	15	+44
Nov 21-24	52	28	+24	70	20	+50	19	53	-34	63	14	+49
Dec 12-15	43	38	+5	61	27	+34	20	50	-30	59	15	+44
1998												
Jan 23-26	46	38	+8	60	29	+31	22	45	-23	56	15	+41
Feb 20-23	44	43	+1	60	31	+29	25	44	-19	56	17	+39

	Government			Mr Blair			Mr Hague			Mr Ashdown		
	Sat	Dis	Net	Sat	Dis	Net	Sat	Dis	Net	Sat	Dis	Net
Mar 20-23	46	38	+8	62	28	+34	27	43	-16	54	16	+38
Apr 24-27	54	32	+22	68	22	+46	27	42	-15	52	18	+34
May 21-24	52	31	+21	67	23	+44	21	46	-25	51	17	+34
Jun 25 -30	49	38	+11	62	28	+34	23	46	-23	51	18	+33
Jul 17-21	50	35	+15	62	28	+34	24	49	-25	51	20	+31
Aug 21-24	47	40	+7	65	26	+39	23	46	-23	50	20	+30
Sep 18-21	45	41	+4	61	30	+31	20	51	-31	52	18	+34
Oct 23-26	47	42	+5	62	29	+33	25	50	-25	48	23	+25
Nov 20-23	49	37	+12	61	29	+32	27	48	-21	52	21	+31
Dec 11-14	46	40	+6	60	29	+31	24	51	-27	48	21	+27

1999

	Government			Mr Blair			Mr Hague			Mr Ashdown		
Jan 22-25	45	41	+4	59	31	+28	23	50	-27	56	17	+39
Feb 19-22	45	45	0	58	34	+24	23	53	-30	54	17	+37
Mar 19-22	47	41	+6	61	29	+32	24	50	-26	53	18	+35
Apr 23-26	50	37	+13	63	28	+35	21	52	-31	55	18	+37
May 21-24	46	42	+4	58	34	+24	20	55	-35	52	20	+32
Jun 18-21	45	44	+1	57	35	+22	23	50	-27	53	20	+33
Jul 23-26	43	42	+1	55	33	+22	25	48	-23	55	16	+39

	Government			Mr Blair			Mr Hague			Mr Kennedy		
Aug 20-23	39	49	-10	49	39	+10	20	52	-32	21	10	+11
Sep 24-27	47	40	+7	58	34	+24	23	50	-27	24	11	+13
Oct 22-25	42	45	-3	53	37	+16	25	53	-28	23	13	+10
Nov 19-22	44	43	+1	54	36	+18	28	47	-19	28	11	+17
Dec 10-14	45	45	0	57	35	+22	24	54	-30	29	15	+14

2000

	Government			Mr Blair			Mr Hague			Mr Kennedy		
Jan 21-24	37	51	-14	53	38	+15	19	56	-37	28	14	+14
Feb 17-22	35	53	-18	49	42	+7	22	55	-33	26	15	+11
Mar 23-28	37	51	-14	47	43	+4	26	49	-23	30	16	+14
Apr 13-18	38	52	-14	52	41	+11	24	51	-27	34	16	+18
May 18-23	36	49	-13	47	42	+5	27	47	-20	32	15	+17
Jun 22-27	28	62	-34	39	52	-13	29	48	-19	31	17	+14
Jul 20-24	29	59	-30	42	50	-8	29	49	-20	31	19	+12

Source: MORI/The Times

Base: c. 2,000 interviews with British adults aged 18+ each month 1997, c. 1,000 interviews each month from 1998. Quarterly figures 1992-7 based on average of three monthly polls with sample c. 2,000.

Table C: Most Important Issues Facing Britain

Question: What would you say is the most important issue facing Britain today?

Question: What do you see as other important issues facing Britain today?

(Combined answers to both questions. Answers are spontaneous and unprompted)

A	Unemployment/factory closure/lack of industry
B	National Health Service/Hospitals
C	Crime/law & order/violence/vandalism
D	Education/schools
E	Inflation/prices
F	Common Market/EU/Europe/Single European Currency
G	Economy/economic situation
H	Northern Ireland
I	Defence/foreign affairs
J	Pollution/environment
K	Housing
L	Pensions/social security
M	Race relations/immigration/immigrants

	A	B	C	D	E	F	G	H	I	J	K	L	M
1992													
2nd Quarter	56	34	14	24	9	14	28	1	3	13	10	8	5
3rd Quarter	62	25	14	18	10	14	44	1	4	10	13	7	5
4th Quarter	72	26	11	15	8	21	46	1	2	4	14	7	3
1993													
1st Quarter	79	27	28	18	6	9	34	3	5	4	10	8	2
2nd Quarter	70	34	23	20	6	10	34	1	6	4	9	11	3
3rd Quarter	63	33	26	19	5	12	32	1	5	5	8	10	8
4th Quarter	63	34	28	20	6	6	29	2	5	4	9	14	4
1994													
1st Quarter	60	36	30	23	5	7	25	2	7	4	12	9	4
2nd Quarter	62	34	32	22	5	11	23	1	4	5	10	9	3
3rd Quarter	62	35	30	21	5	9	19	2	5	6	10	8	3
4th Quarter	58	36	28	20	5	14	19	2	2	4	10	11	3

	A	B	C	D	E	F	G	H	I	J	K	L	M
1995													
1st Quarter	52	39	24	24	5	21	21	2	2	4	10	9	4
2nd Quarter	50	41	24	30	5	18	19	1	3	4	10	9	4
3rd Quarter	50	41	24	29	4	12	20	1	4	5	11	9	4
4th Quarter	51	41	23	31	4	13	19	2	2	4	10	10	4
1996													
1st Quarter	47	39	25	30	3	14	18	6	3	5	10	9	3
2nd Quarter	44	35	25	30	3	26	15	2	2	4	9	8	3
3rd Quarter	43	34	29	30	3	23	14	3	2	6	8	10	3
4th Quarter	38	40	38	40	4	27	19	1	2	4	8	13	3
1997													
1st Quarter	38	49	26	44	4	32	18	2	2	5	8	13	3
1997													
April 25-28	28	63	27	54	3	43	22	3	2	2	7	17	3
June 20-23	39	51	24	45	2	30	14	4	2	10	8	11	3
July 25-28	34	46	23	49	4	23	19	4	2	7	8	13	4
Aug 21-25	35	47	27	39	5	16	18	2	2	11	9	13	5
Sept 26-29	35	45	28	45	4	21	17	2	2	7	7	12	4
Oct 24-27	32	47	26	36	4	35	14	2	2	7	8	12	8
Nov 21-24	34	47	22	36	4	31	16	1	4	7	8	13	4
Dec 12-15	31	42	16	31	3	28	14	3	2	9	8	20	4
1998													
Jan 23-26	32	42	19	37	3	23	14	8	4	7	10	23	4
Feb 20-23	31	50	14	37	3	16	14	5	26	6	7	19	3
Mar 20-23	34	47	13	42	3	22	19	3	4	7	6	17	3
April 24-27	31	35	21	39	3	23	14	10	5	8	6	13	6
May 21-24	30	49	20	39	5	22	13	11	4	6	7	12	3
June 25-30	33	44	21	33	5	33	13	5	5	8	8	10	3
July 17-21	28	45	19	40	4	22	17	5	3	8	8	13	3
Aug 21-24	36	41	21	33	4	13	26	11	7	7	7	12	4
Sept 18-21	44	40	17	31	6	20	27	1	3	4	9	9	6
Oct 23-26	43	38	20	33	8	23	30	2	4	5	8	12	4
Nov 20-23	35	37	17	32	5	26	21	1	8	5	7	11	6
Dec 11-14	30	34	17	26	6	32	18	2	5	3	8	10	7
1999													
Jan 22-25	26	49	17	32	4	27	19	1	7	6	7	10	4

	A	B	C	D	E	F	G	H	I	J	K	L	M
Feb 19-22	26	39	19	29	4	30	13	3	8	5	7	11	7
March 19-22	25	37	16	29	4	32	15	3	4	5	7	10	5
April 23-26	27	34	20	31	5	15	13	2	28	4	6	7	8
May 21-24	23	33	18	27	3	26	15	★	28	6	9	11	6
June 18-21	19	35	18	29	4	37	16	2	16	5	9	10	7
July 23-26	21	39	16	30	4	30	13	10	7	8	8	7	7
Aug 20-23	24	41	19	30	6	25	13	2	5	6	8	11	10
Sept 24-27	22	39	21	31	4	23	11	3	5	7	8	14	7
Oct 22-25	17	41	16	31	5	34	9	2	5	7	9	12	8
Nov 19-22	21	40	24	29	4	23	13	4	5	8	11	14	5
Dec 10-14	18	41	15	33	3	32	10	2	4	6	8	13	4

2000

	A	B	C	D	E	F	G	H	I	J	K	L	M
Jan 20-25	20	70	24	32	3	22	11	2	4	5	9	12	7
Feb 17-22	19	54	18	32	4	25	11	6	3	3	6	13	12
March 23-28	18	57	20	37	3	20	7	2	2	6	9	12	13
April 13-18	21	53	16	35	2	17	11	2	3	5	10	14	19
May 18-23	23	45	34	30	3	19	11	2	4	5	9	15	16
June 22-27	17	55	23	32	4	24	9	1	3	4	7	12	17
July 20-24	17	51	34	34	5	19	12	1	2	5	7	14	11

★less than 0.5% (but more than 0).

Source: MORI/The Times

Base: c. 2,000 interviews with British adults aged 18+ each month 1997, c. 1,000 interviews each month from 1998. Quarterly figures 1992-7 based on average of three monthly polls with sample c. 2,000.

Table D: Economic Optimism Index

Question: Do you think that the general economic condition of the country will improve, stay the same, or get worse over the next 12 months?

	Improve	Stay the same	Get worse	Don't know	Economic Optimism Index
1992					
2nd Quarter	37	31	25	7	+ 12
3rd Quarter	19	29	46	6	- 27
4th Quarter	19	25	51	5	- 32
1993					
1st Quarter	25	31	40	5	- 15
2nd Quarter	33	32	30	5	+ 3
3rd Quarter	31	33	30	5	+ 1
4th Quarter	26	34	34	6	- 7
1994					
1st Quarter	25	35	36	4	- 10
2nd Quarter	27	36	32	5	- 5
3rd Quarter	26	37	32	5	- 6
4th Quarter	25	36	34	5	- 9
1995					
1st Quarter	20	36	39	5	- 20
2nd Quarter	20	39	35	6	- 15
3rd Quarter	16	41	35	7	- 19
4th Quarter	19	39	36	6	- 17
1996					
1st Quarter	19	39	35	7	- 15
2nd Quarter	23	41	29	7	- 6
3rd Quarter	26	39	28	7	- 3
4th Quarter	24	40	28	8	- 3
1997					
1st Quarter	25	39	24	11	+ 1

1997

	Improve	Stay the same	Get worse	Don't know	Economic Optimism Index
May 9-12	40	35	12	13	+ 28
June 20-23	38	36	19	7	+ 19
July 25-28	35	32	25	8	+ 10
Aug 21-25	29	32	31	8	- 2
Sept 26-29	36	37	19	8	+ 17
Oct 24-27	31	39	24	6	+ 7
Nov 21-24	30	40	24	6	+ 6
Dec 12-15	26	36	30	8	- 4

1998

Jan 23-26	27	38	28	7	- 1
Feb 20-23	29	38	27	6	+ 2
March 20-23	30	36	26	8	+ 4
April 24-27	28	38	27	7	+ 1
May 21-24	26	39	25	10	+ 1
June 25-30	19	36	38	7	- 19
July 17-21	19	33	40	8	- 21
Aug 21-24	18	30	45	7	- 27
Sept 18-21	13	30	50	7	- 37
Oct 23-26	11	25	57	7	- 46
Nov 20-23	16	31	47	6	- 31
Dec 11-14	16	30	46	8	- 30

1999

Jan 22-25	18	35	41	6	- 23
Feb 19-22	21	36	36	7	- 15
March 19-22	26	37	32	5	- 6
April 23-26	23	41	31	5	- 8
May 21-24	25	43	26	6	- 1
June 18-21	23	43	27	7	- 4
July 23-26	26	45	23	6	+ 3
Aug 20-23	19	43	31	7	- 12
Sept 24-27	29	40	24	7	+ 5
Oct 22-25	21	44	28	7	- 7
Nov 19-22	28	42	24	6	+ 4
Dec 10-14	25	45	24	6	+ 1

	Improve	Stay the same	Get worse	Don't know	Economic Optimism Index
2000					
Jan 20-25	27	41	25	7	+ 2
Feb 17-22	22	41	32	5	- 10
March 23-28	25	40	30	5	- 5
April 13-18	20	43	33	4	- 13
May 18-23	22	38	33	7	- 11
June 22-27	18	42	32	8	- 14
July 20-24	23	40	33	4	- 10

Source: MORI/The Times

Base: c. 2,000 interviews with British adults aged 18+ each month 1997, c. 1,000 interviews each month from 1998. Quarterly figures 1992-7 based on average of three monthly polls with sample c. 2,000.

Party Prospects

Labour

As outlined elsewhere in this guide, the Labour party has never governed for two full terms in its 100-year history. Even after the landslide victory of 1945 and the great successes of the Attlee government, the party's majority of over 140 was reduced to just 5 in 1950. It is generally acknowledged that the Labour government simply ran out of steam, and the second term lasted for just 20 months before Attlee (probably unnecessarily) called another general election and was defeated. This swift change in political fortune partly resulted from the recovery of the Conservatives (who accepted much of Labour's legislation) but it is telling that the previous great reforming government, the Liberals after 1906, also lost a massive three-figure majority at the following election, this time for less obvious reasons.

Tony Blair will hope that history does not repeat itself, and thus far most of the signs are promising. In particular Labour's opinion poll ratings are impressive when compared with any previous government; the opinion polls section reveals leads over the Conservatives that stood at 30% even two years into the government (April 1999). This figure is greater than the opinion poll lead recorded immediately before the 1997 landslide and would appear to suggest that a second massive Labour victory is possible. After all, at the same stage of the 1945 Labour government, Labour and the Conservatives were neck-and-neck (the next election in 1950 saw a Labour lead of just 2.5%), and the 1966 Labour government was no less than 20% behind (with Labour duly losing the 1970 election). Even at the time of Blair and Gould's anguished memo's (April/May 2000), later leaked to the press, Labour remained 15–20% ahead in the polls, ratings which would have been greeted as extraordinary by any previous administration – indeed they were roughly comparable to the post-Falklands leads held by Mrs Thatcher and the Conservatives in 1982.

So in the face of continuing poll leads and helped by the current electoral bias which would give them a comfortable majority of up to 60 even 2–3% ahead, why does Labour remain worried? The main reason is that in the elections which have taken place since 1997, 'real votes' have stacked up somewhat differently to the opinion polls. Labour were 8% behind the Conservatives in the only national election to have taken place in the period (the European election of June 1999), suffered serious reverses in the local elections of 1999 and 2000, failed to gain a majority in the new Scottish parliament and Welsh Assembly and finished a poor third in the London mayoral race. Some have claimed that these results prove that the opinion polls are simply wrong. But there is a more complex explanation for the discrepancy, part of which hints at ultimate success for Labour when general election polling day finally arrives.

The first part of this explanation is differential turnout, that Labour voters have simply stayed at home in elections which have taken place since 1997, while Conservatives have streamed to the polls. This particularly seemed the case in the European elections, where the overall turnout in Britain was just 23% and stories were legion of voters arriving at polling stations *Daily Mail* or *Telegraph* in hand demanding to 'vote against Europe'. In traditional Labour areas, polling stations remained eerily quiet, and when the votes were counted the Labour support had apparently disappeared. Many have since argued that this effectively constituted a protest against the government by Labour's 'core' voters. Some have gone on to claim that unless the Blair government takes more notice of Labour's heartlands, there will be a similar mass abstention at the general election. Yet a powerful alternative hypothesis is that voters simply did not view the Euro elections (and local elections) as important, and in the absence of an overriding reason to vote, failed to do so. Labour voters in particular lacked such a reason, with their party in power and the election campaign (for the Euro elections at least) comfortably the worst fought by the party since 1983. Conservative voters meanwhile were eager both to display their anti-Euro views and to give the government a bloody nose. When it comes to the general election, the situation is likely to be very different. Voters may claim to be turned off by wall-to-wall campaigning, but it does serve to emphasise the importance of the contest. The campaign will also remind electors that the alternative to Labour is the Conservatives. And it is clear from contests even since 1997 that the one factor that motivates Labour voters above all others is opposition to the Tories.

Evidence for this assertion is provided by both by-election contests and those for the Scottish Parliament and Welsh Assembly. In the parliamentary by-elections, Labour's vote has fallen heavily in safe seats such as Leeds Central and Tottenham, while their share of the vote actually increased in the Conservative-held marginals of Beckenham and Eddisbury. It is significant that Labour's campaign in Eddisbury was not only more high profile than those in their heartland areas, but also that it concentrated on highlighting Conservative policy (fox-hunting on that occasion). This tends to suggest that Labour supporters are still prepared to go to the polls if they believe it may stop the 'old enemy', particularly if they are reminded about the threat posed. This pattern is supported by the elections in Scotland and Wales, where Labour did extremely badly against the nationalist parties, losing Islwyn and Rhondda, yet simultaneously winning far more unlikely constituencies which until recently were solidly Conservative, such as Eastwood and Cardiff North. This all suggests that in 'Labour against Conservative' contests, Labour do remain well ahead. It is where Labour find themselves in different battles, campaigning against nationalists, Liberal Democrats (as in many local council contests) or left wing independents (as in the London mayoral campaign) that their problems begin and the polls seem so wrong. But of course the national general election battle (and most of the local battles) will be viewed as Labour versus Conservative. And in this context, which is reflected by the opinion polls, a second Labour term seems highly probable.

The Labour government has not had an entirely smooth ride since May 1997. Issues as diverse as pensions, welfare reform, foxhunting, petrol prices and the Euro have all proved troublesome, while arguably Labour's greatest political achievement, devolution, has created some of the biggest problems of all. But it has been Labour's economic record which has been central to the party's continued strong position and favourable prospects. Keeping to Tory spending limits for the first two years of the government may not have been popular with Labour activists, but in that time Gordon Brown amply demonstrated his 'tough' credentials to the City while the state of the public finances improved. As a result Labour have avoided repeating past crises, where governments initially boosted public spending only for cuts to be introduced after a loss of economic confidence two or three years in. The financial sector now trusts Labour to an extent that would have been unimaginable in previous decades, with little negative reaction to the comprehensive spending review in July 2000 when Brown promised an extra £43 billion to improve public services, such as health, education and transport. And of course famine followed by feast is a far better election-winning formula than feast followed by famine, as previous election results testify.

Labour's new-found reputation for economic competence has been underlined by the fall in unemployment to levels last seen in the 1970s. It is also the case that many families in Britain are better off than at any time in the past. The feel-good factor engendered by rising affluence was central to the Conservatives' success in the 1950s, played a part in the 1980s, and for the first time it is apparent during a period of Labour government. While both the national economy and individual circumstances remain favourable, Labour's position will remain strong, regardless of short-term (and quickly forgotten) difficulties such as backbench revolts or leaked memo's. The only cloud on Labour's horizon would appear to be the Euro, with the Conservatives hoping to make political capital by contrasting Labour's likely support for entry to the single currency when the referendum arrives with the apparent hostility of much of the British public. Could this be enough to turn an election if the issue became dominant? Labour will hope not to find out, by delaying a referendum (and an official position) until after the election. However there remains the suspicion that the pro-Euro case has simply not been made yet, and if it were the whole issue may not automatically be the 'Tory issue' it appears to be at present.

Two of Labour's misjudgements since coming to power have centred on devolution and pensions. Both have had serious electoral consequences in those elections which have taken place, but are likely to be less important (for differing reasons) when the general election arrives. Devolution was Labour's 'unfinished business' from the late 1970s when a combination of parliamentary opposition and referendum reverses put an end to the then government's plans. In this respect the 'New' Labour government proved it was not so new after all, by including legislation for fresh referendums in the first Queen's speech after coming to power. Cunningly, the Welsh referendum (which overwhelmingly rejected devolution in 1979) was timetabled for a week after the Scottish referendum, widely expected to deliver a clear 'yes' vote. The wisdom of this timetable was demonstrated when the referendum results were declared in September 1997; 'yes' votes were duly delivered, though by the narrowest possible margin in Wales. But this was only the start of Labour's problems. After Welsh Secretary Ron Davies was forced to resign (see key events), a bruising contest to replace him saw the Blair-backed Alun Michael defeat Rhodri Morgan partly as a result of trade union block votes, and the impression that London or Millbank had interfered in a Welsh contest was never shaken off. When the Assembly elections came, the unthinkable happened and Labour lost the Rhondda to Plaid Cymru, whose new suffix 'the Party of Wales' was far more in tune with the nationalist dynamic unleashed by the devolution process. Labour failed to gain a majority in the new Assembly, and though they opted to govern as a minority, Michael was forced to resign minutes before being picked off by an opposition-sponsored confidence vote. Rhodri Morgan's resulting ascent to the position of First Secretary seems to have finally placated Labour's critics, and the party may not suffer lasting damage in the general election, though the whole episode has amply demonstrated the dangers of inter-fering with devolved institutions.

Meanwhile in Scotland, Labour's selection procedures led to Dennis Canavan standing and winning as an independent in elections to the Scottish Parliament, while the new system of proportional representation encouraged the Labour vote to splinter: significant support was garnered by Scottish Socialist Labour and the Greens. Since the election a form of right-wing nationalism appears to have been developing, as demonstrated by the rise to political prominence of bus magnate Brian Souter (who held his own referendum on Clause 28) and Cardinal Thomas Winning, who joined the condemnation of Labour's liberal policies. Meanwhile in London, the new Assembly and Mayor promised by Labour provided the scene for another dismal election performance, with Ken Livingstone (like Rhodri Morgan, narrowly defeated by union block votes in an electoral college) romping to victory as an Independent on a 'vote London' platform.

Thus while Labour have successfully delivered devolved institutions, the party has failed to understand the regional / national political dynamic they have unleashed. Elections in London, for the Welsh assembly and Scottish Parliament have been seen by electors as an opportunity to elect represen-tatives to defend the interests of London, Wales and Scotland, against the government if necessary. While this has been understood by nationalist parties and Ken Livingstone, Labour inappropriately believed they could continue setting a central framework for selecting candidates, several of whom ultimately paid the electoral consequences of being seen as puppets of central government. But will this matter in a general election? In all like-lihood, it will not, as the overriding context of a general election is the selection of a national government, and issues such as the state of the economy are centre-stage rather than who appears best to defend the interests of, for example, London.

Labour's other serious misjudgement so far has come on pensions. In many ways this has been an 'error of spin' since in reality most of Britain's 11 million or so pensioners have received rises in incomes greater than the headline 75 pence per week announced in Gordon Brown's 2000 budget. For example winter fuel payments and free television licenses (given to the over-75s) are together worth £5 per week. But the perception has been of a derisory rise in the basic pension, which does not come close to keeping up with the increases in living standards enjoyed by much of the working population. It is no surprise that the Conservatives have campaigned hard on this issue, promising large increases if they win the next election. Given that older voters are far more likely to vote than younger electors, particularly in local elections (where it is possible that a majority of voters are pensioners), their anger towards Labour over the issue is likely to have been a very large part of the explanation for Labour's local reverses in May 2000. Yet in the general election it will be different, as more electors of working age will undoubtedly turn out and, as a result, the proportion of the voting population who rely on the pension will be far lower. Indeed, this large (and growing) differential in the composition of voters between general and other elections seems likely to be a major part of the explanation for the opinion polls / real votes discrepancy outlined above. Thus the Conservative strategy of appealing to pensioners is likely to prove far more successful in local elections than general elections, though in any event political expediency will doubtless dictate a somewhat larger increase in the pension at the next budget.

So what will be Labour's agenda at the general election? Almost certainly it will be one which concentrates on the extra public spending promised by Gordon Brown in July 2000, probably contrasted with claims of possible Conservative cuts. It is interesting that this agenda chimes with opinion poll findings (see opinion polls, table C) which suggest that the issues of health and education have remained as important as they were during the 1997 election campaign, when they played an important role in Labour's victory. This is not automatically good news for the party, as the government will need to demonstrate that they have delivered on their 1997 key pledges on class sizes and waiting times. But this is more natural territory for Labour than crime and immigration, which were becoming more important to electors through 2000 as Labour's opinion poll lead started to fall. These are the issues, together with Europe and the Euro, which remain dangerous for Labour, and they will need to find some way of neutralising them. However, the most important issue of all at the election is likely to be the state of the economy. If Labour can continue to persuade electors of their competence in this area, that elusive second term must be well within the party's reach.

The Conservatives

The landslide defeat of May 1997 traumatised the Conservative Party. The Tories slumped to 165 seats, their lowest ebb since the 1906 wipe-out, and their share of the vote at 30.7% was much the lowest in any democratic national election. Even so, the bedraggled party could not console itself that the only way was up – at the time of writing the Conservatives' parliamentary strength stands at 162, reflecting two defections to Labour and one by-election loss to the Liberal Democrats, and for much of the first three years of the 1997 parliament Labour's lead was even greater than in May 1997.

John Major stepped aside quickly and maintained his dignity, but the Conservative leadership contest was anything but dignified. The much anticipated clash between Michael Portillo and Michael Heseltine did not take place, as the Michaels were ruled out respectively by electoral defeat and health problems. There was instead a confusing, three-round battle in which the winner, William Hague, at first backed another candidate and the front-runner Ken Clarke did a deal with his ideological opposite John Redwood. Hague won a fairly decisive victory over Clarke in June 1997.

Hague's first forays as leader were not impressive; his handling of the situation caused by the sudden death of Princess Diana was clumsy, and he engaged in maladroit photo opportunities at the Notting Hill carnival and with a baseball cap. His strengths proved to be more in the House of Commons, where he performed well at Question Time and in set piece speeches, and internal party reform. His public image remains very poor; it is difficult to shake off a bad image once established in the public mind, and his star turn as a teenage Tory during the 1977 party conference started him off with the image of being a slightly strange politically obsessed 'Tory boy'.

Despite these handicaps, Hague – a product of McKinsey's management consultants – has reformed the structure of the Conservative Party in the most radical way since Rab Butler's reforms of the 1940s. The changes have been made with the assistance of Party Chairmen Cecil Parkinson and Michael Ancram, and Archie Norman of ASDA as Chief of Staff. The anomalous distinction between the professional Central Office and the voluntary National Union has been swept away, and the structure of Central Office has been rationalised. New organisations have replaced moribund or stale branches – in 1997 Conservative Future replaced the youth and student sections which had become notorious for factional warfare, and the constituency discussion groups were remodelled as the Conservative Political Forum in 1998. New sections also deal with ethnic minority issues and business liaison, and the 'Conservative Network' is a national organisation aimed at young professionals. An Ethics and Integrity Committee was established to combat sleaze, but it did nothing to save the party from the embarrassment of Lord Archer's abortive campaign to be London mayor.

The bureaucratic distinctions between research and press sections in Central Office have grown blurred as the Conservatives have adopted the 'War Room' campaigning approach used by Clinton and Blair. Three of the most important Central Office figures are former associates of David Owen in the SDP, and came to the Conservatives via the Social Market Foundation think tank – Rick Nye, Director of Research, Andrew Cooper, Head of Political Operations, and Danny Finkelstein as policy adviser to Hague. All three have a keen interest in US Republican politics, and British Conservatism is influenced to a perhaps unprecedented degree by American approaches.

Hague has also democratised the Conservative Party to some extent, although it is plebiscitary rather than directly democratic. There were two ballots of the party membership in 1998, the first to validate Hague's election as leader, and the second to approve the party's policy on the Euro. Both passed overwhelmingly. The reformed leadership election system, in which ordinary members have a vote for the first time, incidentally makes it harder for leaders to be ousted in internal coups like those which toppled Heath in 1975 and Thatcher in 1990.

Conservative policy has been under review as well. It is always difficult to formulate policy after a long period of power – new ideas risk the riposte that the party failed to do anything when they had the opportunity, and old ideas face the charge that the party is stale and has learned nothing. The severity of the defeat lent a certain desperation to the search for a new approach, and the party has veered around somewhat since 1997. At first, the Conservatives proclaimed a more inclusive, tolerant, less arrogant approach – Michael Portillo was in the vanguard of this change ('New Portillo, New Danger'). The failure to reap dividends led in 1999 to a US-modelled search to define a 'kitchen table Conservatism' that appealed to a broad mass of ordinary people, and then to the conference theme (modelled on Ontario) of a 'Common Sense Revolution'. At the time of writing in summer 2000, the Conservatives seem to be rowing back from Common Sense.

The most successful campaigns the Conservatives have run have involved exploitation of populist issues as they arise, such as asylum seekers, Clause 28 and the right to shoot burglars. The Conservatives have also tapped into a vein of rural discontent with what is perceived as a 'metropolitan elite' and the problems facing farming.

While issues like asylum and Clause 28 have struck a chord with many voters and the popular press, they have also alienated liberal-minded Tories such as Shaun Woodward, the MP for Witney, who defected to Labour in 1999. Steve Norris, the party's mayoral candidate in diverse London, also dissociated himself from some of these socially conservative hot button issues. The Tories have also developed more resonant slogans on Europe, such as 1999's 'In Europe, not run by Europe' and the 'Keep the Pound' campaign. The increasingly Eurosceptic tone of the party's policy and rhetoric led to the breakaway of the Pro-Euro Conservatives, although this party made little impact on the 1999 Euro election. The Pro-Euro Tories promise to run 50 candidates, targeted at leading Eurosceptic Tories, and gain the opportunity for a national Party Election Broadcast. The Conservatives are perhaps more worried that by playing the anti-Europe card they may steer voters into the arms of the UK Independence Party which can take an unequivocal position on the EU: withdrawal is 'the love that dare not speak its name' for many Tories. A local council by-election in Bexley also warned that campaigning on asylum may fuel support for the British National Party.

The Conservatives' electoral position is described in other chapters. They have remained poorly placed in the polls and by-elections, and did badly in the 1998 local elections. The 1999 local elections saw some recovery in their heartlands, and the European Parliament election of June 1999 was a surprisingly good victory for the party. They made considerable gains in the May 2000 local elections. Leaders with a clear regional profile, such as Harold Wilson in 1964 or Neil Kinnock in 1987, often give an electoral bonus in their home region. Hague's Yorkshire identity seems to have helped the Conservatives somewhat in Yorkshire and the Pennine towns. The party's image as hostile to change seems, however, to be a handicap in London and other economically dynamic areas.

The Conservatives face the problem, common to many opposition parties, of constructing a viable policy on taxation and public spending. The 'tax guarantee' of 1999 was an obvious hostage to fortune and was rescinded in 2000. The Tories criticised the Comprehensive Spending Review as a Labour reversion to 'tax and spend' politics, but Labour can easily retort by asking the Conservatives which public spending projects they would cut to pay for tax cuts. Many Conservative policies designed to appeal to particular interest groups such as the countryside lobby will also cost money, and Labour can play what used to be the old Tory game of 'costing' the other side's promises and then warning the electorate of the consequences for tax rates or spending cuts elsewhere.

Conservative expectations for the next election are mixed. There is official, public confidence in outright victory – as of course there must be. A far gloomier picture of an election result in 2001 'remarkably unchanged' since 1997 emerged from a leaked advertising tender document in April 2000, but some observers thought this may have been cunning 'spin' to generate Labour apathy in the local elections. Nevertheless, Central Office has always been quite good at hard-headed assessment of electoral prospects and they have been reading the same polls and election results as everyone else.

A crucial indicator of what the Conservatives expect will be in their pattern of targeting. It has been reported that the campaign will focus to an unprecedented extent on marginals, with even the candidates from 'hopeless' seats encouraged to work in the target seats. If they are serious about winning, their target list will include about 175 seats, which would put them back to 1992 levels, and involve all the seats in our constituency section. A more limited aim would see a concentration on the front line seats that were unexpected losses in 1997. These decisions affect election-eering strategy on the national level too. Some observers see populist campaigning as a means of gathering a kind of inverse rainbow coalition of anti-Europeans, rural people discontented with their lot, social conserva-tives, and those generally uneasy with 'modernisation'. If people who feel strongly on any one of this basket of issues are inspired to go to the polls and vote Conservative then it will lead to a good enough result in a low-turnout general election to see Hague through and gain enough MPs to challenge for national power in 2005/6. Only one Conservative leader has ever failed to become Prime Minister – Austen Chamberlain – and before speculating too much about the intriguing possibility of a Portillo-Widdecombe lead-ership election (with Portillo as the left wing candidate) one should remember that Hague may well have two chances to get to Downing Street. 2001/2 seems a slim chance, but slim chances sometimes come good.

The Liberal Democrats

The Liberal Democrats were junior partners to New Labour in the rout of the Conservatives in May 1997. Their haul of 46 seats was the best centre showing – as an independent force rather than part of a coalition – since 1929, although their share of the vote was lower than the Alliance had reached in 1983 and 1987 and lower than the Liberals managed in 1974.

There are two reasons why the Liberal Democrats managed to win so many seats despite a falling share of the vote. One is simple arithmetic – the Conservative share fell much more, and therefore the Liberal Democrats benefited from a favourable 'swing' in the clutch of seats where they were challengers to the Tories. In marginal Portsmouth South, for instance, the Liberal Democrat share of the vote fell by 2.5% but the Conservatives were defeated as their vote fell 11.4%. The other reason is tactical voting. In seats where Labour challenged the Tories, the Liberal Democrat vote often fell to very low levels and Labour supporters returned the favour in many Lib Dem target seats. Take, for example, the neighbouring seats of Mitcham & Morden and Sutton & Cheam in south west London:

% vote	Mitcham and Morden			Sutton and Cheam		
	1983	1997	Change	1983	1997	Change
Conservative	42.7	29.7	−13.0	57.1	37.8	−19.3
Labour	28.8	58.4	+29.6	7.6	15.5	+7.9
Centre	27.4	7.6	−19.8	35.2	42.3	+7.1

The question for the Liberal Democrats, and Labour, is whether this pattern can be sustained when there is not an unpopular Conservative government to eject. Paddy Ashdown enjoyed cordial relations with Tony Blair, and had moved his party towards closer relations with Labour from his Chard speech after the 1992 election. New Labour's final abandonment of any pretensions to effect a socialist change in society removed a symbolic barrier to co-operation, and actually placed the Liberal Democrats to the left of Labour on economic issues. The parties were in considerable agreement on consti-tutional reform. Had Labour won a narrow victory in 1997 Liberal Democrats might have joined the Cabinet, but in the event their participa-tion in government was limited to membership of a special Cabinet committee.

Paddy Ashdown announced his resignation as party leader in January 1999, although the election of his successor was delayed until after the Euro election of June. Charles Kennedy won comfortably although Simon

Hughes put up a respectable challenge. The Liberal Democrats edged away from the close alignment Ashdown had formed with Labour, criticising the government's Home Office policies among others, but relations stayed warm enough to make it conceivable for the parties to form a coalition government if future circumstances permit it. Such a coalition was indeed formed after the elections for the Scottish Parliament in 1999, and for the first time since 1945 Liberals have exercised executive power.

The relationship with Labour – some in New Labour muse about the possibility of reconstructing the Lib-Lab hegemony of Edwardian times – is the central question of Lib Dem politics. Electorally, it is double-edged. The party still seems (see by-elections) able to attract tactical voters from Labour sympathisers, perhaps attracted by the party's image of being more radical than New Labour. The risk is that closeness to Labour puts off the voters the Liberal Democrats need most in its parliamentary seats, many of which are in affluent and conservative areas, but in the by-elections this has not damaged them so far.

The Liberal Democrats have built up a powerful political position in local government over the years. The elections of 1999 and 2000 dented the position, as seats and councils were lost to the Conservatives in southern England in particular, but the losses were not drastic. However, they have gathered strength against Labour in many city areas, gaining Liverpool and Sheffield councils and making serious inroads in the inner cities and council estates in previously Labour-Conservative battlegrounds such as Southampton and Norwich. There is an inbuilt tension in the party between its parliamentary corps, most of whom won their seats from Conservatives and feel sympathy for the Labour agenda, and urban councillors who have battled against Labour.

The centre parties have always performed poorly in European elections, and June 1999 was no exception. They only led in three constituencies – Orkney & Shetland, Oldham East & Saddleworth and Birmingham Yardley – and were thrashed in the south west where many seats are vulnerable to the Conservatives. The portents, therefore, are mixed as the next general election looms. Some losses to the Conservatives might be expected, and there are few Labour seats where they were serious challengers in 1997. More than other parties, the Liberal Democrats depend on personal votes and local activism, which should help the new arrivals of 1997 (and Sandra Gidley of Romsey) resist any adverse movement of opinion, but threaten the seats where popular incumbents are retiring (like Ashdown's own Yeovil). Only 5 of the 46 MPs inherited their seats from a Liberal predecessor, including Torridge where former MP Emma Nicholson had been elected as a Conservative in 1992.

Kennedy also needs to establish himself as a heavyweight political figure. Ashdown, though not a celebrated Commons figure, spoke with authority on the Balkans (the government valued his support over Kosovo) and had a favourable public profile. Kennedy will be helped by the equal broadcasting rules that come into force during the formal election campaign – his profile will rise sharply and his quick wit may well be an asset in campaign conditions. The party has some formidable election strategists, including Chris Rennard whose string of by-election triumphs now includes the remarkable result in Romsey. While the main battle is between Labour and the Conservatives, the Liberal Democrats are a potentially important factor. If the national result is close, their MPs will hold the balance. If they hold most of their 1997 gains, it will reflect a very significant change in British electoral politics. If they do badly, as in 1999, Conservative gains from the Liberal Democrats could save William Hague's bacon – or even put him into Downing Street.

Changes to Electoral Law

By the time the general election is called, there are likely to have been two major sets of changes to the framework governing elections in Britain. The first, the Registration of Political Parties Act, was in place by 1999. The second, more radical, change concerns national election spending and was expected to become law by autumn 2000 (though at the time of going to press this was uncertain as a result of likely opposition). To a great extent however, neither of the two changes will alter the traditional local campaign, as this is largely based on successive Representation of the People Acts, most recently changed in a major fashion in 1983. In this short section, we will introduce the key elements of the two pieces of legislation passed since the last general election and then summarise some of the existing regulations governing local campaigning, particularly those relating to election spending.

The Registration of Political Parties Act enables political parties to centrally register both their name (on a 'register of political parties'), and party emblem. This act was passed in time to be implemented nationally for the 1999 European elections. Only registered parties are able to put forward candidates in that party name, a stipulation which aims to prevent the candidatures of 'bogus' party candidates who have in the past been able to confuse the electorate and siphon off several thousand votes from the main parties, occasionally affecting constituency outcomes.

For example, in Slough in 1992, Labour candidate Eddie Lopez was defeated by Conservative John Watts by just 514 votes. But a second 'Labour' candidate, whose name was at the very top of the ballot paper, secured 700 votes, possibly preventing a Labour victory. More famous was the case of Richard Huggett, who stood as a 'Literal Democrat' in Devon and East Plymouth in the 1994 European election, securing a far greater vote (10,203) than the margin (700) by which the Liberal Democrats trailed the Conservatives. It was this case more than any other which highlighted the need for legislation, though change had still not come about by 1997. In that election, an Independent Conservative gained over 1,700 votes in Hove, an Independent Labour candidate took nearly as many in Falmouth and Camborne, and even more votes were attracted by bogus 'New Labour' candidates in Cardiff and Hackney. In all there were 13 cases of such candidates attracting over 1,000 votes (not including Liberal or Socialist Labour candidates), often in constituencies where the corresponding 'official' party candidate performed worse than the national average for no other obvious reason.

The new legislation also enables candidates to have their party emblems printed on ballot papers, again to make it easier for voters to connect individual candidates with one of the main parties. In 1999, the only difficulties with the new legislation surrounded a dispute between various left wing groups over ownership of the 'socialist' label. Perhaps the irony of the Euro elections was that despite the implementation of this legislation, which appeared to be aimed at helping the main parties, 'others' attracted a record 18% of the vote across Britain.

Meanwhile, a separate Political Parties, Elections and Referendums Bill was proceeding through parliament as this guide went to press. This Bill has resulted from the deliberations of the Neill Committee on Standards in Public Life (which replaced the earlier Nolan Committee) since the last general election. A key aim is to restore confidence in political parties by removing the veil of secrecy over party political donations (large donations of £5,000 and over will in future have to be declared), but as important for the general election is the clause of the Bill that will limit national party spending for the first time. Previously, there had been fairly stringent limits on how much individual candidates could spend on their local campaigns, but no limit at all on national spending, as a result of the original legislation being passed over a century ago when, to all intents and purposes, the national campaign did not exist. Thus in 1997 both of the two main parties were able to raise and then spend millions on national advertising, leader's tours, private polling, focus group research and so on, with no formal checks. It is estimated that the Conservatives spent £20 million on their national campaign last time, Labour about £13 million and the Liberal Democrats less than £1 million. Given that the new bill seems likely to set the national spending cap at the £20 million figure, such inequality may not be reduced, though any further escalation in spending will be prevented.

Of course the transparency which will now surround party donations (as well as the ban on donations from outside the UK) may well make it much harder for parties to raise such huge sums in the future, which could have the effect of reducing the intensity of the national campaign. It is also interesting to note that it is proposed that the national spending limit will apply for 365 days before the election, a change which reflects the present-day reality of election campaigns, but one which appears totally at odds with the existing provisions of the Representation of the People Act governing local campaign spending.

Existing rules on local campaign spending are just as stringent as the new laws on national campaigning, if not more so. The maximum permissible spending per candidate, a regulation which dates back to the 1883 Corrupt Practices Act, has remained at a relatively low level, currently working out at approximately £8,000 per candidate per constituency (the exact formula takes into account the number of electors per constituency, and the limit is also higher in rural constituencies). In reality this amount barely covers two or three leaflets to all electors in a constituency, with little room to spare. Local campaign expenditure can only be authorised by the candidate's duly appointed agent, who is required to retain all bills and receipts and submit a full record of expenditure on the campaign to the local returning officer approximately a month after the date of the election. It is interesting to note that the maximum local spend by 639 Labour candidates (the number who stood in 1997) would be approximately £5 million, which is only a quarter of the proposed spending cap on national level campaigning, perhaps reflecting prevailing views on the importance of each. The costs of local (and national) campaign spending are of course borne by the candidates and parties themselves, though there is in effect a state subsidy consisting of free party election broadcasts on a national level and the free delivery of one leaflet to each elector on a local level. It should also be added that all local candidates are required to deposit a sum of £500 with their nomination papers (the deadline for which is two weeks before the date of the election), which they will forfeit if they receive less than 5% of the vote. The size of the deposit was raised, and threshold lowered, in 1985.

Because most major party candidates spend very close to their local spending limit (particularly in marginal constituencies), tensions during campaigns can often run high between local parties, who regularly suspect their rivals of not reporting the full costs of their campaign. It was within such an atmosphere that the successful Labour candidate (now MP) Fiona Jones and her agent from the Newark constituency were initially convicted of presenting fraudulent election expense accounts for the 1997 election, though they were later exonerated on appeal (see chronology section). It was the opinion of many political analysts that had the convictions been maintained, the result would have been a flood of petitions from defeated candidates after the next election. A major reason for the lack of such appeals at present is precisely because no successful parliamentary candidate had been convicted of such fraud for a period of 75 years; before Newark no appeal had even been made since 1929.

The date at which local candidates start to use up their legal spending allowance has remained somewhat unclear, though this is generally taken either as the date of the publication of the notice of the election, three weeks before polling day (soon after the declaration of the election by the Prime Minister) or the date when a 'prospective' parliamentary candidate is officially 'adopted' by a local party as their candidate. This latter procedure is purely a formality, since in reality most candidates have been selected many months (or even years) earlier, but it avoids the accusation that their local campaign (and thus election spending) has already commenced. In any event, these dates mark out the 'official campaign period', traditionally the focus of all campaign efforts but in reality now only the culmination of a much longer election campaign, as reflected by the year-long national campaigning period defined by the Political Parties, Elections and Referendums Bill. This official recognition of the long campaign is long overdue, and tallies with the fact that most electors claim to make up their mind as to how they will vote several months before the actual date of the election. However, if national campaign spending is to be capped over a year, it does seem somewhat anomalous that local parties, on the proviso that they do not formally announce their candidate, are still able to spend heavily on literature or telephone canvassing two or three months before a likely election date without using any of their limited spending allowance. One conclusion from all this could be that the rules on local campaign spending are in urgent need of reform, but for the moment radical change is not on the political agenda.

As well as the changes to campaign spending which have taken place, there may also be changes to the framework surrounding the voting process before the next election, following the report of a Home Office working party group and a series of local pilots in the 2000 local council elections. The working party recommended the easing of rules on postal voting, suggesting that in future absentee votes should be available on demand rather than requiring a reason (such as illness or immobility). A local pilot in Newcastle saw the number of electors requesting a postal vote on this basis rise to 30,000, well over 10% of the electorate, and a far higher total than the 5,000 who applied before the rules were relaxed. If this rule is eased for the general election, it is worth bearing in mind that the deadline for postal vote applications will probably remain two-and-a-half weeks before polling day, (usually only a week after the election is called) which is often too soon for many voters to respond, unless local political parties are particularly well-organised.

Other electoral pilots tested in May 2000, such as the successful all-postal ballots (which in some cases doubled turnout) and the unsuccessful weekend voting and supermarket voting (which made virtually no difference to levels of turnout), are unlikely to be repeated at this general election. The other change that may come about is the introduction of a 'rolling electoral register', resulting from growing unease about the accuracy of the electoral register, currently published each year in February on the basis of an October census date. Electors must be included on this list to be allowed to cast their vote, but it is accepted that the register becomes increasingly outdated as the year progresses, and is more inaccurate in urban areas, where there is greater population movement. In all, the present register is probably no more than 95% accurate, which reduces the maximum possible turnout, implying that in reality general election turnouts are a few points higher than the official figures suggest. A rolling register could be kept up-to-date throughout the year and will help improve official turnout levels. This may not of course prevent a fall in the numbers voting at the forthcoming general election, when overall turnout (as a result of apathy rather than inaccuracy of the register) is widely expected to drop below 70% for the first time since 1918.

Retiring MPs

As ever, there will be a significant number of Members of Parliament standing down at the next election (over 50 had been announced by the time of going to press), including some notable political figures. Tony Benn was first elected in 1950, but will end half a century in the House of Commons knowing his son (Hilary Benn – Leeds Central) will maintain a distinguished line. For the Conservatives, a number of prominent leavers are headed by John Major, likely to continue his career in the Lords alongside former Prime Ministers Callaghan and Thatcher, and his former deputy Michael Heseltine, who is to be replaced by Daily Telegraph columnist Boris Johnson. A host of 'knights of the shires' to stand down include Sir Richard Body, who like Benn first contested a parliamentary election in 1950. Meanwhile former Liberal Democrat leader Sir Paddy Ashdown is also bowing out, along with former Labour MP and brief leader of the SDP, Robert Maclennan.

The number of retiring MPs has been increased by the election of a significant number to the Scottish Parliament or Welsh Assembly. Prominent names who will withdraw from Westminster as a result of devolution include Donald Dewar, Jim Wallace, Rhodri Morgan and Ron Davies. The list does not include Alun Michael, Labour's former Welsh leader, who now returns to concentrate on Westminster.

One final point to note about the retirements announced so far is that they may contribute to a fall in the number of women in the Commons – although only six of the 50 MPs who have confirmed they will stand down are women, all bar two of the replacements so far selected are men. This may change, as there are a number of local parties yet to select, and, as in 1997, a further raft of retirements and new candidates will almost certainly be announced shortly before the election.

The replacements so far selected include a number of defeated Conservatives from 1997, and also two former Labour MEPs, Wayne David and Tony Cunningham.

Labour

	Retiring MP	Replacement
Aberavon	John Morris	Hywel Francis
Ashton-under-Lyne	Robert Sheldon	David Hayes
Bassetlaw	Joe Ashton	John Mann
Birmingham Perry Barr	Jeff Rooker	
Caerphilly	*Ron Davies	Wayne David
Cardiff West	*Rhodri Morgan	Kevin Brennan
Chesterfield	Tony Benn	
Dagenham	Judith Church	John Cruddas
Dundee East	*John McAllion	Iain Luke
East Lothian	*John Home Robertson	Anne Picking
Edinbugh North and Leith	*Malcolm Chisholm	Mark Lazarowicz
Fife Central	*Henry McLeish	John MacDougall
Glasgow Anniesland	*Donald Dewar	John Robertson
Glasgow Cathcart	John Maxton	
Gloucester	Tess Kingham	
Greenock and Inverclyde	Norman Godman	David Cairns
Leigh	Lawrence Cunliffe	
Merthyr Tydfil	Ted Rowlands	David Harvard
Midlothian	Eric Clarke	David Hamilton
Morley and Rothwell	John Gunnell	Colin Challen
Newcastle-under-Lyme	Llin Golding	Paul Farrelly
Rhondda	Allan Rogers	Chris Bryant
Sheffield Heeley	Bill Michie	Meg Munn
Strathkelvin and Bearsden	*Sam Galbraith	
Wolverhampton South West	Jenny Jones	Rob Marris
Workington	Dale Campbell-Savours	Tony Cunningham
Wrexham	*John Marek	Ian Lucas

Conservative

	Retiring MP	Replacement
Bedfordshire North East	Sir Nicholas Lyell	Alastair Burt
Bedfordshire South West	Sir David Madel	Andrew Selous
Bexhill and Battle	Charles Wardle	
Billericay	Teresa Gorman	John Baron
Boston and Skegness	Sir Richard Body	Mark Simmonds
Bridgwater	Tom King	Ian Liddell-Grainger

Cities of L'don and W'minster	Peter Brooke	Mark Field
Devon East	Sir Peter Emery	Hugo Swire
Epsom and Ewell	Sir Archibald Hamilton	Chris Grayling
Fareham	Sir Peter Lloyd	Mark Hoban
Faversham and Mid Kent	Andrew Rowe	Hugh Robertson
Henley	Michael Heseltine	Boris Johnson
Hertford and Stortford	Bowen Wells	Mark Prisk
Huntingdon	John Major	Jonathan Djanogly
Leominster	Peter Temple-Morris★★	Bill Wiggin
Norfolk South	John MacGregor	Richard Bacon
Rayleigh	Michael Clark	Mark Francis
Sutton Coldfield	Sir Norman Fowler	Andrew Mitchell
Wealden	Sir Geoffrey Johnson Smith	Charles Hendry
Yorkshire East	John Townend	Greg Knight

★★Temple-Morris has defected to Labour, but Leominster is a solid Tory seat.

Liberal Democrats

	Retiring MP	**Replacement**
Argyll and Bute	Ray Michie	Paul Coleshill
Caithness and Sutherland	Robert Maclennan	
Edinburgh West	★Donald Gorrie	John Barrett
Orkney and Shetland	★Jim Wallace	Alistair Carmichael
Southport	Ronnie Fearn	
Yeovil	Sir Paddy Ashdown	David Laws

★will continue to sit in Scottish Parliament or Welsh Assembly.

Independents

	Retiring MP
Brent East	Ken Livingstone
Tatton	Martin Bell

London

Conservative Targets

Target No	Constituency		Labour Lead
C11	Romford	649	1.5%
C16	Harrow West	1,240	2.4%
C23	Enfield Southgate	1,433	3.1%
C42	Wimbledon	2,990	6.2%
C45	Finchley and Golders Green	3,189	6.3%
C47	Ilford North	3,224	6.6%
C50	Upminster	2,770	6.7%
C51	Putney	2,976	6.8%
C53	Croydon Central	3,897	7.0%
C55	Bexleyheath and Crayford	3,415	7.1%
C56	Hammersmith and Fulham	3,842	7.1%
C83	Brent North	4,019	10.5%
C93	Battersea	5,360	11.3%
C101	Hendon	6,155	12.3%
C105	Hornchurch	5,680	12.9%
C117	Enfield North	6,822	14.3%
C134	Ealing North	9,160	16.4%
C139	Harrow East	9,734	17.1%
C189	Eltham	10,182	23.4%

(Liberal Democrat held)

			Lib Dem Lead
C3	Kingston and Surbiton	56	0.1%
C29	Sutton and Cheam	2,097	4.5%
C31	Carshalton and Wallington	2,267	4.7%
C34	Richmond Park	2,951	5.2%
C58	Twickenham	4,281	7.4%

Labour Targets

Target No	Constituency	Conservative Lead	
L8	Uxbridge	724	1.7%
L10	Chipping Barnet	1,035	2.1%

London is a very large region, with more constituencies than Scotland, and a profusion of marginal seats. It is not just metropolitan laziness that lends great media interest to general elections in London. As well as its importance to the overall result, London has also demonstrated considerable independence in its voting behaviour.

London has produced two extreme results in recent general elections – 1987 and 1997. In the 1980s prosperity, underpinned by a boom in well-paid service employment and an extraordinary rise in the paper value of property, created a strong background for Thatcherite conservatism. The Conservative position was also helped by an adroit political campaign against the 'loony left' in Labour local government whose gesture politics and deteriorating standard of local services alienated many traditionally Labour voters. While the rest of Britain swung a little to Labour in 1987, the Conservatives managed the extraordinary feat of improving on their landslide showing in 1983 by achieving a broad favourable swing and winning seats from Labour. London has never been a very Labour city, particularly in the outskirts now grouped into greater London, and seemed to be very Conservative in the mid 1980s.

Labour came back strongly in 1992, as the recession exposed the limitations of the 1980s boom and the party reformed itself. It was one of Labour's better areas and the party managed to win back several of the classic marginals (Dulwich, both Lewisham seats, Ilford South, Hampstead & Highgate), some more recent losses (Walthamstow, Feltham & Heston, Greenwich, Woolwich) and most significantly expand into some seats never before won by the party (Streatham, Hornsey & Wood Green, Croydon NW).

London was again Labour's best region in 1997 with an 11% swing in inner London and 14.3% in outer London. The marginals won in 1992 all had enormous swings that render the seats of limited interest in the coming context. Labour's majority in Streatham was 41% of the vote, making it on paper a safer seat than Barnsley West & Penistone in the former mining district of South Yorkshire. Some of the gains of 1997 have similarly swung all the way past our list of marginal seats, mainly the working class seats that the Tories were unable to win before 1979 or 1983 and were somewhat fortunate to hold in 1992. Labour's gains in Edmonton (30% majority), Hayes & Harlington (34.8%), Mitcham & Morden (28.7%) and Brentford & Isleworth (25.7%) were by crushing margins. These seats, all designated 'Key Seats' by Labour in the run up to 1997 and the focus of much media and campaigning interest during that election, should be safe next time. Many of these seats have traditionally strong Labour constituency organisations.

The main attention in 1997 was instead on the massacre of previously safe Conservative seats in outer London. Labour won a swathe of seats across the northern suburbs, including the ousting of Michael Portillo and bizarre gains such as Harrow West; the Lib Dems knocked out five adjacent Tory seats in the south western suburbs. The Conservatives held only 11 seats, their worst showing ever in the region by some margin, and Labour had 58. How far can the Conservatives recover, and can Labour consolidate its new strength in the suburbs?

The focus in the mid-term of the Blair government has been on the travails of London Labour. The party's share of the vote has collapsed from nearly half to around a third in the Euro and GLA elections, and only an eighth in the fiasco of the London Mayoral election. The gains have been scattered for the most part among minor parties. The Greens, helped by Ken Livingstone's endorsement, did very well in the GLA election with over 10% of the vote, but had also managed 7.7% in 1999. The Lib Dems also picked up in 2000 (but not 1999) and various Labour rebels and socialists drew off votes. The wallflowers at this party have been the Tories. Their gains have been by default of Labour's failures, and they have not advanced far from the electoral ghetto of 1997. Labour held on in unlikely seats like Brent North in the 1999 Euro elections. It seems that Labour, despite the Mayoral election, is still performing relatively well in London.

The social changes that were transforming London even in the 1980s gathered momentum over the 1990s. London is very different from the rest of England and has a kind of rude republican equality and liberty quite well expressed by its new Mayor, Ken Livingstone. According to the 1991 census 14 of the 20 most non-white constituencies are in London, ranging from inner city seats to comfortable suburbs. London is home to large Asian and Afro-Caribbean communities, as well as a multitude of other minorities from across the world, including Africa, Ireland, Portugal and Poland. London is also a welcoming environment for gay people, who form a significant proportion of the metropolitan population. While lacking in the traditional mainsprings of Labour support like unionised heavy industry, London has become increasingly hostile to the 'forces of conservatism'.

Susan Kramer's Mayoral campaign won some admirers for the London Lib Dems, and there are a few seats, apart from the five southern marginals, where the party is a significant factor. Although the Lib Dems only hold one seat in inner London (Southwark North and Bermondsey), they are a considerable presence in several others. In 1990 and 1994 they menaced Labour in several inner city seats but their challenge seems to have slipped back in 1998 except in Islington, where in the Islington South and Finsbury constituency they outpolled Labour 55-32 despite Chris Smith's over-whelming 41-point majority in 1997. The Lib Dems won control of the borough in 1999 thanks to a gain from Labour at a by-election. Once upon a time Islington was an SDP area – the fledgling party had a majority on the council in 1981-82 and for a while all three of the borough's MPs. Smith's seat is the number one Lib Dem target in inner London, but they have failed before (even when defending the seat in 1983) and it would be a major upset if they won. More distant prospects, where Lib Dems can secure respectable showings (30%+) in local elections are Bethnal Green & Bow, Hackney South & Shoreditch, Leyton & Wanstead, Streatham, Vauxhall and Walthamstow. In most of these the party's share of the vote had receded since 1994.

In outer London, the Lib Dems probably maximised their showing in 1997. There was only one seat where a plausible challenge failed, and that was Orpington (whose dalliance with Liberalism in 1962-70 seems to have vaccinated it against more serious Liberal revivals). However, in the 1998 Bromley borough elections the Lib Dems nosed ahead of the Tories, by all of 0.1%, in the Orpington wards. A victory there next time is an outside chance but one that would give a great deal of satisfaction to Liberals, as the Tory MP is John Horam, dubbed a 'dirty double-rat' by Dennis Skinner for leaving Labour for the SDP and then defecting to the Tories.

One seat deserving a special note is Bethnal Green and Bow. It is just outside our definition of a marginal, but it was one of only two seats (see also Bradford West) which swung towards the Conservatives in 1997. London's ethnic diversity has tended to help Labour overall, but it has created problems here. Labour's Oona King was at a disadvantage to Tory Kabir Choudhury in appealing to the many Bengali electors in the seat, and also faced opposition from the BNP, who saved their deposit in a seat with a significant minority fascist tradition. The Lib Dems are a force in local elections, but a traditional Liberal also stood in 1997. Added to complex ethnic politics, parts of the constituency have been physically and demographically transformed by the Docklands development. It is a fascinating place that pays little attention to the wider trends of London or England, and well worth watching. But for the most part the constituencies that matter are the marginal ones.

Battersea

Labour majority 5,360 (11.3%)

Conservative target 93

MP Martin Linton

1997 (Turnout 69.0%)			
	Labour	24,047	50.7%
	Conservative	18,687	39.4%
	Liberal Democrat	3,482	7.3%
	Referendum	804	1.7%
	UK Independence	250	0.5%
	Other	127	0.3%

Battersea, though Labour in 1983, was a somewhat surprising Conservative loss in 1997. It has been the scene of some comprehensive social engineering by the Conservative controlled Wandsworth council, aided by its proximity to Chelsea and the West End which has attracted many upwardly mobile professionals. The riverside and Battersea Park areas deserve their reputation as 'south Chelsea', while the area near Clapham Junction station (Northcote) has also moved up in the world since the days of 'Up the Junction'. The constituency stretches down as far as Balham, also an increasingly expensive but hardly fashionable corner. Interspersed with the upwardly mobile terraces and avenues are some grim council estates where Wandsworth's right to buy policies have been less enthusiastically taken up. The Doddington Estate is notorious for the corrupt methods by which it was built in the 1960s; the council leader responsible, Sidney Sporle, was jailed for taking bribes.

Labour's problem was not that Battersea was overwhelmingly Conservative, it was that it seemed that a hard-line and intransigent form of Conservatism had taken over the area and voted down the line for Tories in local and general elections, while the still substantial Labour vote was a scattered and demoralised force. John O'Farrell's *Things Can Only Get Better* is a grimly hilarious account of Labour's string of defeats in Battersea, culminating in the loss of the seat in 1987 and humiliation in the council elections of 1990. It was not even considered a key seat, despite its marginality on paper, and it was a major surprise when Martin Linton won in 1997. Linton, previously a journalist for the Guardian and author of many thoughtful articles about politics and elections, is a keen electoral reformer.

In most parts of the country, Labour did significantly worse in the Euro election of 1999 than in the local elections of 1998. In Battersea, however, the Tories led by 21.7% in 1998 but only 1.3% in 1999. We can presume that Battersea voted Conservative by a fair margin in the GLA election of May 2000. Wandsworth's Toryism is the Toryism of winners rather than losers; the confidence of successful and aspirational voters rather than the sullen defensiveness of those whom change is leaving behind. The paradox of such a seat voting overwhelmingly for Tories in local elections but supporting New Labour nationally is not so difficult to resolve.

Bexleyheath and Crayford

Labour majority 3,415 (7.1%)

Conservative target 55

MP Nigel Beard

1997 (Turnout 76.1%):			
	Labour	21,942	45.5%
	Conservative	18,527	38.4%
	Liberal Democrat	5,391	11.2%
	Referendum	1,551	3.2%
	BNP	429	0.9%
	UK Independence	383	0.8%

Bexleyheath and Crayford, in the far south east of London where the capital shades into Kent, was supposed to be a pretty safe Conservative seat when the Crayford wards were added to Bexleyheath in 1997. The main battle was thought to be for the Tory nomination, and Thatcherite David Evennett won out over the centrist Bexleyheath MP Sir Cyril Townsend. The large London swing carried the seat over into the Labour column and Nigel Beard defeated Evennett by a respectable margin.

Bexleyheath is a very suburban area, with many commuters travelling on the rather poor trains into central London. There are few extremes of wealth or poverty in the area. Its wards are mostly quite mixed politically although with Conservatism predominating. Crayford, added in 1997, tends to be Labour although Bostall, another additional ward, is rather Conservative. Overall, Labour held a three point lead in the 1998 borough elections, but lagged by 10 points in Euro 99 and a similar margin in 2000. If Labour win the next election, the party might well be able to overcome such a relatively shallow midterm trough in Bexleyheath and Crayford, and frustrate David Evennett again.

Brent North

Labour majority 4,019 (10.5%)

Conservative target 83

MP Barry Gardiner

1997 (Turnout 70.5%):	Labour	19,343	50.7%
	Conservative	15,324	40.1%
	Liberal Democrat	3,104	8.1%
	Others	403	1.0%

Brent North is essentially the suburban parts of Wembley – the stadium and the shopping centre are in Brent South. It is a quiet and comfortable place for the most part, shading into Harrow on its north side at Sudbury, served by the upper reaches of the Jubilee and Bakerloo lines. Along with Harrow, this is London's premier Asian residential area. The area is close enough to the cultural and shopping facilities of Southall to keep up community links, and also provides high quality 1930s family housing and a pleasant environment. By 1991 the non-white population was 41.3% in Brent North, but the seat was still safely Conservative, reflecting its very middle class composition.

Brent North broke a record in May 1997. The swing to Labour, 18.8%, was the sharpest to take place in a seat undisturbed by a defection or a by-election since 1945. The Conservatives were completely shell-shocked by the loss of the seat, and Labour's victories have continued here since. Although Labour were lagging 48–39% in the wards of Brent North in the 1998 council elections, this is perhaps deceptive. Most of the component wards of Brent North had swings of over 10% to Labour between 1994 and 1998 – in Roe Green (across the road from Hendon) it reached 18.8%. Labour's positive national image was at last able to secure a strong vote for the party in local elections, where Labour had for long been struggling against the disastrous record of the council in 1986–90. Brent North was still Labour in the 1999 Euro election – the only unlikely Labour gain to remain this loyal – but was probably Tory in the 2000 GLA election. With the loss of 1974–97 Tory MP Rhodes Boyson's personal vote, it now looks a tough nut for Tory candidate Philip Allott to crack.

Carshalton and Wallington

Lib Dem majority 2,267 (4.7%)

Conservative target 31

MP Tom Brake

1997 (Turnout 73.3%):			
	Liberal Democrat	18,490	38.2%
	Conservative	16,223	33.5%
	Labour	11,565	23.9%
	Referendum	1,289	2.7%
	Green	377	0.8%
	Others	479	1.0%

While Sutton and Cheam is uniformly middle class, the other half of the London Borough of Sutton is more varied. In the north it contains the borough's part of the large St. Helier estate, which elects Labour councillors, and industrial areas around Beddington and the Wandle valley. Carshalton and Wallington are middle class suburbs between Sutton and Croydon. To the south are the wealthy Carshalton Beeches and Woodcote areas, and an isolated and unpleasant council estate at Roundshaw on the site of the old Croydon airport.

Demographically, it could be a Tory-Labour marginal, but local politics has produced Liberal Democrat ascendancy in all parts of the constituency – even inroads into St. Helier. This was translated from local to national politics in 1997 with the victory of Tom Brake. Unlike in Richmond, the 1998 local elections were better for the Lib Dems than 1997 (they led by 22.7%). The Tories led 37–23% in 1999 but were probably behind again in the 2000 GLA election. Labour won 23.9% of the vote in 1997, rather high for a Con-Lib Dem marginal, and Liberal Democrat strategy must be to squeeze this in the next general election. Brake has not let up campaigning since being elected and is a very attentive constituency MP who stands a reasonable chance of capitalising on his advantages and retaining the seat.

Chipping Barnet

Conservative majority 1,035 (2.1%)

Labour target 10

MP Sir Sydney Chapman

1997 (Turnout 70.9%):			
	Conservative	21,317	43.0%
	Labour	20,282	40.9%
	Liberal Democrat	6,121	12.3%
	Referendum	1,190	2.4%
	Others	655	1.3%

Chipping Barnet was one of the few suburban seats in north London to resist the Labour tide in 1997. Labour narrowly won Barnet (a larger area) in 1945, but it proved a safe berth for Tory high-flier Reginald Maudling in 1950-79 and since then for his successor Sydney Chapman. The swing in 1997, at 14.1%, was massive but a bit lower than in neighbouring seats such as Hendon and Enfield Southgate, which saved Chipping Barnet for the Conservatives.

Chipping Barnet consists of some rather uniform suburban territory at the edge of London, with no particularly poor areas and a small extremely wealthy area at Totteridge village. Arkley ward is mostly Labour, Totteridge mostly Conservative, but there are no real strongholds for either party and in a good Labour year like 1994 or 1998 all wards are closely fought.

The Conservatives have extended their lead from 2.1% in 1997, to 8.1% in 1998 to 13.9% in 1999 and about 20% in 2000, and start favourites even if Sir Sydney Chapman bows out at the next election. Labour, however, are not out of contention as suburban London seems to be a growth area for the party.

Croydon Central

Labour majority 3,897 (7.0%)

Conservative target 53

MP Geraint Davies

1997 (Turnout 69.6%):	Labour	25,432	45.6%
	Conservative	21,535	38.6%
	Liberal Democrat	6,061	10.9%
	Referendum	1,886	3.4%
	Green	595	1.1%
	UK Independence	290	0.5%

This constituency occupies a middle band of the London Borough of Croydon, from the town centre eastwards (Croydon East might be a better name). The centre of Croydon has a striking skyline of office towers and flyovers, and boasts a large shopping centre that serves a wide area of south London, Surrey and even Sussex – but there are few voters here. Croydon's new tramlines weave through the constituency, uniting its disparate parts. Furthest is New Addington, a massive council estate housing 14,000 electors on a hill overlooking London, surrounded by fields and even farms. It was the council base of the Labour MP Geraint Davies. On the way to New Addington the tram meanders through the Conservative Fairfield and Heathfield wards, with northern branches to the more mixed areas of Addiscombe and Woodside. It is a large seat, and despite its name 46% of the voters come from the abolished Croydon NE seat, not the old Central. The new territory is more marginal than the polarised wards of the old seat.

Labour's victory in 1997 was surprising. It was based on a solid vote in New Addington, plus a lead in most of the wards formerly in Croydon NE, and a respectable showing in the most upmarket areas of the seat. Of these, persuading New Addington to turn out again may be the hardest part. In the 1998 borough elections the Tories led by 48–40%, and in the Euro elections by 40–29%. A rough estimate of the 2000 GLA result would have the Tories ahead by perhaps 7 points. It seems that Labour has lost a little support since 1997 but has not slumped as it has in some marginals. The Conservative MP for Croydon NE in 1992–97, David Congdon, tries again to win Central.

Ealing North

Labour majority 9,160 (16.4%)

Conservative target 134

MP Stephen Pound

1997 (Turnout 72.3%):

Labour	29,904	53.7%
Conservative	20,744	37.2%
Liberal Democrat	3,887	7.0%
UK Independence	689	1.2%
Green	502	0.9%

Ealing North has been a hard-fought marginal seat since its creation in 1950, and it fell to Labour in 1997 on a typically large London swing. It is a rather unpretentious working class place, although it has the wealthy district of Pitshanger in the east which had previously kept Acton so Conservative. It lies on both sides of the A40 main road out of London towards Oxford. Many of the wards are quite marginal and prone to high swings in local elections. Its Labour MP Stephen Pound, in a witty maiden speech in 1997, described it as 'a mixture of hamlets, towns, villages and communities, bound together by many things — but most of all by the Boundary Commissioner' and rather devoid of interesting landmarks and local history, except for a curious incident in 1889 when a circus elephant, with its last breath, staggered out of the seat into Acton rather than die in Ealing North.

London has little manufacturing industry left, but there is still an industrial tone to Ealing North, particularly in the areas around Park Royal and Northolt. Ealing North has the largest Polish population in Britain, because of the Polish Air Force presence at Northolt during the war. Ealing North also boasts a large open space, spared from the developers in the 1930s, around Horsenden Hill. Labour were 5.6% in the 1998 Ealing borough elections in North, but it was one of the party's better performances in 1999 with a lead of 4.3%. The Conservatives probably led somewhat in the 2000 GLA elections and their candidate is Charles Walker but Labour start favourites. This is perhaps the only constituency where the populist slogan 'Keep the Pound' has pro-Labour connotations.

Eltham

Labour majority 10,182 (23.4%)

Conservative target 189

Labour MP Clive Efford

1997 (Turnout 75.2%):	Labour	23,710	54.6%
	Conservative	13,528	31.2%
	Liberal Democrat	3,701	8.5%
	Referendum	1,414	3.3%
	Others	1,075	2.4%

Eltham is a collection of middle London suburbs on the hills south and west of Woolwich town centre: Eltham itself and Plumstead are the best known. Eltham's wards are a mixture of small council and ex-council estates and private developments. It is peculiar for a halfway-out London seat in not having changed much demographically; it is still mainly skilled working class and lower middle class, and it is the least ethnically mixed seat in inner London. It has also not changed into a Labour stronghold like Hornsey or Streatham and remains marginal. In the past it was one of the largest constituency Labour Parties in the country, based on strong Co-op and union movements in the area.

Eltham has a bad reputation as one of the most racist areas of London. Stephen Lawrence was murdered on its streets in 1993 and there have been other attacks; Brian Cathcart in his study of the murder said of Eltham then that 'by London's standards it was a place with a distinctly ugly streak.' The seat was highly marginal in 1992 and the incumbent Tory MP Peter Bottomley left it for Worthing. Clive Efford, a taxi driver and Labour councillor for Well Hall ward, gained the seat by a wide margin (over 10,000 votes) in 1997. Since then, Labour has led in all the mid-term elections in Eltham; by 16% in 1998, 5% in 1999 and about 2% in 2000. It seems like a pretty solid bet for a Labour hold.

Enfield North

Labour majority 6,822 (14.3%)

Conservative target 117

MP Joan Ryan

1997 (Turnout 70.4%):	Labour	24,148	50.7%
	Conservative	17,326	36.3%
	Liberal Democrat	4,264	8.9%
	Referendum	857	1.8%
	BNP	590	1.2%
	UK Independence	484	1.0%

Enfield is as far north as you can get and still be in Greater London. The northern seat of Enfield is a rather peculiar marginal constituency, which has so far during its existence been won by the party that formed the government. When the Conservatives held it during the 1980s it seemed to be becoming a safe seat, but Labour dealt a knockout blow in 1997. Despite neighbouring Edmonton being a designated target marginal seat and getting the full treatment of top name visits and outside volunteers, the swing in Enfield North, just over 16%, was a bit larger. It is a rather volatile constituency.

Enfield North was created by a merger of Labour Enfield East and the bulk of Tory Enfield West, and the join still shows. East Enfield, down by the Lea river and various parallel canals, highways and railway lines, is an industrial area and the wards down here – Enfield Lock, Enfield Wash and Ponders End – are strongly Labour. Up by the old town centre and further west Enfield is strongly Tory. Labour won 50.7% of the vote in Enfield North in 1997 and still led by 4.3% in 1998, but the Tories pulled ahead by a little over 6% in Euro 99 and probably around 10% in 2000. Labour's sharp and witty Joan Ryan defends the seat against Tory candidate Nick De Bois, a marketing manager who fought Stalybridge and Hyde in 1997.

Enfield Southgate

Labour majority 1,433 (3.1%)

Conservative target 23

MP Stephen Twigg

1997 (Turnout 70.7%):			
	Labour	20,570	44.2%
	Conservative	19,137	41.1%
	Liberal Democrat	4,966	10.7%
	Referendum	1,342	2.9%
	Others	518	1.1%

Enfield Southgate's ejection of Michael Portillo in 1997 was one of the most celebrated moments of the election; Brian Cathcart's book about election night 1997 was called *Were You Still Up for Portillo?* Southgate was in the middle of the band of north London where Labour achieved their highest swings in the country. It consists of a slice of suburbia stretching from just south of the North Circular Road to the edge of greater London – Arnos

Grove, Palmers Green, Southgate and Winchmore Hill. Most were true-blue until the late 1980s, when Labour started winning the southern wards. Like other London suburbs it has become more and more racially mixed, with a growing population of Indian origin and upwardly mobile Cypriots moving up from Tottenham and Edmonton. Labour were also helped by a poll showing them closing on Portillo the weekend before the election that attracted Lib Dem tactical voting.

The Conservatives have come out ahead in every contest in Southgate since 1997; narrowly (43–40%) in the 1998 local elections, and by more comfortable margins in Euro 1999 and the 2000 GLA elections. Conservative candidate John Flack replaces Portillo, who has since been returned for the truly safe Kensington and Chelsea seat, and must be reasonably confident of replacing Labour MP Stephen Twigg. And yet . . . demographic change continues in Labour's favour, Twigg is a popular MP and Southgate's Labour Party is quite strong and has been experimenting with a new style of constituency organisation.

Finchley and Golders Green

Labour majority 3,189 (6.3%)

Labour marginal 45

Conservative target

MP Rudi Vis

1997 (Turnout 68.2%):			
	Labour	23,180	46.1%
	Conservative	19,991	39.7%
	Liberal Democrat	5,670	11.3%
	Referendum	684	1.4%
	Green	576	1.1%
	UK Independence	205	0.4%

This seat had a special place in the 1997 roll of honour for Labour as it was the former stronghold of Margaret Thatcher. It is mostly a product of inter-war growth and depends heavily on the erratic Northern Line of the London underground. East Finchley is an increasingly Indian area, and the seat as a whole is 21.2% non-white, but the most prominent local minority is the Jewish community – particularly in the Golders Green area. Many residents commute into central London but there are large local employers, including McDonalds' UK headquarters. Finchley and Golders Green is an affluent area in the top ten seats in the country for professional and non-manual workers, and has some of the intellectual sheen of neighbouring Hampstead and Highgate which has gradually become a safe Labour seat.

Labour MP Rudi Vis was famously unprepared for his surprise victory in 1997; he had to find someone to teach his economics classes at the University of East London at very short notice after winning. The next election is a rematch between Vis and the defeated Tory John Marshall, previously MP for Hendon South 1987–97. Labour's strong performance was repeated in the Barnet borough elections in 1998, when the party was still well ahead (5.3%) and consolidated its advantage in the previously marginal St Paul's and Woodhouse wards. Labour were only one point behind even in Euro 99; voters here scorned the Thatcher legacy with a low (3.1%) UKIP vote. In the 2000 elections for the GLA Labour probably lagged by about 11 points.

The demographic and political shifts in outer London have transformed places like this from safe reservoirs of Tory support to the new front line of the major party battle. In the long term it may even follow other middle London seats like Streatham and Hornsey and become a reliable Labour seat, but for now it is still vulnerable to a national Tory recovery.

Hammersmith and Fulham

Labour majority 3,842 (7.1%)

Conservative target 56

MP Iain Coleman

1997 (Turnout 68.7%):			
	Labour	25,262	46.8%
	Conservative	21,420	39.6%
	Liberal Democrat	4,728	8.8%
	Referendum	1,023	1.9%
	New Labour	695	1.3%
	Green	562	1.0%
	Others	336	0.5%

This seat has seen its share of titanic electoral confrontations; Fulham East in 1933, Hammersmith South in 1949 and Fulham in 1986 in by-elections; and the repeated 'Battles of Barons Court' in the 1950s and 1960s in general elections. It is still a close fight. In 1997, Labour council leader Iain Coleman beat Matthew Carrington, Tory MP for Fulham 1987–97. There will be a rematch between Coleman and Carrington at the next election.

Fulham has been climbing the social ladder for decades and now has the reputation of being London's most overpriced residential area. The steady advance of Conservatism in the area is concentrated in a group of wards south of Fulham Broadway, which have swung relentlessly to the right. Sulivan, for instance, has seen its Tory lead stretch, against the trend, from 5 points in 1986 to 34 points in 1998. The northern wards around Hammersmith Broadway have, by contrast, followed the London trend towards Labour. Ravenscourt Park and Brook Green are both sought-after areas; the latter has had several million-pound house sales recently. Labour gained both wards in 1998. It seems that different sorts of people are moving into each end of the seat.

Labour still led by 1.6% in 1998, but were 5.3% behind in 1999 and well adrift – perhaps 18 points down – in the 2000 GLA election. Labour will need to call upon every resource to win this marginal seat again.

Harrow East

Labour majority 9,734 (17.1%)

Conservative target 139

MP Tony McNulty

1997 (Turnout 71.4%)			
	Labour	29,923	52.5%
	Conservative	20,189	35.4%
	Liberal Democrat	4,697	8.2%
	Referendum	1,537	2.7%
	UK Independence	464	0.8%
	Other	171	0.3%

Harrow East was a Labour seat in the previous landslide victories of 1945 and 1966, and duly fell in 1997. An enormous swing in 1997 gave Labour's Tony McNulty a much larger majority than his two predecessors, and he could hold on even if Labour's national majority disappears at the next election. Even in the Euro election of 1999 Labour had a relatively healthy 4.5% lead, in an election where the Tories would have enjoyed an overall majority. The Tories were probably a little ahead in May 2000.

The East is less exclusive and wealthy than West, although it actually has fewer council tenants and rather more terraces. It includes the Wealdstone district of Harrow, stretches up to the Barnet border at Stanmore and adjoins Brent North at Kenton. It is about a third non-white, mostly Asian, and rather similar to Brent North. Several tube lines weave through it. Harrow East was affected by a local issue, the future of Edgware Hospital, in 1997 which helped Labour then, but Labour have a strong position and Tory, Peter Wilding, a difficult task.

Harrow West

Labour majority 1,240 (2.4%)

Conservative target 16

MP Gareth Thomas

1997 (Turnout 72.2%)	Labour	21,811	41.5%
	Conservative	20,571	39.2%
	Liberal Democrat	8,127	15.5%
	Referendum	1,997	3.8%

Until 1997 the idea of Labour representing the lush suburbs of Harrow West was preposterous. Gareth Thomas's victory was, to those who know Pinner and Harrow-on-the-Hill, one of the most unbelievable results of the evening. The seat also includes tracts of suburbia around Headstone Lane and Rayner's Lane. Labour had never won here, and failed to come within 9,000 votes of the Conservatives even in 1945. Unlike Harrow East, it has no Labour history and until recently no Labour wards.

Labour's victory was rounded out in May 1998 with the capture of Harrow Borough Council, the first time the party has had a majority on the authority. The wards making up Harrow West contributed to the win, and Labour were still 0.5% ahead in the seat, even gaining a councillor in the Harrow-on-the-Hill ward. This proved that the 1997 result was not a total freak and that Labour had gathered a strong core of support in Harrow West. The Conservatives led by 8.5% in Euro 99 – not overwhelming in so marginal a seat – and probably around 19% in 2000.

Danny Finkelstein, former director of the Conservative Research Department and one-time close associate of David Owen in the SDP, has what should, at least in theory, be the easy task of regaining the seat for the Tories.

Hendon

Labour majority 6,155 (12.3%)

Conservative target 101

MP Andrew Dismore

1997 (Turnout 65.7%)			
	Labour	24,683	49.3%
	Conservative	18,528	37.0%
	Lib Dem	5,427	10.8%
	Referendum	978	2.0%
	UK Independence	267	0.5%
	Other	153	0.3%

Hendon is the first part of London to greet people arriving from the north on the M1; an untidy tangle of flyovers and the Brent Cross Shopping Centre, a revolutionary development when it opened in 1976. Hendon is a creation of the 20th Century; most of the private housing sprang up during the interwar period and is crisscrossed by arterial roads. There is a large old-fashioned council estate at Watling (Burnt Oak) and on the site of the old airfield the large, confusing and rather slummy 1970s Grahame Park estate, but also a prosperous suburb at Mill Hill. Like Finchley and Golders Green, the constituency has a prominent Jewish community.

Labour has only won Hendon (North) in the landslide elections of 1945 and 1997 – even in 1966 Tory MP Ian Orr-Ewing held on by a whisker. However, at the next election Labour might well hold Hendon even if the party's majority nationally is slashed. Thanks to an enormous swing in 1997, the Labour lead here was 12.3% – the Conservatives would be doing well to overhaul this nationally. In Hendon, however, Labour support seems to be holding up well – the party was still ahead by a full 8.3% in the 1998 borough elections, only 0.5% behind in the Euro election and 5.5% behind in the GLA elections in 2000. Labour does not have to recover, or bring to the polls (turnout in 1997 was rather low), too much extra support to hold Hendon.

Hornchurch

Labour majority 5,680 (12.9%)

Conservative target 105

MP John Cryer

1997 (Turnout 72.2%)			
	Labour	22,066	50.2%
	Conservative	16,386	37.3%
	Liberal Democrat	3,446	7.8%
	Referendum	1,595	3.6%
	Others	448	1.0%

A lot of London's population is drawn from the top and bottom of the social and income scale, and a large range of cultures, but there are areas that are resolutely ordinary places, inhabited mainly by skilled manual and lower middle class white people. One such is Hornchurch, north and east of the huge, threatened Ford motor production plant at Dagenham and home to many of its workers. Most of its wards are mixed and marginal. Hornchurch has long been a critical marginal, prone to large swings, and was duly a Labour gain on a 16% swing in 1997. John Cryer is the son of the late Bob Cryer MP and Ann Cryer, another new MP of 1997 (Keighley). He is well to the left of the 1997 intake and a participant in most of the major rebellions in this parliament, and also an assiduous worker on behalf of his constituency.

Like other Havering borough seats, party lines are blurred in local elections, and in 1998 Labour's 43–23% lead over the Tories should be seen in the context of a 32.6% vote for 'Resident' candidates. The Conservatives led by 41.5% to 31% in the Euro elections, and were ahead again in 2000. Robin Squire, a genial and very moderate Conservative, represented the constituency from 1979 to 1997 and will hope to regain the seat next time.

Ilford North

Labour majority 3,224 (6.6%)

Conservative target 47

MP Linda Perham

1997 (Turnout 71.6%)	Labour	23,135	47.4%
	Conservative	19,911	40.8%
	Liberal Democrat	5,049	10.3%
	BNP	750	1.5%

Ilford North is a pretty uniform stretch of suburban London strung out along the A12 and the further reaches of the Central Line. There is one large council-built estate at Hainault but a lot of it has been sold under 'right to buy' and the gap between it and 1930s semi-detached suburbia at Fullwell and Barkingside is not so great. It is an Essex equivalent of the Metroland that sprawled over Middlesex in the 1930s. Its main local peculiarity is the high number of London cabbies who live in the area.

The seat now extends up to Woodford Bridge after the abolition of the Wanstead and Woodford constituency, long famous for sending Churchill to parliament. A previous Ilford North was Labour in 1945 and October 1974, but did not contain the Conservative areas from Woodford which are now included.

Labour's Linda Perham did very well to win a seat that is basically Conservative, and gave the Tories a 3.8% lead in the 1998 borough elections. Their lead stretched to 11.9% in Euro 99 and more in 2000. Conservative Vivian Bendall, the MP from a 1978 by-election until 1997, challenges again.

Kingston and Surbiton

Liberal Democrat majority 56 (0.1%)

Conservative target 3

MP Edward Davey

1997 (Turnout 75.3%)	Liberal Democrat	20,411	36.7%
	Conservative	20,355	36.6%
	Labour	12,811	23.0%
	Referendum	1,470	2.6%
	UK Independence	418	0.8%
	Others	200	0.4%

This seat sounds like a very suburban district, and so it is for the most part. Kingston is one of the largest shopping centres in southern England and has a flourishing university, but outside the central area it gets suburban pretty quickly. Surbiton sprang up as a result of the main line railway (Victorian Kingston refused to have the main line put through their town), and other settlements like Tolworth hug the A3 Kingston Bypass, a 1930s arterial road. There are pockets of Labour support in Tolworth in particular but for the most part the battle is between Lib Dems and Tories.

The Liberal Democrats won the seat from the Conservatives by a margin of only 56 votes in 1997. Their MP Edward Davey would seem to be one of the most obvious single-term members of the 1997 parliament, particularly as the Lib Dems went on to lose control of Kingston council in 1998 and came third in Euro 99. It would, however, be premature to mark this down as a certain Conservative gain. Adding up the votes in the component wards in 1998 actually stretches the Lib Dem lead to 1.2%. Davey is also an assiduous constituency MP. In the May 2000 GLA elections the South West district turned in a very strong Lib Dem performance and the minuscule swing to the Tories would have made this seat no more than 'too close to call'. The Conservatives have selected the former MP for Dover, the abrasive David Shaw, as their candidate. Shaw was a rancorous presence in previous parliaments, and most Labour MPs would feel great satisfaction if he did not return. Much depends on whether the sizeable 23% of Labour voters here in 1997 share this dislike.

Putney

Labour majority 2,976 (6.8%)

Conservative target 51

MP Tony Colman

1997 (Turnout 71.4%)			
	Labour	20,084	45.7%
	Conservative	17,108	38.9%
	Liberal Democrat	4,739	10.8%
	Referendum	1,518	3.5%
	UK Independence	233	0.5%
	Others	313	0.6%

Although Putney's election night count, with an angry shouting match between defeated Tory David Mellor, James Goldsmith and pro gun lobbyists, was exceptional, the Putney result curiously enough was not. Tony

Colman, whose dignified contribution to election night went unnoticed by the TV cameras, won the seat for the Labour Party. Gloss aside, Putney was a major party contest in 1997 and will be again. The swing to Labour was 11.2%, very near the average for inner London.

Putney has tended to move according to long-term trends. It was a citadel of 'villa Toryism' from 1918 to 1964, when the Labour London County Council finally managed to build the Tories out of Putney through large council housing projects in Roehampton. Left wing MP Hugh Jenkins held the seat until his defeat by Mellor in 1979. Then the Conservatives managed to sell off a lot of the former council houses and capitalise on Putney's environmental advantages (transport links, the river, parks) and the demographic changes of the 1950s and 1960s went into reverse. Putney looked safely Tory by the end of the 1980s. Labour's new ascendancy in Putney is unlikely to be as long-lived.

In the 1998 local elections, Putney showed the largest Tory majority in a Labour seat anywhere in the country, a massive 29% (60–31%). The Tories won every ward in the seat, including the former council estate wards of Roehampton and Parkside. Despite this Putney probably shifted little in its preferences over that year, as there are many voters who vote Conservative in local elections and Labour in general elections because of the generally positive reputation of the Tory Wandsworth Council. The Tories only led by 5% in Euro 99, but in the 2000 GLA election their lead was back up over 20%. Their candidate Michael Simpson probably starts the favourite in the next general election.

Richmond Park

Liberal Democrat majority 2,951 (5.2%)

Conservative target 34

MP Jenny Tonge

1997 (Turnout 77.3%)			
	Liberal Democrat	25,393	44.7%
	Conservative	22,442	39.5%
	Labour	7,172	12.6%
	Referendum	1,467	2.6%
	Others	379	0.7%

Richmond Park is an outer London seat consisting, as its name might suggest, a series of districts bordering on the largest of the London Royal Parks. The main centre of the seat is Richmond, a pleasant and prosperous town — it is ungenerous to call it a suburb — by the Thames. North lies Kew and the highly favoured residential suburbs of Palewell and Barnes, which are surprisingly close to central London. The new accessions to the seat in 1997 consisted of the northern half of the abolished Kingston seat, which had been represented by Norman Lamont for 25 years (see Harrogate & Knaresborough) comprising the wealthy Tudor Drive, Kingston Hill and New Malden areas and the central wards of Canbury and Cambridge. The seat has two Millionaire's Rows, at Richmond Hill and Coombe, and other than the depressing Ham estate little of it is shabby. It is the fifth most 'professional/ managerial' seat in the country.

That Richmond Park was lost by the Conservatives in 1997 may seem bizarre, but many observers were surprised that Jeremy Hanley, the jovial Tory MP for Richmond and Barnes 1983–97, held on for so long. The Lib Dems have been practising pavement politics in Richmond for a quarter of a century now and took a firm grip of the borough council in 1986. The wards transplanted from Kingston were supposed to have made the seat safer for the Tories, but they were swamped. The Lib Dem lead in the 1998 borough elections was 3%, less than in 1997. The result in the 1999 Euro election was an unconvincing Conservative win, with 39% compared to about 20% each for Lib Dem and Labour (Labour's vote was considerably up on 1997 reflecting the lack of tactical voting). In the 2000 GLA elections the Lib Dems seem to have been ahead by a similar margin to 1997 when Jenny Tonge, a doctor, won the seat by 5.2%. She faces opposition from Tory Tom Harris, and starts as the favourite.

Romford

Labour majority 649 (1.5%)

Conservative target 11

MP Eileen Gordon

1997 (Turnout 70.5%)			
	Labour	18,187	43.2%
	Conservative	17,538	41.6%
	Liberal Democrat	3,341	7.9%
	Referendum	1,431	3.4%
	Others	1,622	3.8%

Romford is an almost entirely suburban constituency on the fringes where London spreads out into Essex. It is uniformly middle class but unglamorous. The 'town' is big enough in itself to act as a centre for areas of east London and Essex. It was a safe Conservative seat from its creation in its modern form in 1974 until 1997, when to near universal surprise it fell to Labour.

Like other seats in the outer London borough of Havering, the picture of what has happened since 1997 is obscured by a powerful Residents political organisation whose support cannot be straightforwardly translated into national political terms. While the Tories led Labour 44–32% in Romford in 1998, 'others' polled 16%. Residents won 11.8% in the GLA elections in 2000 across the whole of Havering and Redbridge, and their support was presumably concentrated in Havering. There was no such distraction in the Euro election of 1999 and the Conservatives were easy winners, with a 45–27% lead over Labour and another 9% voting UKIP. It seems improbable that Labour's Eileen Gordon could hold Romford. The likely winner is Conservative candidate and local councillor Andrew Rosindell, a devout Thatcherite and almost self-parodic Essex Man stereotype, but perennially popular in his Chase Cross ward. He has converted Chase Cross, which he gained from the Lib Dems in 1990, into the ward with the highest Conservative share of the vote in London – 81% – and won a 20% swing from Labour between 1994 and 1998. Rosindell is clearly a formidable campaigner.

Sutton and Cheam

Liberal Democrat majority 2,097 (4.5%)

Conservative target 29

MP Paul Burstow

1997 (Turnout 75.1%)			
	Liberal Democrat	19,919	42.3%
	Conservative	17,822	37.8%
	Labour	7,280	15.5%
	Referendum	1,784	3.8%
	Others	287	0.6%

The Lib Dem triumph in Sutton in 1997 reflected a long history of activism, from the victory of Graham (now Lord) Tope in a 1972 by-election to taking control of the council in 1986. Much of the constituency is composed of 1930s vintage outer London suburbs, with some nuances of demographic difference between its wards. Cheam, with its scattered Tudor buildings, is posher than Sutton's 1960s town centre despite its association with Tony Hancock's ménage. Nearly all the wards are Liberal Democrat in local elections, except the southern, most affluent, part of Cheam. The central Sutton town wards return massive Lib Dem leads.

There are no reservoirs of Labour support (it has three of the five weakest Labour wards in London) but the party managed an almost respectable 15.5% in 1997 spread thinly across the area. The Lib Dems enjoyed a massive 23.1% lead in 1998, were 20 points adrift in Euro 99 and probably back in the lead in the 2000 GLA elections. Paul Burstow for the Lib Dems and Olga Maitland for the Tories face off for the third time in a row. They have very contrasting political styles – Burstow is a grassroots politician with long council experience and a near obsessive concern for local issues. Olga Maitland is an ex-gossip columnist and a flamboyant campaigner for assorted right wing causes who was rebuked by the Speaker in 1994 and affected grand indifference to her eviction in 1997. It should be another divisive election in Sutton.

Twickenham

Liberal Democrat majority 4,281 (7.4%)

Conservative target 58

MP Vincent Cable

1997 (Turnout 78.1%)	Liberal Democrat	26,237	45.1%
	Conservative	21,956	37.8%
	Labour	9,065	15.6%
	Others	886	1.5%

On paper, Twickenham – the seat includes several other areas such as Hampton and Teddington – is the safest of the five Lib Dem seats in south west London, but it may not prove to be so in fact. Liberal Democrat strength in local elections in the borough of Richmond seems to have peaked. The party lost six council seats to the Tories in Twickenham in 1998 and their lead (4.5%) in the seat was less than at the general election. This is a reversal of the pattern in previous elections, and contrasts with the picture in Sutton borough. In Euro 1999 the Lib Dems trailed behind Labour in third place in Twickenham, with Labour's share of the vote rising by 6% since 1997, a sign that the Lib Dem hold is dependent on tactical voting.

Vincent Cable was a special adviser to John Smith when Smith was in the Labour Cabinet in the 1970s, but then joined the SDP. He is one of the leading Liberal Democrat economic thinkers. His main challenger is Tory candidate Nick Longworth who replaces defeated MP Toby Jessel.

Upminster

Labour majority 2,770 (6.7%)

Conservative target 50

MP Keith Darvill

1997 (Turnout 72.1%)			
	Labour	19,085	46.2%
	Conservative	16,315	39.5%
	Liberal Democrat	3,919	9.5%
	Referendum	2,000	4.8%

The Upminster seat was marginal when first created in 1974, but swung strongly to the Conservatives and looked safe for Sir Nicholas Bonsor. Like many Conservative MPs for hitherto safe seats in outer London he was unexpectedly out of a job on 2 May 1997.

Most Londoners have heard of Upminster, but few have been there. It is at the far east end of the District Line and is a familiar sight on destination boards. It is the eastern seat of the outer borough of Havering, which has more to do with Essex than London. Upminster is a variegated collection of suburbs, stretching from Harold Hill in the north (a big council built estate which saw the first large scale sale of council houses in the early 1970s), through the wealthy areas of Cranham and Emerson Park to Upminster itself. Harold Hill produces three safe Labour wards, and Harold Wood has some Labour elements, but the party enjoys little support in the other four wards. The Havering Residents' main strongholds in local politics are in Upminster. In 1998 the Cranham wards were virtual one party (or no party?) states for them. This makes analysis from local elections misleading, as these affluent areas provide much of the Tory vote in general elections. In the 1999 Euro elections the Tories led by 12% and it was the strongest UKIP area in London. The Conservative candidate for a seat that ought to be pretty easy to regain is Angela Watkinson.

Uxbridge (see by-elections)

Conservative majority 724 (1.7%) in May 1997

Conservative majority 3,766 (11.8%) in July 1997

Labour target 8

MP John Randall (previously Sir Michael Shersby)

1997 Gen Elec (Turnout 72.3%)			
	Conservative	18,095	43.6%
	Labour	17,371	41.8%
	Liberal Democrat	4,528	10.9%
	Referendum	1,153	2.8%
	Other	398	

Uxbridge is the main centre in the outer London Borough of Hillingdon. While it is administratively part of London and is served by the tube, Uxbridge has its own telephone code and a certain sense of independence from the metropolis. As well as Uxbridge town, the seat contains the straggling suburb of Hillingdon on the A40 and stretches down the Colne valley (not to be confused with the one in Yorkshire) to the towns of Yiewsley, Cowley and West Drayton. Labour used to be strong enough in Uxbridge to hold the seat even in Tory years such as 1951 and 1955, but since then have only won it in 1966 – despite by-elections in favourable circumstances for the party in 1972 and 1997. Uxbridge is well located near Heathrow and by a tangle of motorways and has become increasingly well off.

The Conservatives did very well again in Uxbridge in the 1998 local elections, enjoying swings of around 10% since 1994 in some wards and leading 50–33%. Hillingdon council elections have seen some wild swings over the years, but this went markedly against the pattern in London. While not safe, exactly, the Conservatives can now count Uxbridge as a pretty reliable prospect.

Wimbledon

Labour majority 2,990 (6.2%)

Conservative target 42

MP Roger Casale

1997 (Turnout 73.3%)			
	Labour	20,674	42.8%
	Conservative	17,684	36.6%
	Liberal Democrat	8,014	16.6%
	Referendum	993	2.1%
	Green	474	1.0%
	Others	505	1.0%

Although Labour won a seat called Wimbledon in 1945 it then included parts of what is now Mitcham and Morden, so in a real sense Labour's gain on a swing of over 17% in 1997 was unprecedented. Modern Wimbledon includes some affluent metropolitan areas like Wimbledon village, home of the tennis tournament, and the commuter suburb of Raynes Park. There are a few dowdier areas east of the main railway line down towards the South Wimbledon tube station.

The London borough of Merton, half of which is Wimbledon, has been one of Labour's growth areas in the 1990s. Labour won the council for the first time in 1990 and has stayed comfortably in charge since. Adding up the votes in 1998 produced a small (1.4%) Conservative lead in Wimbledon, which was extended to 6.3% in Euro 99. But coupled with Wandsworth in the 2000 GLA elections it produced the largest swing in London to the Tories. Labour's Roger Casale has been an imaginative MP who has explored new methods of constituency service but faces a tough challenge from the Conservative candidate Stephen Hammond.

South East

....

Conservative Targets

Target No	Constituency		Labour Lead
C7	Milton Keynes North East	240	0.5%
C26	Gillingham	1,980	3.9%
C28	Sittingbourne and Sheppey	1,929	4.2%
C35	Hastings and Rye	2,560	5.2%
C38	Chatham and Aylesford	2,790	5.7%
C44	Reading West	2,997	6.2%
C46	Thanet South	2,878	6.4%
C48	Hemel Hempstead	3,636	6.6%
C59	Reading East	3,795	7.6%
C60	Brighton Kemptown	3,534	7.7%
C62	Hove	3,959	8.2%
C63	Dartford	4,328	8.3%
C71	St Albans	4,459	8.8%
C77	Portsmouth North	4,323	9.5%
C82	Watford	5,792	10.5%
C84	Welwyn Hatfield	5,595	10.6%
C87	Gravesham	5,779	10.9%
C98	Medway	5,354	12.0%
C138	Bedford	8,300	17.0%
C161	Milton Keynes South West	10,292	20.3%
C162	Luton North	9,626	20.3%
C171	Dover	11,739	21.7%
C180	Stevenage	11,582	22.5%
C187	Crawley	11,707	23.2%
C190	Luton South	11,319	23.5%

(Liberal Democrat held)

			Lib Dem Lead
C1	Winchester	2	0.0%
C10	Eastleigh	754	1.4%
C20	Lewes	1,300	2.6%
C65	Portsmouth South	4,327	8.4%
C69	Isle of Wight	6,406	8.8%
C80	Oxford West and Abingdon	6,285	10.3%
C124	Newbury	8,517	15.1%

Labour Targets

		Conservative Lead	
L2	Bedfordshire South West	132	0.2%
	Witney*	7,028	12.5%

*Witney was effectively gained by Labour after 1997 when MP Shaun Woodward defected from the Conservatives.

Liberal Democrat Targets

	Labour Lead	
Hastings and Rye (3rd)	3,150	6.4%

(Conservative held in 1997)

	Con Lead in 1997	
Romsey**	8,585	16.6%

**Romsey was gained by the Liberal Democrats after 1997 at a by-election.

Even in the reduced circumstances of 1997, the south east of England was still the Conservative party's heartland, electing 63 Tories to 30 Labour MPs and 7 Liberal Democrats. 15% of all constituencies are in the south east, but it returned 38% of the Conservative parliamentary delegation in 1997 and it was the only region in which they registered over 40% of the vote. The long-term growth in the parliamentary representation of the area has been a boon to the Conservatives.

The south east has a majority of the remaining safe Conservative seats;

eight seats (New Forest West, Hampshire North East, Wokingham, Chesham and Amersham, Surrey East, Surrey Heath, Arundel and South Downs, and Horsham) had a Tory vote exceeding 50% in 1997. Only five other seats in the entire country (two in London, two in the West Midlands and John Major's Huntingdon) were this strong in support for Major's government – if voting for John Redwood in Wokingham can be interpreted in that way.

In the landslide victory of 1987 the Conservatives managed 92 of the 93 seats, and were hardly worse off in 1992 (92 out of 94). Labour's showing in the region in the 1980s was exceptionally poor. Labour were wiped out in 1983 but managed to gain Oxford East in 1987. Labour strength seemed confined to local elections; the party was in control of Oxford, Southampton, Stevenage, Crawley and Slough for most of the time, and gained Brighton and Reading a bit later, but could not break through at parliamentary level. While the Alliance and Liberal Democrats could manage a respectable showing in many places, and win local elections, they were truly competitive only in a few seats.

All this changed in 1997. Seat after seat tumbled to Labour and some cherished Liberal Democrat ambitions were also fulfilled. Despite the wipe-out in 1983 the general swing and a few advantageous boundary revisions in 1997 produced a few Labour seats which now seem pretty safe: both the Southampton seats have five figure Labour majorities, and Brighton Pavilion gave Labour a two to one majority over an incumbent Tory MP. Oxford East and Slough are also no longer marginals according to our definition (Labour leads exceed 25%) and the Conservatives would be doing exceptionally well if they won any of them, or even came close.

However, most Labour seats in the south east do come within our rather generous definition of a marginal seat and are included in the detailed analysis. Many of them centre around the post-war New Towns circling London: Stevenage, Welwyn Hatfield, Crawley, Hemel Hempstead, Milton Keynes, and the Essex New Towns covered by our East Anglia and Essex region – all of which were Labour gains in 1997 and all except Crawley have been Labour before. Only Bracknell of the New Towns stayed Tory in 1997.

Another group of Labour seats in the south east are towns with substantial manufacturing industry, but tend to be rather unglamorous, workaday places: Slough, Dartford, Gravesham, Bedford, Watford, Dover, Medway (Rochester); Portsmouth North, and the larger and more varied towns of Luton and Reading which have two seats each. Labour have won them before, and mostly not just in years of national triumph although Dartford is the only one that has ever seemed safe. All these form familiar Labour territory, but Labour also revived in areas where the party had been presumed long extinct such as St Albans (last won in 1945), Sittingbourne (1966), Gillingham (1945) and Brighton Kemptown (1966). In Bedfordshire South West, and Wycombe, however, previously Labour seats stayed with the Conservatives.

Some Labour gains in 1997 were unprecedented. The common factor of these (except Crawley) was that they were seaside constituencies: Hastings & Rye, Thanet South, Brighton Pavilion. Many of these seats in all regions swung violently against their traditional Conservative allegiance in 1992 and 1997, but have since shown signs of rejecting Labour government almost as decisively, unlike the New Towns.

Liberal Democrat seats in the south east are a scattered collection. There is a clump around Southampton (Eastleigh, Romsey, Winchester) and the outposts of Isle of Wight, Portsmouth South, Oxford West & Abingdon, Newbury and Lewes. Most of these, with the possible exceptions of Newbury and Oxford, were won by thin margins in 1997 and are at risk from a Conservative revival. There is no common factor other than local activity or a fortuitous by-election in the recent past. The Liberal Democrats missed Eastbourne, scene of a by-election victory in 1990, by 3.8% and slightly more surprisingly came within 4.8% of a sensational win in Surrey South West against Cabinet minister Virginia Bottomley. There were more distant prospects in Guildford (8.4%) and Worthing East & Shoreham (9.9%) that did not come off. In all of these the Conservatives were miles ahead in the 1999 Euro election and, except in Guildford, the Liberal Democrats have fallen back in local elections. Labour won some previous Liberal Democrat prospects like Gillingham, Hastings & Rye and St. Albans.

The creeping advance of the Liberal Democrats into previously safe Labour wards in the inner cities and even in peripheral council estate areas has continued, and spread beyond Liverpool and Sheffield into the south east. Bizarrely, the Liberal Democrats would have won both Southampton Itchen and Southampton Test in May 2000, two seats traditionally hard fought between Labour and the Conservatives but with five figure Labour majorities in 1997. The result in Oxford East in the 2000 local election was also rather strange. Labour would have held the seat on 35% of the vote thanks to a three way split between Liberal Democrats on 25% and Conservatives and Greens on about 19% each. The Greens are also a significant factor in cosmopolitan Brighton, with 19% of the Euro election vote in the Pavilion constituency.

If history is any guide, Labour's gains in the south east – and those of the Liberal Democrats – should melt away. The only time the Conservatives have ever lost the region was in 1906 to the Liberals, and this was promptly reversed in January 1910. Even in 1945, 42 Conservatives opposed 22 Labour MPs. Labour's toehold proved impossible to sustain in the 1950 and 1951 elections. The pattern was repeated in 1970 when Labour was wiped out in Kent for the first time since 1935. Will it happen again in 2001 or 2002, or does New Labour offer a different enough political formula to hold on? The south east has always been relatively Conservative because of its high income and private sector driven economic dynamism, but can Labour now gain credit for these?

The prospects in each marginal are analysed below, but there are a few other seats worthy of a mention. The Conservatives held Wycombe, Folkestone and Hythe, and Canterbury with under 40% of the vote against split opposition, and Labour also ran them pretty close in Basingstoke (4.2% lead). If Labour recovers particularly strongly from mid-term blues, these seats would be vulnerable, particularly the boom town of Basingstoke in north Hampshire where the party suffered no losses in 1999 and only one in 2000 in the local elections. The swing there was 6.6% in the Euro elections, resulting in a Conservative lead (17.3%) lower than in some currently Labour-held seats.

Bedford

Labour majority 8,300 (17.0%)

Conservative target 138

MP Patrick Hall

1997 (Turnout 73.5%)	Labour	24,774	50.6%
	Conservative	16,474	33.7%
	Liberal Democrat	6,044	12.3%
	Referendum	1,503	3.1%
	Other	149	0.3%

Bedford has only been a Labour seat at times of national landslide – 1945, 1966 and 1997. In the first two, the win was by microscopic margins (288 votes and 378 votes respectively) and the seat included more rural territory than it does now, but Patrick Hall's 1997 gain is undoubtedly impressive. As well as the padding of an 8,300 majority, Hall can draw some confidence from Labour's ability to top the poll even during a bad national election such as Euro 99, when the party was ahead 1.2%. Labour were still the largest party on Bedford borough council after the May 2000 elections, in which the party only shed one seat.

Bedford is a gritty, culturally diverse town, with many black and Italian residents. It is on the far fringe of the London outer metropolitan area and bears some resemblance to East Midland industrial towns. The smaller town of Kempston, across the River Ouse from Bedford, is also in the seat. The wards that make up the seat are a patchwork of Labour, Liberal Democrat and Conservative inclined areas and many are close fought. The outcome in the constituency as a whole in May 2000 was a nail-biting three-way fight, with Labour nosing ahead on 35.4%, to the Conservatives on 33.9% and the Liberal Democrats on 30.2%. The Liberals and successors have tended to do better in local elections than general, and the party in Bedfordshire has a radical tinge. Labour notional holds in both 1999 Euro and 2000 local elections, two pretty bad showings for the party, should mean that Patrick Hall is the likely winner in the battle against Tory Nicky Attenborough.

Bedfordshire South West

Conservative majority 132 (0.2%)

Labour target 2

MP David Madel (retiring)

1997 (Turnout 75.2%)			
	Conservative	21,534	40.7%
	Labour	21,402	40.5%
	Liberal Democrat	7,559	14.3%
	Referendum	1,761	3.3%
	UK Independence	446	0.8%
	Others	162	0.3%

This constituency is based around Dunstable and extends up through rather bleak hills and villages to Leighton Buzzard and Linslade. It is not a pretty part of the world and not a typical Home Counties seat. It is rare in having been a Labour seat in previous elections (1950 and 1966 as South Beds which included parts of Luton) but not in 1997. It is represented by moderate Tory David Madel whose service since 1970 must have contributed enough personal votes to provide his 132 vote margin over Labour. Madel is retiring at the next election and is replaced by Andrew Selous as the Conservative candidate. Selous is an underwriter and accountant who was 'blooded' in the safe Labour seat of Sunderland North in 1997 – Labour's showing in the 2000 local elections here was calamitous, although the Euro elections were not as bad (a Conservative lead of 15.2%). A Conservative hold looks the most likely outcome.

Brighton Kemptown

Labour majority 3,534 (7.7%)

Conservative target 60

MP Desmond Turner

1997 (Turnout 70.4%)			
	Labour	21,479	46.6%
	Conservative	17,945	38.9%
	Liberal Democrat	4,478	9.7%
	Referendum	1,526	3.3%
	Others	704	1.6%

Since Brighton was split into two seats in 1950, Kemptown has always been the more marginal of the two. Pavilion used to be safely Conservative, while Kemptown narrowly elected Labour MP Dennis Hobden in 1964 (by seven votes, against a Tory MP who spent most of his time looking for the Loch Ness Monster) and 1966. Kemptown is still marginal, but Pavilion has swung over to being a relatively safe Labour seat.

Kemptown is east Brighton, from the Palace Pier to the Marina and beyond along the sea front, and inland among the terraces and council estates around the racecourse and the downs. A distinctive feature of Kemptown is that the gay vote has been recognised as a major electoral factor for some time. Brighton is, in terms of lifestyle and values, one of the most metropolitan parts of Britain: Kensington and Soho by sea. It has swung a long way to Labour, and the Greens have also done increasingly well. Keeping Clause 28 is not a popular cause here.

Why, then, is Kemptown marginal? The answer is that it includes some very Conservative smaller beach and retirement communities along the coast – Rottingdean (part of Brighton) and now Peacehaven from Lewes district, below Roedean school and the cliffs. The new Kemptown produced a larger Labour majority than the old one ever did, but it is still vulnerable to a national Tory recovery and Labour lagged 11.6% behind in the Euro election. Geoffrey Theobald, a Conservative Brighton councillor, takes on long-time Labour local politician Desmond Turner next time. It remains to be seen whether, in its political orientation at least, the new Kemptown really does swing both ways.

Chatham and Aylesford

Labour majority 2,790 (5.7%)

Conservative target 38

MP Jonathan Shaw

1997 (Turnout 70.8%)			
	Labour	21,191	43.1%
	Conservative	18,401	37.4%
	Liberal Democrat	7,389	15.0%
	Referendum	1,538	3.1%
	UK Independence	493	1.0%
	Other	149	0.3%

Rochester and Chatham run together and are interdependent, but they have been parted for parliamentary purposes since 1983. Chatham is now paired with a semi-rural tail stretching down south westwards including Snodland and Aylesford itself, a growth area by the M20 motorway to the north west of Maidstone. This area has little in common with Chatham but Kent has consistently posed problems for the Boundary Commissioners in creating constituencies that make some sense. Chatham and Aylesford is not the silliest ever result of their deliberations.

Chatham is a quite traditional working class town, sprawling along the steep hills and valleys that punctuate the Medway conurbation. The Labour Luton ward comprises tightly packed terraces and Wayfield is a peripheral estate. Some of the other wards, such as Lordswood and Horsted, were Conservative gains in May 2000, and Walderslade is reliably Tory. Chatham is less Labour than it looks, reflecting the military tradition that lingers on after the closure of the naval yard (now being converted into a waterside development and heritage site). The growth areas, at least in 1997, were less Tory than they looked and the seat was a surprising Labour gain for Jonathan Shaw.

Chatham's civic motto is 'Loyal and True'. As a Labour seat, however, it is anything but, and Tory Sean Holden must be pretty confident of winning. A slight cloud on the horizon is the rather small swing (7.4%) to the Conservatives in the 1999 Euro election that left them 9 points ahead. Labour should not be throwing in the towel yet, even in seats like this one.

Crawley

Labour majority 11,707 (23.2%)

Conservative target 187

MP Laura Moffatt

1997 (Turnout 72.5%)			
	Labour	27,750	55.0%
	Conservative	16,043	31.8%
	Liberal Democrat	4,141	8.2%
	Referendum	1,931	3.8%
	UK Independence	322	0.6%
	Other	230	0.5%

Labour never had a seat in West Sussex before 1997, but now Crawley is one of the more likely 'gain' seats to survive any electoral setback. It consists purely of the New Town. The London to Brighton rail line passes through the edge of Crawley at Three Bridges, and the town lies to the west. It has a relatively high proportion of public sector housing, reflecting its planned origins. In most of the estates the housing is of high quality and mingles with woods and parks; for instance Tilgate, a Labour area, is set on the east edge of town. Further west are areas that are still growing, at Pound Hill for instance, but the housing here is private (though often less generously dimensioned than the post-war New Town estates) and Labour less dominant. The economy is modern and diverse; the growth of Gatwick Airport has brought many jobs to Crawley but to see outward mail post-marked 'Gatwick' can do little for civic pride.

Labour held Crawley easily in the 1999 Euro election, with 36.5% to 30.9% for the Conservatives but a UKIP vote of 13.3%, very high for a seat with Crawley's demographics. Labour suffered only one loss here in the May 2000 local elections and remain dominant in local politics. It would be a big surprise if Laura Moffatt was to lose to Conservative candidate Henry Smith, and would probably indicate a comfortable overall Tory majority.

Dartford

Labour majority 4,328 (8.3%)

Conservative target 63

MP Howard Stoate

1997 (Turnout 74.6%)			
	Labour	25,278	48.6%
	Conservative	20,950	40.3%
	Liberal Democrat	4,872	9.4%
	BNP	424	0.8%
	Others	515	1.0%

Dartford, in recent years, has been best known for a big hole in the ground, but its famous tunnel under the Thames has been joined by an awesome and graceful bridge linking Kent to Essex. Dartford is an unpretentious town, very much within London's orbit, and almost a mirror image of the industrial landscape across the river in Thurrock. Most of it tends towards Labour, although there are some Conservative areas in the south and west, plus the two rural wards from Sevenoaks attached to Dartford for parliamentary purposes. The Labour vote was solid enough for the party, unusually in southern England outside London, not to sink into third place in 1983, and to win the seat back after 18 years represented by Conservative Bob Dunn (who is trying again at the next election).

Dartford lies between two extraordinary monuments to consumerism – Lakeside mall in Thurrock (which has a local newspaper) and the even newer Bluewater centre near Greenhithe, east of Dartford in a former gravel pit. The malls have created thousands of jobs – unemployment is low and has been falling relatively fast – and widened opportunities for Dartford people, but created some problems for the town centre.

Labour did well in the borough elections of May 1999, polling 52% in the town to 39% for the Conservatives (allowing for the rural areas this suggests little change since 1997), but lagged by 6.7% in the Euro election. The Lib Dems are barely organised in the town, running only one candidate and polling a mere 78 votes in the local elections. Labour MP Howard Stoate is a doctor: 'critical but stable' is the diagnosis for marginal Dartford and it remains to be seen whether Conservatism here is really dying or only in remission.

Dover

Labour majority 11,739 (21.7%)

Conservative target 171

MP Gwyn Prosser

1997 (Turnout 78.6%)			
	Labour	29,535	54.5%
	Conservative	17,796	32.8%
	Liberal Democrat	4,302	7.9%
	Referendum	2,124	3.9%
	UK Independence	443	0.8%

Dover is the main point of entry to the UK for travellers not arriving by air; it is still the world's busiest ferry port and the Channel rail link emerges just to the west of the town. It has very close links with France, and perhaps as a result the share of the vote for the Eurosceptic minor parties has been a little lower than in other depressed coastal towns. While not particularly anti-Europe, Dover is a town where the politics of asylum and immigration have had a big impact, and there are simmering resentments in the town which the BNP has tried to exploit.

The town is not the entire constituency; there are also the Georgian town of Deal and some inland villages. Dover and Deal towns elect Labour majorities, but most of the villages and suburbs are Conservative, despite one or two Labour remnants of the Kent coalfield. In 1997 Gwyn Prosser unseated Tory David Shaw, who has since retreated to the suburban groves of Kingston & Surbiton (see London) and is replaced by Paul Watkins next time. Prosser won by a large margin but Dover is not particularly safe. Labour suffered a bad result in the seat in the 1999 Euro election, ending up 4.9% behind the Conservatives. It is one of the seats more amenable to right wing populism of the sort that has become the staple of Tory politics, and could be a rather unpleasant seat to defend for Labour.

Eastleigh

Liberal Democrat majority 754 (1.4%)

Conservative target 10

MP David Chidgey

1997 (Turnout 76.6%)

Liberal Democrat	19,453	35.1%
Conservative	18,669	33.7%
Labour	14,883	26.8%
Referendum	2,013	3.6%
UK Independence	446	0.8%

Eastleigh is a suburban area wrapped around the north and east of Southampton. Its main town, from which it draws its name, was once a working class town centred on a major railway junction and engineering works, but it has become a commuting centre, looking south to Southampton and north to London. The M27 motorway links the town to the rest of the constituency; Hedge End is an expanding, recently built satellite town of Southampton, and further south lie the old villages of Bursledon, Botley and Hamble and the little town of Netley on Southampton Water. Labour support appears patchily and inconsistently in different parts of the seat, but for the most part, the battle is between the Liberal Democrats, who control the council, and Conservatives in local elections. Even in May 2000 the Lib Dems were further ahead (44%) of the Conservatives (31%) and Labour (25%) than in 1997. The Conservatives led 36-22-22 in the Euro election.

The election result in 1997 was affected by the dramatic by-election in 1994 in which the Conservatives crashed from first to third. Labour were able to resist a tactical squeeze in 1994, with the result that the Lib Dem bar charts did not point clearly to a tactical vote in 1997 and it was a three-way marginal. Labour were only 8.3% behind the Lib Dems in third place in 1997, but would be lucky to escape a squeeze next time. The Lib Dem position in the local elections is very strong and the avuncular David Chidgey has now effectively had two terms as MP. Conor Burns, a Southampton councillor and former student political activist, has the Conservative nomination – a promising one on paper but on closer inspection an uphill struggle.

Gillingham

Labour majority 1,980 (3.9%)

Conservative target 26

MP Paul Clark

1997 (Turnout 72.0%)	Labour	20,187	39.8%
	Conservative	18,207	35.9%
	Liberal Democrat	9,649	19.0%
	Referendum	1,492	2.9%
	UK Independence	590	1.2%
	Others	558	1.1%

Gillingham is the largest single element of the Medway Towns. While fascinating politically, it is itself a relatively dull residential area to the east of Chatham, extending across flatter land than the other two towns to the Labour Twydall estate and the more Conservative suburbs of Rainham and Parkwood.

There have been ward boundary changes in the Medway Towns and it is difficult to arrive at a precise estimate of the local election result in Gillingham. It would also be somewhat futile, as voting behaviour here differed widely between local and general elections on the same day in 1997. The Conservatives, reflecting their national lead, were ahead in Gillingham in May 2000, thanks in large measure to an overwhelming lead in the Hempstead Valley growth area. They also led, although by a relatively unimpressive 9.4% from Labour, in the Euro election.

Gillingham is a traditionally Conservative seat, a surprising Labour win in 1997 of the sort which will be very difficult to hold at the next election even if there is not much of a national swing. Tim Butcher, the Conservative candidate, is the favourite, but Labour's Paul Clark cannot be ruled out. The Liberal Democrats are probably well past their peak in Gillingham.

Gravesham

Labour majority 5,779 (10.9%)

Conservative target 87

MP Chris Pond

1997 (Turnout 76.7%)	Labour	26,460	49.7%
	Conservative	20,681	38.8%
	Liberal Democrat	4,128	7.8%
	Referendum	1,441	2.7%
	Others	543	1.0%

Gravesham is, for some reason, the name of the borough council that governs the Gravesend area, and is therefore also the name of the identical parliamentary constituency. North Kent is a functional part of the world, and the Thames estuary here is dominated by industrial development and marshland. Gravesend itself is a very old town, but it wears its history lightly. The borough also includes Northfleet, a mainly Labour town, and some very Conservative suburbs and villages – Shorne voted Conservative by more than three to one in May 1999.

Gravesend has been a key marginal for many years. It is the truest bellwether seat in the country. Since 1918 – not just since 1945 – it has been won by the party which has gone on to form the government – with the exceptions only of 1929 and 1951. Its unusual deviance in these elections is perhaps accounted for by the fact that the national 'winner' in each case was elected with fewer votes than its main opponent. The council was so finely balanced that the Conservatives ran it on successive mayoral casting votes for eight years, but it is now more comfortably Labour. Labour were about ten points ahead in May 1999, pretty much the same lead they enjoyed in 1997, but lagged 6.5% in the Euro election in June.

Although typical in many ways, Gravesend has been most unusual in its consistent scorn for third party politics. The Lib Dems polled a measly 7.8% in 1997 and in the 1999 local elections only managed 14.5% in their best ward, Northfleet West. Another tight two party contest is in prospect in Gravesham at the next election. It is a rematch of the 1997 contest between low pay campaigner Chris Pond and the former backbench Conservative MP for the seat, Jacques Arnold.

Hastings and Rye

Labour majority 2,560 (5.2%)

Conservative target 35

Liberal Democrat target

MP Michael Foster

1997 (Turnout 69.7%)			
	Labour	16,867	34.4%
	Conservative	14,307	29.2%
	Liberal Democrat	13,717	28.0%
	Referendum	2,511	5.1%
	Liberal	1,046	2.1%
	Others	621	1.3%

Hastings is a depressed town tucked in the far corner of East Sussex; unlike sleepy Eastbourne it is not a retirement centre and it lacks the elegance and excitement of Brighton. Unemployment, particularly long term unemployment, is a severe problem. It stood at 5.3% in April 2000 in Hastings & Rye, higher than in some very working class seats such as Stoke-on-Trent Central. The seat also contains, as its name might suggest, the bijou Cinque Port of Rye as well as Winchelsea, a pretty half-abandoned mediaeval new town, and some beach areas.

Labour won the seat for the first time in 1997 on only 34.4% of the vote, so it might be assumed that the tenure of Michael Foster is pretty short term. This assumption may not be sustained. There was indeed an almost three way split in 1997, with a strong Lib Dem showing based on their previous second placed challenge to the Tories; Foster may benefit in the next election from some Labour supporters who had cast misguided tactical votes in 1997. Labour support has remained strong in Hastings since the election; the party gained the council in 1998 and held it in 2000 and the Conservatives are still a very marginal force in Hastings politics. Different wards are contested each year in local elections, making exact comparisons difficult. The outlying areas are stronger for the Tories, but Labour still elected one of the three district councillors for Rye in May 1999. However, like many seaside towns, there was a high UKIP vote (12.2%) in the 1999 Euro elections and the Tories were 11% ahead of Labour then. Mark Coote contests the seat for the Tories, as the unseated MP Jacqui Lait now represents Beckenham. It promises to be another exciting and unpredictable contest next time.

Hemel Hempstead

Labour majority 3,636 (6.6%)

Conservative target 48

MP Tony McWalter

1997 (Turnout 76.7%)			
	Labour	25,175	45.7%
	Conservative	21,539	39.1%
	Liberal Democrat	6,789	12.3%
	Referendum	1,327	2.4%
	Other	262	

Hemel Hempstead has an unusual electoral history. It was a fortress of Conservatism for many years, deviating only in a freak Liberal gain in 1923, until October 1974 when Labour won for the first time. The reason for the trend to the left over such a long time was the growth of the New Town at Hemel Hempstead itself, which caused an influx of working class voters and council tenants. This raised the Labour vote in the town, and raised the electorate in the seat so that boundary reviews gradually cut off more and more outlying Tory territory. Although there was a low swing in 1979, Labour did extremely badly in 1983 and 1987; the Conservatives and the SDP invaded previously solid Labour areas of the New Town.

In 1997 the only other significant element in the constituency apart from the town was the suburb of Kings Langley, on the Watford road. There was also a big recovery in Labour support in precisely this sort of seat – New Towns in southern England – and Labour duly won only its second general election victory in Hemel Hempstead.

The two main parties were still very competitive in the May 1999 elections for the borough council of Dacorum, the strangely named local authority for Hemel Hempstead and towns to its west, but in the Euro elections the Conservatives had a rather large lead of 12.4%. It will be a tough fight; of the New Town seats Hemel Hempstead is the most likely to revert to the Conservatives. Paul Ivey, a Bedfordshire councillor, challenges Labour's Tony McWalter.

Hove

Labour majority 3,959 (8.2%)

Conservative target 62

MP Ivor Caplin

1997 (Turnout 69.7%)			
	Labour	21,458	44.6%
	Conservative	17,499	36.4%
	Liberal Democrats	4,645	9.7%
	Referendum	1,931	4.0%
	Ind Con	1,735	3.6%
	Green	644	1.3%
	UKIP	209	0.4%

When Labour won control of Hove borough council in 1995 it was regarded as an outlandish example of a mid-term result that could not possibly be repeated in a general election. John Prescott made a special trip to Hove to celebrate with the new council leaders. But in 1997 Tony Blair, in his plane, had to grapple with the idea of Labour Hove and assumed that someone was having a joke at his expense.

Hove's reputation as a staid, Conservative place depended in part on its oft-stressed distinction from seedy, sinful Brighton. In fact, the border between the two towns was never very apparent to the naked eye and they always shared a football club; now 'Hove, actually' is more than ever just a state of mind. Its borough council has been merged with Brighton. Much of Hove's property is cheaper than central Brighton's and it has been affected by the same social trends that have transformed the Brighton Pavilion constituency, although it is still by a long chalk a much older and less cosmopolitan place. In the east of the seat is the Portslade area, some of which is industrial, but Labour now have a presence throughout Hove. In the council elections of May 1999 Labour were still ahead in Hove by a small margin.

The Conservatives led by a big margin, 16.7%, in the Euro election and it is obviously possible that Hove and other seaside towns will swing back sharply. It is also possible that the Labour trend in the Brighton area will continue, as it may be different in origin from the strong showing in more traditional resorts. Labour MP Ivor Caplin is an astute local politician. The Conservative contender is Jenny Langston, who must hope that the right is not split in Hove as it has been in recent general elections by Independent Conservatives. It still seems strange to write a sentence like 'Hove is a crucial marginal seat that Labour have realistic hopes of holding.'

Isle of Wight

Liberal Democrat majority 6,406 (8.8%)

Conservative target 69

MP Peter Brand

1997 (Turnout 71.7%)			
	Liberal Democrat	31,274	42.7%
	Conservative	24,868	34.0%
	Labour	9,646	13.2%
	Referendum	4,734	6.5%
	UKIP	1,072	1.5%
	Island Ind	848	1.2%
	Green	544	0.7%
	Others	173	

The Isle of Wight has the largest electorate of any seat in Britain, but it seems to prefer this to being paired with territory from the mainland, and it is really not big enough to divide into two seats. The island is a diamond shape sheltering Southampton from the Channel and creating that port's double high tides. It is best known for holidays and prisons, although it also boasts a royal palace and a yachting festival. The main towns are Cowes and Newport on the Medina river, and the Ryde to Shanklin resorts of the east coast.

The island has long been stony ground for Labour, although now at least the party can elect a few councillors, and better than doubled its share of the vote in 1997. The Liberals gained it in 1974 and held it until Tory Barry Field won in 1987. Field became rather disaffected in the 1992–97 parliament and did not stand again, and Dr. Peter Brand won Wight back for the Liberal Democrats. As in some centre party hopes in the south west, the victory was rather by default – in this case actually with a lower share of the vote than in 1992, Labour and the anti-Europeans picking up votes.

Wight shares some of the characteristics of the south west in its geographical remoteness and outdated economic base, and like the south west saw a fearful Liberal Democrat collapse in 1999. The party lost overall control of the unitary council, and in the Euro election came third, with 17% of the vote to 18% for Labour and 42% for the Conservatives. The UKIP accounted for another 12%. Andrew Turner, a grant-maintained schools campaigner, tries again for the Conservatives against Dr. Brand and unless Brand can squeeze the Labour vote back down again Turner stands a good chance of winning.

Lewes

Liberal Democrat majority 1,300 (2.6%)

Conservative target 20

MP Norman Baker

1997 (Turnout 76.4%)	Liberal Democrat	21,250	43.2%
	Conservative	19,950	40.6%
	Labour	5,232	10.6%
	Referendum	2,481	5.0%
	UKIP	256	0.5%

The Brighton metro area produced a dire set of results for the Tories in 1997. The three town seats went Labour, and the Liberal Democrats administered the punishment in outlying Lewes. Lewes, on paper, is the easiest for the Conservatives to win back.

Lewes is the county town of East Sussex – an attractive town set among the hills north of Brighton; it is to the brash seaside town as Bath is to Bristol, or Winchester to Southampton. Lewes town is too small to be a constituency by itself, so the seat also includes some surrounding countryside, the troubled ferry port of Newhaven, the resort town of Seaford, and even Polegate, a small town on the edge of Eastbourne. It seems improbable for such a place to have spurned the Conservatives, but the Liberal Democrats have a history of activism here and first won the local council in 1991.

The Conservatives failed to recover any of their 1995 losses in Lewes in the May 1999 local elections, but went on to score a convincing win in the Euro election, with a lead of 26.5%. They would be disappointed if their candidate Simon Sinnatt failed to win the seat with a comfortable majority, but the Liberal Democrats have reserves of strength. Few of the 1997 Lib Dem intake have made a national, as opposed to local, impact, but the Lewes MP Norman Baker has established himself as a record-breaking parliamentary questioner and scourge of the executive. While not universally popular, he upholds a celebrated parliamentary tradition of awkwardness.

Luton North

Labour majority 9,626 (20.3%)

Conservative target 162

MP Kelvin Hopkins

1997 (Turnout 73.2%)			
	Labour	25,860	54.6%
	Conservative	16,234	34.3%
	Liberal Democrat	4,299	9.1%
	UKIP	689	1.5%
	Other	250	

Both Luton seats returned large Labour majorities in 1997, reflecting the national swing and the traditional marginality of the town. Glamorous Luton is not, but it is a productive place with a modern economic base. As early as 1969 it was a test-bed for social research about the apparently 'instrumental' attitudes and voting behaviour of skilled workers. It has been won by the winning party in the general election in every election since 1951, and since it was divided in 1974 both seats have moved in tandem.

North is a rather more polarised place than South; it contains both the high class residential area of Icknield (the only Conservative ward in the town) and the estates of Leagrave and Sundon Park. It was previously the seat of John Carlisle, one of the most right wing Conservative MPs in the House, but has now switched to the relatively left wing Kelvin Hopkins, who rebelled several times in the 1997 parliament. Labour did well in Luton in the borough elections of May 1999, and won seven out of eight wards in North, with no change since 1995. Labour also led by half a point in the Euro election. Although Luton did not vote in May 2000, Labour support held up best in similar places like Reading, and Hopkins seems well placed to survive next time against Conservative Amanda Sater.

Luton South

Labour majority 11,319 (23.5%)

Conservative target 190

MP Margaret Moran

1997 (Turnout 70.4%)	Labour	26,428	54.8%
	Conservative	15,109	31.4%
	Liberal Democrat	4,610	9.6%
	Referendum	1,205	2.5%
	UKIP	390	0.8%
	Green	356	0.7%
	Other	86	

The southern edge of Luton contains the large Vauxhall motors plant, the biggest single employer in the town, and the rapidly developing airport, where 7,000 people work. The airport is something of a success story, having been given a facelift in 1999 and nearly trebled passenger numbers in five years. The seat also contains the town centre, dominated by an outsize Arndale Centre, and the large Asian quarter of Luton. South is a working class area, but some more rural leavening is provided by two South Bedfordshire wards in a strip of territory between Luton and Harpenden. Labour won a massive majority in 1997, and has held on well since. There were no Labour losses in Luton in the 1999 local elections, although the Liberal Democrats maintained their hold on the three eastern suburban wards. In the Euro election Labour were 7.6% ahead. The Conservative challenger Gordon Henderson would be ill-advised to give up the day job; it would be a sign that the Conservatives were on course for a large majority if Luton South ejected Labour MP Margaret Moran after only one term.

Medway

Labour majority 5,354 (12.0%)

Conservative target 98

MP Bob Marshall-Andrews

1997 (Turnout 72.2%)	Labour	21,858	48.9%
	Conservative	16,504	36.9%
	Liberal Democrat	4,555	10.2%
	Referendum	1,420	3.2%
	UKIP	405	0.9%

Medway was not a particularly surprising gain for Labour in 1997. It is based around the City of Rochester, which was the core of a seat Labour usually won between 1945 and 1979. Rochester's Cathedral and attractive old-fashioned High Street of small shops may suggest old-world conservatism, but it has many working class suburbs which run together with Chatham, and there is heavy industry in the lowlands along the Thames. Labour MP Bob Marshall-Andrews, a prominent barrister, won the seat; Marshall-Andrews is one of the highest profile dissidents of the parliament; he is convenor of the 'Old Testament Prophets' group of traditional Labour MPs. However, he is far from a knee-jerk rebel and has only rarely gone into the division lobbies against the government, even in most of the larger rebellions of the parliament.

The Medway Towns were a bad area for Labour in the 2000 local elections, but the losses in seats were worse than the loss in votes. Within the Medway constituency the Conservatives led by something like nine points, but the Lib Dems left many wards uncontested. There was a strong difference in turnout between Conservative and some marginal wards, where turnout was well over 30%, and some Labour wards with dismal turnout – Temple Farm with 19%. The Conservatives led by 5.5% in Euro 99. Labour cannot go into the next election totally confident of holding Medway. The Conservative candidate is Mark Reckless. Mr Reckless is taking a risk; Bob Marshall-Andrews QC has won tougher cases for the defence than this one.

Milton Keynes North East

Labour majority 240 (0.5%)

Conservative target 7

MP Brian White

1997 (Turnout 72.8%)			
	Labour	20,201	39.4%
	Conservative	19,961	39.0%
	Liberal Democrat	8,907	17.4%
	Referendum	1,492	2.9%
	Green	576	1.1%
	Other	99	0.2%

If local election results were replicated in general elections, the Liberal Democrats would be a far stronger force than even their doubled number of seats (46) won in 1997. North East Milton Keynes is a classic example of a constituency where locally both Labour and the Conservatives have been left trailing; the Liberal Democrats won no fewer than 9 out of the 10 seats contested in 2000, attracting an overall majority of the vote and nearly 70% in the two Newport Pagnell wards.

Yet the much vaunted third-party 'breakthrough' at a national level has never arrived, precisely because constituencies such as this vote differently in different sets of elections. Thus despite strong third party hopes after the seat's creation at the 1992 election, it was the Conservatives who triumphed, and Labour who finished second. Last time, a swing in excess of 14% saw Labour capture the seat, while the Lib Dems were reduced to fewer than 9,000 votes.

This is currently Labour's third most vulnerable seat, but much of the territory is archetypal 'New' Labour, particularly the endless dormitory housing estates in Bradwell and Linford. This may just be the sort of area where, having avoided the economic crises which have beset previous Labour governments, Labour attracts voters who still feared voting for them in 1997. Conservative candidate Marion Rix will look to squeeze the local Lib Dem vote in the villages towards Olney, but former councillor Brian White may yet surprise everyone again by holding on against the odds.

Milton Keynes South West

Labour majority 10,292 (20.3%)

Conservative target 161

MP Phyllis Starkey

1997 (Turnout 71.4%)			
	Labour	27,298	53.8%
	Conservative	17,006	33.5%
	Liberal Democrat	6,065	11.9%
	Other	389	0.8%

When rapidly expanding Milton Keynes was divided in 1992, Labour always fancied their chances in the new South West constituency. The seat includes areas of traditional Labour strength in Wolverton and Bletchley, as well as the inevitable new housing estates around the somewhat bizarre 'centre' of Milton Keynes itself and, more importantly, none of the rural areas which so often hinder the party's chances elsewhere. Labour's failure here in 1992 (Barry Legg's majority exceeding 4,500) proved symbolic of the party's general failure to make a breakthrough that year, but there was to be no repeat in 1997 when former Oxford City Council leader Phyllis Starkey was elected with what looks to be a comfortable majority of over 10,000.

Since 1997 this has been one of the very few Labour gains which have been held in both European and local elections. Even when Labour's vote elsewhere dived in May 2000, they out-polled the Conservatives in Milton Keynes South West by approximately 5%, all of which means that Conservative candidate Iain Stewart will have his work cut out when the general election is called.

Newbury

Liberal Democrat majority 8,517 (15.1%)

Conservative target 124

MP David Rendel

1997 (Turnout 76.7%)			
	Liberal Democrat	29,887	52.9%
	Conservative	21,370	37.8%
	Labour	3,107	5.5%
	Referendum	992	1.8%
	Green	644	1.1%
	UKIP	302	0.5%
	Other	174	

David Rendel won a stunning Liberal Democrat victory in the by-election here in May 1993, but Lib Dem success did not come out of the blue. They had run the Tories close in 1974 and taken over the council in 1991, and the tactical position was clear because Labour have never amounted to much in Newbury.

Newbury town is strong in high-tech industry and services, and has become so prosperous that there is nearly no unemployment and wages, even for very menial jobs, are high. Newbury is also close enough to London to house some metropolitan commuters and the west Berkshire countryside is an attractive part of the world; the constituency extends over a sparsely populated hinterland. Newbury's problems are the envy of other towns – how to reconcile massive demand for new housing and employment with the pleasant local environment, and how to continue to attract business to a high-wage economy.

The Conservatives will be hoping that the result next time will see a continued recovery from the by-election disaster. They led by 44 to 28 in the Euro election, although Labour bounced back to 10% in the absence of tactical voting. In the local elections of May 2000 the Liberal Democrats held on to West Berkshire council, although with a majority severely reduced by Conservative gains. The result is likely to be closer than in 1997; local councillor Richard Benyon challenges again for the Tories.

Oxford West and Abingdon

Liberal Democrat majority 6,285 (10.3%)

Conservative target 80

MP Evan Harris

1997 (Turnout 77.1%)			
	Liberal Democrat	26,268	42.9%
	Conservative	19,983	32.7%
	Labour	12,361	20.2%
	Referendum	1,258	2.1%
	Green	691	1.1%
	UKIP	258	0.4%
	Others	377	

'Oxwab' was one of the easier Lib Dem wins in 1997 as former Cabinet Minister John Patten retired and was replaced by Liberal Democrat doctor Evan Harris. The seat contains the historic centre of Oxford and nearly all the colleges and university buildings. It extends up through the villas of North Oxford along the Banbury and Woodstock Roads to Wolvercote and Kidlington. It also extends southwards to the nearby market town of Abingdon, which has seen a lot of recent development of high tech industry and distribution services along the A34 corridor. Every part of the seat has a strong local Lib Dem organisation, although in the student and academic wards of Oxford the Green Party has become a force to be reckoned with – Green gains were instrumental in depriving Labour of control over Oxford in May 2000. Many Labour-inclined people in west Oxford are experienced tactical voters in general elections; the pattern has been visible since 1987.

Oxwab was one of the least disastrous Lib Dem showings in the 1999 Euro election, the Conservatives leading 34–27. The Conservatives recovered little in Oxford and Cambridge in the May 2000 elections, and Labour's clumsy interventions over Oxford selection procedures caused rattling of port glasses at High Tables and cannot have impressed many student voters. The way looks clear for Evan Harris, a doctor and NHS expert, to win a second term.

Portsmouth North

Labour majority 4,323 (9.5%)

Conservative target 77

MP Syd Rapson

1997 (Turnout 70.1%)			
	Labour	21,339	47.1%
	Conservative	17,016	37.6%
	Liberal Democrat	4,788	10.6%
	Referendum	1,757	3.9%
	UKIP	298	0.7%
	Other	72	

Labour's gain in Portsmouth North was one of the first results to be announced on election night in 1997, and the 14% swing with which long-time local leader Syd Rapson won the seat was an indication of what would happen in many southern marginals. North was Labour in 1974 but became overwhelmingly Tory in the Thatcher years before swinging back with considerable violence. The defeated Tory MP was Peter Griffiths, first elected for Smethwick in a notorious campaign in 1964. The constituency is, to coin a phrase, exactly what it says on the tin – the northern half of the city of Portsmouth, straddling the channel between the mainland and Portsea Island. It is low-lying and flat, except for a ridge in the far north from which forts have long guarded the city.

The Conservative candidate Chris Day needs a 4.8% swing to regain the seat. Most of the wards in Portsmouth North are quite marginal. In the 2000 local elections the Conservatives led 49–38, a similar lead to that in the 1999 Euro elections. Nearly all the margin came from safe Tory Drayton & Farlington and the turnout in Labour Paulsgrove and Nelson was extremely anaemic; the two wards together only contributed a couple hundred more votes than Drayton & Farlington. The Conservatives must feel pretty confident of regaining this marginal even if they don't manage to win nationally, but if the Labour vote can be brought out to the polling stations – as it was not in 1999 and 2000 – Rapson will be in again.

Portsmouth South

Liberal Democrat majority 4,327 (8.4%)

Conservative target 65

MP Mike Hancock

1997 (Turnout 63.8%)			
	Liberal Democrat	20,421	39.5%
	Conservative	16,094	31.1%
	Labour	13,086	25.3%
	Referendum	1,629	3.2%
	Liberal	184	0.4%
	UKIP	141	0.3%
	Other	140	

About half of the Portsmouth South constituency thinks of itself as Southsea, a patchily elegant but not totally successful Hampshire version of Brighton's Regency grandeur. The rest is decidedly Portsmouth, with the working class central ward of Charles Dickens, the university area and the tightly packed terraces of Fratton near the football ground of Portsmouth FC. One might speculate that had there not been a by-election here in 1984, which the SDP won, Portsmouth South might have followed Brighton and Hove into the Labour column. But after the 1984 victory the Alliance and Lib Dems have remained competitive, Mike Hancock losing out by a whisker to Conservative David Martin in 1987 (205 votes) and 1992 (242 votes) and winning in 1997. The win was despite a fall in the Lib Dem share of the vote; it arose through a swing of over 10% from Conservative to third placed Labour.

The Conservatives led by about 40 to 35 from the Lib Dems, with 25% for Labour, in the May 2000 local elections. People obviously vote differently for different sorts of elections, as the Lib Dems were third in the Euro elections in 1999. Mike Hancock was re-elected as a city councillor in the Fratton ward by a massive margin. Portsmouth South as a constituency does not habitually produce massive majorities, and Hancock's 4,327 lead was large by recent comparison. He should win again, if by a smaller margin against Tory Philip Warr (formerly a Bournemouth councillor). The Labour

Party is still a significant force in the seat, even if Labour has little chance of victory next time.

Reading East

Labour majority 3,795 (7.6%)

Conservative target 59

MP Jane Griffiths

1997 (Turnout 70.2%)			
	Labour	21,461	42.7%
	Conservative	17,666	35.2%
	Liberal Democrat	9,307	18.5%
	Referendum	1,042	2.1%
	UKIP	252	0.5%
	Others	492	

Labour's gains in Reading in 1997 were unexpected. Both seats combine some very Conservative suburbs with urban areas from a prosperous town of the sort that had often turned against Labour. East is slightly the more urban seat. It contains the railway station, the town centre and the eastern and northern parts of the town, and the satellite town of Woodley from the Wokingham district. Woodley is a growth area near the M4 and on a commuter line into Reading and Waterloo; while Tory it has an opposition presence and Labour used to be able to win the Bulmershe ward. Woodley, and the only reliable Tory ward in Reading (Thames) were outvoted in the Labour surge of 1997.

Labour's victories in Reading seem more durable than many of the surprises in the Home Counties. Reading's Labour vote showed rare resilience in the local elections of 2000, and adding up the votes in Reading East produces a continuing Labour lead. At the parliamentary level, however, Reading East has been one of the most quarrelsome areas, with attempts to deselect sitting MP Jane Griffiths, disciplinary action and infighting. So far this has not had any impact on Labour's vote. If Reading East can put this dissension behind it, Griffiths should be able to mount a strong defence of the seat against Tory candidate Barry Tanswell.

Reading West

Labour majority 2,997 (6.2%)

Conservative target 44

MP Martin Salter

1997 (Turnout 70.1%)			
	Labour	21,841	45.1%
	Conservative	18,844	38.9%
	Liberal Democrat	6,153	12.7%
	Referendum	976	2.0%
	BNP	320	0.7%
	UKIP	255	0.5%

Reading is a flourishing place, with strong light industry, IT and fast links into London. Most of the town centre of Reading is in the East constituency; this seat is a collection of outlying residential districts, varying from the council estates along the Southampton road which have long been Labour wards to the smarter areas on the A4 west of the town. The West constituency spills over into parts of the West Berkshire district, including some suburbs indistinguishable from the town (Theale and West Tilehurst) and the plush commuter villages up the Thames as far as Pangbourne. The traditional political geography would call the town areas closely fought, the outer areas strongly Tory, adding up to a safe seat. It fell on a huge 15% swing to Labour in 1997.

Labour was still strong in Reading West in the 2000 local elections, winning six out of seven town wards (the other, Tilehurst, is a Lib Dem stronghold). Party competition is less regular in the West Berks wards but Labour's weakness there probably narrowly fails to outweigh the majority in the town; this is the most surprising Labour victory of 2000. The party was only 2.5% behind the Tories in the 1999 European elections. Unlike Reading East, in this seat there was no dissension over MP Martin Salter, who had distinguished himself in this area, in which the drone of overflying planes is background noise, by his opposition to 'part-privatisation' of air traffic control. Salter is a genial, laddish, approachable MP who is popular and hard working; loyal but no robot. Stephen Reid is the Conservative prospective candidate. He was the luckless Tory who defended Eastleigh in the 1994 by-election and failed to regain it in 1997. If he fails again in Reading it will not be his fault; Labour was so far been able to maintain a strong position in Reading and are well positioned to defend the parliamentary seats.

Romsey (see by-elections)

Conservative majority (1997) 8,585 (16.6%)

Liberal Democrat majority (2000) 3,311 (8.6%)

MP Sandra Gidley (previously Michael Colvin)

1997 (Turnout 76.4%)			
	Conservative	23,834	46..0%
	Liberal Democrat	15,249	29.4%
	Labour	9,623	18.6%
	UKIP	1,824	3.5%
	Referendum	1,291	2.5%

The Romsey constituency has had a dramatic history since its creation in 1997. When created, it seemed to be a very safe Conservative seat (it was number 273 on the Lib Dem target list based on 1992 figures). About half the population comes from the generally affluent though rather straggling northern suburbs of Southampton: Chandler's Ford, Hiltingbury, Chilworth and North Baddesley; and the only reliably Tory ward of the city, namely Bassett. Romsey itself is a growing historic town a few miles outside Southampton. The seat also includes some villages up the river Test towards the downs to the east of Salisbury Plain.

All parts of the somewhat ill-assorted seat were Tory even in 1997; Labour has not elected a district councillor anywhere in the seat for many years, and although the Lib Dems had some local strength in Romsey town and a foothold in Chandler's Ford they were well behind the Tories in 1997 despite a 12% swing. When Michael Colvin died in a house fire, the seat looked safe for his Tory successor. While the Tories did well in the 2000 local elections nationally, they lost the parliamentary seat to Lib Dem Sandra Gidley. Gidley was clearly a popular candidate; her reasonable demeanour and calm manner befitting a pharmacist went down well even among people who did not know her from her local political activities in Romsey town. She does not have long to build up a personal vote and in all probability faces the same fate as other late midterm by-election winners like Elizabeth Shields (Ryedale, 1986) and David Bellotti (Eastbourne, 1990); but Charles Kennedy, and Tony Blair, have reason to smile on Romsey's new member.

St Albans

Labour majority 4,459 (8.8%)

Conservative target 71

MP Kerry Pollard

1997 (Turnout 77.5%)			
	Labour	21,338	42.0%
	Conservative	16,879	33.2%
	Liberal Democrat	10,692	21.0%
	Referendum	1,619	3.2%
	Others	277	

Hertfordshire is best known as a modern county full of New Towns, but it has a very old town at its heart. St. Albans is a historic place, with the ruins of Roman Verulam and a fine cathedral, and its fast rail links into the City make it a favoured location for the discerning commuter as well as a centre in its own right. This makes it sound a rather Conservative town, probably with a Liberal Democrat presence, and this is what it seemed until 1997 when Labour pulled off a stunning victory, surging from a bad third to a clear first.

St. Albans includes some solid Labour areas such as Ashley and Sopwell on the edge of the town, and the large council-built estate of London Colney, but the Conservatives are surprisingly feeble in some of the more affluent parts of the town where Labour and Liberal Democrats poll well. The only reliably Conservative element of the seat is St. Stephen's, an out of town ward on the way to Watford.

Although the Conservatives led by nearly 10 points in the Euro election, the 2000 local elections presented a confusing picture. Allowing for wards not voting this time, the three parties were pretty much dead level, with perhaps Labour slightly behind the other two. Since 1999, when there were all-out elections, Labour lost one seat but the Conservatives dropped two in the district. At midterm, particularly considering the wounds inflicted on the Labour Party elsewhere, this was a heartening result for Labour and Kerry Pollard, and a warning for the high-flying young Tory candidate Charles Elphicke. For Labour to be doing better in St. Albans than in, say, Hyndburn in Lancashire, is strange but just one of the curiosities of politics at the turn of the century. We shall see if the next general election solidifies this picture or reverts to more traditional patterns.

Sittingbourne and Sheppey

Labour majority 1,929 (4.2%)

Conservative target 28

MP Derek Wyatt

1997 (Turnout 72.3%)			
	Labour	18,723	40.6%
	Conservative	16,794	36.4%
	Liberal Democrat	8,447	18.3%
	Referendum	1,082	2.3%
	UKIP	472	1.0%
	Other	644	

This is a very mixed seat. Sittingbourne is an expanding town on the main Victoria to Dover railway line and is the largest single element of the seat. New privately owned estates are springing up around Milton Regis and Kemsley. It is set on what is now the A2, but was Watling Street in Roman times and a pilgrimage route to Canterbury, and has a fine High Street but is for the most part a humdrum but pleasant town. There is also a certain amount of Kent countryside around Newington, and the rather isolated Isle of Sheppey projecting into the bleak Thames estuary opposite Southend. Sheerness is a ferry port; despite an impressive Victorian Gothic Conservative club in its centre it is a Labour town and property is exceptionally cheap. There are also desultory Sheppey seaside resorts and industrial towns. It is flat, marshy countryside that needs strong sea defences.

This seat is basically what used to be called Faversham, less the eponymous town. It was a continual source of frustration to Conservatives as Labour MP Percy Wells held on with hair-raisingly narrow majorities throughout the 1950s thanks to one of the most active constituency Labour Parties in the country. It finally fell in 1970 and the Conservatives built up a large lead which disappeared in 1997 on a 14.5% swing, propelling the rather surprised Derek Wyatt into parliament as a Labour MP.

The Conservatives were marginalized in elections for Swale, the borough covering the area, in the mid 1990s but have made a bit of a recovery since then, principally against Labour. They gained some quite surprising victories in 2000, even in Sheppey. They also led by 10 points in the Euro election, and Labour would be fortunate indeed if they could hold off the Conservatives as well as they did in the 1950s. Adrian Lee, a Conservative apparatchik, has a reasonable chance of gaining the seat.

Stevenage

Labour majority 11,582 (22.5%)

Conservative target 180

MP Barbara Follett

1997 (Turnout 76.8%)			
	Labour	28,440	55.3%
	Conservative	16,858	32.8%
	Liberal Democrat	4,588	8.9%
	Referendum	1,194	2.3%
	Others	306	

Stevenage was the first post-war New Town and it is generally regarded as one of the most successful. It lies in mid-Hertfordshire, up the A1 and King's Cross main line from London, and as well as having its own industries has become an acceptable refuge for people priced out of London property. The modern town centre is ringed by residential neighbourhoods on three sides and to the east, by the A1M, is a long strip of industrial and commercial territory.

The only Tory ward is Woodfield, on the far north of the town, and the Lib Dems won Manor, in the east. All the rest are Labour, sometimes over-whelmingly, and the other parties did not offer full slates of candidates in May 2000. Stevenage is not quite big enough for its own parliamentary seat and extends out to a few villages and small towns in the surrounding area such as Walkern and Knebworth, where Labour votes are pretty minimal. Stevenage was one of the few places where the SDP had a strong appeal without much of a prior Liberal tradition – the new party almost won the seat in 1983 but Labour re-emerged as the main challenger to the Tories in 1992 and had a massive victory in 1997 with a swing of nearly 14%. Labour still clearly had the advantage in 1999, with a 3.5% Euro election lead, and 2000.

The elegant Barbara Follett, a long time Labour activist, was a style consultant to other Labour MPs, and is married to the novelist Ken Follett. Their struggle with a champagne bottle was one of the highlights of election night 1997, but since then Ken Follett has exchanged the champagne for sour grapes and turned against Tony Blair. Mrs Follett has associated herself with her husband's criticisms, and distanced herself somewhat from her Blairite reputation – and presumably from ministerial office. She is unlikely to lose Stevenage to Tory Graeme Quar, or any centre resurgence.

Thanet South

Labour majority 2,878 (6.4%)

Conservative target 46

MP Stephen Ladyman

1997 (Turnout 71.6%)			
	Labour	20,777	46.2%
	Conservative	17,899	39.8%
	Liberal Democrat	5,263	11.7%
	UKIP	631	1.4%
	Green	418	0.9%

As well as seven Cabinet ministers, five former Conservative Cabinet ministers tasted personal defeat in May 1997. Jonathan Aitken was among them, and his ignominy only deepened with the collapse of a libel case he had brought against the *Guardian*, and his subsequent imprisonment. Aitken's defeat in the election owed little to his own sleaze; the swing in neighbouring Thanet North was almost as large, and the Conservatives fared badly in most seaside constituencies. Thanet South is based around the town of Ramsgate, plus Broadstairs and some inland areas in this northeastern corner of Kent. As well as the Thanet wards, the seat includes several wards from Dover district, including Sandwich, where the drug company Pfizer has a large complex employing several thousand people, which has protected the area somewhat from the scourge of unemployment. Labour need some political Viagra if they are to hold Thanet South, as their vote seems to have grown somewhat limp since 1997. Although the party maintained control of Thanet council in May, by a reduced majority after the landslide of 1995, the Conservatives were 16.8% ahead in the 1999 Euro election. Thanet did not vote in 2000, but the Conservatives did well in similar areas in the local elections then. Stephen Ladyman, who defeated Aitken, faces a strong Tory challenge from former Federation of Conservative Students activist Mark Macgregor, who fought the unpromising territory of West Ham in 1997.

Watford

Labour majority 5,792 (10.5%)

Conservative target 82

MP Claire Ward

1997 (Turnout 74.6%)			
	Labour	25,019	45.3%
	Conservative	19,227	34.8%
	Liberal Democrat	9,272	16.8%
	Referendum	1,484	2.7%
	Others	234	

Watford is hardly to be distinguished from outer London towns like Kingston and Romford, but the county boundary puts it into Hertfordshire. The seat has a history of being a crucial marginal with something of a tradition of disappointing the Conservatives – it voted Labour in 1951 when a Conservative gain was expected, and stayed Labour in 1970 as well. From 1979 to 1997 it was the base of Tristan Garel-Jones, a clever player of the Westminster game with a colourful turn of phrase, and on his retirement swung decisively with the tide and elected Labour's Claire Ward. Ward, elected at the age of 24, was just finishing a term as Mayor of the town of Elstree and Boreham Wood having already served on Labour's NEC – a very early start to a political career.

The Conservatives had a five point lead in the 1999 Euro election. Despite an experiment with weekend voting designed to increase turnout in May 2000, Labour lost overall control of Watford borough council although on a comparatively small swing. The Liberal Democrats were the main beneficiary and were a bit ahead in a close three-way split. How this splits in general elections is anyone's guess. The constituency also includes some suburbs outside the borough such as Leavesden and Carpenders Park, which boost the Conservative vote.

Watford is a rather average seat, and has preserved its marginal tradition. Whether it repeats its resistant behaviour to Tory recoveries as in 1951 and 1970 is still to be seen. The Watford Conservatives seem a moderate lot: Michael McManus, a long-serving assistant to Edward Heath, won the Conservative selection contest.

Welwyn Hatfield

Labour majority 5,595 (10.6%)

Conservative target 84

MP Melanie Johnson

1997 (Turnout 78.6%)			
	Labour	24,936	47.1%
	Conservative	19,341	36.5%
	Liberal Democrat	7,161	13.5%
	Others	1,530	

Welwyn Hatfield has been a complex constituency since it was created in 1974. Hatfield is smaller and shabbier than the other London area New Towns; in some ways south Hatfield feels more like an overspill estate than a community in its own right. In the past an aviation centre, Hatfield now depends on education (the University of Hertfordshire) and shopping (the vast American style Galleria mall). Hatfield also contains an attractive district, Old Hatfield, nestling in feudal fashion below Hatfield House. Lord Salisbury would often run the country from Hatfield House when Prime Minister, and Hatfield's connection with aristocratic Toryism continues through Lord Cranborne. Hatfield New Town's ordinary voters, however, are mainly Labour.

Welwyn has more liberal ideological roots. It is in three parts; an old village, the early 20th century Garden City and the post-war New Town. The Garden City was the dream of social reformer Ebenezer Howard, who is commemorated in the form of a large shopping centre next to the railway station. The old area is very Tory, the Garden City a bit less so, and the New Town mainly Labour. The seat also includes outlying Tory areas such as the commuter town of Brookmans Park.

Welwyn Hatfield was the scene of a bitter election campaign in 1997. David Evans, a buffoonish right-winger who tried too hard to become a Commons 'character' had been the MP since 1987. His boorish opinions about Melanie Johnson, his Labour opponent, and the calibre of Tory Cabinet Minister Virginia Bottomley, were leaked shortly before the election; he apologised to Bottomley but not Johnson. His defeat gave pleasure to leading figures in both main political parties. He is not standing again and is replaced by Grant Shapps.

Welwyn Hatfield was Labour's only gain of a local authority in May

2000, but it was by a very small margin. Although ward boundary changes complicate matters, the Conservatives had the edge, slightly, in the popular vote, but by less than the 10.5% lead they enjoyed in the Euro elections. As ever, the seat is a crucial marginal.

Winchester (see by-elections)

Liberal Democrat majority in May 1997, 2 (0.0%);

Liberal Democrat majority in Nov 1997, 21,556 (39.6%)

Conservative target 1

MP Mark Oaten

May 1997 (Turnout 78.6%)	Liberal Democrat	26,100	42.1%
	Conservative	26,098	42.1%
	Labour	6,528	10.6%
	Referendum	1,598	2.6%
	'LD Top'	640	1.0%
	UKIP	478	0.8%
	Others	614	

The 1997 election result – a Lib Dem victory by 2 votes – was the closest since 1931 while it stood, but it was re-run in November 1997 and the Lib Dem Mark Oaten was re-elected by a majority of over 21,000. Winchester now looks one of the safest Lib Dem seats; although this is somewhat illusory because of the odd circumstances of 1997, the Lib Dems are favourites to hold off the Conservatives. During his first interlude as MP Mark Oaten was fanatically attentive to the seat, and he has remained a hard working member. The seat is coterminous with the City of Winchester District, which was a notable Lib Dem victory in the elections of May 2000; they made a net gain of 2 seats from the Conservatives on a high turnout for a local election of 40% (although the Tories were slightly ahead in share of the vote). The Conservatives led by 44-25 in Euro 99.

Winchester is a well-off, attractive cathedral city. It is within an hour's commuting distance of London, but it also has a thriving local economic base of service employment, education and distribution. The constituency includes a large chunk of rural mid-Hampshire, including New Alresford, Bishops Waltham and the Meon Valley, dipping down to the hills above

Fareham and Portsmouth. The Liberal Democrats are fairly strong throughout the seat. Labour have some reserves of support in the city area but none elsewhere, and the majority of Labour supporters in Winchester voted tactically for Mark Oaten at least in November 1997 and will probably do so again at the next election. The Conservative candidate is Andrew Hayes.

Witney

Conservative majority 7,028 (12.5%)

MP Shaun Woodward (Conservative until December 1999, Labour since then)

May 1997			
	Conservative	24,282	43.1%
	Labour	17,254	30.6%
	Liberal Democrat	11,202	19.9%
	Referendum	2,262	4.0%
	UKIP	765	1.4%
	Green	636	1.1%

Witney's brief status as a Labour seat began in December 1999 with the decision of Shaun Woodward to cross the floor in protest at Conservative 'extremism' and 'homophobia'. Most MPs who change parties do not resign their seats, and face ritualistic demands from their spurned parties to do so; Woodward chose not to. He would be ill-advised to defend Witney for Labour, as rural Oxfordshire has been solidly Conservative since 1922. Witney town, an expanding urban centre, has some Labour support but it is swamped by rural west Oxfordshire which is an increasingly popular weekend retreat for Londoners. Unemployment in the constituency is among the lowest in the country, at 0.7%. The Conservative candidate is now David Cameron, a former Treasury special adviser, who was denied at Stafford in 1997. Cameron has now won a safer berth which returned a 24.5% Conservative lead in the 1999 Euro elections (admittedly a smaller than average swing since 1997) and despite the disruption of Woodward's defection is likely to remain a Tory stronghold.

South West

Conservative Targets

Target No	Constituency		Labour Lead
C17	Bristol West	1,493	2.4%
C32	Stroud	2,910	4.7%
C33	Falmouth and Camborne	2,688	5.0%
C70	Wansdyke	4,799	8.8%
C89	Swindon South	5,645	11.0%
C103	Forest of Dean	6,343	12.6%
C115	Gloucester	8,259	14.3%
C130	Swindon North	7,688	15.9%
C149	Exeter	11,705	18.9%
C159	Plymouth Sutton	9,440	19.8%
C164	Bristol North West	11,382	20.6%
C195	Kingswood	14,253	23.8%

(Liberal Democrat held)

			Lib Dem Lead
C2	Torbay	12	0.0%
C4	Somerton and Frome	130	0.2%
C18	Weston-super-Mare	1,274	2.4%
C24	Torridge and West Devon	1,957	3.3%
C25	Northavon	2,137	3.4%
C27	Taunton	2,443	4.0%
C91	Devon North	6,181	11.3%
C92	Cornwall South East	6,480	11.3%
C108	Cheltenham	6,645	13.2%
C109	St Ives	7,170	13.3%
C142	Bath	9,319	17.3%

Labour Target

		Conservative Lead	
L1	Dorset South	77	0.2%

Liberal Democrat Targets

	Labour Lead	
Bristol West (3rd)	4517	7.2%
Falmouth and Camborne (3rd)	4639	8.6%

(Conservative held)

	Conservative Lead	
Teignbridge	281	0.4%
Wells	528	0.9%
Dorset Mid and Poole North	681	1.3%
Totnes	877	1.6%
Tiverton and Honiton	1,653	2.8%

The South West is a varied region. Cornwall is a distinctive part of the country, Celtic rather than Anglo-Saxon, with a small nationalist movement of its own (Mebyon Kernow), a resuscitated language and a peculiar landscape. At the other end, the South West includes Gloucestershire and Wiltshire, parts of which are coming increasingly into the orbit of London work and leisure. Between lie Bristol and its city-region, Somerset and Dorset, and the large county of Devon.

The furthest part of the region, Cornwall and most of Devon, is very much on the periphery of Britain: Penzance is as far from London as Carlisle. It is remote and dependent on several declining industries – first fishing, tin and china clay mining, then tourism. It is poorly served by airports, and communications by rail deteriorate abruptly at Exeter. Cornwall lacks a motorway, or a university, and suffers from an outdated economic base. The Conservatives lost ground here in 1987 and 1992, reflecting the understandable feeling in these parts that the south west was being neglected by London. Somerset shared many of these feelings. The rest of the region was less disenchanted with Thatcher in 1987 and Major in 1992, although Bath and Cheltenham did produce the two most dramatic Conservative reverses of that election. Dorset and Wiltshire continued to lend strong support to the Conservatives, with the party managing to hold Swindon. The Conservatives still dominated the region in 1992, with 38 MPs to 6 Liberal Democrats and 4 Labour, and 47.6% of the vote (down from 50.6% in 1987)

The Conservatives slumped across the region in 1997, being reduced to 22 MPs compared to 15 Labour and 14 Liberal Democrats. It could have been even worse – there were close calls in several Tory seats including Teignbridge and Wells. They were wiped out in Cornwall and Bristol, although Dorset was one of only two counties with 100% Conservative MPs (Surrey is the other; there were 14 such English counties in 1992 and 21 in 1987). Although they won no seats, the Referendum Party and the UK Independence Party polled some of their strongest votes in the area.

The Conservatives came back very strongly in the 1999 Euro elections in the south west, particularly against Liberal Democrat opposition, and will have won all that party's seats in the region and reduced Labour to five, four in the Bristol area plus Plymouth Devonport. There are quite a lot of seats worth watching in the area, particularly if the Conservatives are going to improve their parliamentary position. The last time the Liberals won a swathe of these seats was in 1923, and that was followed at the next election by a sweeping Conservative recovery.

Outside the cities, Labour is quite weak. The party never managed to displace the Liberal Party as the voice of radicalism in these parts even at its high watermark of 1945–51 and puts in some of its worst showings in the rural Lib Dem-Con marginals.

Nearly all the interesting seats are in the list of marginals, but there are a few worth noting otherwise. Conservative strength in Plymouth makes Devonport interesting as well as Sutton; see the profile for Plymouth Sutton. Paddy Ashdown is leaving his seat at Yeovil; David Laws is the new Liberal Democrat candidate but the party has historically been bad at passing seats on when incumbents depart. Conservative Marco Forgione cannot be ruled out despite Ashdown's 21.1% lead in 1997; the Tories led by 15.5% in the Euro election. Liberal Democrat seats at North Cornwall and Truro and St. Austell also looked shaky in 1999 but should survive. The Conservatives were well adrift at Bristol East, even in 1999, and Bristol South after a wobble in 1987 has returned to its safe Labour status. The one Conservative gain anywhere in the country in 1997 was at Christchurch in Dorset; although the seat looks close on paper, the incumbent Liberal Democrat MP had won the seat in a sensational by-election in 1993 which still affected the result in 1997. Diana Maddock is now in the House of

Lords and her successor cannot expect to improve on her showing in 1997. The Conservatives were nearly 50 points ahead of the third placed Christchurch Liberal Democrats in Euro 99. One day, as the Bournemouth-Poole metro area matures, it will surely produce a Labour possible, but that day is not coming any time soon.

Bath

Liberal Democrat majority 9,319 (17.3%)

Conservative target 142

MP Don Foster

1997 (Turnout 75.5%)			
	Liberal Democrat	26,169	48.5%
	Conservative	16,850	31.2%
	Labour	8,828	16.4%
	Referendum	1,192	2.2%
	Green	580	1.1%
	Others	370	0.6%

Bath is recognised as a place of world cultural and historical significance. Its history as a spa goes back to its days as a Roman town called Aquae Sulis, and as if that were not enough modern Bath is a masterpiece of Georgian planning and design. Even the local stone is pleasing to the eye, and there are many dramatic views from the hills which surround the town. Fast rail links into London and the growth of the university have made Bath into an affluent, intellectual, place – in effect, Hampstead-on-Avon. There are a few less favoured parts of the city, such as the Twerton area in the south west, but for the most part Bath is extremely comfortable.

Politically, Bath was in the spotlight in 1992 when it ejected Chris Patten, then Chairman of the Conservative Party, even while his party won nationally. In 1997 it was an unsurprising Liberal Democrat hold for Don Foster, and in May 1999 the party was still dominant in local elections. The Conservatives led by 36.7% to 23.8% in the Euro election, but if Foster can call upon the tactical vote of Labour and Green supporters as he has in the past, he should be safe enough. Foster is now fairly senior among the Liberal Democrats and speaks for the party on education, a key campaigning issue. Bath now seems quite a well-established Liberal Democrat city, and the Conservative candidate Ashley Fox would be very fortunate to unseat Foster next time.

Bristol North West

Labour majority 11,382 (20.6%)

Conservative target 164

MP Doug Naysmith

1997 (Turnout 73.3%)			
	Labour	27,575	49.9%
	Conservative	16,193	29.3%
	Liberal Democrat	7,263	13.1%
	Ind Labour	1,718	3.1%
	Referendum	1,609	2.9%
	Others	887	1.7%

Bristol North West is a classic marginal seat that has changed hands frequently. It is composed of a mixture of areas including dockland (Avonmouth), peripheral council estates like Southmead, and tidy suburbs like Henbury. It extends beyond the city boundary to take in Filton and Stoke Gifford. Filton has generally been known as an aerospace production area (Concorde parts were built here) but it also has a state of the art development housing the Ministry of Defence civilian departments at Abbey Wood, and the University of the West of England. Filton and Stoke Gifford tend towards Labour.

In theory the current Bristol NW is more favourable to Labour than its predecessor, having lost its safest Tory ward at Westbury on Trym to Bristol West; it would have been Labour in 1992. But there was a rather feeble (by 1997 standards only) swing of 7.1% – partly because of an Independent Labour candidate – and it still creeps into the list of marginals. Labour were still doing quite well in 1999 in the Bristol and Northavon portions of the seat in local elections, and held a 2.4% lead in the Euro election. In February 2000, however, the party lost Lockleaze to the Liberal Democrats on a big swing and a higher turnout than May 1999, and in May the Conservatives inflicted a bad defeat in Stoke Gifford. Doug Naysmith, the Labour MP since 1997, has to look over his shoulder at Charles Hansard, the appropriately named Tory candidate, and hope that the Liberal Democrats do not siphon off too much support at the general election.

Bristol West

Labour majority 1,493 (2.4%)

Conservative target 17

Liberal Democrat target

MP Valerie Davey

1997 (Turnout 72.7%)			
	Labour	22,068	35.2%
	Conservative	20,575	32.8%
	Liberal Democrat	17,551	28.0%
	Referendum	1,304	2.1%
	Green	852	1.4%
	Others	291	0.5%

Like many of Labour's most marginal seats Bristol West is a traditionally very Conservative area with demographics to match; 79.5% non-manual workers, the third highest proportion in Britain, in 1991. It combines the university area, wealthy Clifton and suburban Stoke Bishop and Westbury-on-Trym, but also stretches into the inner city; Ashley ward covers most of the St. Paul's enclave and bohemian Montpelier. It has one of the highest concentrations of graduates in the country. The Conservative position in Bristol West had slowly eroded over decades like west end seats in other cities, but until Labour's surge from third to first in 1997 the Liberal Democrats seemed more likely to benefit. There is still a substantial Lib Dem vote, and the party has made local election advances into the formerly safe Labour Ashley ward from its strongholds around Clifton and Cotham in the old west end. The Lib Dems led in the constituency by about 8 points from the Conservatives, with Labour another 8 points behind them, in May 1999. Bristol West is a genuine three way marginal.

Bristol West's Conservative MPs have been relatively liberal figures, and the constituency is not the sort of place where a shift to the populist right is likely to go down well. Pamela Chesters is the new Conservative candidate, and Stephen Williams, who has led the growing Liberal Democrat group on Bristol council, hopes to gain the seat for the Liberal Democrats. Neither challenger can be ruled out.

Cheltenham

Liberal Democrat majority 6,645 (13.2%)

Conservative target 108

MP Nigel Jones

1997 (Turnout 74.0%)	Liberal Democrat	24,877	49.5%
	Conservative	18,232	36.2%
	Labour	5,100	10.1%
	Referendum	1,065	2.1%
	UK Independence	302	0.6%
	Others	727	1.4%

Cheltenham enjoys a pleasing townscape of floral parks, wide avenues and gracious Georgian streets, the product of thoughtful planning and affluence fed by its attractions as a spa and retirement area. The town is also a centre for service sector employment in education and private business, and the massive government GCHQ intelligence establishment is a major influence. Like other spa towns (see also Bath and Harrogate) the Lib Dems are strong and Labour weak. Though prosperous, Cheltenham is not without its problems, as became tragically evident when Liberal Democrat MP Nigel Jones was a victim of an attack at a constituency surgery in which his colleague, Councillor Andrew Pennington, was killed.

Nigel Jones first won Cheltenham in 1992, and increased the small majority he won against John Taylor, then to a considerable 13.2% margin in 1997 against local Conservative John Todman. Cheltenham is still closely contested between Tories and Lib Dems; the Lib Dems lost control of the council in May 1999 when the Tories gained 9 seats, but the results were less overwhelming in 2000. The Conservatives led by an unimpressive 47–41% in the wards that make up the constituency, a contrast to the massive lead the Conservatives enjoyed in the Euro election. The Conservatives will be in no mood to concede Cheltenham and have selected Rob Garnham, but the most likely outcome is another Liberal Democrat victory.

Cornwall South East

Liberal Democrat majority 6,480 (11.3%)

Conservative target 92

MP Colin Breed

1997 (Turnout 75.5%)			
	Liberal Democrat	27,044	47.1%
	Conservative	20,564	35.8%
	Labour	7,358	12.8%
	UK Independence	1,428	2.5%
	Others	1,038	1.8%

Cornwall South East is, for Cornwall, relatively well off. Parts of it, such as Saltash and Torpoint, have become increasingly popular as commuter settlements for Plymouth while others have resisted the decline of the English seaside resort more successfully than most – Looe and Polperro, and the charming double village of Kingsand and Cawsand. Inland is Lostwithiel, an ancient and somewhat austere-looking town which seems more Cornish than the rest. As the most 'English' part of Cornwall South East might be expected to be most Conservative. Not so. The Lib Dems won the seat with a 12% swing and a healthy majority of 11.3%, and this was not a recent flash in the pan – it had switched back and forward between the Liberals (1922–24, 1929–35, 1964–70, Feb-Oct 1974) and Conservatives (1918–22, 1924–29, 1935–64, Oct 1974–97) in its current form and as 'Bodmin'.

The knockout swing in 1997, larger than any other in the south west (except by-election influenced Christchurch), must have in part reflected the loss of the personal vote accruing to moderate Conservative Robert Hicks, MP since 1970 except for a brief interlude in 1974. Hicks retired in 1997, and was replaced as Tory candidate by Warwick Lightfoot, a Kensington councillor and former economic adviser to John Major and Norman Lamont. Lib Dem winner Colin Breed (whose campaign team toyed with the idea of using the slogan 'Breed for Cornwall'), as an experienced Saltash local politician, played the local card strongly against Lightfoot.

Local elections are not organised along thorough party lines in Cornwall, so the main piece of information on voting trends here recently is the 1999 Euro election. The Conservatives led the Lib Dems by a relatively narrow 8 points, less than in Truro or St Ives, and it was the only seat in the south west where their share actually fell between 1997 and 1999. Although the UKIP won 14%, this was the lowest in Cornwall, as was the anti-Europe showing in 1997. The new Conservative candidate Ashley Gray faces a strong incumbent in a seat in which the anti-Europe, anti-Lib Dem winds have not blown as strongly as elsewhere in the south west.

Devon North

Liberal Democrat majority 6,181 (11.3%)

Conservative target 91

MP Nick Harvey

1997 (Turnout 77.9%)	Liberal Democrat	27,824	50.8%
	Conservative	21,643	39.5%
	Labour	5,347	9.8%

North Devon has been a tough fight between Liberals and Conservatives in most elections for nearly half a century now. Its most celebrated MP was Jeremy Thorpe, who represented the seat from 1959 to 1979 and led the Liberal Party from 1967 to 1976. He lives in the constituency and is an honoured local figure, serving as the President of the local Liberal Democrats. North Devon's Liberalism revived in 1992 with the victory of Nick Harvey. Harvey was long the sole Eurosceptic MP in a pro-Europe party, but has recently become more accommodating towards Europe.

The main town in North Devon is Barnstaple, which has some industry, but North Devon also contains other seaside towns and some surprisingly jungly countryside inland. It is a beautiful but rather remote place. The Liberal Democrats held on to control of the council in May 1999; Labour are negligible in all areas although Independent councillors still win elections in town and rural areas. In their June Euro election disaster, though, the Liberal Democrats slumped to 19.4%, only three points ahead of the UKIP and over 20 behind the Conservatives. In that election, though, they were ahead in only three seats in Britain and, strangely, only one (Orkney and Shetland) is currently a Liberal Democrat seat. Nobody expects a wipe-out like that at the general election, and a Conservative candidate faces Clive Allen difficulties in ousting a popular incumbent like Harvey. The last time the Conservatives displaced a Liberal incumbent here, it was while criminal charges were hanging over Thorpe. Harvey is unlikely to face this particular handicap.

Dorset Mid and Poole North

Conservative majority 681 (1.3%)

Liberal Democrat target

MP Christopher Fraser

1997 (Turnout 75.7%)			
	Conservative	20,632	40.7%
	Liberal Democrat	19,951	39.3%
	Labour	8,014	15.8%
	Referendum	2,136	4.2%

This cumbersomely named constituency was a disappointment to the Liberal Democrats at the 1997 election, as former aide to Paddy Ashdown Alan Leaman lost out narrowly to Conservative Christopher Fraser in a seat where the centre had polled strongly in local elections. It was a new creation in 1997; the largest element came from the northern suburbs of Poole, although it spills out westwards to Wareham and the village of Bere Regis. The Poole portion, around Canford Heath, is a recent growth area. The Bournemouth and Poole conurbation now has three seats of its own, plus two more seats with large suburban elements, namely Christchurch and Mid Dorset & Poole North. It is a considerable metropolitan area, and it is unusual in having no real Labour prospects.

All the local authorities contributing to the seat saw Conservative gains from the Liberal Democrats in the local elections of May 1999, and in the Euro election the Conservatives had a massive lead of 28.4%. The Liberal Democrat prospective candidate is Annette Brooke, who has a pretty tough task in trying to win the once-promising seat. Fraser is likely to return with an increased majority.

Dorset South

Conservative majority 77 (0.2%)

Labour target 1

MP Ian Bruce

1997 (Turnout 74.0%)	Conservative	17,755	36.1%
	Labour	17,678	35.9%
	Liberal Democrat	9,936	20.2%
	Referendum	2,791	5.7%
	UK Independence	861	1.8%
	Other	161	0.3%

Weymouth provides an isolated pocket of Labour support in the wilderness of Dorset, but it is not large enough to comprise a constituency of its own and Dorset South includes Swanage and some beautiful Purbeck coastline as well. Labour slashed the Conservative majority to 77 in the 1997 election. The party has never won a Dorset seat in a general election so far, although this seat was briefly Labour after a Eurosceptic independent ran against the official Conservative in a by-election in 1962; a combined Eurosceptic vote of 7.5% in 1997 almost did the same trick. It is the only Labour prospect between Exeter and Southampton (both now seem safe) and no doubt Labour's scattered troops in this area will be encouraged to put their effort into this seat.

Despite some Labour hopes, Ian Bruce is likely to retain the seat for the Conservatives. As in many seaside areas, Labour suffered a large hostile swing in the 2000 local elections, although they are still the largest single party on the perennially hung council of Weymouth & Portland. The Euro election produced a 22.2% Conservative lead.

Exeter

Labour majority 11,705 (18.9%)

Conservative target 149

MP Ben Bradshaw

1997 (Turnout 77.6%)	Labour	29,398	47.5%
	Conservative	17,693	28.6%
	Liberal Democrat	11,148	18.0%
	Liberal	2,062	3.3%
	Green	643	1.0%
	UK Independence	638	1.0%
	Other	282	0.5%

Exeter was one of the most bitter and highly publicised contests in the 1997 election. Labour candidate Ben Bradshaw won the seat comfortably, despite a messy Labour selection procedure and a ferocious campaign against him by right wing moraliser Adrian Rogers for the Conservatives. Bradshaw's success, and that of Stephen Twigg in Enfield Southgate, showed that openly gay candidates could attract votes for the same political reasons as hetero-sexuals – or, for that matter, celibates (as in Maidstone and the Weald).

Exeter is a pleasant city with a vague Trollopean air. It is the sort of cathedral city that used to be Conservative when the Church of England was the Tory party at prayer (see also Chester, Hereford, Oxford, Worcester – all also Tory in 1945). It has a well-regarded university, which affects the political tastes of the electorate by bringing students, and underpaid and overeducated academics, to town; usually to the detriment of the Conservatives and the benefit of Greens, Lib Dems and Labour. The old Liberal Party is still a significant minority force in Exeter as well, at least in local elections. In a very splintered vote in Euro 99, the Conservatives with 29% were half a point ahead of Labour, but the Labour council seems popular with voters and was resoundingly returned to power in May 2000. Conservative candidate Anne Jobson is opposing Bradshaw in the next election, no doubt with more decorum than Rogers managed, but with the probability of a similar result.

Falmouth and Camborne

Labour majority 2,688 (5.0%)

Conservative target 33

Liberal Democrat target

MP Candy Atherton

1997 (Turnout 75.1%)

Labour	18,151	33.8%
Conservative	15,463	28.8%
Liberal Democrat	13,512	25.2%
Referendum	3,534	6.6%
Ind Labour	1,691	3.2%
Others	1,281	2.4%

When Falmouth and Cambourne was created in 1950 Labour won it narrowly until 1970 when it switched to independently minded Tory populist David Mudd, who had a massive 16,600 majority in 1979. Then the Conservatives went into decline; Mudd's share of the vote fell from 57% in 1979 to 50% in 1983, 44% in 1987 and 37% for his successor, Seb Coe, in 1992. West Cornwall definitely saw itself as belonging to the unfavoured periphery of Britain that had failed to benefit from the 1980s boom. This Thatcher-era Tory collapse was more severe than in Manchester or Glasgow but they held the seat thanks to a divided opposition vote.

This constituency is surprisingly ugly for Cornwall. Camborne is not a town on the tourist circuit; it is surrounded by china clay pits gouged out of the land, and has the sullen and dispirited feel of a place that has suffered greatly from unemployment and neglect. The last tin mine closed during the Major government. Falmouth was once a significant port but now depends more on the tourist trade, where it is at a disadvantage compared to prettier places like St Ives and Looe. Its fishermen form a tiny but vocal minority with some sway over the more sentimental voters, and their resentment at EU fishing policy has undoubtedly fuelled the growth of anti-European feeling in west Cornwall. Ironically, Cornwall is a big net beneficiary of EU funding through its regional development budget.

Candy Atherton won Falmouth and Camborne for Labour in 1997, but with a very low share of the vote (33.8%). Coe was ejected with a relatively small (8.1%) further fall in his vote and the Lib Dems slipped to third place. There was a rag tag and bobtail of other candidates, notably Lands End entrepreneur Peter de Savary for the Referendum Party who saved his deposit with 6.6%, and a rebel Labour man who objected to the women only short list used for the selection (3.2%). An old style Liberal, a Cornish Nationalist and a Loony made up the remainder.

Politics in the second-to-last seat in England will continue to be hard fought and somewhat strange. In Euro 99 the Tories were on top, with scarcely more of the vote than Labour managed in 1997, and Labour were in third narrowly behind the Lib Dems at a little under 20%. The UKIP polled a menacing 15.1%. Council elections in the area, in Kerrier and Carrick districts, are not a good indicator for national politics. The perennial resentments of this remote area, ill-served by most recent governments, may now focus on Labour to the benefit of . . . well, who knows? Lib Dem candidate Terrye Jones, a strong candidate denied in 1992 and 1997, is not standing again. The Conservative candidate is Nick Serpell and the UKIP are a force in the seat.

Forest of Dean

Labour majority 6,343 (12.6%)

Conservative target 103

MP Diana Organ

1997 (Turnout 79.1%)			
	Labour	24,203	48.2%
	Conservative	17,860	35.6%
	Liberal Democrat	6,165	12.3%
	Referendum	1,624	3.2%
	Others	332	0.7%

The Forest of Dean is a weird place. Dennis Potter, playwright and son of the Forest, described it as 'rather ugly villages in beautiful landscape, a heart-shaped place between two rivers, somehow slightly cut off from the rest of England.' It is the part of England between the Severn and the Welsh border at the river Wye. Its woods are dense and somewhat spooky, and littered with the remains of a proud industrial past. There are still a few 'freeminers' with the right to dig for coal more or less where they feel like it, but all the pits have now closed. Most of the towns are not twee, hunting and cream teas places, but rather forbidding, with roads looping through bleak estates – see for example Cinderford and Coleford. Other parts are very pretty, particularly along the Wye opposite Tintern Abbey. Some of the Forest in the north west has become commuter country for Gloucester and Cheltenham. It was a reliable Radical Liberal and then Labour citadel for a century from 1880 to 1979 but demographic change gradually pushed it into the Conservative column. As early as 1962 Potter described 'The Changing Forest' in which old working class loyalties were blurring, and Paul Marland's capture of the seat for the Tories in 1979 seemed to close a chapter. But, helped by boundary changes, Diana Organ recaptured the

Forest for Labour in 1997 although apparently on a low swing.

The Forest is hard to measure politically. Labour managed a net gain of two council seats in the May 1999 elections compared to 1995, but the Conservatives hardly feature in local politics and the battle is between Labour and various shades of Independent. This made it difficult for the experts to calculate a 'notional' result on the new boundaries, so the 1997 swing may have been larger than it seems. But in June 1999 Labour suffered the second worst fall in share of the vote compared to 1997 in the south west, and the Tories were 13 points ahead. It is fair to say, now, that the Forest is a critical marginal which both main parties stand a chance of winning. Tory candidate Mark Harper faces the stylish but chilly Blairite Diana Organ at the next election.

Gloucester

Labour majority 8,259 (14.3%)

Conservative target 115

MP Tess Kingham (retiring)

1997 (Turnout 73.6%)			
	Labour	28,943	50.0%
	Conservative	20,684	35.7%
	Liberal Democrat	6,069	10.5%
	Referendum	1,482	2.6%
	UK Independence	455	0.8%
	Other	281	0.5%

Gloucester was Tony Blair's first port of call in his 1997 election campaign tour. It tremendous symbolic significance as the seat that, if Labour won, would produce a single-seat majority in the Commons. Labour did rather better than that, of course, and Gloucester was an easy gain by over 8,000 votes. Gloucester is a crossing point of the wide Severn, and this position has kept a town here, from Roman Glevum to the current manufacturing centre and cathedral city. It also makes it prone to traffic jams and ugly road schemes.

Gloucester seems to allow parties a long lease on its representation. Labour had the seat from 1945 to 1970, and the Conservatives then held it from 1970 until 1997. If the past is a guide, Labour should be all right until the first election of the 2020s, but the sitting MP is not staying around to test the theory. Tess Kingham is a voluntary single-term MP. She rapidly became frustrated with the unsociable hours and boys' club atmosphere of the Commons, and concluded that if the 101 Labour women elected in 1997 could not shift the culture in the first years of the new government, it was unlikely to happen any time soon. Neither Labour nor Conservative have a prospective parliamentary candidate at the time of writing.

Labour kept control of Gloucester in the local elections of 2000 by one seat, after two Conservative gains and despite lagging in the popular vote. The Conservatives had a rather large (12%) lead in the Euro elections, so it will not be plain sailing for Kingham's successor although history seems to be on her (or his) side.

Kingswood

Labour majority 14,253 (23.8%)

Conservative target 195

MP Roger Berry

1997 (Turnout 77.7%)			
	Labour	32,181	53.7%
	Conservative	17,928	29.9%
	Liberal Democrat	7,672	12.8%
	Referendum	1,463	2.4%
	Others	643	1.1%

Kingswood is the urban sprawl to the east of Bristol: the industrial area of Mangotsfield, residential Oldland, Downend and Hanham and a desultory shopping centre at Staple Hill. It also extends into Bristol's eastern fringe at Frome Vale and Hillfields, which is pretty indistinguishable from the rest of the seat. Its lack of distinct identity is reflected in the regularity with which bits of it are swapped and shifted to and from other constituencies at boundary reviews. It is home to a large number of skilled workers in engineering and other trades – a classic 'C2' seat in the jargon used in the 1980s before we had heard of Essex Man and Worcester Woman.

Labour's Roger Berry won the seat (on different boundaries, naturally) in 1992 and held it with a 14% swing in 1997, one of the largest swings outside the London area. Berry is a proud Keynesian economist, which now puts him on the left of the party. He rebelled on benefit cuts for lone parents in November 1997 but is not one of the usual suspects. The May 1999 elections for the South Gloucestershire unitary authority produced broadly positive results for Labour in most of the seat, and in June Labour were 2.8% ahead in the Euro election. Roger Berry seems likely to win a third term when the next election comes.

Northavon

Liberal Democrat majority 2,137 (3.4%)

Conservative target 25

MP Steven Webb

1997 (Turnout 79.1%)			
	Liberal Democrat	26,500	42.4%
	Conservative	24,363	39.0%
	Labour	9,767	15.6%
	Referendum	1,900	3.0%

This seat is the northern area of the defunct county of Avon. It is a strikingly modern part of Britain, dominated by the new private estates of towns like Yate, Chipping Sodbury and Thornbury, out of town office parks and shopping centres, and convenient for transport via the M4 and M5 motorways and the intercity Bristol Parkway station. The satellite town of Bradley Stoke has been an area of rapid growth since the 1980s. Northavon has been a boom area in recent years. Unemployment now stands at a negligible 1.2%, having halved since May 1997.

Northavon is less like a British New Town than it is like an American suburb. That the Conservatives managed to lose such a seat in 1997 is rather amazing. The winner was Lib Dem economist Steve Webb, whose detailed knowledge of the social security system is combined with strong social concern. The Liberal Democrats have been strong in local elections for some time, and first polled the most votes in 1991. They did extremely well in May 1999, almost monopolising the area's representation for the South Gloucestershire local elections. They lagged 15.3% behind the Conservatives in the Euro elections, but this was not uncommon for such areas. The Conservative candidate in the general election is Carrie Ruxton, an unconventional Tory, and although Webb has a strong chance of survival Northavon will be a hard-fought seat.

Plymouth Sutton

Labour majority 9,440 (19.8%)

Conservative target 159

MP Linda Gilroy

1997 (Turnout 67.0%)			
	Labour	23,881	50.1%
	Conservative	14,441	30.3%
	Liberal Democrat	6,613	13.9%
	Referendum	1,654	3.5%
	UK Independence	499	1.0%
	Others	566	1.2%

Sutton is a densely populated constituency in the centre of Plymouth. St. Peter and Sutton wards contain the post-war city centre area and surrounding districts, such as the carefully preserved Barbican and the sordid Union Street area. St Peter is one of the poorest wards in Britain. North of the city centre, among the hills that give Plymouth its distinctive cityscape, is the comfortable Tory area of Compton; north-west are the terraces of marginal Stoke. Plymouth seats often chop and change at the whim of the Boundary Commission; the current Sutton resembles 'Drake', a marginal Tory seat from 1974 to 1997. Labour's Linda Gilroy won an easy victory in the first contest for the new Sutton in 1997 as Tory MP Janet Fookes retired.

The Tories were 5% ahead in June 1999, and Plymouth was one of the Conservatives' best results in May 2000; a large Labour majority on the City council was pretty well reversed. Most of the wards of Sutton are marginal; three wards (Efford, Mount Gould and Sutton) were so close that representation was split between Tory and Labour. The Tories were about 48-38% ahead in the wards that made up the Sutton constituency, an enormous 15% swing since 1997. But in the other Plymouth seat, Devonport, the swing was even larger (18%) and the local result was virtually a tie between the two main parties on 43%; the Tories elected councillors in dockland Keyham and the council estate of Southway. Labour had run Plymouth since 1991 and had accumulated a series of local grievances including some inept planning and parking decisions, which may have contributed to the landslide. Plymouth suffers from its remoteness and has been disappointed with the limited impact of urban regeneration and the amount of funds it receives from the government. It swung wildly against a nationally popular

Conservative government in 1987. Labour face a serious battle against the resurgent Plymouth Tories, whose Sutton candidate is Oliver Colvile.

St Ives

Liberal Democrat majority 7,170 (13.3%)

Conservative target 109

MP Andrew George

1997 (Turnout 75.0%)

Liberal Democrat	23,966	44.5%
Conservative	16,796	31.2%
Labour	8,184	15.2%
Referendum	3,714	6.9%
UK Independence	567	1.1%
Others	674	1.2%

St Ives itself is a small Cornish resort with wide sandy beaches and an artistic community drawn by the clear light and the contrasts of sea, sand and hills; it is also the site of a branch of the Tate Gallery. It is not the largest town in the division; that is Penzance, the end of the Great Western railway line and the commercial capital of west Cornwall. Beyond Penzance is the sinister landscape of Penwith, strewn with mysterious stone circles on dark moors, and the tourist trap of Lands End. The constituency extends out into the sea past Lands End, as it includes the Scilly Isles.

St Ives was won in most elections from 1918 to 1966 by hybrid candidates claiming both Conservative and Liberal credentials. The threadbare flag of 'National Liberalism' still flew over St Ives until the remnants of the party were wound up in 1968 in a meeting in John Poulson's office. From 1970 to 1987 it looked like a safe seat for openly Tory candidates but in 1992 Lib Dem candidate Andrew George secured a 5.8% swing and the seat became a target marginal. The job was completed in 1997 and George won by a comfortable margin of over 7,000 votes.

Like other south western seats, St Ives seems to feel strongly about Europe. The Lib Dems, the most pro-European party, are strong but so are anti-European fringe parties. Referendum and UKIP combined won 8% of the vote in 1997, and UKIP won 15.5% in 1999. The Lib Dems crashed to 24%, 10% behind the Conservatives. In a general election it may well be different; Andrew George is an energetic MP and Cornish MPs have shown themselves capable of amassing personal votes. The Conservative Candidate is Joanna Richardson

Somerton and Frome

Liberal Democrat majority 130 (0.2%)

Conservative target 4

MP David Heath

1997 (Turnout 77.4%)			
	Liberal Democrat	22,684	39.5%
	Conservative	22,554	39.3%
	Labour	9,385	16.3%
	Referendum	2,449	4.3%
	UK Independence	331	0.6%

Somerton and Frome is a constituency of villages and small towns; Frome is the largest town in this constituency, and it is no metropolis. The seat covers some of the traditional heartland of Somerset; villages with excellent names like Curry Rivel and Huish Episcopi, and the puzzling inland town of Milborne Port. The Liberal Democrats have entertained ambitions since the seat was created in 1983, and their dreams finally came true in 1997 when David Heath, the former leader of Somerset county council, gained the seat from the moderate Tory Mark Robinson.

The Conservatives were just short of 20 points ahead in the Euro election, although they had not performed exceptionally well in the May 1999 local elections. Somerton and Frome is certainly on the 'at risk register' of Liberal Democrat seats; 130 votes in such a long-term target is not very impressive, and the Liberal Democrat vote was actually slightly down on 1992. David Heath is very vulnerable to Jonathan Marland, the Conservative candidate.

Stroud

Labour majority 2,910 (4.7%)

Conservative target 32

MP David Drew

1997 (Turnout 78.8%)	Labour	26,170	42.7%
	Conservative	23,260	37.9%
	Liberal Democrat	9,502	15.5%
	Green	2,415	3.9%

Stroud bears some social and political resemblance to the Forest of Dean, across the river, and a physical similarity to Calder Valley in West Yorkshire. Stroud town itself, and the smaller towns of Dursley and Cam, have rather fierce socialist traditions. During poll tax protests in Bath in 1990, Chris Patten is supposed to have complained that the demonstrators were 'bussed in from radical places like Stroud'. Stroud was one of the first local authorities to elect a significant Green group.

The radical tradition, however, is not the dominant one. There are Conservatives in the towns, and the towns are also surrounded by some very Conservative countryside. It was a surprise Labour gain in 1997 for mild-mannered local politician David Drew who enjoyed a swing of nearly 12%. There was a 15.5% Conservative lead in the Euro election, a pretty large swing back although some of the Labour vote seems to have bled away to the Greens who polled 12%. Most seats where the Greens obtain a double-figure percentage are university areas or London seats; Leominster is the only other rural seat.

The Conservatives have recovered strongly in the local elections of 1999 and 2000 and are now the largest party on the council, having been pushed to the margins in the mid-1990s. Their candidate Neil Carmichael stands a good chance of ending Stroud's second period as a rural Labour seat.

Swindon North

Labour majority 7,688 (15.9%)

Conservative target 130

MP Michael Wills

1997 (Turnout 73.6%)	Labour	24,029	49.8%
	Conservative	16,341	33.9%
	Liberal Democrat	6,237	12.9%
	Referendum	1,533	3.2%
	Other	130	0.3%

Swindon North was supposedly a much safer Labour seat than its southern neighbour when the town was divided in the boundary review before the 1997 election, but when the votes were counted it was only a little more inclined to the left. The swing since the estimated result in 1992 was only 7.1%. What explains this comparatively poor showing?

One possibility is that the estimates of the effect of the new boundaries were off-beam; if, as seems possible, there was a Conservative vote in working class areas that did not come out in local elections, as in Harlow and Basildon before 1992; the Tory presence in North may have been understated. Another factor may be the internal rows in the local Labour Party about candidate selection. Some local members regarded Michael Wills as a Blairite foisted upon the constituency.

Swindon is not technically a New Town, but as an Expanded Town it shares many of their characteristics. Swindon was once a railway town, but the works have closed and been replaced by an outlet shopping mall. The employment consequences of the rail works closure was not as bad as it might have been, because the town's economic base had diversified and modernised. Swindon is still growing strongly, as reflected in the extra seat at the 1997 election and frequent reviews of ward boundaries (which make it difficult to compare local elections over a period of time). The largest new private housing development in europe is under construction at Abbey Meads.

Labour had a shock in the Euro elections in 1999, when the Conservatives were 3.6% ahead in North on an embarrassing turnout of 18.4%, and in the May 2000 local elections when the party lost control of the council in all-out elections in the new wards. The Conservatives won seats in the outlying wards of Blunsdon, Highworth and Haydon Wick, but Labour held onto most of the town estate wards despite a dismal turnout in some such as Gorse Hill & Pinehurst. Nick Martin stands a chance of a surprising victory against Wills, who has already become a minister.

Swindon South

Labour majority 5,645 (11.0%)

Conservative target 89

MP Julia Drown

1997 (Turnout 72.9%)			
	Labour	23,943	46.8%
	Conservative	18,298	35.8%
	Liberal Democrat	7,371	14.4%
	Referendum	1,273	2.5%
	Others	277	0.6%

Health administrator Julia Drown pulled off a decisive victory against Conservative Simon Coombs, who had represented the single Swindon seat since 1983, with an estimated swing of 14.6% (although if the boundary estimates for North are wrong the swings in the two seats were in fact rather closer to each other and the national average). Most of the seat is of the same general quasi-New Town type as North, but there are more tradition-ally Conservative areas such as Old Town and Lawns, and a rural element at Wroughton and Chiseldon. Labour did quite badly in the 2000 local elections, as in North, but the benefits were divided between the Conservatives and Liberal Democrats, and the centre party chipped away at the Tory wards too.

The Conservatives were ahead by 10 points in the Euro election, although South's voters were almost as unenthused by the contest as North's, and had some sort of lead in the 2000 local elections. Swindon's growth and modernity means that its political preferences are still rather unformed, and are prone to change as the bulldozers move across this northern corner of Wiltshire. Simon Coombs tries to get back into parlia-ment at the next election and will mount a strong challenge in what probably really is the more vulnerable of the two Swindon Labour seats.

Taunton

Liberal Democrat majority 2,443 (4.0%)

Conservative target 27

MP Jackie Ballard

1997 (Turnout 76.5%)	Liberal Democrat	26,064	42.7%
	Conservative	23,621	38.7%
	Labour	8,248	13.5%
	Referendum	2,760	4.5%
	Other	318	0.5%

Taunton was one of the more expected Liberal Democrat gains of 1997. Jackie Ballard, a local government veteran, ousted David Nicholson, a graduate of the Conservative Central Office and MP since 1987, but by a relatively narrow 4% margin and on a pretty small rise in the Lib Dem (1.9%) and fall in the Conservative (7.3%) votes. Taunton is a less than fascinating town, but it is prosperous for Somerset and has had its growth fuelled by rapid access from the M5 and InterCity railways. Like many towns it has spawned a 'Little America' district of office parks, DIY stores and multiplexes by a motorway junction, and an industrial hinterland with the deceptively bucolic name of 'Norton Fitzwarren' where cider is mass-produced. But Taunton is too small for a seat of its own and the constituency extends far out to the west across the wilds of Exmoor to Dulverton inland from Minehead.

Taunton has less of a Liberal history than most of Somerset; the SDP fought the seat in 1983 and only in 1992 did the Lib Dems come within striking distance. The most notable events in Liberal history in the area involved the execution of a dog called Rinka a few yards within its borders in 1975 and the consequent arraignment of Jeremy Thorpe in Minehead's courtroom in 1978. Ballard is broadly on the community politics 'left' of the party and made a doomed bid for the leadership in 1999. 1999 was a disaster for local Lib Dems; they lost Taunton Deane council in May, and in June were outpolled 45–18 by the Tories in the Euro election. Ballard's Conservative opponent is Adrian Flook, a Wandsworth councillor and banker; if he wins he will surely delight headline writers.

Teignbridge

Conservative majority 281 (0.4%)

Liberal Democrat target

MP Patrick Nicholls

1997 (Turnout 76.9%)	Conservative	24,679	39.2%
	Liberal Democrat	24,398	38.8%
	Labour	11,311	18.0%
	UK Independence	1,601	2.5%
	Green	817	1.3%
	Other	139	0.2%

Teignbridge is in east Devon, between Exeter and Torbay. As its name suggests, it spans the river Teign, from the coast at Teignmouth inland into Dartmoor. It also covers the genteel coastal town of Dawlish, where main line train travellers are carried along a viaduct across the beach, and some Exeter fringe areas such as Kenn valley. Although it sounds like a recipe for a safe Conservative seat, this is Devon and such things cannot be taken for granted. Patrick Nicholls, the pushy and accident-prone Tory MP since 1983, survived only narrowly. He was probably helped by the failure of the Referendum Party to put up against him, in deference perhaps to the xeno-phobic sentiments Nicholls expressed in a local paper.

1999 was a good year for the Teignbridge Conservatives. They increased their council strength from 7 to 19 in May (many councillors in Teignbridge are Independent, and the Tory gains were mainly from the Liberal Democrats, so this was a strong showing). Their main local opponents then crashed to fourth place in the Euro election, the Tories polling 40.2% to 16% for the UKIP, 15.5% for Labour and only 15.1% for the Liberal Democrats. Richard Younger-Ross, narrowly denied in 1997, will have to pick up and dust down a bedraggled local party if he is to win, or even get as close to Nicholls, next time.

Tiverton and Honiton

Conservative majority 1,653 (2.8%)

Liberal Democrat target

MP Angela Browning

1997 (Turnout 77.9%)			
	Conservative	24,438	41.3%
	Liberal Democrat	22,785	38.5%
	Labour	7,598	12.8%
	Referendum	2,952	5.0%
	Liberal	635	1.1%
	Green	485	0.8%
	Other	236	0.4%

Tiverton and Honiton (mostly the old Tiverton seat) is a large rural constituency wrapped around Exeter, sending Conservative frontbencher Angela Browning to parliament. The Honiton and Ottery St. Mary portion is from the very Conservative East Devon district, but Tiverton and Cullompton are in the Mid Devon district, where the Liberal Democrats put up stronger resistance to the Conservatives in the May 1999 district elections. In June, the Conservatives were 26.1% ahead in the Euro election, and the only way in which it was a good showing for the Liberal Democrats was that they maintained second place (unlike Teignbridge or Torbay). Jim Barnard, the Liberal Democrat who obtained a pretty respectable (8.4%) swing against Browning in 1997 tries again, but the Conservatives must be confident that they are past the worst here.

Torbay

Liberal Democrat majority 12 (0.0%)

Conservative target 2

MP Adrian Sanders

1997 (Turnout 73.8%)			
	Liberal Democrat	21,094	39.6%
	Conservative	21,082	39.5%
	Labour	7,923	14.9%
	UK Independence	1,962	3.7%
	Liberal	1,161	2.2%
	Other	100	0.2%

Torbay likes to call itself the English Riviera. True enough, there are sandy beaches and the mild climate of Devon allows palm trees to grow, but it is rather provincial compared to Cannes. The seat includes Torquay and Paignton, but the third Torbay town of Brixham is in the Totnes seat. Torbay is usually one of the first seats to declare its results on election night; Conservative holds in 1987 and 1992 pointed to the disappointment of centre party hopes. In 1997, however, a grey bar appeared at the bottom of the nation's TV screens as 'Recount in Torbay' was all the news hour after hour.

The Liberal Democrats eventually gained Torbay with a majority of 12 over maverick Tory Rupert Allason in 1997. Adrian Sanders, who had been cruelly denied by a 'Literal Democrat' interloper in the Euro election of 1994, at last had some electoral luck. There are entertaining legends about how exactly Allason lost those crucial twelve votes. Sanders has been a good, diligent MP but his council colleagues have done him no favours; Liberal Democrat control of Torbay was punctuated by bitter splits and rows.

Nearly unbelievably, the Liberal Democrats came fourth in the Euro election; the Conservatives on 41.6%, Labour on 16.8%, UKIP on 15.6% were all ahead of the defending party on 15.3%. This very bad result was followed by a sweeping Conservative victory in the all-out local elections of May 2000, with 32 councillors to a forlorn 4 Liberal Democrats. All the portents are for the Conservative candidate Christian Sweeting to overhaul what, since the Winchester by-election, is the shakiest Liberal Democrat seat in the land.

Torridge and West Devon

Liberal Democrat majority 1,957 (3.3%)

Conservative target 24

MP John Burnett

1997 (Turnout 77.7%)			
	Liberal Democrat	24,744	41.8%
	Conservative	22,787	38.5%
	Labour	7,319	12.4%
	Referendum	1,946	3.3%
	UK Independence	1,841	3.1%
	Liberal	508	0.9%

This constituency always proves a problem in alphabetical listings: does it begin with W, D or T? Despite this problem its name describes where it is pretty well. It is a large and sparsely populated seat stretching nearly the entire north-south span of Devon. It is one of the two seats (with Tiverton & Honiton) in the south west to rank among the top 20 agricultural seats in Britain. It has no large urban centres, but a scatter of resort and market towns such as Bideford, Great Torrington and, in the south, Tavistock. The Torrington portion was briefly Liberal under Mark Bonham Carter in 1958-59, but for the most part the moderate Conservatism of Tavistock's last MP as a separate seat (1966-74), Michael Heseltine, has prevailed.

The two traditions of the seat converged in December 1995 thanks to the defection of the sitting Conservative MP Emma Nicholson to the Liberal Democrats. Nicholson did not fight the seat under her new colours in 1997 but handed over to John Burnett, a local farmer and solicitor who had fought the seat in 1987. Under the circumstances, Burnett's victory was less than convincing; the Lib Dem vote was barely changed on 1992 and the Conservative slide of 8.6% seems to have gone mostly to the Referendum and UKIP candidates (who polled 6.4% between them compared to a 3.3% Lib Dem majority). In Euro 99 Euroscepticism was rampant, and on what for the Euro elections was a respectable turnout of 33.5%. The UKIP polled an astonishing 19.2%, coming second to the Tories on 39.4%. Conservative Geoffrey Cox must start as the favourite, but Devon Lib Dems have shown themselves able to accumulate personal votes and Burnett has formidable local credentials.

Totnes

Conservative majority 877 (1.6%)

Liberal Democrat target

MP Anthony Steen

1997 (Turnout 76.0%)			
	Conservative	19,637	36.5%
	Liberal Democrat	18,760	34.9%
	Labour	8,796	16.4%
	Referendum	2,552	4.7%
	Ind Conservative	2,369	4.4%
	UK Independence	999	1.9%
	Others	656	1.2%

South Devon is a beautiful part of England; the scenery is gentler than the rugged Dartmoor country to the north or the Cornish countryside. The Totnes constituency includes the small towns of Salcombe and Kingsbridge to the south, Totnes itself in the north east, and the third Torbay town of Brixham on the coast in the north west. From 1983 to 1997 the seat covering most of this was known as South Hams. The sitting Conservative MP Sir Anthony Steen came here when his Liverpool Wavertree seat was abolished in 1983, and understandably did not return when Wavertree was reconstituted in 1997. Even so, Steen had a close call, with his vote dropping by 14.3% (although the 'Local Conservative' siphoned off some of this).

Torbay seems to have been the epicentre of a Liberal Democrat collapse since 1997; Totnes has been affected. In May 1999 the Conservatives stormed into control of South Hams council (admittedly mostly at the expense of Independents) and in June reduced the Liberal Democrats to fourth in the Euro election (as in Torbay and Teignbridge, except that here the Lib Dems were only 2.3% off coming fifth, behind the Greens!). Despite its closeness in 1997, Totnes looks likely to disappoint Liberal Democrat hopeful Rachel Oliver.

Wansdyke

Labour majority 4,799 (8.8%)

Conservative target 70

MP Dan Norris

1997 (Turnout 79.1%)	Labour	24,117	44.1%
	Conservative	19,318	35.3%
	Liberal Democrat	9,205	16.8%
	Referendum	1,327	2.4%
	UKIP	438	0.8%
	Others	317	0.6%

Wansdyke was a Labour long shot that came good in 1997. It consists of several small towns and surrounding countryside near Bath. Keynsham lies on the A4 and the railway line between Bath and Bristol and is a convenient commuter base for either city. It also includes the southern fringe of the Kingswood area, at Bitton and Hanham Abbots. The other main urban areas are the towns of Radstock and Midsomer Norton, which run together. These towns were the centre of the long defunct north Somerset coalfield and produced enough Labour votes to elect MPs for the Frome constituency in 1929 and 1945. The towns are now somewhat stranded in a hilly part of the country, deprived of a rail link by the 1960s Beeching cuts. Radstock in particular is still a Labour stronghold but was swamped by Conservative rural and suburban areas until Labour candidate Dan Norris, a former Bristol councillor and animal welfare campaigner, managed to win the seat with a massive 14.4% swing in 1997.

Like nearly all the long shot seats, the Conservatives were in the lead by a reasonable margin at the Euro election, leading 38.5% to 27.1%. Local government reform has meant a wholesale redrawing of wards in the area which makes comparison rather difficult, but the Conservative made no net gains in the Kingswood portion or the main part, now in the Bath & North East Somerset unitary council. Chris Watt is the Conservative candidate against Dan Norris next time.

Wells

Conservative majority 528 (0.9%)

Liberal Democrat target

MP David Heathcoat-Amory

1997 (Turnout 77.8%)			
	Conservative	22,208	39.4%
	Liberal Democrat	21,680	38.5%
	Labour	10,204	18.1%
	Referendum	2,196	3.9%
	Other	92	0.2%

Wells is a small city, dominated by an impressive cathedral and Bishop's Palace. The constituency also includes most of the Mendip council area except Frome. Among the Mendip hills lies the mysterious town of Glastonbury, which has become a New Age theme park on the basis of a rather fanciful legend about Jesus travelling to the area. Glastonbury Tor has a strange habit of appearing on the skyline at totally unexpected places. Shepton Mallet, a centre for part of rural Somerset, is in the seat too, as is an area of the Levels, stretching flatly to the coast at Burnham and Highbridge.

The Liberals have long set their hearts on winning Wells, but have been repeatedly rebuffed, and Conservative David Heathcoat-Amory, now a senior figure in the party and from a famous Somerset political family, defeated Peter Gold who had previously fought Sheffield Hallam. An important element in this outcome was the increase in the Labour vote; their candidate was Michael Eavis, the local farmer who organises and hosts the Glastonbury rock festival.

The Conservatives were over 30 points clear in the Euro election and are unlikely to be defeated by Liberal Democrat aspirant Graham Oakes.

Weston-super-Mare

Liberal Democrat majority 1,274 (2.4%)

Conservative target 18

MP Brian Cotter

1997 (Turnout 73.7%)	Liberal Democrat	21,407	40.1%
	Conservative	20,133	37.7%
	Labour	9,557	17.9%
	Referendum	2,280	4.3%

Weston-super-Mare gave Jeffrey Archer and John Cleese to the world – Archer's family, strangely, took over a flat from the Cleese family. Archer wears the town's name with pride in his peerage, although whether Weston is so proud of the connection is another matter. For the most part Archer's Conservatism has prevailed, but in 1997 Weston came into line with the Cleese tradition by voting for the Liberal Democrats. It was yet another Conservative defeat in a seaside resort constituency. Weston is quite close to Bristol and has been able to counteract the decline of the English holiday resort and its own dubious charms in this respect (cynics call it Weston-super-Mud) by developing as a commuting and day trip centre.

As with many south western seats, the Liberal Democrats melted down in 1999. Weston-super-Mare and the neighbouring safe Tory seat of Woodspring are part of North Somerset unitary council, which the Conservatives gained in May 1999 while the Lib Dems collapsed from being the largest single party on the council to third, behind Labour who did well. The same pattern applied in June, with the Lib Dems third and over 30 points adrift of the Conservatives. Brian Cotter must hope that his party's fortunes revive and that he can command a personal vote, and squeeze Labour's growing support here; Conservative candidate John Penrose has grounds for some optimism.

East Anglia and Essex

Conservative Targets

Target No	Constituency		Labour Lead
C13	Harwich	1,216	2.3%
C14	Norfolk North West	1,339	2.3%
C15	Castle Point	1,143	2.4%
C19	Braintree	1,451	2.6%
C125	Peterborough	7,323	15.1%
C141	Norwich North	9,470	17.2%
C143	Great Yarmouth	8,668	17.7%
C169	Waveney	12,093	21.5%
C170	Ipswich	10,436	21.6%
C175	Harlow	10,514	22.0%
C200	Basildon	13,280	25.0%

(Liberal Democrat held)

			Lib Dem Lead
C22	Colchester	1,581	3.0%

Labour Targets

			Conservative Lead
L5	Bury St Edmunds	368	0.7%
L12	Norfolk Mid	1,336	2.3%
L14	Billericay	1,356	2.5%

Liberal Democrat Target

	Conservative Lead	
Norfolk North	1,293	2.2%

East Anglia and Essex were strongholds of the Conservatives during the 1970s and 1980s, and even after 1997 its parliamentary delegation was still majority Conservative: 24 Conservatives, 14 Labour and one Lib Dem. This marked a considerable Labour recovery – the party was reduced to one seat in the region in 1987 and was only up to 4 in 1992 – but it was much less impressive than the Labour triumph of 1945 in the region. Then, Labour won 18, plus one for the allied Common Wealth Party, to one Liberal and eight Conservatives. The east is the one region with a substantial number of seats that were Labour in 1945 but Conservative in 1997 (Norfolk SW, Norfolk S, Norfolk N, Chelmsford, Cambridgeshire and Sudbury). It used to be a very traditional agricultural region, with a regional capital at Norwich, some ports and resorts and a scatter of market towns. While there is still a great deal of arable farming, East Anglia is more dependent on trade, particularly with Europe, and has developed high-tech industry particularly around Cambridge.

Essex is technically in the south east rather than East Anglia, but it is linked with the region. Southern Essex is strongly influenced by London, including wealthy commuter towns, New Towns and industrial sprawl. Northern Essex is more rural and less ravaged by development.

Both parts of the region have grown in population, causing a steady increase in the number of parliamentary constituencies, from 27 in 1955–70, 31 in 1974–79, 36 in 1983–92 and 39 now. Each new allocation has been a long-term benefit to the Conservatives. By the 1990s the region sent a concentration of senior Tories to Westminster – John Major, Brian Mawhinney, Richard Ryder, John MacGregor, John Gummer and Gillian Shephard were said to comprise an 'East Anglian mafia'.

Like London, another economically dynamic region, Anglia and Essex swung to the Conservatives in 1987 but then exceeded the national movement to Labour both in 1992 and 1997. Unlike London, the Conservatives have made some headway in recovering from their losses since then, particularly along the coast. East Anglia is a rather Eurosceptic region, electing one UKIP list MEP in 1999, and Labour seem to have suffered. Both Southend seats looked marginal in 1997 but racked up colossal Conservative leads in the 1999 Euro and 2000 local elections. The

Conservatives also superficially look exposed in many rural seats but should be able to hold on, although Norfolk South West is worth noting. It once oscillated between Labour and Conservative on tiny majorities, often going the 'wrong' way at elections, but had large Tory majorities in the 1970s and 1980s and was held by Gillian Shephard in 1997 despite a big swing. Could it revive its strange traditions? There was, admittedly, no sign that it was about to do so in the 1999 local elections.

In closer detail, there are three apparently safe Labour seats (majorities over 25%) in the region on 1997 figures, although there is not a single seat the Conservatives did not win at some point in the 1980s. The three are Thurrock, Cambridge and Norwich South. The latter two have seen considerable Lib Dem activity in local elections, and in May 2000 Labour trailed them by 20 points in the Norwich South city wards (there are also two South Norfolk wards in the seat). In Cambridge Labour enjoyed only a slim lead in the constituency as the Lib Dems gained the City Council and the Greens polled well. The Lib Dems are also locally active in South Norfolk and maintained control of the council in 1999; the Tories held the seat with only 40% of the vote in 1997 against split opposition.

Basildon

Labour majority 13,280 (25.0%)

Conservative target 200

MP Angela Smith

1997 (Turnout 71.6%)			
	Labour	29,646	55.8%
	Conservative	16,366	30.8%
	Liberal Democrat	4,608	8.7%
	Referendum	2,462	4.6%

Basildon won emblematic status in 1992 when the Conservatives held the seat early on election night with a small adverse swing. It was not the first time the seat had disappointed Labour – its predecessors stayed Tory in 1964 and swung sharply to the right in 1979. Basildon is a large New Town in south Essex, but this seat is not identical to the town. New Town neighbourhoods such as Pitsea and Laindon are in the Billericay seat, and this 'Basildon' seat also includes the eastern reaches of Thurrock borough around Stanford-le-Hope, whose private estates and massive oil refinery nestle in a bend of the Thames.

There was a 13.2% swing from Labour to Conservative in comparable wards between May 1999 and May 2000, one of the best Conservative showings. Not all the Thurrock wards are contested every year, but as far as one could tell the Tories nosed ahead in the constituency as a whole by a couple of hundred votes in 2000. Labour were still 2.2% ahead in the Euro elections, so this must be a worrying performance for the party, although Basildon is undoubtedly volatile in local elections – the Tories won everything in May 1992 and nothing in May 1994. Labour's Angela Smith defends the seat against Conservative Dominic Schofield, and cannot take victory for granted on the basis of recent results.

Billericay

Conservative majority 1,356 (2.5%)

Labour target 14

MP Teresa Gorman

1997 (Turnout 72.1%)			
	Conservative	22,033	39.8%
	Labour	20,677	37.3%
	Liberal Democrat	8,763	15.8%
	Loyal Conservative	3,377	6.1%
	Other	570	1.0%

Paul Richards was very nearly a Labour hero of May 1997 alongside Stephen Twigg and Gisela Stuart, but he fell tantalisingly short of ousting maverick Eurosceptic Tory Teresa Gorman despite an enormous 17.6% swing. Gorman had been one of the anti-Europe 'whipless wonders' of 1994-95 and the saved deposit for a 'Loyal Conservative' showed that, like the Tory whips, many Billericay Tories had tired of her antics. While she suffered from this, her semi-detached attitude to the Major government spared her Eurosceptic competition.

Billericay is essentially outer Basildon. The Basildon district is sharply divided between the New Town and the outlying areas grouped in this seat. Billericay and Wickford are wealthy commuter towns (commuting to the City, not to Basildon) where Labour polls few votes in local elections and the battle is between Lib Dems and Tories. Since 1997 the constituency has also included the New Town neighbourhoods of Pitsea and Laindon, on the east and west edges of Basildon where Labour has stronger support.

Gorman has run into further trouble since 1997 for falling foul of the rules on standards of conduct and declaration of interests; she was temporarily suspended from the Commons and has announced her retirement. There had previously been some speculation that Martin Bell might transfer his sleaze-busting operations here from Tatton, and some hints from the UKIP that a Tory MP might soon transfer allegiance to them. In normal circumstances, Billericay would be an uncomplicated Conservative hold, but if Gorman defected Labour might triumph against divided right wing opposition; and if the man in the white suit rode into town all bets would be off.

Braintree

Labour majority 1,451 (2.6%)

Conservative target 19

MP Alan Hurst

1997 (Turnout 76.1%)			
	Labour	23,729	42.7%
	Conservative	22,278	40.1%
	Liberal Democrat	6,418	11.5%
	Referendum	2,165	1.9%
	Green	712	1.3%
	Other	274	0.5%

Few people thought the Tories were in real trouble in the mid-Essex seat of Braintree in 1997; but in the event Tony Newton joined the cull of seven Tory cabinet ministers who were defeated. The constituency is based around the two towns of Braintree and Witham (the latter dominated by a large brewery) and extends northward into the gentle hills as far as Great Bardfield. To the political historian it is Maldon without the town of Maldon, and will always be associated with flamboyant Labour MP Tom Driberg who represented the seat from 1942–55.

Its recent MPs have been less notorious, but generally well regarded. Newton's un-flashy personal charm and good constituency record won him many admirers. His Labour replacement, Alan Hurst, combines sceptical loyalty to the government with a special concern for rural interests. His Tory challenger, Brooks Newmark, is a businessman and former candidate for Newcastle Central who faces the 'double incumbency' factor. Newton's share in 1997 was boosted by a personal vote, which will vanish from the Tory share next time while Alan Hurst gains one. This is not a massive factor in British politics, worth perhaps 1,000 votes net, but it was noticeable among Tory MPs who gained seats in 1983 and could help Labour's new MPs of 1997. Labour's support in Braintree was strong in the 1999 council elections – a lead of 43–34 over the Conservatives slightly overstates the position thanks to Independents, but the Labour lead was still larger than in 1997. The Tory lead in the Euro election was 40–29, although Braintree was rare in that the Conservative share fell from 1997 to 1999. Braintree is likely to be marginal again, and Labour seem to be able to call upon local strength which may dampen any national movement against the party.

Bury St Edmunds

Conservative majority 368 (0.7%)

Labour target 5

MP David Ruffley

1997 (Turnout 75.0%)			
	Conservative	21,290	38.3%
	Labour	20,922	37.7%
	Liberal Democrat	10,102	18.2%
	Referendum	2,939	5.3%
	Other	272	

'BSE' was good news for the Conservatives in only one sense in 1997 – Bury St Edmunds stayed Conservative, as did the other rural Suffolk seats, but the thin blue line was at its thinnest. The Tories were lucky that a rural lead of 13,202 was spread thinly and advantageously over five seats while the two urban seats in the county were Labour by a combined margin of 22,529; such are the anomalies of first past the post elections.

Bury St Edmunds is an ecclesiastical, quiet, conservative town; the seat bearing its name extends across a wide rural area of Mid Suffolk, including the towns of Stowmarket and Needham Market. Stowmarket is a Labour centre, and the party has some support in Bury itself, but most of it is a thoroughly rural division. Labour did well to win control of the St. Edmundsbury council (whose area is different from the seat) in 1995 but the

Tories regained it in 1999 and improved their position on Mid Suffolk council too. The Tories led 40–23 in the Euro election and the UKIP share at 12% was quite high. As a mainly rural seat it seems an unlikely candidate for a further Labour advance and the new MP in 1997, David Ruffley, should win more comfortably next time.

Castle Point

Labour majority 1,143 (2.4%)

Conservative target 15

MP Christine Butler

1997 (Turnout 72.3%)			
	Labour	20,605	42.4%
	Conservative	19,462	40.1%
	Liberal Democrat	4,477	9.2%
	Referendum	2,700	5.6%
	Other	1,301	2.7%

Castle Point is perhaps the true heartland of Essex. Unlike Basildon and Harlow it is the product of private development rather than planning and as a result it is among the two or three most completely owner-occupied constituencies in Britain. It consists of Benfleet, a residential town by the A13 bordering on Southend, and Canvey Island. The Island is an extraordinary, un-English flat landscape enclosed by a Dutch-built sea wall, with a rather half-hearted seaside resort alongside oil refineries, landfill and sprawling private estates.

Castle Point and its predecessors were heavily Conservative after 1950 until a massive 17% swing turned the seat Labour in 1997. The change was prefigured by a Labour landslide in the 1995 local elections, in which more voters turned out for Labour than in the 1992 general election. Labour also won the 1999 local elections but were miles behind the Tories in the 1999 Euro elections. The Labour MP is Christine Butler. The Conservative MP she surprisingly ejected in 1997, Robert Spink, is challenging again and it would be a major turn up for the book if he failed to resume his parliamentary career.

Colchester

Liberal Democrat majority 1,581 (3.0%)

Conservative target 22

Possible Labour target

MP Bob Russell

1997 (Turnout 69.6%)			
	Liberal Democrat	17,886	34.4%
	Conservative	16,305	31.4%
	Labour	15,891	30.5%
	Referendum	1,776	3.4%
	Other	148	

Colchester is a very ancient town, having been a Roman settlement sacked by Boudicca – perhaps the original Essex Eurosceptic – and then a Norman centre. Currently it is a rather odd mix of garrison and university town, which can give nights on the town here a bit of an edge. The University of Essex is a centre of electoral studies, and there is now something interesting on the doorstep.

Colchester is an area of Lib Dem activity in local elections, and the reunited town seat created in 1997 gave them a chance to translate this into parliamentary success. They managed – just. It was the closest three-way battle in the country with all three main parties winning just over 30%. The picture has been just as confused since, with small Conservative gains from both other parties in May 2000 but the Lib Dems staying strong. It was very different in the Euro election, with the Lib Dems slumping to third, on 19% to 26% Labour and 36% Conservative. Labour's strength will make it difficult for Bob Russell to squeeze the party's vote, and Tory Kevin Bentley will hope to benefit. Colchester will be a fascinating battle in the next election and it would be a brave pundit who would predict victory for any party.

Great Yarmouth

Labour majority 8,668 (17.7%)

Conservative target 143

MP Tony Wright

1997 (Turnout 71.1%)	Labour	26,084	53.4%
	Conservative	17,416	35.6%
	Liberal Democrat	5,381	11.0%

Great Yarmouth is a large town on the east coast of Norfolk. It is primarily a holiday resort but it is affected by the North Sea energy sector, principally gas this far south. Like other coastal towns, Great Yarmouth's Labour Party improved its position in 1992 and achieved a gain on a high swing (13.9%) in 1997 when council leader Tony Wright (not to be confused with the political scientist of the same name from Cannock Chase) was elected against Eurosceptic Michael Carttiss. Carttiss had been given a clear run by the Referendum Party. Next time, Charles Reynolds is the Tory standard-bearer.

However, like other seaside towns Great Yarmouth has swung violently against Labour since 1997. The Conservatives were ahead by 41.1% to 34% in the Euro election and gained seven seats in each of the 1999 and 2000 borough elections, winning control in May 2000. Not all wards are contested each time, but the Conservative lead was probably in double figures in 2000. Great Yarmouth is an economically depressed town. Only 32 UK constituencies had worse unemployment in April 2000, at 8.8%, and even more ominously there are only seven constituencies with smaller falls in the unemployment rate since 1996. Labour need to do something to help places like Great Yarmouth if the party is to regain their loyalty.

Harlow

Labour majority 10,514 (22.0%)

Conservative target 175

MP Bill Rammell

1997 (Turnout 74.4%)	Labour	25,861	54.1%
	Conservative	15,347	32.1%
	Liberal Democrat	4,523	9.5%
	Referendum	1,422	3.0%
	UK Independence	340	0.7%
	BNP	319	0.7%

Harlow was one of the seats in which Conservatism proved popular in the 1980s; in the 1987 election it looked almost safe for moderate MP Jerry Hayes. As in many of the other southern new and expanded town seats Labour took Harlow on a massive swing in 1997 and MP Bill Rammell won a five-figure majority. Hayes had been fending off allegations about his private life, but they seem to have done him little electoral harm; his vote was pretty much the same as that for Conservative council candidates in the synchronous local elections of 1 May 1997.

The New Town is showing its age and parts of the town seem as run down as the streets their residents left in north London 45 years ago. Labour has ruled the council since it was established, remaining dominant throughout the 1980s, but they lost seats heavily to the Conservatives and Lib Dems in 2000. In addition, the constituency also includes several pretty villages in Epping Forest district such as Roydon and Sheering where Labour are weak.

Harlow should be one of the more interesting contests of the next general election. Labour were 1% ahead in the 1999 Euro elections; the Conservatives probably just ahead in the constituency in May 2000. Labour's Bill Rammell has strong local roots, and to confound stereotypes is an articulate pro-European Essex Man. The Conservative challenger, Robert Halfon, is energetic and personable, and speaks with some conviction about 'compassionate Conservatism' providing for the vulnerable in society.

Harwich

Labour majority 1,216 (2.3%)

Conservative target 13

MP Ivan Henderson

1997 (Turnout 70.5%)	Labour	20,740	38.8%
	Conservative	19,524	36.5%
	Liberal Democrat	7,037	13.1%
	Referendum	4,923	9.2%
	Other	1,290	2.4%

Essex is a large and varied county, stretching from Epping, with its tube line, to Harwich, nearly 80 miles away. Harwich is a working trading and ferry port, with links primarily to Holland and Scandinavia. It is a rather charming town, little visited because it is so far off the beaten track. The constituency also includes a strip of coast including the seaside towns of Walton on the Naze and genteel Frinton, stretching down to Clacton-on-Sea. Clacton is a tired, dowdy seaside resort. The Clacton-Frinton-Walton area is a major retirement district and a high proportion of the population are elderly. Labour won most of the wards in Harwich and Clacton towns in the May 1999 local elections but had little support in the smaller centres.

Harwich was safely Conservative from 1931 until 1997, when it suddenly fell to Labour on a swing of over 14%. Harwich based dockworker Ivan Henderson defeated the migrant Tory Iain Sproat, who had abandoned Aberdeen South and been defeated at Roxburgh in 1983 and who returned to parliament for the seemingly safe Harwich in 1992. There are very few seats where it can be said with any confidence that the Referendum Party cost the Conservatives a seat; Harwich may just be one of them as their candidate polled 9.2% compared to a Labour lead of 2.3%. It was the strongest UK Independence party seat in the Eastern Region in the Euro election as well, with 14.8%; the 1997 Referendum candidate Jeffrey Titford was elected an MEP. Harwich has a curiously divided attitude to Europe, relying on trade but with massive fortifications outside the town reflecting fears of invasion in 1802–15, 1914–18 and 1939–45.

The main parties were about level pegging in May 1999 but the Tory lead stretched to 45–23 in June. Iain Sproat is standing again for the Conservatives and must hope that his electoral rejections do not come in threes. The position taken by the UKIP may well be important, as might Henderson's record as an MP. It is hard to imagine Labour ever having won this outpost of Essex in the first place.

Ipswich

Labour majority 10,436 (21.6%)

Conservative target 170

MP Jamie Cann

1997 (Turnout 71.1%)			
	Labour	25,484	52.7%
	Conservative	15,048	31.1%
	Liberal Democrat	5,881	12.2%
	Referendum	1,637	3.4%
	UK Independence	208	0.4%
	Other	107	0.2%

Ipswich is a large and rather independent town, an aspirant for city status and the centre for a considerable rural hinterland. Its independence is apparent in its eccentric political behaviour in the last 30 years. Conservative Ernle Money gained it by 13 votes in 1970 and had a swing in his favour in February 1974, but lost to Labour's Ken Weetch in October 1974. Weetch held the seat well in Labour's disaster years of 1979 and 1983, but lost it to the Tories against the national trend in 1987. The current MP Jamie Cann won it back on a small swing in 1992, and enjoyed a 10.5% swing in his favour in 1997. While par for the course nationally, it was low for a Labour gain of 1992.

Labour led by a small margin, 1.2%, in the Euro election, and the party has also lost considerable ground in local elections. The Conservatives were ahead in the borough, which also includes four wards outside the constituency, on a very high swing since 1996, and cannot be ruled out. Ipswich may yet have surprises up its sleeve. Tory Edward Wild takes on Cann, a socially conservative Labour MP, at the next election.

Norfolk Mid

Conservative majority 1,336 (2.3%)

Labour target 12

MP Keith Simpson

1997 (Turnout 76.1%)	Conservative	22,739	39.6%
	Labour	21,403	37.3%
	Liberal Democrat	8,617	15.0%
	Referendum	3,229	5.6%
	Green	1,254	2.2%
	Other	215	0.4%

Mid Norfolk is a rural seat where the Conservatives had a close call in 1997 but should be able to do a bit better next time. On the map, it is shaped a little like a shapely leg, bent at Norwich and terminating at the shoe-shaped Great Yarmouth. It consists of the rural areas of the Broadland District, including part of the Broads around Acle, and the East Dereham part of the Breckland district. In the Euro election the Conservatives led 42–26, not a massive swing since 1997.

Labour's 2000 meltdown in Broadland was concentrated in the suburban areas in Norwich North, and Aylsham, far up towards the northern edge of Mid Norfolk, was the one ward to survive. In the Breckland council elections in 1999, East Dereham was majority Labour but the rural areas were Conservative. There is less rural radicalism here than in Norfolk N or NW. This is moderate Tory Keith Simpson's first term, and it would be an upset if it was not to be followed by a second after the next election.

Norfolk North

Conservative majority 1,293 (2.2%)

Liberal Democrat target

MP David Prior

1997 (Turnout 76.2%)	Conservative	21,456	36.5%
	Liberal Democrat	20,163	34.3%
	Labour	14,736	25.1%
	Referendum	2,458	4.2%

Norfolk North is a mainly rural seat with a strong agricultural presence hugging the north coast of Norfolk with its string of small seaside resorts, the largest of which is Cromer. Holidaymakers also come to the Broads.

Labour's stronger areas, rather unusually, are in the agricultural areas of Erpingham and the small inland towns. The agricultural workers' vote kept the seat Labour throughout the Tory 1950s, but Labour lost in 1970 and the Conservatives have never lost the seat since. It nearly happened in 1997, but the Conservatives won this seat with an ignominious 36.5% of the vote thanks to a split in the opposition. The Liberal Democrats were a strong second, but Labour were not going to lie down and die and they increased their vote a little to 25.1%. In theory it should be a top Lib Dem target but the Labour vote is very resistant – 19.1% even in the 1983 election. Conservative MP David Prior, a moderate presence in today's Tory party, can probably rely on holding the seat on another minority vote, although Lib Dem Norman Lamb who fought the seat in 1992 and achieved a strong swing in his favour in 1997 cannot be written off and will hope it is third time lucky.

Norfolk North West

Labour majority 1,339 (2.3%)

Conservative target 14

MP George Turner

1997 (Turnout 74.6%)			
	Labour	25,250	43.8%
	Conservative	23,911	41.5%
	Liberal Democrat	5,513	9.6%
	Referendum	2,923	5.1%

There are several rural seats in Norfolk that were usually Labour between the elections of 1945 and 1970: South West, North, and King's Lynn. All then swung strongly to the Tories in the 1970s, but King's Lynn's Tory MP Christopher Brocklebank-Fowler uniquely defected to the SDP and polled well in 1983. After that Labour reasserted itself gradually and swept to a narrow victory in 1997. Norfolk NW is basically King's Lynn and its rural hinterland, plus a stretch of the coastline where the Wash and the North Sea join, around Heacham and Hunstanton.

Labour are dominant in the town of King's Lynn and also enjoy strong support in swathes of the rural areas to the south west and north east of the town, although the area is a patchwork of villages and small towns with their own political traditions and affiliations. The coast is rather

Conservative. There was a tiny swing between the 1997 general election and the May 1999 local elections, although it was enough to deprive Labour of control over the borough council (won in 1995). The Conservatives led by 44–42% in the wards in the Norfolk NW constituency, but Labour and Lib Dems often did not contest each other's rural wards. In the Euro election the Tories led by 46–29%. Norfolk NW is a highly marginal seat, as rural Norfolk often was during 1945–70. Back then, Norfolk seats were given to small swings and this tradition, too, may well revive in future elections. The battle is again between Labour's George Turner, who gained the seat in 1997, and Tory Henry Bellingham, who won the seat from Brocklebank-Fowler in 1983.

Norwich North

Labour majority 9,470 (17.2%)

Conservative target 141

MP Ian Gibson

1997 (Turnout 75.7%)			
	Labour	27,346	49.7%
	Conservative	17,876	32.5%
	Liberal Democrat	6,951	12.6%
	Referendum	1,777	3.2%
	Others	1,107	2.0%

The purist might object to the name of this seat; only 28,000 of its electors are actually in Norwich city council's area, and rather more – 43,000 or so – are in Broadland council's area. The city portion is mainly Labour, with a high proportion of council tenants, but Norwich North is marginal mainly because of the suburban elements. The suburbs are grouped into three townships – Thorpe St. Andrew to the east, and Sprowston and Hellesdon to the north, plus some other adjoining areas. They are mainly Conservative, but not overwhelmingly so with the exception of the Taverham area added to the seat in 1997.

The Conservatives regained Broadland in May 1999, and enjoyed a sweeping victory in May 2000, gaining six seats, mostly in the Norwich suburbs. The Conservative lead in the Norwich North seat was 43–32% in May 2000, but several Broadland seats were not up for election and would only have increased the lead. This was a massive swing, based on

Conservative gains in the suburbs and a slump in turnout in the Labour city wards, and was a clear Tory improvement on the 1999 Euro election when they led by 4.4%. Labour MP Ian Gibson, who gained the seat in 1997, faces a strong potential challenge from Conservative Kay Mason.

Peterborough

Labour majority 7,323 (15.1%)

Conservative target 125

MP Helen Brinton

1997 (Turnout 72.8%)			
	Labour	24,365	50.3%
	Conservative	17,042	35.2%
	Liberal Democrat	5,170	10.7%
	Referendum	924	1.9%
	UK Independence	317	0.7%
	Others	609	1.3%

In the 1960s and 1970s Peterborough was renowned for its very close election results – the Tories held the seat by 3 votes in 1966 and 22 votes in February 1974. More recently it has produced larger majorities, first for the Conservatives and in 1997 for Labour.

Peterborough is a frontier town between the south east, East Anglia and the midlands. As such it has exploited its transport links well and jobs have been created in distributive trades such as Freeman's catalogues and the Post Office. It was designated a New Town in 1968 although it is also a very old town – a Roman centre with a fine mediaeval cathedral. The new estates ring the town to the north, east and south-west (although the south of Peterborough is in the Cambridgeshire NW constituency).

The Conservatives were miles ahead in Peterborough in the May 2000 local elections. Quite how far it is difficult to say as not all wards were being contested and the pattern of the parties' decisions to contest wards is erratic, but they were almost certainly further ahead than they were in the 1992 general election. The city is still growing, and recent growth has tended to be in Conservative areas such as the suburb of Werrington. Peterborough's centre vote is split between old style Liberals and the very weak Lib Dems; it is a very two-party part of the world. Conservative candidate Kevin Hall is in a position to put up a strong fight against Blairite MP Helen Brinton.

Waveney

Labour majority 12,093 (21.5%)

Conservative target 169

MP Bob Blizzard

1997 (Turnout 74.6%)	Labour	31,486	56.0%
	Conservative	19,393	34.5%
	Liberal Democrat	5,054	9.0%
	Other	318	0.6%

'Waveney' is the east coast port of Lowestoft, tucked into the north eastern corner of Suffolk, plus the inland towns of Beccles and Bungay. Although marginal, it has tended to remain with the same party for quite long periods (Labour 1945-59, Conservative 1959-97) despite national swings of the pendulum and was the base of Jim Prior's political career. Now it is the fiefdom of Bob Blizzard, who had previously led the local authority, and managed to 'sweep away' David Porter in 1997.

Labour's gain in 1997 was on a high swing and a very high share of the vote, surpassed only by a few of the party's other gains (e.g. Edmonton). However, Labour's more recent problems in coastal towns apply to Waveney. The Conservatives took a small (0.4%) lead in the 1999 Euro election, a good result in a seat with such a large 1997 Labour lead, and in May 2000 they made significant local election gains. Labour lost ground both in Lowestoft and the inland towns. Not all wards were contested, but as far as one can tell there was a very close balance between the main parties in the constituency. Tory Lee Scott must hope that Labour's big lead in 1997 melts like summer snow.

East Midlands

Conservative Targets

Target No	Constituency		Labour Lead
C5	Kettering	189	0.3%
C6	Wellingborough	187	0.3%
C9	Northampton South	744	1.3%
C39	Newark	3,016	5.8%
C57	Gedling	3,802	7.3%
C78	Broxtowe	5,575	9.6%
C88	Loughborough	5,712	10.9%
C126	Erewash	9,135	15.1%
C129	High Peak	8,791	15.4%
C148	Derby North	10,615	18.9%
C151	Northampton North	10,000	19.3%
C167	Amber Valley	11,613	21.2%
C174	Corby	11,860	22.0%
C188	Derbyshire South	13,967	23.3%
C196	Lincoln	11,130	23.9%

Labour Targets

Target No	Constituency		Conservative Lead
L7	Boston and Skegness	647	1.4%
L9	Bosworth	1,027	2.0%

Liberal Democrat Target

		Labour Lead
Chesterfield	5,775	11.2%

The East Midlands (Northamptonshire, Leicestershire, Lincolnshire, Derbyshire and Nottinghamshire) is a region which has always had its fair share of Labour – Conservative marginals, and at the last general election over a third of seats here changed hands. Labour's success was particularly dramatic in Northamptonshire, where they gained five of the county's six constituencies. Their performance was almost as impressive in Derbyshire (five gains) and Nottinghamshire (three gains); indeed there is a belt containing seven neighbouring constituencies either side of the M1 motorway through Derbyshire, Nottinghamshire and Leicestershire which all turned from blue to red in 1997.

The Conservatives performed particularly well in the East Midlands in 1983, when they increased their number of seats from 20 to 34 and reduced Labour to single figures, comfortably their worst showing since the war. The political behaviour of the East Midlands appeared similar to the south in that the Labour vote steadily disappeared from 1945 onwards; a pattern some put down to the building of the M1 and resulting growth in numbers of London-bound commuters. By 1983, the Conservative lead in the region was 20% and the SDP-Liberal Alliance were just 4% behind Labour. Labour had been reduced to just six seats in the Nottinghamshire/Derbyshire coalfield area plus one each in Derby and Leicester. It is worth remembering that the Conservative triumph of 1983 was so great that they gained all three constituencies in the city of Nottingham, along with two in Leicester; Labour had managed to hold all seats in both cities even in 1979.

After the meltdown of 1983, Labour's recovery in the East Midlands was painfully slow. In 1987 they regained three of the lost seats in Leicester and Nottingham, then the other two in 1992, together with just one solitary gain outside of the main cities: Sherwood, a new seat based on traditional mining areas which should never have gone Conservative in the first place. Before 1997 Labour had failed to make any sort of breakthrough in the smaller towns of the region, many of which they had held until the 1970s. This was all to change of course, with Northampton, Kettering, Corby, Wellingborough, Newark, Loughborough and Lincoln among the towns of 'middle England' to fall to the charms of 'New' Labour on 1st May, 1997. Many of these seats will now form the battleground at the next election, and the Conservatives will certainly need to regain at least some of them if they are to make any sort of national recovery.

Outside of the seats profiled below, it is difficult to see any surprises. Labour now appear rock solid in Leicester and Nottingham, and (the odd by-election apart) always have been in the old coalfield areas further north.

The only exception is the town of Chesterfield, where the Liberal Democrats have been slowly reducing the majority of Tony Benn, in a strikingly contrary pattern to their continuing weakness almost everywhere else in the region. Now that Benn is standing down, it is unclear whether Labour will recover in Chesterfield or if the Lib Dems will make a rare parliamentary breakthrough in a traditional Labour seat. Elsewhere the Conservatives should hold what they were left with in 1997, primarily a number of rural constituencies centred on Lincolnshire and Leicestershire outside of the main towns. Some of the majorities here last time must have given sitting Conservative MPs a fright (for example under 6,000 for Stephen Dorrell in Charnwood, assumed to be a super-safe new seat) but it will be a major shock if Labour gain anywhere which proved beyond them in 1997.

Amber Valley

Labour majority 11,613 (21.2%)

Conservative target 167

MP Judy Mallaber

1997 (Turnout 76.0%)			
	Labour	29,943	54.7%
	Conservative	18,330	33.5%
	Liberal Democrat	4,219	7.7%
	Referendum	2,283	4.2%

The evocative sounding Amber Valley is actually based on the small towns of Alfreton, Ripley and Heanor, all off the A38 a few miles north of Derby. This is very much marginal territory ('middle England' in more than one sense) with the constituency bordering three other key marginals: Derby North, Erewash and Broxtowe. Labour almost won this seat in 1992, when a huge (in pre-1997 terms) swing of 8% left Phillip Oppenheim hanging on by just 712 votes. But there was no way Oppenheim could survive five years later, and in the event a near-12% swing gave Labour's Judy Mallaber a gigantic majority exceeding 11,500.

Since those heady days, things have not been going so well for Labour here. The Conservatives had already made local advances in 1999 (and led narrowly in the Euro election), before an all-out local election in 2000 resulted in their gaining some 20 seats and control of Amber Valley council. On paper this appeared just about the worst Labour result of the local elections, but the headline figure exaggerated the change in vote, and in the constituency the Conservatives were only about 4% ahead, since some of their gains came in wards in the West Derbyshire constituency. Their parliamentary hopeful Gillian Shaw still has a lot of work if she is to unseat Judy Mallaber after a single term.

Boston and Skegness

Conservative majority 647 (1.4%)

Labour target 7

MP Sir Richard Body (retiring)

1997 (Turnout 68.9%)			
	Conservative	19,750	42.4%
	Labour	19,103	41.0%
	Liberal Democrat	7,721	16.6%

Although Labour won a large number of coastal constituencies for the first time in 1997, Boston and Skegness was not one of them. Instead, Conservative Euro-sceptic Sir Richard Body held on by just 647 votes, perhaps saved by the Referendum party refusing to field a candidate against him.

This Lincolnshire constituency was significantly altered prior to the 1997 election, when 23,500 electors from the seaside resorts of Skegness and Ingoldmells (formerly in the constituency of East Lindsey where Labour were extremely weak) were joined with the majority of the old Holland with Boston. Although Labour had never won that constituency either in the post-war period, Labour did gain it way back in 1918, holding the seat until 1924 but then never regaining it. They did however come extremely close in 1966, when Body was elected for the first time by just 300 votes.

There continue to be areas of Labour strength in the town of Boston itself, such as Central, Pilgrim, Skirbeck and Staniland wards, and Labour were the largest party on the balanced Boston Borough council from 1995 to 1999, when the Conservatives were able to regain a number of seats. In the Euro election of 1999, the Conservatives widened their lead over Labour to the huge margin of 47–23%, and it seems likely that they will withstand the retirement of Body, who has spent half a century contesting parliamentary elections, and 34 years representing Boston in the House of Commons. His replacement is Mark Simmonds.

Bosworth

Conservative majority 1,027 (2.0%)

Labour target 9

MP David Tredinnick

1997 (Turnout 76.6%)	Conservative	21,189	40.6%
	Labour	20,162	38.7%
	Liberal Democrat	9,281	17.8%
	Referendum	1,521	2.9%

It is perhaps surprising that Bosworth was held continuously by Labour between 1945 and 1970, and even more surprising that the last Labour MP for the seat was Woodrow Wyatt, before his days as the Thatcherite 'voice of reason'. However, in the early 1980s, the boundaries of the constituency were significantly altered, with the loss of much of the former Leicestershire coalfield (around the appropriately named Coalville) to what is now the Labour constituency of North West Leicestershire. Bosworth is now focused on the comfortable town of Hinckley, along with smaller more working-class settlements such as Barwell and Earl Shilton, which provide the bulk of the remaining Labour vote.

In 1983 and 1987, Labour finished third by some distance in the redrawn Bosworth, but in 1992 their vote advanced by nearly 9% to move into second place, and last time a swing of almost 12% left Conservative MP David Tredinnick clinging on by barely 1,000 votes. Since then the Conservatives have started to make a recovery in local elections, though it is the Liberal Democrats who remain the largest party on Hinckley and Bosworth council. In the Euro elections the Conservatives led by 20% over Labour, and they will certainly be hoping for a more comfortable majority in the next general election.

Broxtowe

Labour majority 5,575 (9.6%)

Conservative target 78

MP Nick Palmer

1997 (Turnout 78.4%)	Labour	27,343	47.0%
	Conservative	21,768	37.4%
	Liberal Democrat	6,934	11.9%
	Referendum	2,092	3.6%

There are a number of marginal constituencies on the edges of Nottingham and Derby which were gained by Labour in 1997. Broxtowe was more unexpected than most; the Conservative majority in 1992 was almost 10,000 and Sir James Lester had sat as MP for the area since 1974. However the constituency does take in the towns of Stapleford and Beeston, where Labour have a significant vote, and the University of Nottingham is also situated nearby. In the event Nick Palmer achieved an above-average swing of nearly 13%, enough to provide him with an almost comfortable majority of 5,500.

Since then, Labour suffered a few losses in the 1999 local council elections, when the Conservatives were ahead across the constituency by a little over 1%. In the European election a month later this lead became 10%, though this was smaller than the Tory leads in the other Nottinghamshire marginals of Gedling and Newark. It is not inconceivable that Palmer will hold on here against Conservative Pauline Latham at the next general election, though it could be a close-run thing.

Chesterfield

Labour majority 5,775 (11.2%)

Liberal Democrat target

MP Tony Benn (retiring)

1997 (Turnout 70.9%)	Labour	26,105	50.8%
	Liberal Democrat	20,330	39.6%
	Conservative	4,752	9.2%
	Other	202	0.4%

Chesterfield has been an oddity in recent general elections, a previously safe Labour seat where the Liberal Democrats have been making steady inroads. There are a number of constituencies where such progress has been made at local elections, only for voters to return to the two main parties at national contests. But in Chesterfield the Lib Dems have moved ahead on both fronts. As a result, Labour's comfortable 1983 majority (over the Conservatives) had been whittled down to less than 6,000 by 1997, the opposite trend to that in most other seats.

Part of Labour's difficulties here may have involved the 'Benn factor': certainly the 1984 by-election which heralded Tony Benn's return to the Commons after a year's absence appears to have been the catalyst for growing Liberal Democrat strength in Chesterfield. Their 1983 vote of under 20% increased to 29% in 1987, 36% in 1992 and almost 40% in 1997. At local council level, the situation is much the same with Labour and the Lib Dems more or less neck and neck in 1999, and the Conservatives almost non-existent, fielding candidates in only a handful of wards. Next time, both Tony Benn and Tony Rogers (the Lib Dem candidate in 1987, 1992 and 1997) will not be candidates, which makes the outcome here all the more unpredictable.

Corby

Labour majority 11,860 (22.0%)

Conservative target 174

MP Phil Hope

1997 (Turnout 77.7%)			
	Labour	29,888	55.4%
	Conservative	18,028	33.4%
	Liberal Democrat	4,045	7.5%
	Referendum	1,356	2.5%
	UK Independence	507	0.9%
	Other	133	0.2%

Corby is the nearest one gets to a 'Scottish colony' south of the border, its former steelworks having acted as a magnet drawing Scottish workers to an unlikely home in deepest Northamptonshire. The town's politics have generally followed a Labour tradition; even in 1999 Labour won 27 of the 29 seats on the district council, and of the 13 wards, three were uncontested and Labour polled over 70% of the vote in a further six. Yet the parliamentary constituency has not been so easy for Labour, and indeed was held by the Conservatives from its creation in 1983 until 1997. How did this come about?

The largest part of the explanation is that the constituency has always included nearly as many rural electors as voters from the town of Corby itself. The Conservatives are as strong in the surrounding villages and public school town of Oundle as Labour are in Corby, and helped by favourable national circumstances, William Powell was able to win the seat for the Tories with a series of small majorities. But Powell's luck ran out in the very different political atmosphere of 1997, Labour's Phil Hope amassing a majority of almost 12,000. Although the Conservatives again led by 5% at the 1999 Euro election, it is difficult to see Andrew Griffith dislodging Hope without first reducing his majority.

Derby North

Labour majority 10,615 (18.9%)

Conservative target 148

MP Bob Laxton

1997 (Turnout 73.5%)			
	Labour	29,844	53.2%
	Conservative	19,229	34.3%
	Liberal Democrat	5,059	9.0%
	Referendum	1,816	3.2%
	Other	195	0.3%

Derby North has always been a marginal constituency; though it had been held continuously by Labour from its creation in 1950, the Conservatives came close in 1959, 1974 and 1979 (when Labour held on by just 214 votes), before Phillip Whitehead was finally defeated by Conservative Greg Knight in 1983. Knight's majority then almost doubled in 1987 before Labour started their recovery in 1992; finally in 1997 the constituency was regained by former Derby council leader Bob Laxton with an above-average swing of 13%.

The constituency includes strongly Conservative territory in Allestree and Darley off the A6 to the north of the centre, but also Labour wards such as Chaddesden and Mackworth to the north-east and north-west. Although the local council is elected annually, not all wards are contested each year, which makes it difficult to detect trends; nevertheless Labour have been slightly ahead in the wards contested in 1998, 1999 and 2000. At the Euro elections, the Conservatives out-polled Labour in Derby North by just 133 votes, and it is difficult to see parliamentary hopeful Barry Holden regaining the seat at the next general election.

Derbyshire South

Labour majority 13,967 (23.3%)

Conservative target 188

MP Mark Todd

1997 (Turnout 78.2%)			
	Labour	32,709	54.5%
	Conservative	18,742	31.3%
	Liberal Democrat	5,408	9.0%
	Referendum	2,491	4.2%
	UK Independence	617	1.0%

It appeared from various statements made to the media during the 1997 election campaign that Edwina Currie was one of the few Conservatives who realised the sheer extent of the likely swing away from the government. Given that she had a small (notional) majority of less than 2,000 in Derbyshire South following boundary changes, her own defeat must have seemed inevitable; in the end a 13% swing gave Labour an enormous majority of almost 14,000 and deprived the Commons of one of its more colourful characters.

Derbyshire South includes the two southernmost wards of the city of Derby (Boulton and Chellaston) and the remaining territory in the county to the south of Derby itself. Much of this is based around the town of Swadlincote, where Labour are strong, but there are also Conservative villages in the constituency such as Etwall, Hilton and Repton, home of a public school. This was not enough to save the Conservatives in 1997, and Labour were still well ahead in the 1999 local council elections, though they were behind by just over 5% in the Euro elections. James Hakewill will take the place of Currie at the next general election, but Labour's Mark Todd should hold on for the time being at least.

Erewash

Labour majority 9,135 (15.1%)

Conservative target 126

MP Liz Blackman

1997 (Turnout 77.8%)	Labour	31,196	51.7%
	Conservative	22,061	36.6%
	Liberal Democrat	5,181	8.6%
	Referendum	1,404	2.3%
	Other	496	0.8%

The constituency of Erewash, named after the eponymous canal and river, which forms its eastern boundary, is based on the Derbyshire towns of Ilkeston, Sandiacre and Long Eaton, lying either side of the M1 motorway between Derby and Nottingham. This is very much marginal territory, and Erewash joined no fewer than five bordering constituencies in being gained by Labour in 1997. Angela Knight had been elected for the Conservatives in 1992, but lasted just one parliamentary term as Liz Blackman won the seat with a majority exceeding 9,000.

Ilkeston (which formed a constituency of its own until 1983) is fertile territory for the Labour Party, but the rest of the division is somewhat mixed, including wards won by the Conservatives in May 1999 such as Breaston, Ockbrook and Borrowash and West Hallam. Overall in the constituency, Labour were 8% ahead in the council elections of 1999, but 9% behind in the Euro election a month later. This whole area is clearly an important barometer of the national mood, and Conservative parliamentary hopeful Gregor MacGregor will hope it swings back to the right next time.

Gedling

Labour majority 3,802 (7.3%)

Conservative target 57

MP Vernon Coaker

1997 (Turnout 75.6%)	Labour	24,390	46.8%
	Conservative	20,588	39.5%
	Liberal Democrat	5,180	9.9%
	Referendum	2,006	3.8%

Gedling contains the north-easternmost suburbs of Nottingham, but formally lies outside of the city boundaries. Until 1983 the constituency took the name of Carlton, but then changed to the same name as the local government borough, most of which lies within the constituency. As well as Carlton, the seat takes in Arnold to the north, and the prosperous small town of Burton Joyce a couple of miles outside the built-up area.

Labour's victory here in 1997 was unanticipated by many, the party were over 10,000 votes behind the Conservatives in 1992 and Labour did not even win Carlton in 1966. In the event a swing of 13% (higher than the national average but about standard for marginals around Derby and Nottingham) propelled the leader of nearby Rushcliffe borough council, Vernon Coaker, into parliament with a respectable, if not entirely safe majority of 3,802. Since then the Conservatives have taken control of the council and in the Euro elections, they led by 16%. Their candidate Jonathan Bullock must be optimistic of regaining this seat, and it certainly looks likely to be an extremely close contest.

High Peak

Labour majority 8,791 (15.4%)

Conservative target 129

MP Tom Levitt

1997 (Turnout 78.9%)	Labour	29,052	50.8%
	Conservative	20,261	35.5%
	Liberal Democrat	6,420	11.2%
	Referendum	1,420	2.5%

The High Peak constituency must be one of the most scenic in England, extending all the way from Glossop, New Mills and Buxton across the 'High Peak' itself to Ladybower and Hathersage. It has generally been held by the

Conservatives, but was gained by Labour in 1966 and also saw a respectable vote for the SDP in 1983, when political theorist David Marquand pushed Labour into third place. In 1992, Labour's vote advanced by 9%, and then at his second attempt Tom Levitt won the seat in 1997 with a comfortable majority of 9,000.

A large proportion of the electorate of High Peak live in towns close to Greater Manchester, and Labour are strong in Gamesley (near Glossop) as well as parts of Buxton and New Mills. The Conservatives' safest areas are the other side of the Snake Pass in Bradwell and Hathersage, and overall the constituency's 28 wards seem unlikely to provide any party with an entirely safe seat. In the 1999 local council elections, Labour were ahead of a split opposition, but the Conservatives led by 8% in the Euro poll a month later. Simon Chapman will hope to regain High Peak for the Conservatives when the general election is called, but this is just the sort of constituency that Labour must hold if Tony Blair is to fulfil his ambition of a second full Labour term.

Kettering

Labour majority 189 (0.3%)

Conservative target 5

MP Phil Sawford

1997 (Turnout 75.5%)			
Labour	24,650	43.3%
Conservative	24,461	42.9%
Liberal Democrat	6,098	10.7%
Referendum	1,551	2.7%
Other	197	0.3%

Northamptonshire proved to be one of the most fertile (and most unexpected) providers of Labour gains at the 1997 general election, with the party gaining no fewer than five of the six parliamentary constituencies in the county. The wins in Corby and Northampton North were expected, but the other three gains were certainly not, with Labour scraping to victory in each of Northampton South, Wellingborough and Kettering by wafer-thin margins.

Kettering had actually been held by Labour from 1945 until 1983, but this was largely because the steel town of Corby was included within the boundaries of the parliamentary seat. As soon as Corby was removed, the Conservatives were able to win here with majorities of around 10,000, and the seat must have seemed a secure base for Roger Freeman's ministerial ambitions. Alas, Freeman joined some of his higher profile colleagues (such as Michael Portillo, Malcolm Rifkind and Michael Forsyth) in being defeated at the polls while serving in the cabinet. Labour's Phil Sawford squeezed home by just 189 votes, making this Labour's most marginal constituency after 1997. Since then, the Conservatives comfortably out-polled Labour by 18% in the Euro election, and were also ahead locally in 1999. Philip Hollobone should regain the seat next time.

Lincoln

Labour majority 11,130 (23.9%)

Conservative target 196

MP Gillian Merron

1997 (Turnout 70.9%)			
	Labour	25,563	54.9%
	Conservative	14,433	31.0%
	Liberal Democrat	5,048	10.8%
	Referendum	1,329	2.9%
	Other	175	0.4%

Lincoln was held by Labour continuously from 1945 until 1973 when MP Dick Taverne resigned from the party and fought the seat in a by-election as a 'Democratic Labour' candidate. Taverne duly won the by-election and narrowly held on in February 1974 against the official Labour party candidate, but then lost by under 1,000 to Margaret Jackson, now Margaret Beckett, in October 1974. However, Labour's troubles were not over as the seat was then lost to the Conservatives in 1979, who held the seat until 1997. The Conservative MP from 1979 was Kenneth Carlisle, who had a majority of over 10,000 in 1983, but just 2,000 by 1992, and even this was whittled away by boundary changes before 1997. Carlisle wisely opted to stand down before the election, when a swing of 11% returned Lincoln to Labour and Gillian Merron to parliament.

Since 1997, Labour have continued to dominate local politics in Lincoln; indeed the Conservatives won just two seats in 1999. Labour even managed to top the poll in the Euro elections, a rarity for a seat gained in

1997 and a result which suggests that this constituency may have finally returned to its pre-1973 status as a reasonably secure Labour seat.

Loughborough

Labour majority 5,712 (10.9%)

Conservative target 88

MP Andy Reed

1997 (Turnout 75.5%)	Labour	25,448	48.6%
	Conservative	19,736	37.7%
	Liberal Democrat	6,190	11.8%
	Referendum	991	1.9%

Loughborough was held by Labour from 1945 until 1979, but then like Bosworth it swung to the right, partly as a result of the boundary changes which created the new constituency of North West Leicestershire. By 1987 Conservative MP Stephen Dorrell could boast a majority of 17,600, and even after Andy Reed added 8% to the Labour vote in 1992 that majority remained in five-figures. However, another set of boundary changes then came to Labour's rescue, with the creation of the seat of Charnwood before 1997, which took over 20,000 mainly Conservative voters out of Loughborough. Unsurprisingly, Dorrell followed them, and the result in Loughborough, now more compactly based around the town itself, together with the addition of its smaller Labour-supporting neighbour of Shepshed, was never in much doubt.

Labour remained ahead across the constituency in the local elections of 1999 by a margin of 47–38%, though the Conservatives led by 6.5% in the Euro election. Much of the remaining Conservative strength is based on the villages of Barrow upon Soar, Quorndon and Nanpantan, but any sort of national Labour lead will now probably be enough to hold this more favourably drawn constituency. Neil Lyon will contest the seat for the Tories next time, but Andy Reed should just about start as favourite.

Newark

Labour majority 3,016 (5.8%)

Conservative target 39

MP Fiona Jones

1997 (Turnout 74.4%)			
	Labour	23,496	45.2%
	Conservative	20,480	39.4%
	Liberal Democrat	5,960	11.5%
	Referendum	2,035	3.9%

Newark hit the headlines after the 1997 election, when its new MP Fiona Jones was initially convicted of submitting false election expenses and disqualified from office, before being cleared on appeal and reinstated to the Commons. In many ways, Jones was a somewhat unlikely victor in the first place. Newark had been a Labour seat from 1950 until 1979, but then the new constituency of Sherwood was created, taking in much of the former Nottinghamshire coalfield areas which provided the old Newark with most of its Labour votes. As a result, Conservative Richard Alexander was able to build a majority of 13,500 by 1987, though the Labour vote did advance by 8% in 1992. Last time a swing of 10% was enough to see off Alexander after 18 years as the local MP.

Much of the constituency is highly unlikely Labour territory, including the prosperous town of Newark itself, the small cathedral city of Southwell, which in local terms is dominated by Liberal Democrats, and a large rural area where the Conservatives are very strong. Labour only really pile up votes in the town of Retford up the A1 to the north, and overall in the 1999 local elections they were in third place, some 23% behind the Conservatives. This lead was more or less replicated in the Euro election a month later. Conservative hopeful Patrick Mercer must start as favourite to regain the seat next time.

Northampton North

Labour majority 10,000 (19.3%)

Conservative target 151

MP Sally Keeble

Labour	27,247	52.7%
Conservative	17,247	33.4%
Liberal Democrat	6,579	12.7%
UK Independence	464	0.9%
Other	161	0.3%

Labour were able to gain both Northampton seats in 1997; in North a swing of over 13% was comfortable enough to see off Conservative Euro-rebel MP Tony Marlow after 18 years as the constituency's MP. The seat itself is compact, including a mix of older housing stock towards the centre and newer estates to the north. Locally the Liberal Democrats have made some headway, winning a number of wards such as Boughton Green and Kingsthorpe, but nationally such areas were always likely to find 'New' Labour attractive, and so it proved with former Southwark council leader, Sally Keeble, amassing a majority of exactly 10,000 at the last general election.

Since May 1997, Labour have maintained their strength, leading by approximately 20% over the Conservatives in local council elections in 1999, and indeed the Liberal Democrats also polled more votes than the Tories across the constituency. In the Euro election this was reversed with the Conservatives narrowly ahead, but their new parliamentary hopeful John Whelan seems unlikely to regain the seat at the first attempt.

Northampton South

Labour majority 744 (1.3%)

Conservative target 9

MP Tony Clarke

Labour	24,214	42.4%
Conservative	23,470	41.1%
Liberal Democrat	6,316	11.1%
Referendum	1,405	2.5%
UK Independence	1,159	2.0%
Other	541	0.9%

Northampton South always seemed a more unlikely target for Labour than its northern counterpart, partly due to the sprawling new housing estates to the south and east of the centre, but mainly because the constituency also includes 11,400 rural electors among whom the Conservatives remain strong. Since its creation in 1974, the seat had appeared a secure base for Conservative Deputy Speaker, Michael Morris, but even he could not withstand a swing of over 13% in 1997, which was enough to overturn his seemingly impregnable 1992 majority of more than 15,000.

In the local elections of 1999, Labour remained ahead of the Conservatives by 45-34% in the Northampton part of the seat, which would probably just about be enough to outvote the solidly Conservative rural electors from South Northamptonshire and hold the seat if repeated in a general election. This did not happen in the Euro election, when the Conservatives led by 14.5%, and their parliamentary hopeful Shailesh Vara must be optimistic. However like many new Labour MPs, Tony Clarke should have the benefit of a small incumbency factor at the next election, and the new estates of Northampton may prove more fertile territory for the Labour government than more traditional Labour areas in other parts of the country. A shock 'Labour hold' should not be totally ruled out here.

Wellingborough

Labour majority 187 (0.3%)

Conservative target 6

MP Paul Stinchcombe

1997 (Turnout 74.8%)			
Labour	24,854	44.2%
Conservative	24,667	43.8%
Liberal Democrat	5,279	9.4%
UK Independence	1,192	2.1%
Other	297	0.5%

Wellingborough was yet another unexpected Labour gain in 1997, though the constituency had been held by Labour from 1945 to 1959 and again from 1964 to 1969. Following a by-election victory in 1969, Peter Fry steadily built up a large majority for the Conservatives, increasing his lead to over 14,000 in 1987. This swing to the right was probably connected with the loss of industry in the towns of Wellingborough and Rushden, and the days of Labour victories here seemed to be over. But then Phil Sawford (now Labour MP for Kettering) increased Labour's vote by 7% in 1992, and last time a nationally average swing of 10% was enough for Paul Stinchcombe to defeat Fry by less than 200 votes.

Perhaps even more surprising than Labour gaining the parliamentary seat in 1997 was the gain of the local council in 1999, from its previously balanced state. Although most of their gains were made from Independents, Labour's local vote held up or even slightly increased from 1995 to 1999, a pattern strikingly contrary to that almost everywhere else. However this run of success did not survive the Euro election, when the Tories led Labour by 41–30%. In the next general election, Peter Bone, who became the first Conservative to lose Pudsey in three quarters of a century last time, will hope to have better fortune by regaining a constituency which is Labour's second most marginal in Britain.

West Midlands

Conservative Targets

Target No	Constituency		Labour Lead
C8	Rugby and Kenilworth	495	0.8%
C21	Shrewsbury and Atcham	1,670	3.0%
C36	Warwick and Leamington	3,398	5.6%
C49	The Wrekin	3,025	6.7%
C64	Stafford	4,314	8.3%
C79	Birmingham Edgbaston	4,842	10.0%
C81	Wolverhampton South West	5,118	10.5%
C94	Stourbridge	5,645	11.4%
C95	Burton	6,330	11.6%
C102	Wyre Forest	6,946	12.6%
C112	Redditch	6,125	13.7%
C118	Worcester	7,425	14.4%
C123	Tamworth	7,496	15.0%
C155	Staffordshire Moorlands	10,049	19.7%
C157	Dudley North	9,457	19.8%
C160	Birmingham Hall Green	8,420	20.1%
C166	Halesowen and Rowley Regis	10,337	21.2%
C172	Coventry South	10,953	21.9%

(Liberal Democrat held)

			Lib Dem Lead
C104	Hereford	6,648	12.6%

Labour Targets

			Conservative Lead
L4	Lichfield	238	0.5%
L6	Meriden	582	1.1%

Liberal Democrat Targets

		Labour Lead
Shrewsbury and Atcham (3rd)	6,646	12.0%
Birmingham Yardley	5,315	14.1%

The West Midlands is not short of electoral interest, with the Conservatives looking to regain a large number of likely and unlikely losses suffered in 1997. Many of the seats gained by Labour were (as in the East Midlands) in constituencies based on small or medium-sized towns, such as Shrewsbury, Burton, Stafford and Wyre Forest (centred on Kidderminster). There is also a large belt of important marginals to the west and south of Birmingham itself, extending from Wolverhampton South West and the Wrekin down through Dudley North, Halesowen and Rowley Regis, Stourbridge and Worcester, and across to Redditch, Warwick and Leamington, and last and most unlikely of all, Rugby and Kenilworth. Many of the contests in these seats could be extremely close come the next general election, and they will certainly be an important pointer to national fortunes.

Historically, Labour have tended to do a little worse in the West Midlands region than should have been the case given the industrial and social make-up of the region. The Conservatives have always been able to hold a solid number of constituencies, mainly in rural areas but a few in urban areas such as Coventry, Wolverhampton and Birmingham itself. For their part, Labour have found gains difficult to come by in the past (for example just three in 1964, four in 1966 and none at all in 1987) though their biggest breakthrough before 1997 came in the two elections of 1974, when a significant number of voters must have heeded the call by former Conservative MP Enoch Powell to vote Labour: in these elections the Tory vote in the West Midlands plummetted and Labour were able to gain 11 seats. However virtually all of these gains were wiped out in 1979, and as elsewhere Labour then declined further to reach a post-war low in 1983.

Labour did manage to gain seven seats in 1992, including three in Birmingham (Northfield, Selly Oak and Yardley), one in Wolverhampton plus Warwickshire North, Nuneaton and Cannock and Burntwood. All of these seats now appear beyond the range of the Conservatives (for example, government minister Mike O'Brien has a majority close on 15,000 in the previously marginal Warwickshire North), though Labour remain vulnerable to the Liberal Democrats in Birmingham Yardley. In the main, it will be the constituencies gained by Labour in 1997 which will form the electoral battleground when the next general election is called, with up to ten seats which could realistically go to either of the two main parties. It will be a major surprise indeed if Labour holds onto Rugby and Kenilworth, Shrewsbury, Warwick and Leamington, or The Wrekin, but the marginals listed above from Stafford (majority 8%) to Tamworth (majority 15%) are all in the balance, a group which includes Labour's emblematic 1997 gain of Birmingham Edgbaston. Beyond that list, the Conservatives will do well to make further gains, though of course they must if they are to form a majority government. It should be noted that in the May 2000 local council elections, Labour performed worse in parts of the West Midlands than anywhere else in the country. It seems plausible that this was connected with uncertainty over the Rover plant in Longbridge, but this is a politically volatile area, and it would not be totally unexpected if Labour did do worse here at the general election than in other regions.

Birmingham Edgbaston

Labour majority 4,842 (10.0%)

Conservative target 79

MP Gisela Stuart

1997 (Turnout 69.0%)			
	Labour	23,554	48.6%
	Conservative	18,712	38.6%
	Liberal Democrat	4,691	9.7%
	Referendum	1,065	2.2%
	Other	443	0.9%

Birmingham Edgbaston will forever be remembered as 'Labour's Basildon': it was the first marginal constituency in 1997 to declare its result in front of the watching nation, and Labour duly gained the seat for the first time with a swing of exactly 10%, thus announcing that 18 years of Conservative government were over.

In many ways this is unlikely Labour territory. Edgbaston contains affluent and leafy neighbourhoods to the south west of the city centre (as well as an international cricket ground, the University of Birmingham and BBC Pebble Mill), and Labour failed to win here even in 1945. However, urban areas have been swinging to the left for many years, and the 'urban

Conservative MP' has been becoming an increasingly endangered species. Having said all that, the Conservatives have done well here since 1997; they led by 10% in the 1998 local elections, 12% in the 1999 local elections, 13% in the Euro elections and no less than 23% in May 2000, when they gained the one normally Labour ward (Quinton). The battle between Labour incumbent Gisela Stuart and Conservative hopeful Nigel Hastilow will certainly be one to watch.

Birmingham Hall Green

Labour majority 8,420 (20.1%)

Conservative target 160

MP Steve McCabe

1997 (Turnout 71.2%)			
	Labour	22,372	53.5%
	Conservative	13,952	33.4%
	Liberal Democrat	4,034	9.6%
	Referendum	1,461	3.5%

Birmingham Hall Green was one of the last of the urban Conservative seats to be lost by the party, when a Labour scotsman, Steve McCabe, gained the constituency in 1997 on a larger-than-average swing of 14%. Birmingham therefore joined Manchester, Liverpool, Glasgow, Cardiff, Leeds and indeed virtually all other cities in sending an entirely Labour delegation to Parliament. Indeed, the Conservatives have almost no urban MPs left at all outside London and (if it can be considered urban), Bournemouth.

Hall Green itself had never fallen to Labour since its creation, Andrew Hargreaves enjoying comfortable majorities of 7,600 in 1987 and 3,600 in 1992. But elsewhere in Birmingham, the Conservatives were gradually losing seats (Northfield, Selly Oak and Yardley in 1992) and Hall Green was always likely to be the next in line.

Predictably, Labour were able to stack up a large majority of 8,000 in 1997, but since then they have fallen behind, trailing the Conservatives narrowly in 1998 (40–39%) and 1999 (39–37% in the locals, 35–31% in the Euros) but more dramatically in May 2000 (44–29%). Conservative Chris White could regain a rare 'city seat' for his party next time.

Birmingham Yardley

Labour majority 5,315 (14.1%)

Liberal Democrat target

MP Estelle Morris

1997 (Turnout 71.2%)			
	Labour	17,778	47.1%
	Liberal Democrat	12,463	33.0%
	Conservative	6,736	17.8%
	Referendum	646	1.7%
	UK Independence	164	0.4%

Birmingham Yardley has been a third party stronghold in council elections for many years now, with the Liberal Democrats taking no less than 61% of the vote across the constituency in the May 2000 local elections. They were extremely confident of gaining the parliamentary seat at the last general election, starting just 5% behind, but despite a small increase in their vote, their chances were dashed by Labour's strong national performance.

The constituency (lying to the east of the city centre along the A45) was actually held by the Conservatives from 1979 to 1992 and was regarded as a standard two-party marginal before that. Now however it seems that Conservative hopes here have receded, and their vote seems likely to be squeezed further by the Lib Dems.

Since 1997, Labour MP Estelle Morris has been elevated to ministerial rank, but this will not necessarily end Liberal Democrat hopes. Yardley was one of only three constituencies in the entire country where they led in the 1999 Euro elections, and their perennial candidate here, councillor and businessman John Hemming, will hope it is third time lucky for him.

Burton

Labour majority 6,330 (11.6%)

Conservative target 95

MP Janet Dean

1997 (Turnout 75.1%)

Labour	27,810	51.0%
Conservative	21,480	39.4%
Liberal Democrat	4,617	8.5%
Other	604	1.1%

Since they last won the seat in 1945, Labour had come close in Burton without regaining the seat; the Conservatives held on by just 300 votes in 1966 and prominent Conservative MP Ivan Lawrence won by just under 6,000 in 1992. But even Lawrence could not withstand the Labour tidal wave in 1997, a slightly below average swing resulting in Staffordshire councillor Janet Dean more or less reversing the 1992 result with a majority of 6,330.

The constituency is a mix of Burton-upon-Trent and a rural strip running in a north westerly direction through and beyond Uttoxeter. There are safe Labour wards in Burton itself, but equally safe Conservative wards in villages such as Tutbury and Hanbury. In the East Staffordshire council elections in May 1999 (almost all of which is included in the constituency), Labour were marginally ahead of the Conservatives, but this result was dramatically reversed in the following month's Euro elections when the Conservatives led by 15%. A close contest is in prospect next time, and it will be one of the handful which will feature two women, as the Conservatives have selected Maggie Punyer.

Coventry South

Labour majority 10,953 (21.9%)

Conservative target 172

MP Jim Cunningham

1997 (Turnout 69.8%)

Labour	25,511	50.9%
Conservative	14,558	29.0%
Liberal Democrat	4,617	9.2%
Socialist	3,262	6.5%
Referendum	943	1.9%
Others	1,233	2.5%

Labour have been engaged in battles on a number of fronts over the last few years. In addition to the main struggle for national power with the Conservatives and a growing number of mainly northern spats for local control with the Liberal Democrats, there have been a small number of confrontations of an altogether different sort on Labour's left front, one of which persists in Coventry.

Labour have never entirely seen off the Socialist challenge of their former MP Dave Nellist, who following his expulsion from the party, polled over 10,000 votes in 1992 and still managed 3,000 in 1997. Since then, Socialist candidates have continued to win St Michael's ward in the centre of Coventry, and attracted a surprisingly high number of votes in the Euro elections. However the real threat for Labour in Coventry South is the more traditional danger on their rightward flank. The Conservatives led in the constituency by 11% in the 2000 local council elections, and their prospective parliamentary candidate Heather Wheeler must be in with a chance of repeating that result when the general election is called. If Labour continues to have to fight this constituency on two fronts, such an outcome is all the more likely.

Dudley North

Labour majority 9,457 (19.8%)

Conservative target 157

MP Ross Cranston

1997 (Turnout 69.5%)

	Labour	24,471	51.2%
	Conservative	15,014	31.4%
	Liberal Democrat	3,939	8.2%
	Socialist Labour	2,155	4.5%
	Referendum	1,201	2.5%
	Others	1,028	2.1%

Labour's results in the local council elections of 2000 were poor in many areas, but nowhere worse than parts of the West Midlands. In Dudley North, their vote dropped from just over 51% in both 1997 and 1999 down to 38%, with the Conservatives capturing the previously Labour ward of Gornal with a majority of 1,200 votes and taking almost 48% of the vote overall.

This brought to an end a run of success which started when Labour gained Dudley West in a by-election in late 1994, with a gigantic swing of 29%. Since then the constituency boundaries have been radically changed, and the new Dudley North is very mixed, including traditionally Conservative Sedgley, divided Coseley and strongly Labour wards in the centre of Dudley itself. On balance, the constituency should be retained by Ross Cranston when the general election is called, but this part of the West Midlands seems to have been regularly associated with volatile results, and the Conservatives cannot be entirely discounted.

Halesowen and Rowley Regis

Labour majority 10,337 (21.2%)

Conservative target 166

MP Sylvia Heal

1997 (Turnout 73.6%)			
	Labour	26,366	54.1%
	Conservative	16,029	32.9%
	Liberal Democrat	4,169	8.6%
	Referendum	1,244	2.6%
	Green	361	0.7%
	Other	592	1.2%

According to the constituency tables, Halesowen and Rowley Regis is the seat the Conservatives must gain if they are to form another majority government after the next election. Probably for this reason, the residents of Downing Street, Halesowen have recently found fame courtesy of one national newspaper, their political opinions filling many column inches since the last general election in an attempt to predict the result of the next. In line with many of the individual views expressed, their local council ward has swung firmly to the Conservatives since 1997, as indeed have all wards in Halesowen. This is a little surprising as the town of Halesowen appears a slightly downmarket kind of place, though it sees itself as a separate entity from the Birmingham-West Midlands conurbation and politically has tended to incline to the right in the past.

However, this is not the whole story as the constituency also includes 30,000 voters further into the West Midlands conurbation in three wards around Rowley Regis, which are far more Labour-inclined and have remained that way in the local elections of both 1999 and 2000. These areas (part of the borough of Sandwell) will almost certainly keep the constituency in the Labour column next time, even if Halesowen continues to back the Conservatives. All of which is good news for Sylvia Heal, the short-term MP for Mid Staffordshire, who should be able to rely on a more stable parliamentary base in this more urban part of the region.

Hereford

Liberal Democrat majority 6,648 (12.6%)

Conservative target 104

MP Paul Keetch

1997 (Turnout 75.2%)			
	Liberal Democrat	25,198	47.9%
	Conservative	18,550	35.3%
	Labour	6,596	12.6%
	Referendum	2,209	4.2%

Hereford had been a potential Liberal target for many years before their eventual breakthrough in 1997. They finished less than 3,500 votes behind the Conservatives in February 1974 and a mere 1,100 adrift in October of the same year. Decades earlier, the Liberals had managed to win the seat in their landslide victory of 1906 and gained it again in 1929, the last time they won a significant number of parliamentary seats before 1997. For 20 years from 1974, Colin Shepherd held on to the seat for the Conservatives with a series of low majorities, which peaked at just under 5,000 in 1979. It seemed as though the Liberals/Alliance/Liberal Democrats would never regain Hereford, continually falling just short of victory.

Finally in 1997, Shepherd could avoid defeat no longer when his vote dropped by 12%, and former Hereford councillor Paul Keetch won the seat by 6,600 votes, ironically a larger majority than Shepherd ever achieved himself. Since then however the Lib Dems have been completely massacred in the 1999 Euro election, receiving less than 15% of the vote in Hereford and finishing behind Labour in third place. Clearly they will need to continue squeezing the Labour vote to hold on in the forthcoming general election, though this is one constituency where any perceived national relationship between the Liberal Democrats and Labour could have voters returning in droves to the new Conservatives candidate, Virginia Taylor.

Lichfield

Conservative majority 238 (0.5%)

Labour target 4

MP Michael Fabricant

1997 (Turnout 77.5%)			
	Conservative	20,853	42.9%
	Labour	20,615	42.4%
	Liberal Democrat	5,473	11.3%
	Referendum	1,652	3.4%

Lichfield was part of the Mid Staffordshire seat which was gained so spec-
tacularly by Labour in a by-election back in 1990, when the Poll Tax was
driving voters from the Conservatives to Labour, and there still seemed a
realistic chance that Neil Kinnock would soon become Prime Minister.
After the most recent boundary changes, Lichfield was able to form the basis
of its own constituency, and calculations by the experts put the
Conservatives roughly 20% ahead of Labour in the 1992 election, which
should have been enough for Labour to have gained the seat in 1997 had
they achieved anything above the average 10% swing in their favour. In the
event, the swing in Lichfield was a little less than the average, and Michael
Fabricant was able to hang on by the extremely tight margin of 238 votes.

Lichfield itself, lying within easy commuting reach of Birmingham, is a
rather Conservative place, and it is probably not all that surprising that it was
able to resist the Labour tide in 1997. There are some areas of Labour
strength in Burntwood, which was previously linked with Cannock in a seat
gained by Labour in 1992, but these are more than likely to be outvoted by
the more numerous Conservative wards in the constituency. In the Euro
elections of 1999, the Tories out polled Labour by almost 20%, and it is
difficult to believe that Labour have not missed their best opportunity of
gaining this seat.

Meriden

Conservative majority 582 (1.1%)

Labour target 6

MP Caroline Spelman

1997 (Turnout 71.7%)

Conservative	22,997	42.0%
Labour	22,415	41.0%
Liberal Democrat	7,098	13.0%
Referendum	2,208	4.0%

Unusually for a Tory seat in 1997, Labour has won the constituency called Meriden relatively frequently in the past (1955, 1964, 1966, 1974 twice), but in a sense the current seat was a new invention in 1983 when nearly half the old Meriden vanished into Warwickshire North.

Meriden is sandwiched between Birmingham and Coventry. Meriden itself is a village that claims, as do some other midland settlements, to be the very centre of England, but most of the seat's population is divided between some vast Birmingham overspill estates like Chelmsley Wood, and some extremely prosperous commuter villages like Knowle and Dorridge south of Solihull. It is a very divided seat, but the Conservative minority in the estates is much stronger than the Labour presence in the villages. Meriden comprises half the borough of Solihull, which the Conservatives gained in May 2000 (although it is somewhat strange for them to have lost it in the first place) and it would be truly surprising if Labour managed to overhaul the new Conservative MP Caroline Spelman's majority of 582 votes. The May 2000 elections produced a 60-22 Conservative lead over Labour, compared to 47–18 in Euro 99; leads of this size must be regarded with some respect!

Redditch

Labour majority 6,125 (13.7%)

Conservative target 112

MP Jacqui Smith

1997 (Turnout 73.5%)

Labour	22,280	49.8%
Conservative	16,155	36.1%
Liberal Democrat	4,935	11.0%
Referendum	1,151	2.6%
Other	227	0.5%

The success of 'New' Labour at the 1997 general election was particularly marked in England's new towns. In the south, Milton Keynes, Harlow, Stevenage, Crawley and Basildon were all gained, and in the midlands Labour won the newly created constituency of Redditch with a comfortable 6,000 majority.

Although dominated by new housing estates, Redditch itself has become fertile territory for Labour in recent years. In 1995, they took almost 60% of the local election vote, and even in the 1999 council elections, the Labour lead over the Conservatives in the borough of Redditch remained a healthy 8%. However, this result was reversed in the Euro elections a month later, and in May 2000 the Conservatives led in the borough by fully 12%. Conservative support is strongest in West and rural Feckenham, as well as the single ward included from the District of Wychavon (Inkberrow) where Labour polled just 7% in 1999. These rural areas will not provide enough voters for Karen Lumley to count on gaining Redditch for the Conservatives next time, unless the new Labour appeal to new towns proves short-lived.

Rugby and Kenilworth

Labour majority 495 (0.8%)

Conservative target 8

MP Andy King

1997 (Turnout 77.1%)			
	Labour	26,356	43.1%
	Conservative	25,861	42.2%
	Liberal Democrat	8,737	14.3%
	Other	251	0.4%

One of Labour's most remarkable gains at the 1997 general election was Rugby and Kenilworth. To the west of this rather oddly shaped constituency, prosperous Kenilworth has always been safely Conservative in national elections, and even when chalking up huge and unlikely gains elsewhere in the local elections of 1995, Labour failed to win a single local council seat here. To the east, Rugby is a mixed town politically, with a local authority never controlled outright by Labour since the local government map was redrawn in 1973. Although there are Labour wards in the town, notably Benn, Newbold and New Bilton, Conservative support becomes stronger the further one travels out, particularly to the south west in Bilton and then surrounding villages such as Dunchurch and Thurlaston. Overall in the borough of Rugby, the Conservatives had 14 local council seats in 1999, only slightly fewer than Labour's 18.

In the Euro elections of 1999, the Conservatives led Labour by 40%–23% and it is difficult to see how Andy King can possibly see off the challenge of David Martin to retain this improbable Labour seat should there be any sort of Conservative recovery at the general election.

Shrewsbury and Atcham

Labour majority 1,670 (3.0%)

Conservative target 21

Liberal Democrat target

MP Paul Marsden

1997 (Turnout 75.3%)			
	Labour	20,484	37.0%
	Conservative	18,814	34.0%
	Liberal Democrat	13,838	25.0%
	Referendum	1,346	2.4%
	UK Independence	477	0.9%
	Others	385	0.7%

Shrewsbury was one of Labour's least anticipated 1997 gains; the party had never won here before and finished third in 1992 as indeed they had done for many years. In the event, it was the sheer size of the national swing which catapulted 29-year old Paul Marsden into Parliament at the expense of Conservative whip Derek Conway, himself originally selected at a similar youthful age some 14 years earlier.

In fact the result here should not have been totally unexpected, as in 1995 Labour had been comfortably ahead in local elections to the borough of Shrewsbury and Atcham, which shares the same boundaries as the parliamentary constituency. This lead persisted into 1998, but by 1999 the Conservatives moved back in front with a narrow 2.5% lead, which was extended to 17% in the Euro elections and almost 10% in the 2000 local council elections. There is also a sizeable Liberal Democrat vote here, and where this goes next time could determine the ultimate outcome. Their candidate will be Jonathan Rule, while the Conservatives have selected Anthea McIntyre.

Stafford

Labour majority 4,314 (8.3%)

Conservative target 64

MP David Kidney

1997 (Turnout 76.6%)			
	Labour	24,606	47.5%
	Conservative	20,292	39.2%
	Liberal Democrat	5,480	10.6%
	Referendum	1,146	2.2%
	Other	248	0.5%

The constituency of Stafford became a possible Labour gain at the boundary changes before the last election when 23,000 mainly rural voters were moved to the new Stone constituency. In a wise move the local euro-sceptic Conservative MP Bill Cash decided to follow them, avoiding, given the national landslide, what would have been inevitable defeat. In the event the swing in Stafford was slightly below average, but even this could not stop former local councillor David Kidney winning the seat for Labour for the first time since their first national landslide in 1945.

The constituency still includes some territory outside its main town, but much of this is centred on Penkridge where Labour could still win the odd council seat in 1999. The town of Stafford itself is politically marginal and although Labour have a number of strong wards, they lost control of the council in 1999. The Conservatives were also 12% ahead in the Euro elections and their parliamentary hopeful Philip Cochrane will be able to count on areas of strength to the south east of Stafford beyond the River Penk and some rural areas running down to Penkridge. A close battle is on on the cards.

Staffordshire Moorlands

Labour majority 10,049 (19.7%)

Conservative target 155

MP Charlotte Atkins

1997 (Turnout 77.3%)			
	Labour	26,686	52.2%
	Conservative	16,637	32.5%
	Liberal Democrat	6,191	12.1%
	Referendum	1,603	3.1%

Staffordshire Moorlands is based on the towns of Leek and Biddulph, now joined by Kidsgrove on the northern edges of Stoke-on-Trent; it is one of the clearer cases of a seat which was won by Labour at the last boundary review rather than at the election itself. The alterations replaced 26,000 largely rural voters with 18,000 from Kidsgrove, almost exactly recreating the old Leek constituency, which was held by Labour from 1945 to 1970. The result in 1997 was never really in much doubt, Charlotte Atkins piling up a majority in excess of 10,000.

The Conservatives did manage to win here in the Euro elections when they polled 37% to Labour's 30%, and much of their strength comes from the remaining rural territory outside the main towns. But in an even year this would no longer be enough; in Kidsgrove for example the Conservatives failed to poll more than 15% of the vote in any of the four wards in May 1999, and they did scarcely any better in Biddulph. Their parliamentary hopeful Marcus Hayes will have an uphill struggle in what again seems a reasonably safe Labour seat.

Stourbridge

Labour majority 5,645 (11.4%)

Conservative target 94

MP Debra Shipley

1997 (Turnout 76.5%)	Labour	23,452	47.2%
	Conservative	17,807	35.8%
	Liberal Democrat	7,123	14.3%
	Referendum	1,319	2.7%

Stourbridge is a somewhat mixed and extremely marginal constituency on the south west edge of the West Midlands conurbation. It includes Labour territory such as Lye and Wollescote, and Quarry Bank and Cradley, but also affluent suburbs to the south east of Stourbridge centre which back the Conservatives, and similar areas to the west, which locally at least back the Liberal Democrats.

In the 1999 local council elections, Labour would have held the seat by just 2%, but this became an 11% deficit in the Euro elections of 1999 and an 18% deficit by the May 2000 local elections. With a higher turnout in the general election, the result here could be extremely close and a pointer to the national outcome. The Conservatives have selected Stephen Eyre as their prospective candidate to take on Debra Shipley, who gained what was then a newly created constituency in 1997, on a swing of 11%.

Tamworth

Labour majority 7,496 (15.0%)

Conservative target 123

MP Brian Jenkins

1997 (Turnout 74.2%)	Labour	25,808	51.8%
	Conservative	18,312	36.7%
	Liberal Democrat	4,025	8.1%
	Referendum	1,163	2.3%
	UK Independence	369	0.7%
	Other	177	0.4%

The constituency of Tamworth was created in 1997, though it is extremely similar to the old seat of South East Staffordshire, which was held by Conservative David Lightbown from 1983 to 1995. Lightbown's death prompted a 1996 by-election shortly before the last general election, which was won by Labour's Brian Jenkins with a swing of over 20%. As with Wirral

South a few months later, it was an early indication that the Conservatives were in serious trouble. Much of the constituency consisted of rapidly expanding estates in and around Tamworth, and it seemed clear that the 'new middle class' they contained had finally decided to make the leap from the Conservatives to 'New' Labour.

Jenkins duly won the slightly altered seat in 1997 with what looks a comfortable majority of 7,500, though Labour have been having problems here since then. In the Euro elections of 1999 they trailed the Conservatives 39–34%, while in local elections to the borough of Tamworth, Labour led comfortably in 1999 only for the Conservatives to make significant gains in May 2000. Considering that the constituency also includes approximately 15,000 mainly rural voters from the district of Lichfield, where the Conservatives could gain vote shares as high as 91% in 1999, this seat may be more vulnerable than it looks. Conservative Luise Gunter should provide Jenkins with a strong challenge at the general election.

Warwick and Leamington

Labour majority 3,398 (5.6%)

Conservative target 36

MP James Plaskitt

1997 (Turnout 75.7%)			
	Labour	26,747	44.5%
	Conservative	23,349	38.9%
	Liberal Democrat	7,133	11.9%
	Referendum	1,484	2.5%
	Green	764	1.3%
	Others	614	1.0%

The twin centres of both medieval Warwick and the Royal Spa of Leamington exude affluence and hardly appear the basis of a Labour seat. Indeed the constituency was the political base of Conservative Prime Minister Anthony Eden for many years until his fall from grace in 1957. But the former Labour leader in Oxfordshire, James Plaskitt triumphed in 1997 by an almost comfortable 3,000 votes, adding this to other historic English seats (such as Worcester and Chester) which were captured for the very first time by Labour at the last general election.

Away from the tourist trail, both Warwick and Leamington do include solid Labour wards, in the estates to the west and north of Warwick and the Willes ward of Leamington. But there is also strong Conservative support in surrounding rural villages such as Radford Semele and Leek Wootton as well as in twee Henley-in-Arden, in the district of Stratford-on-Avon, where Labour are extremely weak. The Euro elections of 1999 saw the Conservatives lead Labour in the constituency by more than 16%, and their parliamentary hopeful David Campbell Bannerman must be optimistic of re-establishing traditional allegiances (and a famous political name) here next time.

Wolverhampton South West

Labour majority 5,118 (10.5%)

Conservative target 81

MP Jenny Jones (retiring)

1997 (Turnout 72.5%)			
Labour	24,657	50.4%
Conservative	19,539	39.9%
Liberal Democrat	4,012	8.2%
Other	713	1.5%

Wolverhampton South West will be remembered as the seat of right-wing Conservative Enoch Powell from 1950 until 1974, though he had a worthy successor after 1974 in Nick Budgen, who kept the Conservative flag flying after Powell called on electors to vote Labour and then promptly defected to the Ulster Unionists. However, even Budgen could not withstand the tide in 1997, with former local councillor Jenny Jones achieving the once unthinkable and gaining the seat for Labour with a swing of 10%.

In some ways this was a surprise. The constituency includes some extremely affluent suburbs to the west of the town centre, such as Tettenhall Regis and Tettenhall Wightwick, where the Conservatives recorded over 70% of the vote in the May 2000 local elections. Only the central wards of Graiseley and St.Peter's provide reliable Labour leads, yet this was enough in the landslide year of 1997. In the Euro elections of 1999, normal service was restored as the Conservatives led by 11%, and this margin was doubled in the local council elections of May 2000, giving David Chambers hope that he can regain the mantle established by Powell and Budgen after a short interlude.

Worcester

Labour majority 7,425 (14.4%)

Conservative target 118

MP Mike Foster

1997 (Turnout 74.6%)			
	Labour	25,848	50.1%
	Conservative	18,423	35.7%
	Liberal Democrat	6,462	12.5%
	UK Independence	886	1.7%

Worcester had never been won by Labour before May 1997. From 1961 until 1992, the constituency was held by Conservative 'wet' Peter Walker, a member of the Cabinet under both Edward Heath and Margaret Thatcher. Peter Luff then took on the Conservative mantle, winning the seat by 6,000 votes from Labour in the 1992 election. However, this figure was almost certainly reduced by boundary changes, which removed approximately 10,000 mainly rural electors from the seat, now based to a greater extent; on the city of Worcester itself. Wisely, Luff followed the minority of his electors to the newly created Mid Worcestershire, where he could rely on a near-10,000 majority even in 1997. Meanwhile, back in Worcester, a nationally average swing of 10% swept Michael Foster into parliament with a majority of almost 7,500.

Foster has gained a certain amount of fame or notoriety since his election for introducing a private members bill in the Commons to ban fox hunting with hounds. For various well-documented reasons, the bill ran out of parliamentary time despite a huge majority in its support at second reading (411–151). Back in Worcester, Labour's narrow local election lead of 1998 became a narrow deficit in 1999, and they also trailed the Conservatives by over 8% at the 1999 Euro elections. Foster will hope that he does not follow the fate of his bill and run out of time in Worcester; he probably just about starts as favourite against Conservative Richard Adams, but this could be a close and hard-fought battle.

The Wrekin

Labour majority 3,025 (6.7%)

Conservative target 49

MP Peter Bradley

1997 (Turnout 76.6%)

Labour	21,243	46.9%
Conservative	18,218	40.2%
Liberal Democrat	5,807	12.8%

It had been wrongly assumed before the last election that the seat called The Wrekin would automatically fall to the Conservatives as a result of boundary changes. The creation of the stand-alone constituency of Telford appeared to take away most of the Labour voters from the formerly oversized and extremely marginal Wrekin division, though it did at least end the worries of Bruce Grocott, who had originally gained the seat from the Conservatives in 1987 and could now pile up a majority of over 11,000 in Telford in 1997. However, to confound the pundits, the now reduced and more Conservative Wrekin (which had also taken in electors from solidly Tory Ludlow and Shropshire North) also managed to elect a Labour MP in 1997, with Peter Bradley defeating former Leicester East MP Peter Bruinvels by 3,000 votes.

The new Wrekin constituency still contains a number of small towns close to Telford itself, such as Arleston, Donnington and Hadley where Labour is able to rely on a solid vote. It seems though that in 1997, Bradley must have been able to take a fair vote from the large rural area in the constituency, which includes the town of Newport (a Liberal Democrat stronghold in local elections). Whether this vote can be retained at the next general election must be in some doubt; in the Euro elections the Conservatives led Labour 39–30% and their new standard-bearer Jacob Rees-Mogg will certainly hope for a better result than the 9% he achieved in Fife Central in 1997.

Wyre Forest

Labour majority 6,946 (12.6%)

Conservative target 102

MP David Lock

1997 (Turnout 75.4%)			
	Labour	26,843	48.8%
	Conservative	19,897	36.1%
	Liberal Democrat	4,377	8.0%
	Referendum	1,956	3.6%
	Liberal	1,670	3.0%
	UK Independence	312	0.6%

Wyre Forest includes the towns of Kidderminster, Stourport-on-Severn and Bewdley, once the political base of Conservative inter-war Prime Minister Stanley Baldwin. It was one of many 'small town' constituencies in the Midlands to fall to Labour in 1997 (along with Kettering, Wellingborough, Loughborough, Stafford, Warwick and Leamington among others) and could perhaps truly be described as 'middle England'.

Since 1997 however, strange events have been afoot in Wyre Forest District, virtually all of which lies within the constituency. In the 1999 local council elections, 'Health Concern' candidates won 7 seats in their battle to maintain services at Kidderminster Hospital, and in May 2000 they added another 11 seats, leaving the group close to overall control of the council, and the Labour vote reduced to less than 20%. How much effect all this will have on a general election contest remains to be seen, but it may benefit Conservative candidate Mark Simpson rather more than the sitting Labour incumbent David Lock. A possible early indicator was the Euro election result in the constituency, when the Conservatives led Labour by 43–25%, a far wider margin than in the nearby marginal seats of Worcester and The Wrekin.

Yorkshire

Conservative Targets

Target No	Constituency		Labour Lead
C37	Shipley	2,996	5.7%
C52	Selby	3,836	6.8%
C61	Leeds North West	3,844	7.8%
C66	Bradford West	3,877	8.5%
C68	Colne Valley	4,840	8.6%
C76	Scarborough and Whitby	5,124	9.4%
C90	Calder Valley	6,255	11.1%
C96	Pudsey	6,207	11.8%
C106	Batley and Spen	6,141	13.1%
C111	Brigg and Goole	6,389	13.7%
C113	Keighley	7,132	13.9%
C128	Leeds North East	6,959	15.3%
C131	Elmet	8,779	16.2%
C145	Cleethorpes	9,176	18.2%
C150	Dewsbury	8,323	19.3%
C178	Halifax	11,212	22.2%

(Liberal Democrat held)

C107	Harrogate and Knaresborough	6,236	13.1%
C146	Sheffield Hallam	8,271	18.2%

Possible Liberal Democrat Targets

		Labour Lead	
Leeds North West (3rd)	8,005	16.2%
Colne Valley (3rd)	10,530	18.7%

In the past Yorkshire (including Humberside) has been one of the more stable regions politically – few seats change hands (for example only three in 1966, four in 1979 and one in 1992) and both main parties have a large number of constituencies that they can usually rely upon. As everywhere else however, Labour did finally make a significant number of gains last time, notably in West Yorkshire where the Conservatives lost nine seats and as a result were completely wiped out. The Conservatives also lost three seats in normally solid North Yorkshire (Harrogate, Scarborough and Selby), with their county-wide vote here dropping by 13%. They also lost Sheffield Hallam, their only seat in South Yorkshire.

Yorkshire's marginals could well prove to be more fertile ground for the Conservative Party at the next general election. It has often been the case that the leader of a major party can attract additional support in their own region, as demonstrated by an impressive Labour performance in Wales in 1987 (the first election in which Neil Kinnock was leader); by a series of gains made by the Liberal Democrats in the South West under Paddy Ashdown's leadership; and even by a slightly higher than average swing to Labour in the North East in 1997, a region where the party already polled heavily. William Hague is a Yorkshireman who also has his constituency in the region, and it would be surprising if there was not some sort of electoral bonus for the Conservatives here when the election arrives.

Conservative prospects in Yorkshire are enhanced further by a cluster of seats in West Yorkshire based on the towns to the south and west of Leeds/Bradford, many of which Labour struggled to gain in the first place and some of which have turned heavily away from Labour since the 1997 election. This 'Pennine belt' actually crosses into the North West region, with Labour also potentially in trouble in the East Lancashire constituencies of Rossendale and Hyndburn as well as Oldham East and Saddleworth, some of which was originally on the Yorkshire side of the border. Many of these seats contain former industrial areas, accounting for previous Labour strength, but now attract a significant number of affluent commuters as well as those coming to retire. Both of these groups have traditionally been reservoirs of Conservative support, and it would not be a great surprise if Labour were to lose a number of these constituencies at the general election.

Labour are arguably more likely to hang on to Leeds North East and Leeds North West, even though these seats were traditional Conservative strongholds. Demographic change in urban and suburban areas has long been working to Labour's advantage, and these seats contain few of the safe Labour areas where the party may struggle to bring out its voters next time.

Over in Bradford, it is difficult to see Labour holding Shipley, and the result in Bradford West, now suddenly a marginal after its pro-Tory swing last time, is totally unpredictable. Meanwhile Labour may struggle to hold Scarborough and Whitby, with coastal constituencies showing signs of swinging as violently away from Labour next time as they did towards the party in 1997. In the former Humberside, the seats of Brigg and Goole and Cleethorpes will be true barometers of national feeling, the first in particular could go either way.

The Liberal Democrats will look to hold on to their two gains of 1997, Harrogate and Sheffield Hallam, which are of a completely different character to the seats held by the Liberals in the region in 1983 (Colne Valley and Leeds West). They will hope to continue to benefit from Labour supporters voting tactically to keep the Tories out; a major factor in 1997 with the Labour vote actually falling in these two constituencies compared with their national vote rising by some 9%. Realistically the Lib Dems will not add to this return of two seats, and their vote may even be squeezed further in Leeds North West despite their lead in local elections. It should also be noted that in local elections they have pulled ahead in two other Sheffield seats: Heeley and Hillsborough, though it would be a major surprise if such patterns were repeated in a national contest.

It is difficult to see any other seats changing hands that are not profiled below. Labour's 1992 gain of York was held with a remarkable majority of over 20,000 in 1997, though their lead in Wakefield (held by Labour since 1945 but marginal in the past) was smaller. In the Euro elections, Labour were out-polled by the Conservatives in Wakefield, all three constituencies in Bradford and also their safe Don Valley seat, though no-one seriously believes this pattern will be repeated at a general election. Meanwhile the Conservatives are surely unlikely to lose any more seats, even though a swing of 16% cut their majority in Beverley and Holderness to just 1,211 last time. This is of course another coastal constituency (including Hornsea and Spurn Head) which saw a huge swing to Labour last time, and it seems likely that it will now see a significant Conservative recovery.

Batley and Spen

Labour majority 6,141 (13.1%)

Conservative target 106

MP Mike Wood

1997 (Turnout 73.1%)	Labour	23,213	49.4%
	Conservative	17,072	36.4%
	Liberal Democrat	4,133	8.8%
	Referendum	1,691	3.6%
	BNP	472	1.0%
	Green	384	0.8%

Batley and Spen, like several other small-town 'Pennine Belt' seats, has proved an extremely tough nut for Labour to crack. Conservative MP Elizabeth Peacock held on by just 1,362 votes in 1987, then actually increased her majority (despite a national swing to Labour) in 1992, before finally being defeated in 1997 on a swing of 7.4%, again significantly lower than the national average.

The constituency includes the town of Batley itself, which has a substantial Asian population, together with the smaller towns of Cleckheaton and Birstall, just south of the M62 motorway. At a local government level all three main parties continue to win wards, and all three polled over 30% of the vote in May 2000. However, previous patterns suggest that the local Lib Dem vote here is more likely to switch to the Conservatives than Labour in national contests. Thus even though Labour remained ahead in the council elections of 1998, 1999 and 2000, Peacock has opted to stand again, and must have some chance of defeating Labour MP Mike Wood when battle recommences.

Bradford West

Labour majority 3,877 (8.5%)

Conservative target 66

MP Marsha Singh

1997 (Turnout 62.9%)	Labour	18,932	41.5%
	Conservative	15,055	33.0%
	Liberal Democrat	6,737	14.8%
	Socialist Labour	1,551	3.4%
	Referendum	1,348	3.0%
	Green	861	1.9%
	Others	1,084	2.4%

Something very unusual has been happening in Bradford West. At the last general election, it was one of two constituencies (along with Bethnal Green and Bow) which against the tide actually swung to the Conservatives. Since then, Labour has lost the previously rock-solid University ward, where they gained almost 70% of the vote in 1995. How can these changes be explained?

The answer seems to be inextricably bound up with Bradford's complex ethnic and political mix. Much of the city's non-white population is concentrated in Bradford West, but whereas the Conservative candidate at the last general election and a growing number of the party's local council candidates are from the dominant Muslim community, the Labour MP Marsha Singh is of Sikh origin. It seems that this choice of candidates is paying rich electoral dividends for the Conservatives; in local elections they moved ahead across the constituency in 1999 when they captured the 70% non-white University ward. In the parliamentary contest, 1997 candidate Mohammed Riaz will fight again, the outcome as unpredictable as anywhere in the country.

Brigg and Goole

Labour majority 6,389 (13.7%)

Conservative target 111

MP Ian Cawsey

1997 (Turnout 73.5%)	Labour	23,493	50.2%
	Conservative	17,104	36.5%
	Liberal Democrat	4,692	10.0%
	Referendum	1,513	3.2%

Brigg and Goole is a somewhat curious constituency, which was created at the last boundary review. The seat takes in a large chunk of the former constituency (and borough) of Boothferry centred on the town of Goole itself, along with the Isle of Axholme to the south. It then laps around Scunthorpe as far as the town of Brigg, which for parliamentary purposes had previously been connected with first Scunthorpe and then Cleethorpes.

Labour's victory in 1997 was something of a surprise, though there are strong areas of support in Goole, as well as an unusually strong rural Labour vote in some of the nearby villages. The Conservatives poll strongly in

South Axholme as well as in Brigg itself, and they were probably just about ahead in the 1999 local council elections, though it is difficult to be exact since the former boroughs of Boothferry and Glanford have now been replaced by the differently constituted East Riding and North Lincolnshire. It is undisputed that the Conservatives led by 18% at the Euro elections, and the second battle between their standard bearer Donald Stewart and Labour's Ian Cawsey promises to be much closer than the first.

Calder Valley

Labour majority 6,255 (11.1%)

Conservative target 90

MP Christine McCafferty

1997 (Turnout 75.4%)			
	Labour	26,050	46.1%
	Conservative	19,795	35.1%
	Liberal Democrat	8,322	14.7%
	Referendum	1,380	2.4%
	Green	488	0.9%
	Other	431	0.8%

Calder Valley was the focus of Pete Davies' 'This England', an account of the 1997 election campaign. The constituency itself runs along the eponymous river from Brighouse as far as the Lancashire border, taking in the towns of Elland, Hebden Bridge and Todmorden on the way. This is another seat which Labour have found difficult; Donald Thompson held on fairly comfortably against strong challenges in 1987 and 1992, but he was swept away in 1997 by local councillor Christine McCafferty on a swing only fractionally below the national average.

Labour has been behind in the constituency in all contests since 1997, with a local election vote that has halved since 1995. The Liberal Democrats continue to do well here in local elections, and were just about ahead across the constituency in both 1998 and 1999. The Conservatives then took a narrow lead in May 2000, pushing Labour into third place. Tory success in the Euro elections (a lead of 12.5%) together with previous patterns here suggest (as in neighbouring seats) that local Lib Dem voters are more likely to defect to the Conservatives than Labour in national contests, whatever the views of their national leadership. If this pattern persists, Sue Robson-Catling stands a good chance of regaining the seat for the Tories.

Cleethorpes

Labour majority 9,176 (18.2%)

Conservative target 145

MP Shona McIssac

1997 (Turnout 73.4%)			
Labour	26,058	51.6%
Conservative	16,882	33.4%
Liberal Democrat	5,746	11.4%
Referendum	1,787	3.5%

Cleethorpes was one of many seaside towns to fall to Labour in 1997, when former Wandsworth councillor Shona McIsaac defeated Brigg and Cleethorpes MP Michael Brown by over 9,000 votes. As with many other coastal constituencies, it had already started to move away from traditional allegiances, the Labour vote advancing in 1992 by fully 12%, three times the national average.

As well as Cleethorpes itself, the seat takes in Barton-upon-Humber some miles to the north-west, as well as industrial Immingham, before curling around Grimsby to take in a number of villages. It is this part of the constituency, the 'Wold Parishes' and Humberston, where the Conservatives are at their strongest; Labour support grows again in Cleethorpes to reach its peak in the terraced streets around Grimsby Town FC. In the local elections of 1999, Labour led in the constituency by a narrow margin, but this was clearly reversed in the Euro elections with the Conservatives ahead by 15%. Their candidate Stephen Howd will hope this marks the start of a recovery for his party along Britain's coastline.

Colne Valley

Labour majority 4,840 (8.6%)

Conservative target 68

Possible Liberal Democrat target

MP Kali Mountford

1997 (Turnout 76.8%)	Labour	23,285	41.3%
	Conservative	18,445	32.7%
	Liberal Democrat	12,755	22.6%
	Socialist Labour	759	1.3%
	Green	493	0.9%
	UK Independence	478	0.8%
	Other	196	0.3%

Colne Valley is a historic constituency name and has been the scene of some famous electoral battles, such that its former MP David Clark (before he moved to South Shields) was able to write a book on its history. It was here that Victor Grayson won on a socialist label in a by-election in 1907, and also this seat that provided the base for Labour's first chancellor, Philip Snowden. In the 1960s and 1970s, Labour and the Liberals became engaged in a succession of titanic electoral battles; then after Richard Wainwright had held the seat for the Liberals from 1974, Conservative Graham Riddick won a rare three-way contest in 1987.

Riddick was defeated in 1997 by Sheffield councillor Kali Mountford, thus re-establishing Labour's pre-eminence in the towns to the south and west of Huddersfield. But in local elections, the Liberal Democrats have continued to lead, by 2% in 1998, 14% in 1999 and 15% in 2000, and they now hold all but one ward, while Labour cannot claim a single success in the last two council elections. Whether this will have much bearing on a general election remains to be seen, but both Conservative Philip Davies and Liberal Democrat Gordon Beever will believe they are in with a chance of victory, as befits this fascinating seat.

Dewsbury

Labour majority 8,323 (19.3%)

Conservative target 150

MP Ann Taylor

1997 (Turnout 70.0%)			
	Labour	21,286	49.4%
	Conservative	12,963	30.1%
	Liberal Democrat	4,422	10.3%
	BNP	2,232	5.2%
	Referendum	1,019	2.4%
	Ind Labour	770	1.8%
	Green	383	0.9%

Dewsbury has been held by Labour's Ann Taylor since 1987, but extremely low swings in both 1992 and 1997 have resulted in the constituency never quite shaking off its marginal status. The seat borders Batley and Spen, which has been similarly resistant to the strong Labour advances made elsewhere. As in Batley, there is an Asian population in Dewsbury itself, and the suspicion that recent voting behaviour reflects some sort of ethnic polarization is reinforced by the strong showing for the extreme-right British National Party in 1997.

Unlike most other marginal seats, Labour have managed to stay ahead across Dewsbury constituency in all local elections since 1997. In May 1998, the lead was 7.5%; it then increased to 15% in 1999 before dropping to 3.5% in 2000. Even in the Euro elections, the Conservatives only out-polled Labour by a mere 11 votes, which suggests that Taylor should hang on whenever the general election is called.

Elmet

Labour majority 8,779 (16.2%)

Conservative target 131

MP Colin Burgon

1997 (Turnout 76.7%)	Labour	28,348	52.4%
	Conservative	19,569	36.2%
	Liberal Democrat	4,691	8.7%
	Referendum	1,487	2.7%

Elmet constituency is made up of the eastern wards of the metropolitan borough of Leeds, which largely comprises territory outside of the city itself. Before 1983 the constituency (together with what is now Selby) formed the oversized division of Barkston Ash, which was held by the Conservatives by 116 votes in 1945 and more comfortably after that. Elmet is rather more marginal, though it was held by Spencer Batiste for the Conservatives from 1983 to 1997. The constituency includes one ward on the outer edge of the city of Leeds, the council estates of Whinmoor, where Labour are traditionally strong, and also the town of Garforth, along with Swillington, Barwick and Kippax which are all generally Labour-inclined. However, Elmet also includes the comfortable and strongly Conservative town of Wetherby, which is enough to swing the balance in all but the best Labour years.

Labour's vote in Elmet has gradually been falling since the mid 1990s: from almost 60% in the 1995 local elections, their share fell to 52% in the 1997 general election (still enough to win by 9,000 votes), 50% in the 1998 local elections, 47% the year after and 40% in May 2000, when the Conservatives led by 6%. On this last occasion the voters of Wetherby succeeded in out-polling all the other wards of the constituency, and Labour MP Colin Burgon must hope this pattern is not repeated at the next general election. The Conservative hopeful is Michael Hayman.

Halifax

Labour majority 11,212 (22.2%)

Conservative target 178

MP Alice Mahon

1997 (Turnout 70.5%)	Labour	27,465	54.3%
	Conservative	16,253	32.1%
	Liberal Democrat	6,059	12.0%
	UK Independence	779	1.5%

Halifax was first won by Alice Mahon in 1987, but as a result of a slight swing back to the Conservatives in 1992, it became a rare Labour-held 'key seat' at the 1997 election, and is still not totally safe. It is interesting to note that in Halifax, the general election result in 1997 was almost identical to the local election result two years earlier, partly because unlike in many neighbouring constituencies the Liberal Democrats are weak here both nationally and locally.

Since 1997, the Conservatives have been amassing some large leads in council elections, 48–34% in 1998, 45–38% in 1999 and most recently 55–31% in 2000. Indeed Labour won just one of the nine wards in the constituency in May 2000 (Ovenden) while losing three others to the Tories. Conservative general election hopeful Derek Squirrell will also have been buoyed by a 13% lead in the Euro elections, despite the UKIP polling an above-average 8%. If William Hague continues to exert an appeal to small-town England (particularly in Yorkshire) then Labour could be in trouble here.

Harrogate and Knaresborough

Liberal Democrat majority 6,236 (13.1%)

Conservative target 107

MP Phil Willis

1997 (Turnout 72.9%)			
	Liberal Democrat	24,558	51.5%
	Conservative	18,322	38.5%
	Labour	4,151	8.7%
	Other	614	1.3%

Although always held by the Conservatives, Harrogate had for some time seemed a possible Liberal Democrat target. They had already taken what looked to be fairly similar seats in Bath and Cheltenham in 1992, and Labour remained extremely weak here. Then in 1997 the MP for 23 years, Robert Banks, stood down and was replaced by former Chancellor of the Exchequer Norman Lamont, whose own seat of Kingston-upon-Thames had been effectively abolished by the boundary commission. It was not a happy move for Lamont. His Liberal Democrat opponent Phil Willis had been leader of Harrogate borough council for some years and Lamont's candidature allowed the Lib Dems to campaign on their strongest trump card: local knowledge. In the event the swing away from the Conservatives here was almost 16%, with Willis able to rake up a majority of over 6,000.

There seems no reason why Willis should not follow Don Foster in Bath and Nigel Jones in Cheltenham by building up a reasonably secure parliamentary base here. Locally, the Lib Dems are in a strong position; they originally gained control of the council in 1990, became the biggest party in 1991 and remained well ahead in council elections in 1998 and 1999. Labour certainly offer no threat, though it is true that the Conservatives did increase their vote in 1999 and were well ahead in the Euro election, when the Lib Dem performance was poor across the whole country. Andrew Jones will hope to have better luck for the Conservatives at the next general election than Norman Lamont at the last, but it would probably take a significant national recovery for Phil Willis to be dislodged.

Keighley

Labour majority 7,132 (13.9%)

Conservative target 113

MP Ann Cryer

1997 (Turnout 76.3%)	Labour	26,039	50.6%
	Conservative	18,907	36.7%
	Liberal Democrat	5,064	9.8%
	Referendum	1,470	2.9%

Keighley was a Labour target in both 1987 and 1992, but as elsewhere the party had to wait until May 1997 before ultimately tasting victory. An average 10% swing saw Gary Waller defeated by Ann Cryer, wife of the late Labour MP for Bradford South, Bob Cryer and mother of another new Labour MP, Hornchurch's John Cryer.

The constituency includes not only the Labour-supporting town of Keighley, but also the strongly Conservative town of Ilkley as well as a good portion of rural territory, including the postcard village of Haworth, home of the Bronte sisters. This results in a highly marginal constituency, which the Conservatives must regain to have any chance of forming another government. Local election results have not been particularly promising, with the Conservatives ahead by just 2% across the constituency in 1998 and not even that in 1999. The Euro elections were somewhat better (a lead of

11.5%), which gives some grounds for optimism to general election standard-bearer Simon Cooke.

Leeds North East

Labour majority 6,959 (15.3%)

Conservative target 128

MP Fabian Hamilton

1997 (Turnout 71.8%)			
	Labour	22,368	49.2%
	Conservative	15,409	33.9%
	Liberal Democrat	6,318	13.9%
	Referendum	946	2.1%
	Socialist Labour	468	1.0%

Leeds North East was the constituency where Labour left winger Liz Davies was first selected and then promptly deselected before the last general election. These internal ructions appeared to have little impact when the electors of the seat finally had their say; Fabian Hamilton (who had contested the constituency in 1992, adding over 11% to the Labour vote) gained the seat with an above average swing of 12% and a majority of almost 7,000.

This is certainly a constituency of contrasts, including the inner-city area of Chapeltown, but also wealthy neighbourhoods in North Leeds such as Moortown and Roundhay. For over 30 years the seat was represented by right-wing Conservative MP Keith Joseph, and a Labour victory here would have seemed unlikely. Yet suburban constituencies such as this have been slowly but surely turning away from the Conservatives in recent years, and it is notable that Labour were still ahead here by 7% even in the local elections of 1999. May 2000 saw an almost perfect three-way split locally, and the Conservative lead in the Euro elections may encourage their candidate Owain Rhys not to abandon all hope.

Leeds North West

Labour majority 3,844 (7.8%)

Conservative target 61

Possible Liberal Democrat target

MP Harold Best

1997 (Turnout 69.7%)			
	Labour	19,694	39.9%
	Conservative	15,850	32.1%
	Liberal Democrat	11,689	23.7%
	Referendum	1,325	2.7%
	Others	818	1.7%

One of Labour's most impressive gains in 1997 came in Leeds North West, where they started the campaign in third place (a position they had been in for the last three elections). Despite this handicap, and Liberal Democrat attempts to claim it was they who were best placed to defeat the Conservatives, the swing to Labour was almost identical to neighbouring Leeds North East, producing a majority of almost 4,000 for left-winger Harold Best, the first time Labour had ever won this seat

Election battles since 1997 have remained complex, with all three parties winning the town of Otley (and Wharfedale) some miles to the north west in successive local elections, and Labour also losing Headingley ward to the Liberal Democrats. Overall in the constituency, a narrow Labour lead in the council elections of 1998 became a narrow Lib Dem lead in both 1999 and 2000, with the Conservatives topping the poll at the Euro elections. All three parties will therefore take an element of recent success into the next general election campaign. The Conservative hopeful is Adam Pritchard.

Pudsey

Labour majority 6,207 (11.8%)

Conservative target 96

MP Paul Truswell

1997 (Turnout 74.3%)

Labour	25,370	48.1%
Conservative	19,163	36.3%
Liberal Democrat	7,375	14.0%
Referendum	823	1.6%

Pudsey had never been a Labour seat before 1997, and for a time in the 1980s it seemed as if the Liberals were more likely to provide any serious challenge to the Conservatives. But Labour's Paul Truswell achieved one of his party's best results in the country at the last election, a 19% increase in the Labour vote ending an unbroken period of Conservative domination which had lasted for three-quarters of a century.

The constituency includes not just Pudsey itself (which is squeezed somewhat precariously between Leeds and Bradford) but also suburban areas to the north, including Horsforth and the towns of Yeadon and Guiseley, which is famous for the original Harry Ramsden's fish and chip restaurant. This is not necessarily fertile territory for Labour, indeed in local elections Horsforth remains strongly Liberal Democrat, while Aireborough ward was gained by the Conservatives in May 2000. Overall, a narrow Conservative lead in the 1999 local council elections became a 12% lead in the Euro elections and then a 17.5% advantage in 2000. Their hopeful is John Procter, and this could prove to be an extremely close contest.

Scarborough and Whitby

Labour majority 5,124 (9.4%)

Conservative target 76

MP Lawrie Quinn

1997 (Turnout 71.6%)

Labour	24,791	45.6%
Conservative	19,667	36.2%
Liberal Democrat	7,672	14.1%
Referendum	2,191	4.0%

Scarborough was one of many seaside resorts to fall to Labour for the first time in 1997. It was a completely unanticipated gain, though Lawrie Quinn was able to accumulate a majority of over 5,000, large enough for him to contemplate holding on next time. The size of the majority was a result of the huge swing of 14.7%, considerably above both the Yorkshire and national average, but very much in line with anti-Tory swings in other coastal seats (14.2% in Tynemouth further up the east coast, 16% in Morecambe, 16.4% in Hove). It was clear that these previously solid Conservative seats (which were always aberrant: Labour performed much worse than they should have done given the social profile of the population) had rejected their traditional allegiance in a decisive way, perhaps because of growing economic difficulties, for which the blame was squarely placed on the governing party.

The question now is whether Labour can hold on to seats like this after they too have been in government. The signs are not particularly promising; in the Euro elections the Conservatives led by a massive 23% in Scarborough and Whitby, their largest lead in any Labour marginal in the region. In the local elections just before that, Labour also did badly here, declining from being the biggest group on the local council down to third place behind the Conservatives and Independents. All this will have encouraged John Sykes, Conservative MP from 1992 to 1997, to contest the seat again next time.

Selby

Labour majority 3,836 (6.8%)

Conservative target 52

MP John Grogan

1997 (Turnout 74.9%)			
	Labour	25,838	45.9%
	Conservative	22,002	39.1%
	Liberal Democrat	6,778	12.0%
	Referendum	1,162	2.1%
	UK Independence	536	1.0%

Selby is a sprawling constituency including some 29 local government wards, all lying within the district of the same name. Only the towns of Selby and Tadcaster contain a significant number of electors, with a large number of smaller settlements, scattered from the outskirts of Castleford in the south west of the constituency as far as to the edges of York, providing the bulk of the electorate. This would appear to make Selby an unlikely Labour constituency, and in all probability it would not be but for the (now highly rare) presence of a large coal mine to the south east of Selby itself.

The Selby coalfield was opening up as others closed, and it is note-worthy that after John Grogan added 6% to the Labour vote in 1987, his vote again advanced by twice the national average in 1992. Then Grogan finally won the seat in the 1997 landslide with a third successive above-average swing.

Will this growing Labour strength in Selby be reversed? The 1999 local election results provided a mixed message; although Labour narrowly lost overall control of the council, they were still 7.5% ahead of the Conservatives, a greater margin than their general election lead. It would certainly be a mistake to assume that Michael Mitchell will automatically regain the parliamentary seat next time.

Sheffield Hallam

Liberal Democrat majority 8,271 (18.2%)

Conservative target 146

MP Richard Allen

1997 (Turnout 72.4%)	Liberal Democrat	23,345	51.3%
	Conservative	15,074	33.1%
	Labour	6,147	13.5%
	Referendum	788	1.7%
	Other	125	0.3%

Sheffield Hallam was one of the biggest Liberal Democrat triumphs of the 1997 election; they overturned a previous (notional) Conservative majority of over 8,000 to build up a similar lead of their own. Labour's vote actually fell here by 5%, a very similar pattern to that in Harrogate, the other seat gained by the Lib Dems in Yorkshire.

Hallam itself is not the sort of inner city urban constituency one might expect to find in Sheffield. Instead it includes affluent suburbs such as Dore to the south of the centre along the railway line. Perhaps unsurprisingly it had been safely held by the Conservatives since the war, though the Liberals started to come within striking distance from 1987.

Since 1997 the Liberal Democrat run of success in Sheffield has continued with the gain of the council from Labour. In 1999 they actually increased their share of the vote in Hallam from 51% at the general election to 57.5%, though this figure slipped back a little in May 2000. Perhaps more impressively, the Lib Dems would have also won Sheffield Heeley and Hillsborough on both the 1999 and 2000 local election results, taking a higher proportion of the vote in both than in Hallam itself. It seems unlikely that this success could be replicated nationally, but Richard Allen must be favourite to hold this constituency against Conservative John Harthman.

Shipley

Labour majority 2,996 (5.7%)

Conservative target 37

MP Christopher Leslie

1997 (Turnout 76.3%)

Labour	22,962	43.4%
Conservative	19,966	37.8%
Liberal Democrat	7,984	15.1%
Referendum	1,960	3.7%

Perhaps no single result better encapsulated the unpredictable nature of a general election than the 1997 defeat of eminent backbench Tory MP, Sir Marcus Fox, by an unknown 24-year old, Chris Leslie. It provided a stark reminder of the absence of any significant incumbency factor in parliamentary elections: voters had decided it was time for a change, whether or not Fox had been a hard-working MP for 27 years. The 'For Sale' notice that appeared outside the local Conservative Club soon after only emphasised the rather brutal nature of British politics.

However the Labour reign here could be a short one. They have been well behind the Conservatives in all elections since 1997, with only Shipley East ward providing Labour victories in local council elections. Meanwhile in the Euro elections of 1999, the Conservatives led by the huge margin of 20%, with another 7% picked up by the UK Independence Party. Shipley constituency (which includes Baildon, Bingley and the southern part of Rombalds Moor) has never been natural Labour territory, and David Senior must be favourite to regain the seat for the Conservatives next time.

North West

Conservative Targets

Target No	Constituency		Labour Lead
C12	Lancaster and Wyre	1,295	2.2%
C40	Wirral West	2,738	5.8%
C75	South Ribble	5,084	9.2%
C99	Morecambe and Lunesdale	5,965	12.1%
C116	Bury North	7,866	14.3%
C119	Bolton West	7,072	14.4%
C120	Wirral South	7,004	14.6%
C132	Crosby	7,182	16.3%
C136	Blackpool North and Fleetwood	8,946	16.6%
C140	Chorley	9,870	17.1%
C147	City of Chester	10,553	18.8%
C154	Warrington South	10,807	19.6%
C168	Rossendale and Darwen	10,949	21.4%
C173	Oldham East and Saddleworth (3rd)	11,880	22.0%
C182	Blackpool South	11,616	22.6%
C186	Pendle	10,824	23.0%
C194	Hyndburn	11,448	23.7%
C198	Bury South	12,381	24.6%

(Liberal Democrat held)

C100	Southport	6,160	12.2%

(Independent held)

	Tatton	11,077	22.7%

Liberal Democrat Targets

Oldham East and Saddleworth	3,389	6.3%
Rochdale	4,545	9.5%

The North West (including Lancashire, Cheshire, Merseyside and Greater Manchester) has traditionally played a key role in national general election fortunes, due to the large number of marginal constituencies within its bounds. For example when Harold Wilson ended 13 years of unbroken Conservative rule in 1964, almost a quarter of the 59 constituencies gained by Labour were in this region. In 1970, it was the Conservatives who gained 15 seats in the North West as Wilson was defeated. Interestingly the same pattern was not repeated in 1979; Labour's vote in the North West fell by just 2% in Thatcher's first triumph and only seven seats changed hands. But the Conservatives then won another raft of constituencies in 1983 (including Bury North and Bolton West) and it was these seats that Labour found so difficult to win back in the following two general elections. Indeed Labour made but a single breakthrough in 1987 (Manchester Withington) and their eight gains in 1992, including the East Lancashire trio of Hyndburn, Pendle and Rossendale, were simply not enough for the party to dislodge the Conservatives from power.

The 1997 election finally saw breakthroughs in established marginals such as Chester, Chorley and Blackpool South, but Labour went one stage further by mopping up another raft of constituencies which had hitherto been seen as Conservative by right. These included Morecambe and Wirral West, hardly bastions of the left, where government ministers Mark Lennox-Boyd and David Hunt tasted the bitter pill of defeat after long and distinguished parliamentary careers. In total the Conservatives were reduced to holding just seven seats of 70 in the region, even managing to lose rock solid Tatton to Independent Martin Bell.

It is difficult to see the Conservatives losing any more seats here at the next election, though Cheadle remains a possible Liberal Democrat target and Labour are only 1,200 votes behind in Eddisbury (see by-elections) and 2,500 adrift in Altrincham and Sale West. It is more likely that the Conservatives will make advances, but beyond Tatton (surely an immediate regain), Lancaster and Wyre and Wirral South, Labour must be confident in holding most of their 1997 gains. Indeed the next most likely Tory successes could be in East Lancashire, where a series of spectacular local election results appear to have returned both Hyndburn and Rossendale and

Darwen to marginal status. As a long-shot, watch out for Wallasey, at the depressed northern end of the Wirral, where the Conservatives were over 20% ahead in the May 2000 local elections, despite Angela Eagle's 19,000 majority in 1997.

The region is not without interest for the Liberal Democrats; they will be keen to hold on to Southport, which has oscillated between themselves and the Conservatives in recent elections, and also to win back Rochdale. They may be disappointed in both constituencies, but results since 1997 suggest they have a better chance in Oldham East and Saddleworth, scene of some ferocious electoral battles in recent years. After a number of near misses, Hazel Grove was won by such a huge majority last time (almost 12,000), that the constituency appears to have temporarily lost its marginal status. Finally, the Lib Dems continue to make extraordinary inroads into Labour's vote at a local level in Liverpool, so much so that they would have notionally gained all five constituencies in the city in both 1999 and 2000. The Lib Dems have of course failed to turn such local strength into national success on many previous occasions, and Labour will hope that this pattern continues.

Blackpool North and Fleetwood

Labour majority 8,946 (16.6%)

Conservative target 136

MP Joan Humble

1997 (Turnout 71.6%)			
	Labour	28,051	52.2%
	Conservative	19,105	35.5%
	Liberal Democrat	4,600	8.6%
	Referendum	1,704	3.2%
	Other	288	0.5%

Blackpool North and Fleetwood appeared a less good target for Labour than its southern counterpart in 1997, but the sheer size of swing, both nationally and in Blackpool, swept former Lancashire County Councillor Joan Humble into Parliament with a comfortable majority of nearly 9,000.

The seven northern wards of Blackpool included in the constituency are less good for Labour than those in Blackpool South, and Labour was 6% behind the Conservatives here in the 2000 council elections. However, the fishing port of Fleetwood is of a different character altogether, containing a number of strong Labour wards. Indeed, after the 1999 local elections, the town could account for 15 of the party's 19 councillors on Wyre District. The other four were elected in the wards around Cleveleys, but this is more marginal territory and would support the Conservatives in an even year. Overall, the Conservatives were ahead by 6% in the 1999 Euro elections and have selected Alan Vincent to fight what could be a close contest next time.

Blackpool South

Labour majority 11,616 (22.6%)

Conservative target 182

MP Gordon Marsden

1997 (Turnout 67.7%)	Labour	29,282	57.0%
	Conservative	17,666	34.4%
	Liberal Democrat	4,392	8.6%

Labour had never won a general election contest in Blackpool before 1997. But for many years, the tide had slowly been turning against the Conservatives, and it was no surprise that after losing by less than 2,000 votes in 1992, History Today editor Gordon Marsden won at his second attempt, though the size of his majority (in excess of 11,000) might have raised a few eyebrows.

This constituency has always been a better bet for Labour than its northern neighbour, containing the centre of the famous tourist town together with a number of working-class wards, and only a small amount of Conservative territory around Stanley Park and Squires Gate airport. It was notable that Labour would have held the seat on the basis of both the 1999 Euro elections and 2000 council elections, making this appear one of the safest of Labour's 1997 gains. Conservative candidate David Morris will surely have his work cut out here.

Bolton West

Labour majority 7,072 (14.4%)

Conservative target 119

MP Ruth Kelly

1997 (Turnout 77.4%)			
	Labour	24,342	49.5%
	Conservative	17,270	35.1%
	Liberal Democrat	5,309	10.8%
	Socialist Labour	1,374	2.8%
	Referendum	865	1.8%

Bolton West is a mixed constituency on both sides of the M61 motorway, which includes strong areas of Labour support in the working-class towns of Blackrod and Westhoughton, but also areas inclined to the Conservatives such as Deane-cum-Heaton, on the western fringes of Bolton itself. Labour narrowly failed to gain the seat in 1987 and 1992, but finally succeeded at the third attempt in 1997, when Ruth Kelly defeated Tom Sackville with a swing of 11%.

Election results since May 1997 indicate that this will not be an automatic 'Labour hold' next time. Conservative hopeful James Stevens will have been heartened by a 6% lead in the Euro elections, and the fact that Labour failed to win a single ward in local council elections in May 2000. To add to the uncertainty, the Liberal Democrats have been making strong local inroads into both Conservative and Labour territory, and would notionally have won the seat in 2000, even though in the 1997 general election contest they took barely 10% of the vote.

Bury North

Labour majority 7,866 (14.3%)

Conservative target 116

MP David Chaytor

1997 (Turnout 78.1%)			
	Labour	28,523	51.8%
	Conservative	20,657	37.5%
	Liberal Democrat	4,536	8.2%
	Referendum	1,337	2.4%

Labour gained both Bury constituencies in 1997, after the Conservatives had resolutely held out in the previous two elections. Bury North had always been slightly safer than South, as it includes not only most of Bury itself, but also Ramsbottom and Tottington towards the Lancashire border, which contain a large number of natural Conservative voters. However even they could not prevent the defeat of social security minister Alistair Burt on an 11% swing last time – close to the national and regional average.

In the 1999 Euro elections Labour trailed by 5%, a deficit which increased to almost 10% in the 2000 local council elections. Even though Burt has now moved down to the more fertile Tory terrritory of North East Bedfordshire, his replacement John Walsh must have at least a slight chance of defeating the present incumbent David Chaytor after a single term, especially if the Conservatives mount a strong campaign nationally. In any event, Labour's respectable 1997 majority in Bury North is likely to be reduced.

Bury South

Labour majority 12,381 (24.6%)

Conservative target 198

MP Ivan Lewis

1997 (Turnout 75.7%)			
	Labour	28,658	56.9%
	Conservative	16,277	32.3%
	Liberal Democrat	4,227	8.4%
	Referendum	1,216	2.4%

Bury South was near the top of Labour's target list in 1997, and duly fell with a swing of 13%, slightly above the national and regional average, and enough for Labour to win with a huge majority exceeding 12,000. The constituency itself is not really based on the town of Bury (which lies within Bury North), but rather the working-class town of Radcliffe together with more prosperous commuter territory to the north and south of the M60 motorway, including Whitefield, Prestwich and Sedgley Park.

This was one of the very few of Labour's 'gain seats' of 1997 which the party held in the 1999 Euro elections, and in a reverse of the pattern in Bury North, Labour then strengthened its position in the local elections of May 2000, extending their lead to 11%. It is plausible that the tough asylum policies of the Conservatives have not played well with the large number of

Jewish voters in the constituency, and this can only be to the advantage of the local Jewish MP, Ivan Lewis.

Chorley

Labour majority 9,870 (17.1%)

Conservative target 140

MP Lindsay Hoyle

1997 (Turnout 77.6%)			
	Labour	30,607	53.0%
	Conservative	20,737	35.9%
	Liberal Democrat	4,900	8.5%
	Referendum	1,319	2.3%
	Other	143	0.2%

Labour finally triumphed in Chorley in 1997 after failing to come anywhere near dislodging popular Conservative MP Den Dover in 1983, 1987 and 1992. The constituency is based around the town of Chorley itself, which is usually inclined to Labour, and also includes the Labour stronghold of Adlington. However the seat also takes in a large number of Conservative-inclined villages such as Charnock Richard and Brindle and Hoghton, which all result in a highly marginal constituency.

The parliamentary seat shares the same boundaries as the local government borough, where Labour lost control in 2000. However, the Conservative lead barely exceeded 4%, and it is noticeable that Labour performed far better in some surrounding villages such as Eccleston and Heskin, and Withnell, than they had in the early 1990s. The continued wider appeal of 'New' Labour should ensure that Lindsay Hoyle (son of former Labour whip Doug, now Lord Hoyle) is able to fight off the challenge of Peter Booth when battle recommences.

City of Chester

Labour majority 10,553 (18.8%)

Conservative target 147

MP Christine Russell

1997 (Turnout 78.1%)			
	Labour	29,806	53.0%
	Conservative	19,253	34.2%
	Liberal Democrat	5,353	9.5%
	Referendum	1,487	2.6%
	Others	358	0.6%

Chester is another marginal constituency which Labour narrowly failed to gain in the general election of 1992, when sometime celebrity Gyles Brandreth held on by just 1,100 votes. There was to be no repeat however in 1997, a swing of just over 11% giving Labour victory here for the first time, and with an unlikely 10,000 majority.

Chester itself is very mixed politically – Labour is strong in the centre ,and wards towards and in Blacon, but the Conservatives hit back in rural wards such as Christleton and Mollington and the Liberal Democrats have been making strong local inroads in wards to the east of the city centre. In the local elections of 1999, Labour led by approximately 9%, but the Conservatives narrowly polled more votes in the Euro elections, and the 2000 local elections then produced a three-way split, reflecting the composition of the council. Assuming an improved Labour performance at the general election, the odds do not favour Conservative candidate David Jones, but this is unlikely ever to become an entirely safe Labour seat for former local councillor Christine Russell.

Crosby

Labour majority 7,182 (16.3%)

Conservative target 132

MP Claire Curtis-Thomas

1997 (Turnout 77.2%)			
	Labour	22,549	51.1%
	Conservative	15,367	34.8%
	Liberal Democrat	5,080	11.5%
	Referendum	813	1.8%
	Others	332	0.7%

Crosby should have been the result which heralded Labour's triumph of May 1997. The early declaration saw a swing of 18%, with the Labour vote advancing by more than 22%; a constituency which few believed the party could gain was won with a large majority exceeding 7,000. Crosby's place in election folklore was denied by a single factor, the absence of TV cameras, which instead signalled the landslide with the later and more predictable result from Birmingham Edgbaston.

Yet the result here should probably not have been such a total surprise. Coastal constituencies had been slowly moving away from their traditional Conservative allegiance for many years, and Crosby (which stretches north from the Liverpool conurbation as far as the town of Formby) had been lost before when Shirley Williams famously gained the seat for the SDP in a by-election in 1981. However, the third party vote almost totally subsided in Crosby in 1997, and this contest is now a straight two-party battle. Conservative candidate Robert Collinson will have been given hope by the party's 13% lead at the Euro elections and 7% lead in the most recent local elections; next time a close result is likely and with luck the media may be around to report it.

Hyndburn

Labour majority 11,448 (23.7%)

Conservative target 194

MP Greg Pope

1997 (Turnout 72.3%)			
Labour	26,831	55.6%
Conservative	15,383	31.9%
Liberal Democrat	4,141	8.6%
Referendum	1,627	3.4%
Other	290	0.6%

Hyndburn was not a Labour gain of 1997; in fact the constituency was won five years earlier when Greg Pope defeated Kenneth Hargreaves by 2,000 votes. However a slightly lower than average swing to Labour in 1997, together with a significant Conservative advance over the last two years (including the gain of Hyndburn District Council) must make this a marginal worth watching next time.

The constituency is based on a number of small East Lancashire towns between Blackburn and Burnley, notably Accrington but also Oswaldtwistle, Church, Clayton-le-Moors and Great Harwood. This is territory where William Hague's Conservatives are demonstrating a strong appeal, and the Conservatives increased their lead in the parliamentary constituency from 6.5% in the 1999 Euro elections to almost 14% in the 2000 local council elections. Finishes in Hyndburn have been close in the past (the 1983 count famously went to six recounts) and the Conservatives may be in with an outside chance of regaining the seat at the next general election, despite the huge size of Pope's majority in 1997.

Lancaster and Wyre

Labour majority 1,295 (2.2%)

Conservative target 12

MP Hilton Dawson

1997 (Turnout 74.9%)			
	Labour	25,173	42.8%
	Conservative	23,878	40.6%
	Liberal Democrat	6,802	11.6%
	Referendum	1,516	2.6%
	Green	795	1.4%
	UK Independence	698	1.2%

Lancaster and Wyre was a newly created constituency at the last election, including the historic city of Lancaster south of the River Lune, farming areas around Garstang, and wealthier suburbs of Blackpool such as Poulton-le-Fylde and Thornton. Despite a Labour vote that had become very strong in Lancaster itself by the mid 1990s, it was a major surprise that Labour won the parliamentary constituency in 1997, Hilton Dawson defeating Wyre MP Keith Mans by 1,295 votes. The fact that the size of the Labour majority was smaller than the Referendum party vote will give Conservative candidate Steve Barclay hope that the result can be reversed next time.

Labour's fortunes in the constituency have not been good since 1997. The party lost control of both Lancaster and Wyre councils in 1999, and the Conservatives now hold all but one of the local council wards in the Wyre section of the constituency. In Lancaster, the Greens made spectacular advances in 1999, gaining no fewer than five council seats at Labour's expense; then in the Euro elections the Labour vote in the constituency fell to under 24%, with the Greens picking up over 11%. It is clear that this vote will need to be squeezed if Labour are to have any chance of holding Lancaster and Wyre at the general election.

Morecambe and Lunesdale

Labour majority 5,965 (12.1%)

Conservative target 99

MP Geraldine Smith

1997 (Turnout 72.3%)	Labour	24,061	48.9%
	Conservative	18,096	36.7%
	Liberal Democrat	5,614	11.4%
	Referendum	1,313	2.7%
	Other	165	0.3%

Morecambe had never been a Labour seat before 1997, and it was a measure of Labour's landslide that not only did the party triumph here for the first time, but they won comfortably, with a 19% advance in their vote. Indeed Britain's seaside resorts were very much part (if largely unnoticed) of the 'New Labour coalition' in 1997, with once rock solid Tory resorts like Blackpool, Scarborough, Ayr, Hove and Hastings all turning red for the first time.

Labour's ability to retain these seats next time will play a key role in the overall result, but some of the signs in Morecambe since 1997 have not been promising. In the 1999 Euro Elections, the Conservatives romped home with a 15% lead, despite a vote of over 10% for the UK Independence Party, who finished third. In the council elections of the same year, Labour's impressive local gains of 1995 were more or less reversed, though the beneficiaries were not the Conservatives but 'Morecambe Bay Independents', who now control the local council.

Victory for Conservative candidate David Nuttall at the next election is more likely than Independence for Morecambe Bay, but it should be noted that in national terms this seat is now a safer bet for Labour than Bradford West, and Geraldine Smith may well turn out to be more than a single-term MP.

Oldham East and Saddleworth

Labour majority 3,389 (6.3%)

Liberal Democrat target

Conservative target 173

MP Phil Woolas

1997 (Turnout 73.9%)			
	Labour	22,546	41.7%
	Liberal Democrat	19,157	35.4%
	Conservative	10,666	19.7%
	Referendum	1,116	2.1%
	Others	616	1.1%

Labour's triumph in 1997 did not arrive purely at the expense of the Conservatives; in the North West the party gained two seats from the Liberal Democrats. In the case of Oldham East and Saddleworth, the gain was notionally from the Conservatives, but the constituency is largely based on the former Littleborough and Saddleworth division (minus the town of Littleborough itself), which was won by Liberal Democrat Chris Davies in a hard-fought by-election in 1995.

Davies must have been disappointed to lose 'round two' to his adversary Phil Woolas in 1997, but he has now moved on to the European Parliament, heading the Liberal Democrats' North West regional list in 1999. His candidature probably accounted for his party polling the most votes in Oldham East and Saddleworth in the Euro elections; remarkably this was one of only three constituencies the Lib Dems 'won' in the whole country. In local elections the Lib Dems have continued to make gains, taking fully 60% of the vote in council elections in the constituency in May 2000. They have selected Howard Sykes as their new parliamentary challenger, while Conservative candidate Craig Heeley cannot be entirely discounted either. In any event, another hard fought battle on the eastern edges of Greater Manchester seems inevitable.

Pendle

Labour majority 10,824 (23.0%)

Conservative target 186

MP Gordon Prentice

1997 (Turnout 74.5%)	Labour	25,059	53.3%
	Conservative	14,235	30.3%
	Liberal Democrat	5,460	11.6%
	Referendum	2,281	4.8%

Pendle is one of three East Lancashire constituencies gained by Labour in 1992 which must still be regarded as marginal. The seat is largely based on Nelson and Colne, and has been held by a succession of notable MPs: Labour's Sydney Silverman (whose private member's bill led to the abolition of capital punishment) from 1935 until 1968, Conservative David Waddington (later Home Secretary) from 1968 until 1974, Labour's Doug Hoyle from 1974 until 1979 and Conservative minister John Lee for 13 years after that. To add to the sense of marginality, the Liberals have been strong locally for many years, regularly polling over 30% in local council elections.

In the Euro elections of 1999, the Conservatives led Labour 35–31%, however it was Labour who led in the local council elections in May 2000. Indeed, Labour were still making gains here in 2000, the opposite pattern from that in nearby Rossendale and Hyndburn. This suggests that 'right to roam' campaigner Gordon Prentice should see off Conservative challenger Rasjid Skinner for the time being at least.

Rochdale

Labour majority 4,545 (9.5%)

Liberal Democrat target

MP Lorna Fitzsimons

1997 (Turnout 70.0%)	Labour	23,758	49.4%
	Liberal Democrat	19,213	40.0%
	Conservative	4,237	8.8%
	Others	874	1.8%

Rochdale had been held for the Liberals by larger-than-life MP Cyril Smith from a by-election in 1972 until 1992, after previously looking like a fairly typical solid Labour seat. In retrospect it is perhaps surprising that Liz Lynne managed to hold the seat (albeit narrowly) in 1992, especially given that Smith's final majority was less than 3,000. However there was to be no repeat five years later when Labour challenger and former NUS president Lorna Fitzsimons triumphed in a sometimes bitter contest with a majority exceeding 4,500.

In general elections here the Conservative vote has been heavily squeezed by the Liberal Democrats, and their recovery in the absence of tactical factors in the 1999 Euro elections resulted in Labour comfortably topping the poll. But even in local council elections, Labour remained only 7% behind the Lib Dems in 2000, a far narrower margin than in neighbouring Oldham East and Saddleworth and one which suggests that Labour should hold on next time. The new Liberal Democrat hopeful is Paul Rowen.

Rossendale and Darwen

Labour majority 10,949 (21.4%)

Conservative target 168

MP Janet Anderson

1997 (Turnout 73.4%)			
	Labour	27,470	53.6%
	Conservative	16,521	32.3%
	Liberal Democrat	5,435	10.6%
	Referendum	1,108	2.2%
	Other	674	1.3%

Like its geographical neighbour, Hyndburn, Janet Anderson gained Rossendale and Darwen in 1992 when she defeated government minister David Trippier by just 120 votes. In 1997, Anderson's majority was extended to almost 11,000, and yet as with its neighbour, recent results must give the Conservatives some hope that they can record a surprise victory here when the next general election is called.

The constituency includes most of the borough of Rossendale, which the Conservatives gained in the 2000 local council elections; indeed Labour held just one ward as a blue tide swept this part of east Lancashire. Also included in the seat are six wards in Darwen, where the three parties were closely matched in the most recent local elections. Overall, the Conservatives took approximately 50% of the vote across the constituency in May 2000, their lead of 12% double that recorded in the previous year's Euro elections. Their new candidate George Lee must be more confident than the formal 'target number' suggests.

Southport

Liberal Democrat majority 6,160 (12.2%)

Conservative target 100

MP Ronnie Fearn

1997 (Turnout 72.1%)	Liberal Democrat	24,346	48.1%
	Conservative	18,186	35.9%
	Labour	6,125	12.1%
	Referendum	1,368	2.7%
	Others	571	1.1%

The town of Southport seems to many to be out of place in Merseyside, and in general elections its numerous close battles between the Conservatives and Liberal Democrats have been wholly out of keeping with the rest of this metropolitan county. The Conservative vote here has always been very strong (they never polled fewer than 22,000 votes in any post-war general election until 1997), but the Labour vote has slowly been squeezed by the Liberals and then Liberal Democrats, who as a result started to come close from 1974 onwards. In 1987, the constituency was finally gained at his fourth attempt by Ronnie Fearn, only to be promptly regained by the Conservatives five years later. However Fearn then won again in 1997 on a 9% swing to oust Matthew Banks after one term.

Since 1997 the Lib Dems have remained narrowly ahead in local council elections; they won five out of the seven council wards in 1999 and in May 2000 led the Conservatives by 47–40%. However, in the 1999 Euro election the third party vote collapsed, the Conservatives won by a landslide and Labour almost claimed second place. The Liberal Democrats must hope the same pattern is not repeated at the general election when Fearn stands down.

South Ribble

Labour majority 5,084 (9.2%)

Conservative target 75

MP David Borrow

1997 (Turnout 77.1%)			
	Labour	25,856	46.8%
	Conservative	20,772	37.6%
	Liberal Democrat	5,879	10.6%
	Referendum	1,475	2.7%
	Others	1,249	2.3%

South Ribble constituency, which was created by the boundary changes of 1983, is based on the town of Leyland, together with rural and suburban areas to the west and east. It was a Labour target in 1992, but like so many constituencies in the North West and elsewhere the Conservatives hung on fairly comfortably; however fortunes were firmly reversed in 1997 when former minister Robert Atkins was defeated on a swing of 12% by the former leader of Preston borough council, David Borrow.

In the local elections of 1999, both Labour and the Conservatives emerged with 15 council seats in the constituency, with the Liberal Democrats taking 12. Most of Labour's support is concentrated in Leyland itself, along with lower Penwortham towards Preston (previously in the ultra-marginal Preston South constituency). The Conservatives can count on big leads in Hutton and Longton, and while the Lib Dems have gained wards such as Farington in local elections, their vote tends to subside in national contests. In the Euro elections the Conservatives were ahead by over 12%; their candidate Adrian Owens must be in with a chance in what could be an extremely tight battle.

Tatton

Independent majority 11,077 (22.7%)

Conservative target

MP Martin Bell

1997 (Turnout 76.5%)	Independent	29,354	60.2%
	Conservative	18,277	37.5%
	Others	1,161	12.4%

No constituency produced a more enduring image of the 1997 general election than Tatton, where former BBC correspondent Martin Bell, permanently attired in a white suit, took on former minister Neil Hamilton and romped to victory with over 60% of the vote. This was all the more extraordinary as Tatton is usually one of the Conservatives' safest seats in the whole of England – based on the affluent Cheshire towns of Knutsford, Wilmslow and Alderley Edge together with a large rural area in between. Prior to 1997 it seemed inconceivable that this constituency could ever be lost by the Conservative Party.

Bell's victory would not have been possible without a range of factors, notably the nationally-engineered withdrawal of Labour and Liberal Democrat candidates, who had already been selected by their local parties. Although there have been occasional previous instances of local pacts (such as those between the Conservatives and Liberals in Huddersfield and Bolton some decades ago), it has become standard practice in recent general elections for the major parties to field candidates in all seats. When Labour and the Lib Dems agreed to pull out and support an independent candidate, the writing was on the wall for Hamilton, though the sheer size of Bell's majority seemed to stun all concerned.

When normal party competition returned in the 1999 Euro elections, the Conservatives polled an overall majority of the votes cast, and with Martin Bell promising to retire after a single term there is surely no prospect of Conservative candidate George Osborne not re-establishing the natural order in Tatton.

Warrington South

Labour majority 10,807 (19.6%)

Conservative target 154

MP Helen Southworth

1997 (Turnout 76.2%)			
	Labour	28,721	52.1%
	Conservative	17,914	32.5%
	Liberal Democrat	7,199	13.1%
	Referendum	1,082	2.0%
	Other	166	0.3%

Warrington South was first gained by Labour with a majority of less than 200 votes in 1992; however boundary changes before 1997 left the new constituency looking a decidedly dubious prospect and as a result MP Mike Hall followed a minority of his electors to the new Weaver Vale division. In the event the new Warrington South did not prove a difficult proposition for Labour; on an above average swing of 12% it was won comfortably with a majority exceeding 10,000.

The constituency is based on areas south of the centre, but also includes areas to the west (Great Sankey and Penketh) and east (Lymm). All in all it is an affluent, politically mixed constituency, and Labour have not had things all their own way since 1997. The Conservatives led here in the 1999 Euro elections, albeit by a wafer-thin margin of 105 votes. Labour have also faced a strong challenge in local elections from the Liberal Democrats, who gained two wards in 2000 to lead Labour by a large margin across the constituency. This success is unlikely to translate into a general election, and the difficult and unlikely task of reversing Helen Southworth's five-figure majority falls to another female candidate, Conservative Caroline Mosley.

Wirral South

Labour majority 7,004 (14.6%)

Conservative target 120

MP Ben Chapman

1997 (Turnout 81.0%)	Labour	24,499	50.9%
	Conservative	17,495	36.4%
	Liberal Democrat	5,018	10.4%
	Referendum	768	1.6%
	Others	315	0.6%

The Wirral South by-election in February 1997 appeared at the time to indicate that the days of the Major government were running out, with Labour's Ben Chapman famously gaining the seat with an 18% swing. In the event the by-election did indeed prove an accurate indicator of events to come, with the same outcome in Wirral South repeated in the general election some nine weeks later.

The Wirral peninsula appears starkly divided into a strongly-Labour urbanised north around Wallasey and Birkenhead, and more prosperous commuter territory to the south and west. However in 1997 Labour's appeal was wide enough to win all four parliamentary constituencies. Wirral South includes Labour-inclined wards running south from Birkenhead such as Bromborough and to a lesser extent Bebington, but also highly prosperous wards such as Heswall where the Conservatives gained 72% of the vote in the May 2000 local elections. Overall, Labour trailed by 13% in the Euro elections, and then finished third in the 2000 local council elections as two wards were won by the Liberal Democrats. Ben Chapman will have his work cut out to fend off the challenge of Tony Millard when the general election is called.

Wirral West

Labour majority 2,738 (5.8%)

Conservative target 40

MP Stephen Hesford

1997 (Turnout 77.0%)	Labour	21,035	44.9%
	Conservative	18,297	39.0%
	Liberal Democrat	5,945	12.7%
	Referendum	1,613	3.4%

Wirral West was surely one of Labour's most unlikely gains in the landslide of 1997. This is prosperous commuter territory, lands where Liverpool's middle class have sought refuge throughout the post-war period. As Conservative support in Liverpool (where they held a majority of seats until 1964) waned, so it increased in the Wirral penninsula, and a Labour break-through here seemed impossible. For over 30 years, Wirral West was the parliamentary base for Selwyn Lloyd, and for 20 years after that for another prominent figure, David Hunt. Labour trailed in the constituency even at the party's 1996 local election highpoint. Yet in 1997 when so many Tory citadels fell, Stephen Hesford joined the ranks of the giant-killers, a near 14% swing resulting in a majority approaching 3,000 and leaving the Wirral an unlikely 'Tory-free zone'.

Labour's success may not be so easy to repeat next time. In the 1999 Euro elections, the Conservative lead in Wirral West was close to 20%, and this increased to 27% in the 2000 local council elections. Indeed from local patterns it is difficult to see how Labour could ever have won this constituency, with the party polling less than a quarter of the vote in all wards bar one (Upton) in May 2000. Labour's performance here in 1997 may have been boosted by the effects of the Wirral South by-election a few weeks earlier, and without such a bad start next time, the Conservative hopeful Chris Lynch must start as favourite to regain the seat.

North East

....

Conservative Targets

Target No	Constituency		Labour Lead
C158	Middlesbrough S'th & E Cleveland	10,607	19.8%
C177	Tynemouth	11,273	22.0%
C179	Stockton South	11,585	22.2%

Labour Target

		Conservative Lead	
L3	Hexham	222	0.5%

The North East (including Durham, Northumberland, Tyne and Wear, the former county of Cleveland and also Cumbria) has fewer marginals than any other region, and the four it does contain are all unlikely to change hands at the next general election. This situation is a result of Labour's traditional and increasing dominance in national elections. Only on one occasion since the war (1959) has Labour failed to win two-thirds of the parliamentary constituencies; even in their meltdown year of 1983 they won 26 out of 36. Since then, the party has mopped up the remaining urban Conservative outposts, starting with Newcastle Central (1987), followed by Darlington and Barrow (1992) and most recently Stockton South, Tynemouth and Middlesbrough South and East Cleveland (1997). All that remains in the blue corner are three large rural constituencies: Westmorland, Penrith and the Border, and Hexham, which was almost lost in the landslide of 1997. Meanwhile the Liberal Democrats cling on to their single seat in Berwick, originally gained in a by-election in 1973.

Media interest since the last general election has focused on the large number of cabinet ministers in the region; as well as Tony Blair, Alan Milburn, Peter Mandelson, Mo Mowlam, Nick Brown and Stephen Byers all have their political bases here. This is probably a result of the concentration of so many safe Labour seats; no fewer than 17, almost half the total number of constituencies in the region, had Labour majorities exceeding 20,000 in 1997. In terms of electoral competition, there is no reason why Labour's dominance should not continue. Even though the party lost control of Hartlepool council in May 2000 and the Liberal Democrats polled most local votes in Blaydon, these results are highly unlikely to be repeated when the national government is at stake. Outside of the featured marginals, only Carlisle provides a realistic chance of a shock result, as the Conservatives gained control of the council in 1999 and are campaigning hard, though as they failed to win the parliamentary seat even in 1983 their chances remain slim. Elsewhere, interest will focus on the likely drop in turnout, though this is highly unlikely to deprive Labour of any of their 'heartland' seats due to the sheer size of majorities that had been amassed by 1997.

Hexham

Conservative majority 222 (0.5%)

Labour target 3

MP Peter Atkinson

1997 (Turnout 77.5%)			
	Conservative	17,701	38.8%
	Labour	17,479	38.3%
	Liberal Democrat	7,959	17.4%
	Referendum	1,362	3.0%
	UK Independence	1,170	2.6%

Hexham was almost Labour's most sensational gain in 1997; this huge rural seat in Northumberland was assumed to be an inpregnable Conservative fortress, and if anything the only threat seemed to come from the Liberal Democrats. In the event, the Lib Dem vote fell, Labour's surged upwards and a huge swing of 14% left Conservative Peter Atkinson clinging on by just 222 votes.

The Labour vote here is concentrated along the Tyne valley, particularly in two towns at opposite ends, Haltwhistle and Prudhoe, while the town of Hexham itself is politically mixed. It is interesting that in 1995, Labour achieved its best performance on Tynedale council since its creation in 1973, winning 18 seats compared with 11 apiece for the other two parties. In 1999, Labour was reduced to 14 seats, with the Conservatives doubling their strength; in percentage terms the Conservatives led 35-24. The task facing Labour candidate, Newcastle councillor Paul Brannen, is even harder as the constituency also includes eight wards from Castle Morpeth borough, including the affluent commuter bases of Ponteland and Darras Hall; in 1999 Labour polled less than 10% here in local elections.

Middlesbrough South and East Cleveland

Labour majority 10,607 (19.8%)

Conservative target 158

MP Ashok Kumar

1997 (Turnout 75.9%)	Labour	29,319	54.7%
	Conservative	18,712	34.9%
	Liberal Democrat	4,004	7.5%
	Referendum	1,552	2.9%

This is essentially the successor to the former Langbaurgh seat, which was gained by Ashok Kumar for Labour in a by-election in 1991, before it was regained by the Conservatives in 1992. Last time a swing of 11% was comfortable enough to return Kumar to parliament with a majority exceeding 10,000.

As the name suggests, this is a constituency of two halves. The slightly larger part is in fact from Redcar and Cleveland borough, including the small towns of Guisborough, Skelton, Brotton, Loftus and the seaside resort of Saltburn. This is highly marginal territory, with the Conservatives slightly ahead in the 1999 local elections. The other part of the constituency contains the southern wards of Middlesbrough, which range from rock-solid Labour areas such as Easterside and Park End to the commuter suburbs of Newham and Nunthorpe, where there is a considerable Conservative vote. Overall, Labour led in the constituency in the 1999 local elections by 38-35%, but in the Euro elections a month later the Conservatives were 10% ahead. Their candidate is Barbara Harpham, leader of the Conservative group on Redcar and Cleveland council.

Stockton South

Labour majority 11,585 (22.2%)

Conservative target 179

MP Dari Taylor

1997 (Turnout 76.1%)			
	Labour	28,790	55.2%
	Conservative	17,205	33.0%
	Liberal Democrat	4,721	9.1%
	Referendum	1,400	2.7%

Stockton South is a constituency with a somewhat peculiar recent history. Labour MP Ian Wrigglesworth defected to the new SDP in 1981, held on by 100 votes in 1983, and was finally defeated in 1987 when all three main parties gained over 30% of the vote. In 1992, the third party vote crumbled, but mainly to the advantage of Conservative MP Tim Devlin whose vote advanced by 10%. Then in 1997 a huge swing of 16% saw the seat finally return to Labour.

Stockton was the eve-of-poll meeting place between Tony Blair and John Prescott after they had each covered thousands of miles on their 1997 campaign buses. The vast crowds which turned up were an early indicator of Labour's landslide, as Stockton South remains theoretically a marginal. Although there are strong Labour areas in Thornaby-on-Tees, the Conservatives poll well in the west Stockton wards of Bishopsgarth, Hartburn and Fairfield and also in expanding Ingleby Barwick. The Liberal Democrats can still win local wards as well, though their vote in general elections has now been squeezed to less than 10%. In 1999, Labour were 4% ahead in local elections, the Conservatives 6% ahead in the Euro elections. Tim Devlin will fight the seat again at the general election, but with a majority of over 11,000, Dari Taylor must start as favourite.

Tynemouth

Labour majority 11,273 (22.0%)

Conservative target 177

MP Alan Campbell

1997 (Turnout 77.0%)

Labour	28,318	55.4%
Conservative	17,045	33.3%
Liberal Democrat	4,509	8.8%
Referendum	819	1.6%
UK Independence	462	0.9%

Tynemouth had been held by the Conservatives from 1950 right up to 1997, first by Dame Irene Ward and more recently by Neville Trotter, who wisely stood down before a swing of 14% finally enabled Labour to make their breakthrough with a majority greater than the Conservatives' in 1983. It appears to be another example of a coastal seat swinging decisively away from the Conservatives, as the constituency includes not only Tynemouth itself but also the seaside resort of Whitley Bay. However, the strongest Labour wards are actually in North Shields, which is more working class and similar sort of territory to that which makes up so many rock solid Labour seats in the North East.

In the aftermath of Alan Campbell's massive victory in 1997, the Labour tide seems to be in retreat here. Annual local elections have seen the Conservatives lead by 2% in 1998, 5% in 1999 and then a massive 23% in 2000, and they also led in the Euro elections, when 1997 candidate Martin Callanan topped the Conservative list. His replacement Karl Poulsen must if anything have a slightly better chance of regaining this seat at the general election than his colleagues in the two Teesside marginals.

Scotland

by Mark Shephard, University of Strathclyde

Conservative Targets

Target No	Constituency	Labour Lead	
C43	Eastwood	3,236	6.2%
C72	Aberdeen South (3rd)	3,920	8.9%
C85	Edinburgh Pentlands	4,862	10.6%
C121	Ayr	6,543	14.6%
C122	Stirling	6,411	14.9%
C133	Inverness East (4th)	7,832	16.4%
C152	Dumfries	9,643	19.5%

(Liberal Democrat held)

		Lib Dem Lead	
C41	Aberdeenshire West and Kincardine	2,662	6.2%
C73	Tweeddale, Ettrick and Laud (3rd)	3,555	9.1%
C127	Edinburgh West	7,253	15.2%
C135	Gordon	6,997	16.6%

(SNP held)

		SNP Lead	
C54	Perth	3,141	7.1%
C74	Tayside North	4,160	9.1%
C110	Galloway and Upper Nithsdale	5,624	13.4%
C114	Moray	5,566	14.0%

Liberal Democrat Targets

	Labour Lead	
Aberdeen South	3,365	7.6%
Inverness East (3rd)	7,823	16.4%

Scottish National Party (SNP) Targets

	Labour Lead	
Inverness East, Nairn and Lochaber	2,339	4.9%
Glasgow Govan	2,914	9.0%
Ochil	4,652	10.6%
Kilmarnock and Loudoun	7,256	15.3%

The 1997 General Election in Scotland was a disaster for the Conservative Party. Opposing devolution and deeply unpopular in the nation, the party lost all of its 11 seats. More importantly, the Conservative Party's share of the Scottish vote dropped below that of the Scottish National Party, effectively challenging the position of the Conservatives as the main opposition party to Labour. In terms of votes, the main beneficiary of the Conservatives' demise was the Labour Party, increasing their vote share from under 40% in 1992 to over 45% in 1997. In terms of seats, the Labour Party made six gains from the Conservatives and one from the Liberal Democrats, taking their total to 56. Meanwhile the Liberal Democrats gained one seat overall taking their total to 10 while the SNP took two seats from the Conservatives to increase their seat share to six.

Much has happened in Scottish politics since 1997, most notably a referendum in favour of devolution and the creation of a Scottish Parliament and Executive. Following the outcome of the referendum, the Conservatives have accepted devolution and have been trying to reclaim lost ground. Although multi-faceted, their strategy has been populist in character and includes a volte-face of position on some of their least popular policies such as university tuition fees, and a hardening of position on high-profile populist issues such as asylum seekers, family values, Europe and law and order. This populist approach has been developing in response to perceived Labour Party weaknesses at Westminster as well as perceived Labour/Liberal Democrat coalition weaknesses in the Scottish Executive. Devolution for Scotland may have created an additional layer of governance for Labour to prove itself, but the down-side of this is that parties such as the Conservatives and the SNP now have an additional layer of governance at which they can level criticism. In short, the new multi-layered system has created a situation in which criticisms and disillusionment with a party in power can be magnified. The next general election will be interesting from this point of view because we have no prior experience of the potential impact of magnification.

Consequently, any analysis of the results of the 1999 Scottish Parliament Elections has to be treated cautiously. Prior to the elections the public could only base their judgement of Labour on the performance of the Westminster Government. In terms of Scotland, performance was most evident on constitutional issues. In particular, Scotland had voted for devolution and the main party to thank on this front was Labour. Emerging unease over mismatches between promises and delivery on key policy areas such as health and education was largely inconsequential in the case of Scotland because these were the very issues that the Scottish Parliament would now be able to address itself. In short, things could get better post-devolution. With the exception of a few marginal seats such as Ayr and Eastwood, the Conservatives posed no real threat to Labour in the Scottish Parliament Elections. Opinion polls showed little evidence of a Conservative revival and support wavered between 10 and 15%. According to the polls the main threat for the Labour Party in Scotland was the SNP. Indeed, on several occasions in the year prior to the 1999 elections the SNP appeared neck and neck with Labour at around 40% support. The Labour Party has been somewhat surprised and concerned over the level of support that devolution has created for the SNP, and at the Holyrood level at least, the SNP look capable of taking numerous key seats in the future.

In the event, little changed at the constituency level during the 1999 Scottish Parliament Elections. Labour managed to hold onto seats such as Ayr, Eastwood, and Govan and only two seats exchanged parties. Labour lost Inverness East, Nairn and Lochaber to the SNP and Aberdeen South to the Liberal Democrats. The Conservatives again failed to gain any constituency seats although they came within 25 votes in Ayr – a seat that they have subsequently taken from Labour in a by-election held on the 16th March 2000. While the SNP and the Conservative Party did well out of the proportional allocations from the regional lists, at the constituency level the main advances were made by the SNP. In 51 out of the 71 constituencies that are comparable the SNP managed to increase their number of votes in 1999 compared with 1997. This represented a remarkable achievement given that turnout was only 58% in 1999 compared with 71% in the 1997 General Election. Meanwhile the SNP's percentage share of the vote also increased in 63 out of 71 constituencies and they increased their number of second placed candidates from 44 to 51.

These advances are even more surprising given the widespread media hostility that greeted the SNP's leader Alex Salmond during the 1999 campaign. The 1999 election took place in the midst of the Kosovo conflict and Salmond was heavily criticised for expressing concerns over the NATO campaign. The SNP also campaigned for a 1p tax increase, the 'penny for Scotland', contributing to damaging portrayals of Salmond as a Teletubby character living in 'La-La Land'. Both incidents helped take the edge off the SNP momentum for the 1999 election. If the SNP can keep a more polished image they should prove more of a threat to future Scottish Parliament Elections. However, Westminster appears to be another matter. ICM polls in June 2000 show that while the SNP are still capable of matching Labour support at the Holyrood level (36% each among those intending to vote), support for the SNP is much lower at the Westminster level (26% compared with Labour's 42%).

In the June 1999 European Parliament Elections, Labour's share of the vote in Scotland dropped to less than 30%. Although it still came first, the SNP came a close second and the Conservatives nearly managed 20% of the vote. Under the new proportional system, Scotland's eight constituencies were combined into one Scottish constituency. Labour lost three of the six seats it had held in the 1994-99 Parliament. Two of these losses went to the Conservatives and one went to the Liberal Democrats. Meanwhile, the SNP broke even with two seats. Held a month after the Scottish Parliament and local government elections, voter fatigue helped contribute to a very low turnout of just 25%. Consequently, the results are not particularly helpful in providing clues about behaviour at general elections when turnout is usually over 70%. Moreover, past practice suggests that voters often vote against the UK government in European Parliament Elections. Such 'second-order' elections represent an opportunity to warn those in power at Westminster of the need to improve performance before the next general election.

So how do the parties fare in Scotland? At the Westminster level, it would seem a case of *plus ça change*. The Labour Party will have to defend the records of two administrations, one in Scotland and one in Westminster. However, despite Labour's inability to convince the electorate that it is fulfilling policy commitments on the improvement of health and education, the position of Labour in Scotland is still holding strong. Their main opponents, the SNP and the Conservatives, have witnessed their own troubles. Both the SNP and the Conservatives have faced damaging internal rows over party organisation matters and the Conservative's drift to the right on issues such as asylum seekers have contributed to party defections, most visibly, Tasmina Ahmed-Sheikh who was the Conservative candidate for Glasgow Govan in 1999. The Labour and Liberal Democrat commitment to scrapping Section 28 may come back to haunt them if the issue is kept alive by businessman Brian Souter's threat of supporting candidates who back family values.

In any event Labour will do well indeed if it can hold Inverness East, Eastwood, Aberdeen South and Glasgow Govan. If things go wrong for Labour the seats to watch include Ochil, Edinburgh Pentlands, Ayr, Stirling, Dumfries and Kilmarnock and Loudoun (see profiles below). Following a by-election (see by-elections), Hamilton South is now technically Labour's most marginal seat, and might also be a contender for the SNP, although it is unlikely that the Nationalists will be able to replicate the degree of support that they achieved on that occasion. If the advance of the SNP at the Scottish Parliamentary level can be reproduced at the Westminster level, then a number of additional seats could be viewed as marginal. Other seats to watch that are not profiled in more detail below include Dundee West (Labour majority over 30% in 1997 but just 0.4% in 1999), Aberdeen North (2.0% Labour majority in 1999) and three constituencies where Labour was just 8–9% ahead in 1999: Renfrewshire West, Linlithgow and Dundee East. In particular, the Dundee seats might be interesting as Labour lost control of Dundee Council in the 1999 local elections for the first time in two decades.

Aberdeen South

Labour majority 3,365 (7.6%)

Liberal Democrat target

Conservative target 72

MP Anne Begg

1997 (Turnout 72.8%)	Labour	15,541	35.3%
	Liberal Democrat	12,176	27.6%
	Conservative	11,621	26.4%
	SNP	4,299	9.8%
	Referendum	425	1.0%

The constituency boundaries of Aberdeen South were substantially modified following the creation of Aberdeen Central before the 1997 election. Although South has lost mainly Conservative areas such as Rubislaw and Rosemount, it has gained numerous affluent suburbs such as Cults, Bieldside and Milltimber, which have benefited the Conservatives and Liberal Democrats. Balancing these new additions are the less affluent areas of Torry and Kincorth which contribute to making the constituency a three-way marginal between Labour, the Liberal Democrats and the Conservatives.

Apart from a near breakthrough for the SDP in 1983, between the late 1960s and early 1990s, the constituency was a two-way marginal between the Conservatives and Labour. In 1992 the constituency contained fewer affluent areas and yet the Conservatives managed their only gain here from Labour in Scotland. Given the changes to the constituency the size of the Labour victory in 1997 represented a significant achievement, but one that could not be replicated in the 1999 Scottish Parliament elections. After coming second to Labour's Anne Begg in 1997, the seasoned campaigner Nicol Stephen managed to defeat Labour's Mike Elrick (a former press officer to John Smith) with a majority of 1,760 (5.1%). Then in the Euro elections, the SNP topped the poll, with the Lib Dems pushed down into fourth place. Given these fluctuations, the seat looks set to continue as one of the least predictable in Scotland at the general election.

Aberdeenshire West and Kincardine

Liberal Democrat majority 2,662 (6.2%)

Conservative target 41

MP Sir Robert Smith

1997 (Turnout 73.0%)	Liberal Democrat	17,742	41.1%
	Conservative	15,080	34.9%
	SNP	5,639	13.1%
	Labour	3,923	9.1%
	Referendum	805	1.9%

Aberdeenshire West and Kincardine is a large rural constituency extending south and west of Aberdeen in the north-east of Scotland. Home to Balmoral and the picturesque Cairngorms, the constituency comprises affluent commuter towns and villages such as Ballater, Aboyne and Banchory. In 1997 the constituency underwent significant boundary changes, and now takes in part of Gordon constituency as well as two thirds of the old Kincardine and Deeside. The main contenders in this seat are the Liberal Democrats and the Conservatives, who alternated control of Kincardine and Deeside throughout the 1990s. The Liberal Democrats' Nicol Stephen captured the seat from the Conservatives in a November 1991 by-election that had been precipitated by the death of the long-standing Conservative MP, Alick Buchanan-Smith. Stephen lost it back to the Conservatives in the 1992 General Election after only 154 days in office.

At the 1997 General Election, the Liberal Democrats' Robert Smith overturned a large notional Conservative majority of 4,437 (10.5%) to win by over 2,500 votes. The Lib Dem position was consolidated in the 1999 Scottish Parliament as Mike Rumbles managed a majority of 2,289 (6.4%). The Labour Party are not popular in this constituency and the Liberal Democrats may suffer from adverse reaction to their coalition links with Labour at Holyrood. However, this may be a seat in which tactical voting by Labour voters saves the day for the Liberal Democrats. The Conservative candidate is Tom Kerr.

Ayr

Labour majority 6,543 (14.6%)

Conservative target 121

MP Sandra Osborne

1997 (Turnout 80.2%)	Labour	21,679	48.4%
	Conservative	15,136	33.8%
	SNP	5,625	12.6%
	Liberal Democrat	2,116	4.7%
	Referendum	200	0.4%

Located on Scotland's west coast, Ayr includes the seaside towns of Ayr and Troon and the more industrial Prestwick which is home to an international airport. Ayr had been held continuously by the Conservative Party since 1950, but its constituency boundaries were altered before the 1997 election, giving Labour a notional majority of 1895 (4.2%). In turn, it was no real surprise that the Conservative MP Phil Gallie was defeated at the 1997

General Election, particularly since he was nursing a majority of only 85 before the boundary changes. In the event Labour's Sandra Osborne won the seat in 1997 with a majority of over 6,500.

Since then, Ayr has proved more problematic for Labour. In the 1999 Scottish Parliament Elections Ayr returned to 'too-close-to-call' form when after several recounts Labour's Ian Welsh defeated Gallie by just 25 votes (0.07%). Pressured by the multiple commitments of family, business and Parliament, Welsh resigned his seat within the year, so precipitating the first Scottish Parliament by-election. The March 2000 campaign was unfortunate timing for the Scottish Labour Party who were ensnared in divisive public battles over the cost of the Parliament buildings and their commitment to repeal Section 28/2a prohibiting the promotion of homosexuality in schools. On the latter issue, a huge billboard and media campaign opposing repeal was financed by the bus tycoon, Brian Souter. The Section 28 issue dominated the by-election and contributed to the huge swing against Labour's candidate Rita Miller who slumped to third place behind the SNP. Conservative candidate, John Scott, gained the party's first constituency seat in the Scottish Parliament with a majority of 3,344 (10.5%). The Conservatives will be hard-pressed to retain such a majority at Westminster, although they are certainly capable of toppling Labour. Either way, Ayr looks set to restore its position as one of the most marginal constituencies in Scotland, and Phil Gallie fights again for the Conservatives.

Dumfries

Labour majority 9,643 (19.5%)

Conservative target 152

MP Russell Brown

1997 (Turnout 78.9%)	Labour	23,528	47.5%
	Conservative	13,885	28.0%
	SNP	5,977	12.1%
	Liberal Democrat	5,487	11.1%
	Referendum	533	1.1%
	Other	117	0.2%

Dumfries is a large constituency on the Scottish/English border, extending from Gretna and the Solway Firth in the south, to Dumfries in the west and

Moffat in the north. Dumfries is mainly a rural seat with agriculture, forestry and tourism dominating the local economies. The constituency used to be one of Scotland's safest for the Conservatives and was held by Sir Hector Munro between 1964 and 1997. The Conservatives' majority of 6,415 over Labour was overturned in 1997 as Labour's Russell Brown squarely defeated Munro's successor Struan Stevenson with a majority of almost 10,000. The 16.5% swing to Labour in Dumfries was one of the largest in the UK.

As well as being caught up in the wave of anti-Conservative feeling that had gripped the nation, support for Stevenson had also suffered because of his public turn of face in favour of the official anti-devolution platform of the Conservative Party. The Labour Party are unlikely to hold onto such a large majority at the next General Election. In the 1999 Scottish Parliament Elections, Labour's Elaine Murray secured a reduced majority of 3,654 (9.5%) over the Conservative candidate David Mundell. Although the Labour majority appears fairly safe on paper, the Conservatives could make a comeback in this seat, particularly if the now pro-devolution Conservative Party can play on enough fears in the rural communities. Their new hopeful is John Charteris.

Eastwood

Labour majority 3,236 (6.2%)

Conservative target 43

MP Jim Murphy

1997 (Turnout 78.2%)			
	Labour	20,766	39.7%
	Conservative	17,530	33.5%
	SNP	6,826	13.1%
	Liberal Democrat	6,110	11.7%
	Referendum	497	1.0%
	Others	523	1.0%

Located to the south of the Glasgow conurbation, Eastwood is largely comprised of a number of affluent areas in towns and villages such as Clarkston, Newton Mearns and Eaglesham. Less affluent areas such as Barrhead and Neilston that have suffered from industrial decline exist in the north of the constituency along the border with Glasgow. Few alterations were made to the constituency prior to the 1997 General Election. In that election Eastwood elected Labour's Jim Murphy, the first time the Conservatives had suffered defeat in this constituency. Eastwood was considered one of the safest Conservative seats in Scotland; Labour's 1997 victory overturned an 11,838 (22.5%) notional Conservative majority on a huge swing of 14%. The plight of the Conservatives was affected little by the Referendum Party as they managed to poll less than 500 votes.

In the 1999 Scottish Parliament elections the Labour majority was reduced to 2,125 (4.7%). Taking the seat for Labour was Ken McIntosh, a New Labourite whose main challenger for the seat was the archetypal Tory, and long-serving local government councillor, John Young. Like the Westminster and Holyrood elections, the 1999 local council elections within Eastwood split fairly evenly between the Conservatives and Labour. Provided the Labour vote does not crumble, tactical voting by the SNP and Liberal Democrats may prove critical in this seat. Raymond Robertson (former MP for Aberdeen South) will hope to regain the seat for the Conservatives.

Edinburgh Pentlands

Labour majority 4,862 (10.6%)

Conservative target 85

MP Lynda Clark

1997 (Turnout 76.7%)			
	Labour	19,675	43.0%
	Conservative	14,813	32.4%
	SNP	5,952	13.0%
	Liberal Democrat	4,575	10.0%
	Referendum	422	0.9%
	Others	305	0.7%

Edinburgh Pentlands extends south-west from Edinburgh along the Pentland hills. Although this constituency contains a diversity of neighbourhoods from depressed council estates such as Wester Hailes to wealthy Edinburgh suburbs such as Morningside, the majority of voters live in desirable surroundings such as Fairmilehead and Balerno. Consequently the Conservative vote is comparatively strong in this constituency. Indeed, the Conservatives held this seat between 1950 and 1997, albeit with some small majorities during the late 1960s and 1970s. Malcolm Rifkind held Pentlands between February 1974 and 1997 and the Labour victory here last time represented a remarkable achievement against one of the most popular and high profile Conservatives in Scotland. Having increased his majority in 1992, few suspected that Rifkind would lose a 1992 notional majority of 4,148 (9%). He was defeated on a 9.8% swing, enough for Lynda Clark to amass a near-5,000 majority.

In 1999, the Scottish Conservative Party leader David McLetchie stood in the Scottish Parliament elections and only managed a small 1.7% swing away from Labour; he was defeated by a 2,885 vote (7.3%) majority. The Conservatives did top the poll here in the Euro elections, but only by 3.7%, with the SNP close behind in third place. Unless the Labour vote declines sharply, Malcolm Rifkind is going to have to work hard to regain the upper hand in this seat.

Edinburgh West

Liberal Democrat majority 7,253 (15.2%)

Conservative target 127

MP Donald Gorrie (retiring)

1997 (Turnout 77.9%)			
	Liberal Democrat	20,578	43.2%
	Conservative	13,325	28.0%
	Labour	8,948	18.8%
	SNP	4,210	8.8%
	Referendum	277	0.6%
	Others	293	0.6%

Edinburgh West contains a large proportion of Edinburgh's affluent suburbs such as Cramond and Barnton. In 1997 its boundaries were extended westward and the constituency now incorporates South Queensferry and Kirkliston. After numerous close calls in this seat, Liberal Democrat Donald Gorrie finally took Edinburgh West from Conservative Lord James Douglas-Hamilton in 1997. Gorrie turned a 1992 Conservative notional majority of 4,291 (8.3%) into an impressive Liberal Democrat majority of over 7,500.

Liberal Democrat Margaret Smith continued the defeat of Douglas-Hamilton in the 1999 Scottish Parliament elections, albeit with a reduced majority of 4,583 (11.0%). The Conservatives only just held this seat in their heyday (1983, 1987, and 1992) and provided the Liberal Democrats are not penalised for their coalition with Labour at Holyrood, this seat is likely to remain their territory. Their new candidate is John Barrett, while Iain Whyte will hope to regain the seat for the Conservatives.

Galloway and Upper Nithsdale

SNP majority 5,624 (13.4%)

Conservative target 110

MP Alasdair Morgan

1997 (Turnout 79.7%)			
	SNP	18,449	43.9%
	Conservative	12,825	30.5%
	Labour	6,861	16.3%
	Liberal Democrat	2,700	6.4%
	Referendum	428	1.0%
	Others	755	1.8%

Situated in the far south-west of Scotland, Galloway and Upper Nithsdale is the largest of the lowland seats. Largely rural and dependent upon agriculture and forestry, the constituency includes Stranraer (which provides ferry links with Northern Ireland), Wigtown, Kirkcudbright and the old mining towns of Sanquhar and Kirkconnell. Like Perth and Tayside North, the SNP took this seat in October 1974, only to lose to the Conservatives in the 1979, 1983, 1987 and 1992 general elections. When Alasdair Morgan regained the constituency in 1997, the SNP had succeeded in pulling off a major coup as the long-standing Conservative MP was Ian Lang – a former Secretary of State for Scotland and high-profile member of the Thatcher and Major administrations. Morgan overturned a 1992 majority of 2,400 (5.5%) to secure a majority of over 5,500.

Like his colleagues in Perth and Tayside North, Morgan also managed to hold out against the Conservatives in the 1999 Scottish Parliament elections. However, the Conservatives' Alex Fergusson did make inroads on the SNP's majority, which was reduced to 3,201 (9.1%) and the Conservatives then topped the poll here in the Euro elections by 7%. Although it might not look it on paper, this seat could provide a greater test of SNP resolve than Tayside North. Peter Duncan is the Tory Hopeful.

Glasgow Govan

Labour majority 2,914 (9.0%)

SNP target

MP Mohammed Sarwar

1997 (Turnout 64.7%)			
	Labour	14,216	44.1%
	SNP	11,302	35.1%
	Conservative	2,839	8.8%
	Liberal Democrat	1,918	5.9%
	Scottish Socialist	755	2.3%
	Others	1,215	3.8%

Glasgow Govan is located on the south bank of the river Clyde, extending in an 'L-shape' west and south of Glasgow city centre. The constituency contains a diversity of neighbourhoods that incorporate both stark industrial areas and some of the city's finest suburbs and parklands (most notably, Pollock Country Park, home to the Burrell Art Collection). The constituency also includes Ibrox, home of Glasgow Rangers FC. While most of the dockland areas are now derelict, the hopes of Glasgow's shipbuilding industry are pinned on the one remaining yard. The Labour Party's main challengers for this seat are the SNP who have secured two by-election victories here in 1973 and 1988. The abolition of the Glasgow Central seat prior to the 1997 General Election precipitated a damaging party selection process in Govan with Mohammed Sarwar eventually being chosen over Mike Watson as the Labour Party candidate. Despite widespread swings to Labour in 1997, the SNP closed the gap in Govan from 5,609 to 2,914.

Labour's fortunes were further dented by allegations of Sarwar's involvement in electoral irregularities. Although eventually cleared of all charges in the spring of 1999, the Sarwar incident, Labour infighting, and uncertainty over the future of the Kvaerner shipyard all proved major headaches for the Labour Party in the run up to the 1999 Scottish Parliament elections. On the night that the results were announced, Donald Dewar appeared very relieved to have held Govan, albeit with a reduced majority of 1,756 (6.7%). The SNP's candidate in 1997 and 1999, Nicola Sturgeon, has steadily whittled down the Labour majority and it could be third time lucky for the SNP at the next General Election.

Gordon

Liberal Democrat majority 6,997 (16.6%)

Conservative target 135

Possible SNP target

MP Malcolm Bruce

1997 (Turnout 71.9%)	Liberal Democrat	17,999	42.6%
	Conservative	11,002	26.0%
	SNP	8,435	20.0%
	Labour	4,350	10.3%
	Referendum	459	1.1%

Gordon is another large rural constituency, located on the north-east coast of Scotland above Aberdeen and sandwiched between Moray and Banff and Buchan. Forestry and agriculture are preponderant in this constituency and a number of towns such as Kintore and Inverurie provide homes to commuters in nearby Aberdeen. Boundaries were shifted northwards in 1997 and the new Gordon constituency supposedly contains a much higher proportion of Conservative voters than it used to. That said, one of the great surprises in 1997 was Liberal Democrat Malcolm Bruce's majority over the Conservatives' candidate John Porter. Turning a 1992 Conservative notional majority of 8,486 (20.8%) into a 1997 Liberal Democrat majority of almost 7,000 represented a remarkable achievement.

Assisting the Liberal Democrats is the fact that the boundary changes have also been beneficial to the SNP. Some of the former Moray and Banff and Buchan constituencies (Nationalist strongholds) now lie within Gordon's boundaries. The effect of this was noticeable in the 1999 Scottish Parliament elections when a swing to the SNP pushed the Conservatives into third place. In the event, Liberal Democrat Nora Radcliffe managed to hold Gordon with a reduced majority of 4,195 (12.5%), but in the Euro elections a month later the SNP topped the poll. If the SNP continue to do well here, they could pose a greater threat to Bruce than the Conservative candidate, Nanette Milne.

Inverness East, Nairn and Lochaber

Labour majority 2,339 (4.9%)

SNP target / Possible Lib Dem target

Conservative target 133

MP David Stewart

1997 (Turnout 72.5%)			
	Labour	16,187	33.9%
	SNP	13,848	29.0%
	Liberal Democrat	8,364	17.5%
	Conservative	8,355	17.5%
	Referendum	436	0.9%
	Others	578	1.2%

Inverness East, Nairn and Lochaber is one of the largest geographical constituencies in the UK, stretching across the highlands and islands from the west coast to the east coast of Scotland. Encompassing islands such as Rum, Eigg and Muck in the west, the constituency includes the western harbour town of Mallaig, the tourist centres of Fort William and Aviemore, with Inverness and Nairn on the east coast. The diversity of interests in this large constituency (from tourism, agriculture and fishing to light industry) are reflected in the close fortunes of the four main political parties. Indeed, in the 1992 election, this constituency was the only four-way marginal in the country, the Conservatives in fourth just 1,741 votes behind the Liberal Democrats in first. However, in 1997, Labour and the SNP extended their share of the vote in comparison with the Conservatives and Liberal Democrats. Labour's David Stewart took the seat with a majority of 2,339 over the SNP's Fergus Ewing (son of Winnie Ewing).

Fortunes were reversed in the 1999 Scottish Parliament elections as Fergus Ewing narrowly defeated Labour's Joan Aitken with a majority of 441 (1.1%). The SNP then widened their lead to over 13% in the Euro elections soon after. Although this seat could still swing one of four ways, particularly if any one of the candidates can strike a chord with the electorate, it looks for the moment to be a tight race between the SNP and Labour.

Kilmarnock and Loudoun

Labour majority 7,256 (15.3%)

SNP target

MP Des Browne

1997 (Turnout 77.2%)			
	Labour	23,621	49.8%
	SNP	16,365	34.5%
	Conservative	5,125	10.8%
	Liberal Democrat	1,891	4.0%
	Others	407	0.9%

Kilmarnock and Loudoun is situated to the south west of Glasgow, sandwiched between the two marginal constituencies of Eastwood and Ayr (see above). Kilmarnock is an industrial town famous for Johnnie Walker whisky as well as supporting light and heavy engineering industries. The textile and knitwear industries are still an important source of employment for many of the villages and towns in this constituency such as Stewarton, Glaston and Darvel. Competition in the textile sector has hit the seat hard over the years and has contributed to making Kilmarnock and Loudoun one of Scotland's highest unemployment areas.

Although the seat has been held continuously by Labour since 1945, the SNP have made substantial inroads during the 1990s. The swing from Labour to the Nationalists was over 8% in the 1992 General Election and more than 4% in the 1999 Scottish Parliament elections. The 1992 result forced the Conservatives into third place and since then the SNP have provided the main challenge to Labour. However, in the 1997 General Election Labour's Des Browne held his ground over the SNP's candidate Alex Neil, securing a majority of over 7,000. If the Conservatives remain unpopular in this seat and the Nationalists are able to build on their 1999 results (in which Labour's Scottish Parliament majority was reduced to 7% and the Euro majority a wafer-thin 48 votes), then the SNP may be in a position to take this seat from Labour.

Moray

SNP majority 5,566 (14.0%)

Conservative target 114

MP Margaret Ewing

1997 (Turnout 68.0%)			
	SNP	16,529	41.6%
	Conservative	10,963	27.6%
	Labour	7,886	19.8%
	Liberal Democrat	3,548	8.9%
	Referendum	840	2.1%

Situated along the Moray Firth, Moray is an odd-shaped constituency on the north-east coast of Scotland and includes the towns of Elgin, Lossiemouth, Forres and Rothes. Moray is largely a rural seat and the main employment sectors are in agriculture, forestry, tourism and fishing. The constituency is also home to a number of whisky distilleries that are famous for malts such as Glenlivet. Although considered a marginal, this seat has been held by Margaret Ewing since the 1987 General Election. The tiny alternating majorities of both the Conservatives and the SNP in the 1970s and 1980s now seem to have given way to more steady majorities for the SNP.

In the 1997 General Election, Ewing effectively doubled her lead over the Conservatives, extending a 1992 majority of 2,844 to over 5,500. The Conservatives had a disastrous result in the 1999 Scottish Parliament elections as a swing to Labour forced them into third place. Once again Margaret Ewing held the seat with a majority of 4,129 (12.3%). The SNP are in a strong position in this seat and the Conservatives will be doing very well indeed if they can recapture it. Moray is very much a Conservative long shot.

Ochil

Labour majority 4,652 (10.6%)

SNP target

MP Martin O'Neill

1997 (Turnout 76.9%)

Labour	19,707	45.0%
SNP	15,055	34.4%
Conservative	6,383	14.6%
Liberal Democrat	2,262	5.2%
Others	379	0.9%

A newly constructed constituency prior to the 1997 General Election, Ochil comprises much of the former Clackmannan seat together with parts of former Perth and Kinross and Stirling. Sandwiched between the Perth and Dunfermline constituencies, Ochil stretches from Bridge of Allan in the west to Loch Leven and the Fife constituencies in the East. The constituency contains both rural and industrial areas and reflects a diversity of interests from industry to agriculture and tourism. The Labour vote remains fairly solid in industrial towns such as Alva, Alloa and Dollar. However, job losses in mining, textiles and the brewery industry have dented Labour's hold on the seat. The SNP managed to make steady inroads on Labour at the 1997 and 1999 elections by fielding one of their most high profile and popular candidates, George Reid. In the 1997 General Election, Ochil was one of the few seats in Scotland to witness a swing away from Labour. The SNP managed a 3.2% swing in their favour, cutting the Labour majority from a notional 7,350 (17%) down to 4,652.

A further swing of 3.55% from Labour to the Nationalists was witnessed at the 1999 Scottish Parliament elections, with Labour's majority reduced to 1,303 (3.5%). Then at the Euro election the SNP topped the poll, if only by 310 votes. Consequently, Ochil is a key target seat for the SNP and Labour will have to campaign hard if they are to keep the Nationalist advance in check.

Perth

SNP majority 3,141 (7.1%)

Conservative target 54

MP Roseanna Cunningham

1997 (Turnout 73.9%)	SNP	16,209	36.4%
	Conservative	13,068	29.3%
	Labour	11,036	24.8%
	Liberal Democrat	3,583	8.0%
	Referendum	366	0.8%
	UK Independence	289	0.6%

Perth is for the most part an affluent rural constituency that extends from Lochearnhead in the west to Perth and Errol in the east. As a link to the highlands, Perth supports a large tourism industry. The SNP's Roseanna Cunningham has stamped her name on this constituency. Having won a 1995 by-election precipitated by the death of the outlandish Conservative Nicholas Fairbairn, Cunningham succeeded in holding this seat for the SNP in the 1997 General Election and then for the 1999 Scottish Parliament. Her main opponent in the 1995 by-election and the 1997 General Election was Conservative candidate John Godfrey, who critics argued had little knowledge of the local terrain. Godfrey came third behind Labour in 1995, and although he managed to come second in 1997 he did not stand in 1999. The Conservatives' new candidate, Ian Stevenson, did manage to reduce Cunningham's majority from 7.1% in 1997 to 5.4% in 1999, and at the 1999 local elections the Conservatives took 11 seats, with the SNP losing control of Perth and Kinross. Their new candidate Elizabeth Smith will stand a much better chance of regaining this seat if Cunningham does not stand. Cunningham is a popular MP who like her predecessor knows how to work this constituency in her own quirky way.

Stirling

Labour majority 6,411 (14.9%)

Conservative target 122

MP Anne McGuire

1997 (Turnout 81.8%)	Labour	20,382	47.4%
	Conservative	13,971	32.5%
	SNP	5,752	13.4%
	Liberal Democrat	2,675	6.2%
	Others	178	0.4%

Stirling is a fairly large constituency that includes the eastern banks of Loch Lomond to the west, Stirling, Dunblane and Callander to the east and extending to Tyndrum and Killin to the north. Much of the constituency is rural and middle-class which favours the Conservatives. However, Labour do well in many of the larger towns such as Stirling itself, where support is buoyed by council house tenants and students attending Stirling University. The boundary changes before 1997 removed the mainly Conservative Bridge of Allan to Ochil (see above) making Stirling even more marginal than it already was following the 1992 General Election.

Nursing a 1992 notional majority of just 236 (0.6%) it was no real surprise that Conservative MP and Scottish Secretary of State, Michael Forsyth lost his seat to Labour's Anne McGuire at the 1997 General Election. McGuire secured a comfortable majority of over 6,000 votes, and fortunes have since been repeated at the 1999 Scottish Parliament elections as Labour's Sylvia Jackson managed to secure a respectable majority of 3,981 (11.1%). Meanwhile, the Conservative vote in Stirling has gone from bad to worse. Second in 1997, the party's candidate in 1999, Brian Monteith, finished third behind the SNP's Annabelle Ewing. The Conservatives will be keen to reclaim ground in this constituency, although it looks as if any breakthrough will be threatened by the SNP.

Tayside North

SNP majority 4,160 (9.1%)

Conservative target 74

MP John Swinney

1997 (Turnout 74.3%)	SNP	20,447	44.8%
	Conservative	16,287	35.7%
	Labour	5,141	11.3%
	Liberal Democrat	3,716	8.2%

Tayside North is a very large constituency to the north of the Perth constituency it borders. An inland constituency that is rural and very pictur-esque, the main activities in the constituency are tourism, agriculture and forestry. Towns in this constituency include, Blairgowrie, Rattray, Forfar, Glamis, Kenmore and Kirriemuir. Since its creation in 1983, Tayside North was held by the Conservatives' Bill Walker until the electoral wipeout in 1997. The Conservatives had lost to the SNP in this area of Scotland during the 1970s and it was no real surprise that the strongly unionist Walker finally lost this seat to the SNP's candidate John Swinney.

After turning a Conservative notional majority of 3,439 (7.6%) into a Nationalist majority of over 4,000, Swinney (like Cunningham in Perth) managed to consolidate the SNP's hold on this seat in the 1999 Scottish Parliament elections with a majority of 4,192 (11%). Swinney was Salmond's deputy leader of the SNP and like Cunningham, his candidacy and presence could pose a severe handicap for the Conservatives at the next general election. However, the SNP did lose control of the Perth and Kinross council in the 1999 local elections and so the possibility of a Conservative upset cannot be ruled out. Their candidate is Murdo Fraser.

Tweeddale, Ettrick and Lauderdale

Liberal Democrat majority 1,489 (3.8%)

Conservative target 73

Possible SNP target

Possible Labour target

MP Michael Moore

1997 (Turnout 76.6%)			
	Liberal Democrat	12,178	31.2%
	Labour	10,689	27.4%
	Conservative	8,623	22.1%
	SNP	6,671	17.1%
	Referendum	406	1.0%
	Others	434	1.1%

Tweeddale, Ettrick and Lauderdale is a large constituency in southern Scotland located to the south of Edinburgh. This is a very rural constituency with only two towns, Penicuik and Galashiels, containing populations over

10,000. The Liberals have held this seat since David Steel won it under its previous guise of Roxburgh, Selkirk and Peebles from the Conservatives in a 1965 by-election. Having peaked in the 1983 General Election, the Liberal Democrats have witnessed a steady erosion of their majority at each successive general election. From a high of 8,539 in 1983, their current majority stands at under 1,500. However, the main challenge to the Liberals in 1997 came from Labour, who succeeded in pushing the Conservatives into third place. The SNP also performed well in 1997 and the Conservatives will have to rally hard in this seat if they are to reclaim ground lost to Labour and the Nationalists. Indeed, in the 1999 Scottish Parliament Elections the Conservatives came fourth behind Labour in third and the SNP in second place. Meanwhile, the Liberal Democrats performed well in 1999 and extended their majority to 4,478 (13.3%). This seat is unlikely to turn blue, but Andrew Brocklehurst will likely make up ground lost in the 1999 elections.

Wales

by **Russell Deacon, University of Wales Institute, Cardiff**

Conservative Targets

Target No	Constituency		Labour Lead
C30	Clwyd West	1,848	4.6%
C67	Monmouth	4,178	8.5%
C86	Conwy (3rd)	4,476	10.8%
C137	Cardiff North	8,126	16.8%
C153	Vale of Glamorgan	10,532	19.5%
C163	Preseli Pembrokeshire	8,736	20.6%
C181	Carmarthen W & S Pembrokeshire	9,621	22.6%
C185	Vale of Clwyd	8,955	22.9%
C191	Cardiff Central (3rd)	9,994	23.7%

(Liberal Democrat held)

C97	Brecon and Radnorshire	5,097	11.9%

Liberal Democrat Targets

Conwy	1,596	3.8%
Cardiff Central	7,923	18.8%

Plaid Cymru Targets

Carmarthen East and Dinefwr	3,450	8.3%
Clwyd West (3rd)	9,497	23.6%
Conwy (4th)	11,717	28.2%
Carmarthen W & S Pembroke (3rd)	15,554	36.5%

To write about elections in Wales over the last half century is to write about the history of the Labour party's electoral fortunes. For generations, in much of Wales the Labour party was the only political party. Voting Labour in Wales became as much a part of Welsh life as rugby and the Eisteddfod. Much of South and North East Wales became a one-party state with virtually no political opposition.

Labour's dominance and success continued right up until the last general election (1997). It was then that Labour's political mastery reached its highest level in Wales since the 1960s. It was then that the cry of a 'Tory free Wales' was finally realised by a combination of seven Labour and one Liberal Democrat gain of existing or notionally Conservative seats. Not since the great Liberal victory of 1906 had there failed to be a single Conservative MP in Wales. It was not, however, the Liberals who benefited significantly from the Conservatives collapse this time, but the Labour Party. After the Liberal Party in Wales declined at the start of the last century Wales had become solidly Labour. From then on in many constituencies the party did not count its majority in hundreds, or thousands but in tens of thousands.

As the Labour party was rebuilt under Kinnock, so Labour fortunes in Wales also improved. At the 1992 election, six of Labour's ten safest seats were in Wales. At the 1997 general election the majorities in these seats increased still further and in ten of its 34 seats it had gained between 69 and 79% of the total vote.

In 1997, the Conservatives who for the last 40 years had been the second party in Wales, were wiped out at a parliamentary level. Their sole political representation in Wales became a handful of local authority councillors bottled up in what had once been some of their safest Welsh seats. Plaid Cymru failed to gain any new seats and only slightly increased their overall vote. By virtue of retaining their four existing seats, in the Welsh speaking heartlands, however, they became the second party in Wales. The Liberal Democrats regained Brecon and Radnorshire and remained, as they had for the previous 50 years, a party of rural Wales.

Any political commentator looking at the results of 1st May 1997 election would have indeed seen it as a 'Labour Day'. It seemed as though the Labour tidal wave which had been gathering in Wales for the previous decade would continue to sweep all before it. Certainly the Labour party believed this to be so. To capitalise on their success the party moved quickly to hold a referendum on a Welsh Assembly. They were well aware of the fact that the 1979 referendum had been used partially as a stick with which to beat the then Labour government. They were determined this time to strike while the iron was hot. This proved to be a successful policy and despite the narrowest of wins for the Yes vote (until the last of the 22 counts the No vote had been in the lead) the Welsh population endorsed a new Assembly. It was a few months after the referendum win that things started to go wrong for the Wales Labour party. Firstly a number of the party's councils became involved in either corruption or mismanagement scandals. In some councils such as Blaenau Gwent and Rhondda Cynon Taff these became a cause celebre in which Labour councils all became publicly tarred with the same brush.

It was over the issue of the Welsh Assembly, however, that the Labour dream began to turn into a nightmare. The party became split over the issue of gender twinning of Welsh constituencies for candidate selection. Many traditional Labour seats simple refused to co-operate, or when election-time came, even to canvass for their 'imposed candidates'. Ron Davies's resignation, as both Welsh Secretary and leader of the Welsh Party, in October 1998 swung the party into an all out civil war. Alun Michael was plucked from the Home Office to stand as Tony Blair's favoured candidate against the Welsh party members' favourite Rhodri Morgan. The bitter selection battle ended only a few months before the Assembly election. It did much to impose on the Welsh electorates' mind that the Wales Labour Party was being run from Millbank and not from Transport House in Cardiff. This was not the ideal setting upon which to campaign for the first elections to a Welsh Assembly.

It was the May 1999 Assembly and council elections that turned Wales from the traditional quasi one-party state into a multi-party one. The unthinkable happened; Labour failed to gain a majority of seats in the new Assembly. Labour's commanding position, expressed in the landslide of May 1997, had been undermined. This reversal was led by Plaid Cymru, which had also now added the English 'The Party of Wales' to its Welsh name. Plaid Cymru traditionally benefits most when there is a Labour government, as its Welsh nationalist and socialist credentials tend to attract disenchanted Labour voters. But even they did not expect the scale of their success. In some constituencies the swingometer went off the scale. They won nine constituency seats outright; their previous high was four seats. Neil Kinnock's former parliamentary seat of Islwyn fell to Plaid Cymru with a swing of over 35%, the same occurred in the Rhondda. Other Labour seats such as Carmarthen East and Dinefwr, Llanelli and Conwy (where they went from 4th to 1st) were also wrestled from Labour by Plaid Cymru. Plaid

Cymru had pushed its vote up from around 10 per cent to 28%. More worryingly for Labour, a NOP/HTV poll in May 1999 indicated that some 38% of Plaid Cymru's new voters were from the Labour party. For the first time ever at an all-Wales election, Plaid Cymru did not lose a single deposit. A month later at the European elections Plaid Cymru's vote rose again to 29.6%, their highest ever, albeit on a turnout of just 28.3%.

Plaid Cymru's success overshadowed the Liberal Democrat achievement of winning Cardiff Central, the first time they had taken control of an urban Welsh seat since the days of Lloyd George. The Conservatives also regained Monmouth. The Conservatives and Liberal Democrats had not, however, profited significantly from Labour misfortunes. The Liberal Democrats gained around the same proportion of votes (12%) as they had in the 1997 general election, whereas the Conservative's share fell from 19.6 to 16%. They gained four fewer Assembly seats than they would have expected, based on their 1997 result. Conservative fortunes appeared to rise slightly in the Euro election of June 1999 where they gained one MEP (22.8%, but on a record low turnout). Since then, however, they have failed to make any gains in local by-elections even in their strongest council, the Vale of Glamorgan.

The 1997 general election illustrated that there were no safe seats for the Conservatives in Wales; two years later the elections gave the message that, in the right circumstances, their were also no safe seats for the Labour party in Wales. In future all seats were up for grabs. It also showed that the Welsh electorate were beginning to be selective in who they supported at different levels of government. For Labour it indicated that the electorate perceived them as being too close to Millbank and New Labour. In February 2000 Alun Michael resigned as First Secretary and leader of the Labour Party in Wales, being replaced by the more popular Rhodri Morgan. In March 2000 Labour restyled themselves as Welsh Labour or Plaid Llafur Cymru, with a dragon's tail emblem replacing the red rose. The Labour Party approaches this general election determined not to repeat the mistakes of 1999. The party, however, is also on the defensive for the first time since 1983. They are defending 34 seats in Wales, seven of which they lost at the Assembly elections. Labour's resources are likely to be stretched to the limit.

The key to the next general election in Wales for both Labour and the Conservatives is what happens to the Plaid Cymru vote. In the absence of retiring leader, Dafydd Wigley, will the party maintain the same appeal? If it does, then both of the main parties are potentially in trouble; if it weakens or collapses, where will the Plaid Cymru voters go? The answer to this question will determine the results of many of the battleground seats.

Brecon and Radnorshire

Liberal Democrat majority 5,097 (11.9%)

Conservative target 97

MP Richard Livsey (retiring)

1997 (Turnout 82.2%)			
	Liberal Democrat	17,516	40.9%
	Conservative	12,419	29.0%
	Labour	11,424	26.6%
	Referendum	900	2.1%
	Plaid Cymru	622	1.5%

Brecon and Radnorshire is the second largest constituency in the United Kingdom. It is mainly rural, containing farming areas and also the Brecon Beacons National Park. The county council, Powys, is run by Independents, and is one of the few county councils in Britain where there was less party competition for council seats in 1999 then there had been in 1973. There is an exception to this around the urban area of Ystradgynlais; this contains around 20% of the constituency's population, and also the majority of the Labour vote.

The current MP Richard Livsey briefly gained national fame for the SDP/Liberal Alliance when he won what had been a safe Conservative seat, in the 1985 by-election. For the next two general elections the seat remained one of the UK's most marginal. In 1987 Livsey retained it by just 56 votes. Then in 1992 Jonathan Evans took it back for the Conservatives by 130 votes. The last election, however, saw Livsey regain the seat with a 5,097 majority. Kirsty Williams won the seat for the Liberal Democrats again at the 1999 Assembly elections, with an increased majority. A month later at the European elections, the Conservatives topped the poll with 38% of the vote, although on a much smaller turnout.

Both parties will have fresh candidates in the next contest. Livsey is stepping down at the general election; Roger Williams a farmer and Powys councillor is seeking to fill his shoes. The former Conservative MP for the seat, Jonathan Evans is now a Welsh MEP and will not be standing again; he is replaced by Peter Gooderham. Both Labour and Plaid Cymru are likely to remain very much in the background.

Cardiff Central

Labour majority 7,923 (18.8%)

Liberal Democrat target

Conservative target 191

MP Jon Owen Jones

1997 (Turnout 70.0%)

Labour	18,464	43.7%
Liberal Democrat	10,541	24.9%
Conservative	8,470	20.0%
Socialist Labour	2,230	5.3%
Plaid Cymru	1,504	3.6%
Referendum	760	1.8%
Others	284	0.7%

Created in 1983, Cardiff Central is geographically the smallest and most urban of all the Welsh constituencies. It also has the largest student population in Wales. In 1983 the seat was one of the great hopes of the Liberal/SDP Alliance, but candidate Michael German (now leader of the Liberal Democrat Group within the Welsh Assembly) finished second to the Conservatives. In 1992, Labour city councillor Jon Owen Jones won it with a majority of 8%, which he increased to 18.8% in 1997. However, unlike in 1992, it was now the Liberal Democrats and not the Conservatives who were in second position.

Initially, Owen Jones was seen as something of a rising star within the Welsh Labour party. He became Welsh whip and was then given a junior ministerial post at the Welsh Office. In 1999, however, with the arrival of the Welsh Assembly he was jettisoned from the government to return to the backbenches. Owen Jones's decline in personal fortune was mirrored by the decline of his own party's fortunes in Cardiff Central. The day of the 1997 Assembly referendum also saw what appeared to be an insignificant council by-election in Cardiff Central. Although Labour held the seat there was a 15% increase in the Liberal Democrat vote. Two years later there was to be an even greater swing to the Liberal Democrats in local council elections, but more importantly, they also won the Assembly seat. Labour's share of the vote fell from 43.7 to 30%, while that of the Liberal Democrats rose from 24.9 to 42.3%. The Liberal Democrats are now keenly working what, with the possible exception of Conwy, is their only realistic target in Wales. Their hopeful is Jenny Willott; Gregory Walker challenges for the Conservatives.

Cardiff North

Labour majority 8,126 (16.8%)

Conservative target 137

MP Julie Morgan

1997 (Turnout 79.7%)			
	Labour	24,460	50.5%
	Conservative	16,334	33.7%
	Liberal Democrat	5,294	10.9%
	Plaid Cymru	1,201	2.5%
	Referendum	1,199	2.5%

Cardiff North has some of the richest wards in Wales, and for generations was true blue territory. One of the suburbs, Whitchurch, even boasts the headquarters of the Conservative Party in Wales. It appeared as though the Conservatives could always count on the voters of Cardiff North to support them. Although the majority over Labour was slender at times, the seat produced two junior ministers at the Welsh Office, Michael Roberts and Gwilym Jones.

In the 1994 council elections, however, the Conservatives lost all of their council seats in Cardiff North. Never before had the Conservatives been so weak in their heartland seat. It was perhaps unsurprising, therefore, that in the general rout of Conservative parliamentary seats in Wales in 1997, Julie Morgan, wife of Rhodri, won the seat with a majority exceeding 8,000.

The Assembly and council elections of 1999 failed to see any significant revival in the Conservatives' fortunes. The majority of council wards remained in Labour hands, Labour won the Assembly seat, and the Conservative vote at 31.4% was even lower than in 1997. It appeared as though the voters of Cardiff North were far happier with the Labour Party than their neighbouring residents in traditional Labour seats. The general election result is likely to depend on whether the 'New' Labour voters of Cardiff North continue to prefer Labour over the Conservatives. The Tory hopefull is Alastair Watson.

Carmarthen East and Dinefwr

Labour majority 3,450 (8.3%)

Plaid Cymru target

MP Alan Wynne Williams

1997 (Turnout 78.6%)			
	Labour	17,907	42.9%
	Plaid Cymru	14,457	34.6%
	Conservative	5,022	12.0%
	Liberal Democrat	3,150	7.6%
	Referendum	1,196	2.9%

Carmarthen East and Dinefwr was created in 1997. Its predecessor seat, Carmarthen had the distinction of being the birthplace of Plaid Cymru's parliamentary fortunes. It was here that Gwynfor Evans won the seat in the spectacular by-election victory of 1966. He lost it to Labour again in 1970, but regained it once more in October 1974. Since Roger Thomas won the seat for Labour in 1979 it has remained stubbornly Labour.

Carmarthen East and Dinefwr is mainly rural and predominantly Welsh speaking. The most recent boundary revisions brought in the Labour supporting Amman Valley from Llanelli, which helped Alan Williams keep the seat Labour, despite a 5.5% increase in Plaid Cymru's vote. It was Plaid Cymru's only realistic target seat in the 1997 elections, and some three months later in September 1997 it was Carmarthen that became the final authority to record an overwhelming Yes vote to the referendum on a Welsh Assembly. It became clear therefore that the constituency had developed strong Welsh nationalist leanings.

Following Carmarthen's endorsement of devolution, it was not long before Plaid Cymru was able to reap some of the benefit. Their 1997 candidate, Rhodri Glyn Thomas, returned in 1999 for victory when he took the Assembly seat with a 15% swing. The party also fared well in the council and European elections, increasing their vote to over 51%. Labour will do very well to hold on here.

Carmarthen West and South Pembrokeshire

Labour majority 9,621 (22.6%)

Conservative target 181

Possible Plaid Cymru target

MP Nick Ainger

1997 (Turnout 76.4%)			
	Labour	20,956	49.1%
	Conservative	11,335	26.6%
	Plaid Cymru	5,402	12.7%
	Liberal Democrat	3,516	8.2%
	Referendum	1,432	3.4%

Carmarthen West and South Pembrokeshire has the distinction of having the longest constituency name in the United Kingdom. It is a mainly rural seat which contains the county town of Carmarthen, the coastal port of Pembroke and the seaside resort of Tenby. It is a new seat having been created by the boundary commission in 1997. The constituencies it came from have Conservative (Pembroke), Labour and Plaid Cymru (Carmarthen) traditions. In 1997 there was a significant swing from the Conservatives to Labour which gave former Pembroke MP Nick Ainger (Labour) a 9,621 majority.

Labour retained the seat in the 1999 Assembly elections but with a much decreased majority of 1,492 votes. The winner was Christine Gwyther, until recently a controversial Welsh agriculture secretary. who went down in history as the first Assembly Member to suffer a vote of censure against them. In 1999 the Plaid Cymru vote sharply increased in the seat, as it did elsewhere in Wales, enabling them to push the Conservatives into third place with just 18% of the vote. In the June European election Plaid Cymru nominally won the seat but on a much reduced poll. Carmarthen West and South Pembrokeshire remains one of the many seats in Wales that on paper should stay in Labour control but with the right prevailing political winds could go to either Plaid Cymru or the Conservatives.

Clwyd West

Labour majority 1,848 (4.6%)

Conservative target 30

Possible Plaid Cymru target

MP Gareth Thomas

1997 (Turnout 75.2%)	Labour	14,918	37.1%
	Conservative	13,070	32.5%
	Plaid Cymru	5,421	13.5%
	Liberal Democrat	5,151	12.8%
	Referendum	1,114	2.8%
	Other	583	1.4%

Clwyd West was a new seat in 1997, running from the coastal resort of Colwyn Bay to the rural areas of Llanrhaedr-yng-Nghinmeirch. It was derived from the seat of Clwyd North West, which itself had come from Flint West in 1983. Part of the seat has had Conservative MPs representing it since 1931, one of whom was the former challenger to Margaret Thatcher's leadership, Sir Anthony Meyer.

After Meyer was de-selected in 1992, Rod Richards achieved victory for the Conservatives, though with a greatly reduced majority. Richards became a minister at the Welsh Office but resigned in 1996 after a sex scandal. In 1997 Gareth Thomas won the seat for the Labour Party, with a majority of almost 2,000, aided by a 'Conservatory' candidate as well as the Referendum Party taking votes off the Conservatives.

In the Assembly election of 1999, Richards, breifly leader of the Conservatives in Wales, failed once more to win the seat as Labour held on. However this time the Plaid Cymru vote shot up to within a few hundred votes of second place. The result of the general election here will depend on the extent to which the Plaid Cymru vote holds up at a Westminster election. If it does, then the seat could potentially go any of three ways. Conservative Jimmy James stands a good chance of ending Wales' status as a Tory free zone.

Conwy

Labour majority 1,596 (3.8%)

Conservative target 86

Liberal Democrat target

Possible Plaid Cymru target

MP Betty Williams

1997 (Turnout 75.3%)

Labour	14,561	35.0%
Liberal Democrat	12,965	31.2%
Conservative	10,085	24.3%
Plaid Cymru	2,844	6.8%
Referendum	760	1.8%
Others	345	0.8%

The constituency of Conwy is centred on the seaside town of Llandudno and includes the university town of Bangor. It is also something of a retirement location, and has one of the oldest population profiles in Wales. Conwy is traditionally a Conservative seat that, on occasions, has been won by Labour. Between 1970 and 1997 it was held by Sir Wyn Roberts (now Lord Roberts) who served at the Welsh Office as Minister of State between 1979 and 1996, making him the longest (continuously) serving minister in one post in the 20th century. Roberts' first and last victories were achieved with majorities of under 1000; all that appeared to have changed over two decades was that it was now the Liberal Democrats in second place as opposed to the Labour Party.

It was not the Liberal Democrats who won in 1997, however; instead the Labour Party came from third place to take the seat. The constituency got its first Labour MP since 1970 and its first female MP ever, Betty Williams. Since then, however, the seat has remained unpredictable. At the 1999 local council elections the Liberal Democrats increased their representation, while in the Assembly elections on the same day they did badly, with Plaid Cymru advancing from fourth place to win the seat by 114 votes. The Conservatives, who polled some 18.5% of the vote, are also not out of the race for future contests; indeed the lesson of Conwy is that the second placed party may not necessarily be the main challenger at the following election. The Conservatives' new hopeful is David Logan; Vicky Macdonald contests for the Liberal Democrats.

Monmouth

Labour majority 4,178 (8.5%)

Conservative target 67

MP Huw Edwards

1997 (Turnout 80.8%)	Labour	23,404	47.7%
	Conservative	19,226	39.2%
	Liberal Democrat	4,689	9.6%
	Referendum	1,190	2.4%
	Plaid Cymru	516	1.1%

Monmouth was the seat of perhaps Wales's most famous Conservative MP in living memory, Peter Thorneycroft, who became Chancellor of the Exchequer and later Chairman of the party. It was also the scene of a significant by-election victory for Labour in 1991; Huw Edwards wrestled the seat from the Conservatives before Roger Evans regained it in 1992. Evans went on to hold a number of ministerial appointments, but this did not help him save his seat in the Labour landslide of 1997. Labour had already taken control of the county council in 1995, and Edwards regained the parliamentary seat with a majority exceeding 4,000.

The constituency contains a number of market towns such as Monmouth and Abergavenny, though there is also much rural farming country next to the English border. It is perhaps the least nationalist of the Welsh constituencies; Plaid Cymru, even in the 1999 Assembly elections, achieved their worst result in Monmouth. The traditional electoral battle has been between Labour and the Conservatives, and in May 1999 the Conservatives' only real sign of recovery in Wales occurred here. They gained control of the council, polled most votes in the Euro election and won their only Assembly constituency in Wales (their other eight seats are all proportional list seats). The general election will once again see Roger Evans (Conservative) face Huw Edwards (Labour); it is bound to be another closely fought contest.

Preseli Pembrokeshire

Labour majority 8,736 (20.6%)

Conservative target 163

MP Jackie Lawrence

1997 (Turnout 78.4%)

Labour	20,477	48.3%
Conservative	11,741	27.7%
Liberal Democrat	5,527	13.0%
Plaid Cymru	2,683	6.3%
Referendum	1,574	3.7%
Green	401	0.9%

Preseli Pembrokeshire is based on the same area as the former district council of the same name. It covers the ferry port of Fishguard, the oil port of Milford Haven and the county town of Haverfordwest. The constituency is largely rural with a significant number of Welsh speaking villages in the northern and north western parts of the constituency. Prior to the 1997 election, part of the new seat (Ceredigion and Pembroke North) had been held by Plaid Cymru, whilst the other part (Pembroke) was held by Labour. Jackie Lawrence easily won the new seat for Labour in 1997, with a majority of over 8,000.

In the Assembly elections Labour retained a substantial majority (2,738 or 9.4%) but the party that had gained most from Labour's lost vote was Plaid Cymru. They had come from fourth position in 1997 to second with almost 25% of the vote. At the same time the Conservative vote fell from 27.7 to 22.6%, putting them in third position, though they did top the poll at the Euro elections a month later when it was Labour who finished third. Once again a previously two-way seat could now potentially go one of three ways; the Conservative candidate is Stephen Crabb.

Vale of Clwyd

Labour majority 8,955 (22.9%)

Conservative target 185

MP Chris Ruane

1997 (Turnout 74.6%)

Labour	20,617	52.7%
Conservative	11,662	29.8%
Liberal Democrat	3,425	8.8%
Plaid Cymru	2,301	5.9%
Referendum	834	2.1%
UK Independence	293	0.7%

The Vale of Clwyd seat was another of the new creations of 1997, made up of part of the old Delyn constituency, which was a Labour marginal, and part of Clwyd North West, which had been the Conservatives' strongest Welsh seat. Although a fifth of the constituency are Welsh speakers, the constituency is centred around the English language dominated coastal towns of Rhyl and Prestatyn. At the 1997 general election Chris Ruane, a former deputy head teacher, won the seat for Labour with a convincing majority of almost 9,000.

Two years later, at the council elections, virtually nothing changed, the Independents remained the largest group with Labour the strongest political party with 14 seats. The Conservatives have just two out of the 48 seats. At the Assembly elections, Plaid Cymru, as elsewhere in Wales saw a large rise in their vote (5.9% to 19.3%). While Labour's Ann Jones easily held the seat, their vote dropped from 52.7 to 37.7%, and the Conservative vote also fell. Conservative candidate, Brendan Murphy will have been boosted by his party's lead in the Euro elections, but Labour should hold on here.

Vale of Glamorgan

Labour majority 10,532 (19.5%)

Conservative target 153

Labour marginal

MP John Smith

1997 (Turnout 80.0%)

Labour	29,054	53.9%
Conservative	18,522	34.3%
Liberal Democrat	4,945	9.2%
Plaid Cymru	1,393	2.6%

The Vale of Glamorgan is one of the most prosperous seats in Wales, and also includes the urban area and traditional Labour stronghold of Barry. In May 1989 John Smith won the seat for Labour in a by-election with a 6,000 majority. This was reversed by the Conservatives in the 1992 general election but only just. Between 1992 and 1997 the Vale of Glamorgan had the distinction of having the smallest majority in Britain, 19 votes. In 1995 the Labour Party easily won control of the new Vale of Glamorgan unitary authority, and it was no surprise when Smith regained his old position as MP in 1997 with a majority of more than 10,000.

Recent electoral fortunes in the Vale have indicated the start of a Conservative recovery. In the council elections of May 1999 the Conservatives won some 16 seats and now govern in coalition with Plaid Cymru. In the Assembly election, the Conservatives' share of the vote actually decreased from 1997, and though the Labour vote fell more dramatically (54% to 35%), they held on to the seat. At the same time Plaid Cymru's vote went up from 6 to 24%, leaving the seat close to becoming a three-way marginal. In May 2000 a council by-election was held in Plaid Cymru's Vale seat which saw a 12.2% rise in the Conservative vote, while the other parties saw their support fall. Although Plaid Cymru held the seat, it did provide an indication to both Labour and the Conservatives that the key to winning the Vale of Glamorgan is in securing the Plaid Cymru vote.

Northern Ireland

Introduction

The 18 seats representing Northern Ireland at the Westminster parliament are contested along very different lines from those in Great Britain, and will reliably return a full slate of 'Other' MPs not affiliated to the mainland parties. The Conservatives had tried to organise in the province but have met little success; their strongest showing in the 1997 general election was 6.8% in Antrim East, and they achieved truly derisory votes in the 1998 Assembly elections.

If the next election were to produce a very close result, the affiliations of Northern Ireland MPs could have implications for the direction of the UK government. This happened in the 1974-79 and 1992-97 parliaments, when every vote mattered. Sinn Fein MPs do not take up their seats, and are therefore not part of Westminster arithmetic. Social Democratic and Labour Party (SDLP) MPs are broadly sympathetic to the Labour Party's philosophy and would not sustain a minority Conservative government. There is a range of views on social and economic matters within the Unionist delegation, and a very pragmatic approach to agreements with other parties at Westminster. Unless a government is doing very badly it should be able to gain support from either the Ulster Unionist Party (UUP) or the Democratic Unionist Party (DUP) in the division lobbies on key votes, but probably not both at the same time.

The politics of Northern Ireland have been transformed since the 1997 election. The 1998 Good Friday Agreement and the establishment of a devolved executive with David Trimble as First Minister and Sinn Fein participation in its work have been revolutionary changes. Their electoral implications are yet to be fully explored, although the Antrim South by-election should provide a clue. David Trimble's support for the Agreement gained the support of a majority of the Unionist community in the 1998 referendum, but there are still deep divisions between pro-Agreement Unionists and those, inside and outside the UUP, who are hostile to it. These divisions could lead to a splintering of Unionist votes in some areas.

The Northern Ireland Constituencies

The basic determinants of who wins a seat in Northern Ireland elections are the religious make-up of the population and which parties choose to contest the seat. In the 1980s the Unionist parties concluded an electoral pact, but this was breaking down in 1997 and is unlikely to be renewed. The SDLP and Sinn Fein compete strongly with each other for the nationalist vote, but if a pact were possible now that Sinn Fein are no longer beyond the pale this would have significant implications.

The basic groups of Northern Ireland seats are as follows:

Strongly Unionist

Antrim East is a coastal seat north of Belfast, including suburbs in the Newtownabbey area plus Carrickfergus and the port of Larne. Anti-Agreement UUP MP Roy Beggs held the seat in 1997, although with only 38.8% of the vote because the Unionist vote was so splintered; the Alliance Party and the Conservatives accounted for over a quarter of the vote between them. The same basic pattern repeated at the 1998 Assembly election and the seat is unlikely to change hands.

Antrim North is the fiefdom of Ian Paisley, leader of the DUP; it is a mainly rural seat around Ballymena. It is a safe DUP seat; Paisley won 46.5% in 1997 (a low total for him), and the DUP team were well ahead of the pack with 37.6% in 1998. The Catholic minority here tends to vote SDLP (16.9% in 1998).

Antrim South is to the north west of Belfast, including some suburbs, Antrim town, Aldergrove airport and the north shore of Lough Neagh. Anti-Agreement UUP MP, the late Clifford Forsythe, had no DUP opponent in 1997 and won very easily. In 1998 the UUP won 30%, as did the anti-Agreement DUP and UKU candidates put together; the nationalist parties were on 25%, and there were also Loyalist and centre candidates. These elections, of course, were under PR so the by-election will be affected by who chooses to stand – but it is not a certain hold for the UUP's David Burnside.

Belfast East is the most Protestant part of the city. DUP MP Peter Robinson has represented East since 1983 although it has substantial votes not only for the UUP but also for the Alliance Party and the Loyalist Progressive Unionist Party, reflecting the very mixed class composition of the seat. Robinson is likely to prevail against divided opposition.

Belfast South is the most liberal, intellectual seat in the city; it contains Queens University and is less sharply divided into segregated residential areas. It is a UUP seat for Martin Smyth, who opposed the Agreement, but minority parties are also strong. A Northern Ireland Women's Coalition candidate was elected to the Assembly in 1998, and the SDLP rather than Sinn Fein polls well among Catholics here. It should continue to send Smyth to parliament, even if the DUP were to oppose him.

North Down is a prosperous middle class Protestant seat east of Belfast. There is hardly any nationalist voting, but it has seen some odd twists and turns within unionism. The MP since 1995 has been Robert McCartney, a 'UK Unionist' who opposes the Agreement and favours integration of the province with Britain. The UUP ran him very close in 1997, with 31.1% to his 35.1%, and a further 20.7% for the Alliance, and 'won' the seat with 32.6% in 1998. It is a possible gain for pro-Agreement unionism at the general election.

Lagan Valley was a strongly UUP seat in the 1997 and 1998 elections, with opposition split between the DUP, nationalist parties and the Alliance. The area lies south west of Belfast and south of the airport. Its MP is Jeffrey Donaldson, a UUP critic of Trimble's leadership.

Londonderry East is a rural seat based around Coleraine and Limavady; it does not include the city. It is represented by anti-Agreement UUP MP William Ross, although he won with only 35.6% in 1997 thanks to a strong DUP challenge. There is also a Catholic minority: 30.8% voted SDLP or Sinn Fein in 1997 and 33.4% did so in 1998, so that this seat is gradually becoming more evenly divided. at this election, however, the most likely threat to the UUP comes from the DUP.

Strangford is south east of Belfast, around the shores of Strangford Lough, and is overwhelmingly Protestant. Its MP is John Taylor, Trimble's UUP deputy, who has been a key supporter at critical moments. He held the seat in 1997 with 44.3%, against 30.2% for the DUP, and in 1998 the gap was down to 1.5%. Taylor can probably hold on by calling upon tactical support from Alliance sympathisers but faces a serious DUP challenge.

Strongly Nationalist

Belfast West has long been a very deprived and troubled area; it contains the Falls Road and was a focal point of conflict between the British Army and the IRA. It is now an overwhelmingly Catholic constituency. Gerry Adams regained the seat for Sinn Fein in 1997 after the SDLP's Joe Hendron held it from 1992 to 1997. Sinn Fein won over 50% of the vote here in 1998, the only such majority for any party in any seat, and Adams will surely win again.

South Down used to be Enoch Powell's seat but boundary changes and social trends have converted it into a nationalist seat where the SDLP are clearly in control, winning 52.9% in 1997 and 45.3% in 1998. Eddie McGrady, the MP since 1987, has a fairly safe seat even if Sinn Fein improve their strength. The constituency is in the far south east of the province and includes Kilkeel and Ballynahinch.

Foyle is the non-sectarian name for the seat based on Derry (Londonderry to Protestants). It has a large Catholic majority and is a strong base for SDLP leader John Hume, although not without a Sinn Fein minority presence.

Newry and Armagh is the base of the SDLP Deputy First Minister Seamus Mallon. South Armagh in particular had a violent history in the troubles, and political opinion here is divided. There is a Protestant, unionist-voting element around Armagh city, and also considerable Sinn Fein support on the border. Mallon is the most likely winner but is not totally invulnerable – in 1998 the SDLP team won 35%, to 26% for Sinn Fein and 31.5% for the scattered unionist parties.

Divided

Belfast North is a patchwork of segregated neighbourhoods. It used to have a large Protestant majority but the Catholic proportion has grown steadily and in 1998 the various unionist parties polled 45.4% to 42.4% for the nationalists. In 1997 pro-Agreement UUP MP won easily as he faced no opposition from the DUP or the Loyalist parties, but the UUP lagged badly in the 1998 election. The SDLP and Sinn Fein votes are dead even; it is possible that Belfast North could change hands on a very low share of the vote.

Fermanagh and South Tyrone is in the rural south west of the province and a long way in every respect from Belfast. It has been precariously balanced between unionist and nationalist for decades, but since 1983 UUP MP Ken Maginnis has won a series of victories against opposition now evenly divided between Sinn Fein and SDLP. In 1998 it was 46.9% unionist and 48.4% nationalist. If the DUP decide to stand against Maginnis for backing the Good Friday Agreement, more or less anyone could win.

Mid Ulster, a rural constituency, elected Martin McGuinness for Sinn Fein in 1997 after several minority wins by the DUP's William McCrea. Sinn Fein led in 1998, although the SDLP and the DUP also polled respectably. Now that McGuinness has established himself here, and become Education Minister in the executive, his record should increase his attraction for SDLP tactical voters and he is likely to win again.

Upper Bann is the constituency of First Minister David Trimble. It lies south of Lough Neagh and the main towns are Portadown and Craigavon. Drumcree is the scene of an annual bust-up over Orange parades. Upper Bann is not overwhelmingly Protestant: SDLP and Sinn Fein combined won 36.3% in 1997 and 38.0% in 1998, but Trimble should be safe enough as long as he can retain the majority of unionist votes while the nationalists are divided.

West Tyrone is a precarious UUP seat, newly created in 1997. It is in the far west, around Omagh and Strabane. It has a nationalist majority approaching two to one, but William Thompson (anti-Agreement) won with just over a third of the vote. Sinn Fein, although a close third in 1997, won the most first preference votes in 1998 with

34.1%, but the divided Unionists totalled 33.2%. It could be close once again.

The Battleground

Labour v Conservative marginals

(Conservative Targets)

Target No	Constituency	Labour Lead		Region
C5	Kettering	189	0.3%	East Midlands
C6	Wellingborough	187	0.3%	East Midlands
C7	Milton Keynes North East East	240	0.5%	South East
C8	Rugby and Kenilworth	495	0.8%	West Midlands
C9	Northampton South	744	1.3%	East Midlands
C11	Romford	649	1.5%	London
C12	Lancaster and Wyre	1,295	2.2%	North West
C13	Harwich	1,216	2.3%	E Anglia & Essex
C14	Norfolk North West	1,339	2.3%	E Anglia & Essex
C15	Castle Point	1,143	2.4%	E Anglia & Essex
C16	Harrow West	1,240	2.4%	London
C17	Bristol West	1,493	2.4%	South West
C19	Braintree	1,451	2.6%	E Anglia & Essex
C21	Shrewsbury and Atcham	1,670	3.0%	West Midlands
C23	Enfield Southgate	1,433	3.1%	London
C26	Gillingham	1,980	3.9%	South East
C28	Sittingbourne and Sheppey	1,929	4.2%	South East
C30	Clwyd West	1,848	4.6%	Wales
C32	Stroud	2,910	4.7%	South West
C33	Falmouth and Camborne	2,688	5.0%	South West
C35	Hastings and Rye	2,560	5.2%	South East
C36	Warwick and Leamington	3,398	5.6%	West Midlands
C37	Shipley	2,996	5.7%	Yorkshire
C38	Chatham and Aylesford	2,790	5.7%	South East
C39	Newark	3,016	5.8%	East Midlands
C40	Wirral West	2,738	5.8%	North West

Target No	Constituency	Labour Lead		Region
C42	Wimbledon	2,990	6.2%	London
C43	Eastwood	3,236	6.2%	Scotland
C44	Reading West	2,997	6.2%	South East
C45	Finchley and Golders Green	3,189	6.3%	London
C46	Thanet South	2,878	6.4%	South East
C47	Ilford North	3,224	6.6%	London
C48	Hemel Hempstead	3,636	6.6%	South East
C49	The Wrekin	3,025	6.7%	West Midlands
C50	Upminster	2,770	6.7%	London
C51	Putney	2,976	6.8%	London
C52	Selby	3,836	6.8%	Yorkshire
C53	Croydon Central	3,897	7.0%	London
C55	Bexleyheath and Crayford	3,415	7.1%	London
C56	Hammersmith and Fulham	3,842	7.1%	London
C57	Gedling	3,802	7.3%	East Midlands
C59	Reading East	3,795	7.6%	South East
C60	Brighton Kemptown	3,534	7.7%	South East
C61	Leeds North West	3,844	7.8%	Yorkshire
C62	Hove	3,959	8.2%	South East
C63	Dartford	4,328	8.3%	South East
C64	Stafford	4,314	8.3%	West Midlands
C66	Bradford West	3,877	8.5%	Yorkshire
C67	Monmouth	4,178	8.5%	Wales
C68	Colne Valley	4,840	8.6%	Yorkshire
C70	Wansdyke	4,799	8.8%	South West
C71	St Albans	4,459	8.8%	South East
C72	Aberdeen South (3rd)	3,920	8.9%	Scotland
C75	South Ribble	5,084	9.2%	North West
C76	Scarborough and Whitby	5,124	9.4%	Yorkshire
C77	Portsmouth North	4,323	9.5%	South East
C78	Broxtowe	5,575	9.6%	East Midland
C79	Birmingham Edgbaston	4,842	10.0%	West Midlands
C81	Wolverhampton South West	5,118	10.5%	West Midlands
C82	Watford	5,792	10.5%	South East
C83	Brent North	4,019	10.5%	London
C84	Welwyn Hatfield	5,595	10.6%	South East
C85	Edinburgh Pentlands	4,862	10.6%	Scotland
C86	Conwy (3rd)	4,476	10.8%	Wales

Target No	Constituency	Labour Lead		Region
C87	Gravesham	5,779	10.9%	South East
C88	Loughborough	5,712	10.9%	East Midlands
C89	Swindon South	5,645	11.0%	South West
C90	Calder Valley	6,255	11.1%	Yorkshire
C93	Battersea	5,360	11.3%	London
C94	Stourbridge	5,645	11.4%	West Midlands
C95	Burton	6,330	11.6%	West Midlands
C96	Pudsey	6,207	11.8%	Yorkshire
C98	Medway	5,354	12.0%	South East
C99	Morecambe and Lunesdale	5,965	12.1%	North West
C101	Hendon	6,155	12.3%	London
C102	Wyre Forest	6,946	12.6%	West Midlands
C103	Forest of Dean	6,343	12.6%	South West
C105	Hornchurch	5,680	12.9%	London
C106	Batley and Spen	6,141	13.1%	Yorkshire
C111	Brigg and Goole	6,389	13.7%	Yorkshire
C112	Redditch	6,125	13.7%	West Midlands
C113	Keighley	7,132	13.9%	Yorkshire
C115	Gloucester	8,259	14.3%	South West
C116	Bury North	7,866	14.3%	North West
C117	Enfield North	6,822	14.3%	London
C118	Worcester	7,425	14.4%	West Midlands
C119	Bolton West	7,072	14.4%	North West
C120	Wirral South	7,004	14.6%	North West
C121	Ayr	6,543	14.6%	Scotland
C122	Stirling	6,411	14.9%	Scotland
C123	Tamworth	7,496	15.0%	West Midlands
C125	Peterborough	7,323	15.1%	E Anglia & Essex
C126	Erewash	9,135	15.1%	East Midlands
C128	Leeds North East	6,959	15.3%	Yorkshire
C129	High Peak	8,791	15.4%	East Midlands
C130	Swindon North	7,688	15.9%	South West
C131	Elmet	8,779	16.2%	Yorkshire
C132	Crosby	7,182	16.3%	North West
C133	Inverness East (4th)	7,832	16.4%	Scotland
C134	Ealing North	9,160	16.4%	London
C136	Blackpool North and Fleetwood	8,946	16.6%	North West
C137	Cardiff North	8,126	16.8%	Wales

Target No	Constituency	Labour Lead		Region
C138	Bedford	8,300	17.0%	South East
C139	Harrow East	9,734	17.1%	London
C140	Chorley	9,870	17.1%	North West
C141	Norwich North	9,470	17.2%	E Anglia & Essex
C143	Great Yarmouth	8,668	17.7%	E Anglia & Essex
C145	Cleethorpes	9,176	18.2%	Yorkshire
C147	City of Chester	10,553	18.8%	North West
C148	Derby North	10,615	18.9%	East Midlands
C149	Exeter	11,705	18.9%	South West
C150	Dewsbury	8,323	19.3%	Yorkshire
C151	Northampton North	10,000	19.3%	East Midlands
C152	Dumfries	9,643	19.5%	Scotland
C153	Vale of Glamorgan	10,532	19.5%	Wales
C154	Warrington South	10,807	19.6%	North West
C155	Staffordshire Moorlands	10,049	19.7%	West Midlands
C157	Dudley North	9,457	19.8%	West Midlands
C158	Middlesbrough S & E Cleveland	10,607	19.8%	North East
C159	Plymouth Sutton	9,440	19.8%	South West
C160	Birmingham Hall Green	8,420	20.1%	West Midlands
C161	Milton Keynes South West	10,292	20.3%	South East
C162	Luton North	9,626	20.3%	South East
C163	Preseli Pembrokeshire	8,736	20.6%	Wales
C164	Bristol North West	11,382	20.6%	South West
C166	Halesowen and Rowley Regis	10,337	21.2%	West Midlands
C167	Amber Valley	11,613	21.2%	East Midlands
C168	Rossendale and Darwen	10,949	21.4%	North West
C169	Waveney	12,093	21.5%	E Anglia & Essex
C170	Ipswich	10,436	21.6%	E Anglia & Essex
C171	Dover	11,739	21.7%	South East
C172	Coventry South	10,953	21.9%	West Midlands
C173	Oldham E and Saddlew'th (3rd)	11,880	22.0%	North West
C174	Corby	11,860	22.0%	East Midlands
C175	Harlow	10,514	22.0%	E Anglia & Essex
C177	Tynemouth	11,273	22.0%	North East
C178	Halifax	11,212	22.2%	Yorkshire
C179	Stockton South	11,585	22.2%	North East
C180	Stevenage	11,582	22.5%	South East
C181	Carmarthen W & S Pembroke	9,621	22.6%	Wales

Target No	Constituency	Labour Lead		Region
C182	Blackpool South	11,616	22.6%	North West
C185	Vale of Clwyd	8,955	22.9%	Wales
C186	Pendle	10,824	23.0%	North West
C187	Crawley	11,707	23.2%	South East
C188	Derbyshire South	13,967	23.3%	East Midlands
C189	Eltham	10,182	23.4%	London
C190	Luton South	11,319	23.5%	South East
C191	Cardiff Central (3rd)	9,994	23.7%	Wales
C194	Hyndburn	11,448	23.7%	North West
C195	Kingswood	14,253	23.8%	South West
C196	Lincoln	11,130	23.9%	East Midlands
C198	Bury South	12,381	24.6%	North West
C200	Basildon	13,280	25.0%	E Anglia & Essex

(Labour Targets)

Target No	Constituency	Conservative Lead		Region
L1	Dorset South	77	0.2%	South West
L2	Bedfordshire South West	132	0.2%	South East
L3	Hexham	222	0.5%	North East
L4	Lichfield	238	0.5%	West Midlands
L5	Bury St Edmunds	368	0.7%	E Anglia & Essex
L6	Meriden	582	1.1%	West Midlands
L7	Boston and Skegness	647	1.4%	East Midlands
L8	Uxbridge	724	1.7%	London
L9	Bosworth	1,027	2.0%	East Midlands
L10	Chipping Barnet	1,035	2.1%	London
L12	Norfolk Mid	1,336	2.3%	E Anglia & Essex
L14	Billericay	1,356	2.5%	E Anglia & Essex
*	Witney	7,028	12.5%	South East

*Witney has technically been held by Labour since the defection of MP Shaun Woodward in late 1999.

Liberal Democrat v Conservative marginals

(Conservative Targets)

Target No	Constituency	Lib Dem Lead		Region
C1	Winchester	2	0.0%	South East
C2	Torbay	12	0.0%	South West

Target No	Constituency	Lib Dem Lead		Region
C3	Kingston and Surbiton	56	0.1%	London
C4	Somerton and Frome	130	0.2%	South West
C10	Eastleigh	754	1.4%	South East
C18	Weston-super-Mare	1,274	2.4%	South West
C20	Lewes	1,300	2.6%	South East
C22	Colchester	1,581	3.0%	E Anglia & Essex
C24	Torridge and West Devon	1,957	3.3%	South West
C25	Northavon	2,137	3.4%	South West
C27	Taunton	2,443	4.0%	South West
C29	Sutton and Cheam	2,097	4.5%	London
C31	Carshalton and Wallington	2,267	4.7%	London
C34	Richmond Park	2,951	5.2%	London
C41	Aberdeenshire West & Kincard	2,662	6.2%	Scotland
C58	Twickenham	4,281	7.4%	London
C65	Portsmouth South	4,327	8.4%	South East
C69	Isle of Wight	6,406	8.8%	South East
C73	Tweeddale, Ettrick & Laud'l (3rd)	3,555	9.1%	Scotland
C80	Oxford West and Abingdon	6,285	10.3%	South East
C91	Devon North	6,181	11.3%	South West
C92	Cornwall South East	6,480	11.3%	South West
C97	Brecon and Radnorshire	5,097	11.9%	Wales
C100	Southport	6,160	12.2%	North West
C104	Hereford	6,648	12.6%	West Midlands
C107	Harrogate and Knaresborough	6,236	13.1%	Yorkshire
C108	Cheltenham	6,645	13.2%	South West
C109	St Ives	7,170	13.3%	South West
C124	Newbury	8,517	15.1%	South East
C127	Edinburgh West	7,253	15.2%	Scotland
C135	Gordon	6,997	16.6%	Scotland
C142	Bath	9,319	17.3%	South West
C146	Sheffield Hallam	8,271	18.2%	Yorkshire

(Liberal Democrat Targets)

	Constituency	Conservative Lead		Region
	Teignbridge	281	0.4%	South West
	Wells	528	0.9%	South West
	Dorset Mid and Poole North	681	1.3%	South West
	Totnes	877	1.6%	South West

Constituency	Conservative Lead		Region
Norfolk North	1,293	2.2%	E Anglia & Essex
Tiverton and Honiton	1,653	2.8%	South West
**Romsey	8,585	16.6%	South East

**Romsey was held by the Conservatives in 1997 but gained by the Liberal Democrats in a subsequent by-election.

SNP v Conservative marginals

(Conservative Targets)

Target No	Constituency	SNP Lead		Region
C54	Perth	3,141	7.1%	Scotland
C74	Tayside North	4,160	9.1%	Scotland
C110	Galloway & Upper Nithsdale	5,624	13.4%	Scotland
C114	Moray	5,566	14.0%	Scotland

Independent v Conservative marginal

(Conservative Target)

Constituency	Independent Lead		Region
Tatton	11,077	22.7%	North West

Labour v Liberal Democrat marginals

(Liberal Democrat Target)

Constituency	Labour Lead		Region
Conwy	1,596	3.8%	Wales
Oldham East and Saddleworth	3,389	6.3%	North West
Hastings and Rye (3rd)	3,150	6.4%	South East
Bristol West (3rd)	4,517	7.2%	South West
Aberdeen South	3,365	7.6%	Scotland
Falmouth and Camborne (3rd)	4,639	8.6%	South West
Rochdale	4,545	9.5%	North West
Chesterfield	5,775	11.2%	East Midlands
Shrewsbury and Atcham (3rd)	6,646	12.0%	West Midlands
Birmingham Yardley	5,315	14.1%	West Midlands
Leeds North West (3rd)	8,005	16.2%	Yorkshire

Constituency	Labour Lead		Region
Inverness East (3rd)	7,823	16.4%	Scotland
Colne Valley (3rd)	10,530	18.7%	Yorkshire
Cardiff Central	7,923	18.8%	Wales

Labour v Plaid Cymru marginals

(Plaid Cymru Targets)

Constituency	Labour Lead		Region
Carmarthen East & Dinefwr	3,450	8.3%	Wales
Clwyd West (3rd)	9,497	23.6%	Wales

Labour v SNP marginals

(SNP Targets)

Constituency	Labour Lead		Region
Inverness East	2,339	4.9%	Scotland
Glasgow Govan	2,914	9.0%	Scotland
Ochil	4,652	10.6%	Scotland
Kilmarnock & Loudoun	7,256	15.3%	Scotland

Sources

We list below the main sources used in the compilation of this guide. In most cases, we have attempted to use (and if necessary reconcile) several sources for each section, rather than rely on a single source. The exceptions to this rule are the data on opinion polls, which is published courtesy of MORI, and the 1999 European election results, which have only been published at the level of parliamentary constituencies (to the best of our knowledge) in the House of Commons Library Research Paper 99/64.

T.Austin (ed) (1997), *The Times Guide to the House of Commons,* May, 1997

D.Butler and G.Butler (2000), *Twentieth Century British Political Facts* ,Basingstoke, Macmillan

D.Butler and D.Kavanagh (1997), *The British General Election of 1997,* Basingstoke, Macmillan

D.Butler and M.Westlake (2000) *British Politics and European Elections 1999* Basingstoke: Macmillan

C.Cook and J.Ramsden (ed) (1997) *By-elections in British Politics* London: UCL Press

D.Denver et al (eds) *British Elections and Parties Review* (volumes 8 and 9) London: Frank Cass

Hansard Society for Parliamentary Government (1997) *Map of the New Parliamentary Constituencies* London: Stanfords

C.Rallings and M.Thrasher *Local Election Handbooks* 1995-1999 Local Government Chronicle Elections Centre / University of Plymouth

C.Rallings and M.Thrasher (1999) *New Britain: New Elections* London:Vacher Dod

C.Rallings and M.Thrasher (ed) (1995) *Media Guide to the New Parliamentary Constituencies* Local Government Chronicle Elections Centre / BBC,ITN,PA News and Sky

The Vacher Dod Guide to the New House of Commons 1997 (1997) London:Vacher Dod Publishing

R.Waller and B.Criddle (1999) *Almanac of British Politics* (6th ed) London: Routledge

D Willetts with R Forsdyke (1999) *After the Landslide* London: Centre for Policy Studies

R Worcester and R Mortimore (1999) *Explaining Labour's Landslide* London Politico's Publishing

Local Election Results

We would like to thank all those local council election departments who sent us results for the 1999 and 2000 local elections on a ward-by-ward basis.

House of Commons Library Research Papers:

Elections to the European Parliament – June 1999 (99/64)

By-elections since the 1997 General Election (99/95)

Unemployment by constituency April 2000 (00/51)

The Local Elections and Elections for a London Mayor and Assembly (00/53)

Newspapers

The *Guardian*

The *Herald*

The *Scotsman*

The *Telegraph*

Web Sites

BBC Election 97 http://www.bbc.co.uk/election97

Election UK http://www.election.co.uk

Scottish Politics http://www.alba.org.uk

Government organisations http://www.open.gov.uk

Predictions

We asked a distinguished panel of authors, academics, pollsters, journalists and other experts for their predictions of how many seats each party would win in the election. Here are the results:

	Lab	Con	LD	Others
Bob Wybrow (former MD Gallup UK)				
Labour majority 123	390	191	47	31
Peter Kellner (*Evening Standard*)				
Labour majority 111	385	205	40	31
Anne Perkins (political journalist)				
Labour majority 70	325	254	50	31
Gerry Hassan (Centre for Scottish Public Policy)				
Labour majority 49	354	249	31	25
Stuart Weir (Democratic Audit)				
Labour majority 21	340	239	50	30
John Blundell (Institute of Economic Affairs)				
No majority	318	273	18	50
Peter Hitchens (*Daily Express*)				
Conservative majority 17	258	338	20	43
Michael Crick (author and journalist)				
Labour majority 185	422	167	41	29
Brian Brivati (Kingston University)				
Labour majority 35	347	246	36	30
Justin Fisher (political academic)				
Labour 117	388	200	41	30
Bob Worcester (MORI)				
Labour majority 127	393	205	33	29
Julia Langdon (political journalist)				
Labour majority 61	360	225	38	38
Lewis Baston (author)				
Labor majority 112	385	219	35	30
Iain Dale (publisher, Politico's Publishing)				
Labour majority 60	358	244	23	31
Simon Henig (author)				
Labour majority 107	383	206	36	34